Identity Politics in the Age of Genocide

While 9/11 and the war in Iraq have substantially changed the international climate in important ways, the Jewish Holocaust nevertheless casts a long shadow over ethics in the Western world. It retains its importance as the pre-eminent symbol of suffering.

In an era of globalization and identity politics, this book explores how Holocaust imagery and vocabulary have been appropriated and applied to reinterpret the history of genocide and other atrocities. The author examines how the Holocaust has impacted on selected ethnic and social groups, and asks whether the Holocaust, as a symbol, is a useful or destructive means of reading non-Jewish history.

This is done by exploring how the Holocaust has reframed representations of identity and history among six distinct groups: American Indians, Australian Aborigines, New Zealand Maori, Armenians, Chinese Americans, and Serbians. The six cases feature background chapters on colonial and other atrocities, many of them genocidal. What follows is a critical engagement with the politics of representing history amongst indigenous and Diaspora groups and the instrumentalization of the Holocaust as a lens through which to do this. Crucial in all cases are attempts to gain public recognition of the group and its claims for apology, compensation, and, ultimately, healing.

Demonstrating both the opportunities and the pitfalls the Holocaust provides to many ethnic and social groups this book fills an evident gap regarding the discursive strategies used in contemporary identity politics. This book will be of interest to students and researchers of international relations, comparative politics, sociology, and Holocaust and genocide studies.

David MacDonald is Senior Lecturer in Political Studies at the University of Otago. He has a PhD in International Relations from the London School of Economics and is widely published in the areas of International Relations, Nationalism, and Holocaust and Genocide Studies. He is the author of *Balkan Holocausts? Serbian and Croatian Propaganda and the War in Yugoslavia*, and co-editor of *The Ethics of Foreign Policy*. He is also Team Leader of the 'Living Together of Hating Each Other' project for the Scholars' Initiative, tasked with creating an impartial history of the Yugoslav conflict.

Routledge advances in international relations and global politics

Identity Politics in the Age of Genocide

The Holocaust and historical representation

David B. MacDonald

 Routledge
Taylor & Francis Group

LONDON AND NEW YORK

First published 2008
by Routledge
2 Park Square, Milton Park, Abingdon, Oxon OX14 4RN

Simultaneously published in the USA and Canada
by Routledge
270 Madison Ave, New York, NY 10016

Routledge is an imprint of the Taylor & Francis Group, an informa business

Transferred to Digital Printing 2009

© 2008 David B. MacDonald

Typeset in Garamond by Wearset Ltd, Boldon, Tyne and Wear

British Library Cataloguing in Publication Data
A catalogue record for this book is available from the British Library

Library of Congress Cataloging in Publication Data
A catalogue record for this book has been requested

ISBN10: 0-415-43061-5 (hbk)
ISBN10: 0-415-54352-5 (pbk)
ISBN10: 0-203-93464-4 (ebk)

ISBN13: 978-0-415-43061-6 (hbk)
ISBN13: 978-0-415-54352-1 (pbk)
ISBN13: 978-0-203-93464-7 (ebk)

Contents

Acknowledgments

This book brings together much of my work over the past ten years, focusing on six of the most interesting cases I have encountered since I began teaching and writing on ethnic conflict, genocide, and the Holocaust. From 1999 to 2002, I tested many of my ideas as a visiting assistant professor at the École Supérieure de Commerce de Paris. My third-year class, 'Genocide and Human Rights in the International System', proved to be an excellent vehicle for exploring concepts of nationalism, genocide, and identity. My thanks to Philippe Nemo for his support and guidance. In 2002 I began a permanent post as Lecturer, then Senior Lecturer, in the Political Studies Department at the University of Otago. Since this time I have offered an honors-level seminar on 'Genocide and Human Rights'. My thanks to my colleagues and students, whose invaluable insight has greatly added to my work, including Robert Patman, Philip Nel, Janine Hayward, Chris Rudd, Marian Simms, and our administrator Geraldine Barrett. My thanks also to the Division of Humanities for their generous financial support.

I completed the conclusions and revised this book while undertaking sabbatical research in the Political Science Department at Concordia University. Many thanks to department head Peter Stoett, and to administrator Jeannie Krumel for her help. My parents, Bruce and Olive MacDonald, have also been highly supportive. Many colleagues around the world have provided illuminating comments and suggestions, which improved the quality of this book. In particular, I would highlight James Mayall, George Schopflin, Spyros Economides, Michael Cox, Frank Chalk, Jim Miller, Dirk Nabers, Ronald Suny, Charles Ingrao, Adam Jones, Sarah Feingold, Nick Bisley, and the late Ari Shachar. Additional thanks to Heidi Bagtazo and Harriet Brinton at Routledge for making the publication process an enjoyable one.

Portions of this book were published previously as journal articles and book chapters. I would like to thank the editors of the books and journals for their kind permission to use some of my previously published work. These are: 'Forgetting and Denying: Iris Chang, the Holocaust and the Challenge of Nanking', *International Politics* (2005) pp. 403–28; 'Daring to compare: the debate about a Maori "holocaust" in New Zealand', *Journal of*

Genocide Research (September, 2003) pp. 383–404 (www.tandf.co.uk/journals); 'Serbs and the Jewish Trope: Nationalism, Victimhood and the Successor Wars in Yugoslavia: 1986–2000', in Wojciech Burszta, Tomasz Kamusella and Sebastian Wojciechowski (eds), *Nationalisms Across the Globe: An overview of the nationalisms of state-endowed and stateless nations* (Poznan: Wyzsza Szkola Nauk Humanistycznych i Dziennikarstwa, 2005) pp. 97–129; and finally 'Globalizing the Holocaust: A Jewish 'useable past' in Serbian and Croatian nationalism', *PORTAL*, vol. 2, no. 2 (2005) pp. 1–31.

I began writing this book shortly after my son Gulliver was born. I thank him and my wife Dana for their understanding, and love, and patience, as I researched and wrote this lengthy study. Without them, this book would never have come to pass.

Introduction

The Holocaust and identity politics

> Holocaust memory lingers like the ground floor of a partially demolished building. The past cannot be cleared away, but neither can it be salvaged. It is overused because it reconfigures not only what we see versus what we remember but also what we remember of the events of yore versus what we need to see of the events of now.
>
> (Barbie Zeliger, *Remembering to Forget* (1998))[1]

Seven years into the 'War on Terror', and America's more recent quagmire in Iraq, the Jewish Holocaust continues to cast a long shadow over politics, ethics, law, and international relations. In some respects, it has come to frame American national identity and foreign policy. Indeed, the bloody insurgency in Iraq seems to have spawned renewed interest in the Holocaust. The December 2006 conference in Tehran promoting Holocaust denial signals the depths to which some leaders will go to deny Israel's legitimacy. It demonstrates how deeply the geopolitical problems of the Middle East are seen to hinge on the horrors of the past and how they are interpreted. And while Iranians spread lies about the Holocaust, neoconservatives David Frum and Richard Perle have provocatively and erroneously declared that America is facing a threat of genocidal proportions: 'There is no middle way for America', they argue, 'It is victory or holocaust'.[2] Into this mix, Iran is a potential target of further US military intervention.

Richard Rubenstein argued of the Holocaust some time ago that 'Few events of the twentieth century have been the object of as much persistent and popular interest ...'[3] This remains true. Despite many post-1945 atrocities, from Vietnam and Cambodia to Rwanda, Yugoslavia, and the Twin Towers, the Holocaust continues to function as a lens through which to interpret these and other events.

This book is about the legacies of the Holocaust on group identity and historical representation. I am interested in the ways the Holocaust as a generator of norms has impacted on state and sub-state identity. Norms can be defined as 'shared expectations about appropriate social behavior held by a community of actors',[4] or as 'social rule[s] that do not depend on government for either promulgation or enforcement'.[5] Morality and ethics in the late twentieth century and after have been strongly influenced by the legacies of the Holocaust. Through its Americanization, nativization, or cosmopolitanization, the Holocaust is seen to provide a universalized standard of good and evil, designed to highlight the roles of victims, perpetrators, and bystanders. I argue that the Holocaust now forms a collective past, shared by many Western nations, upon which leaders freely draw to make foreign and domestic policy decisions. Holocaust imagery has also become a means for substate actors to draw attention to their historical or current predicaments, while helping group members focus on specific agendas.

During the early years of the Clinton administration, we saw a number of phenomena taking place simultaneously:

- First, a process of globalization, of trade, information, and people, which followed the end of the Cold War.
- Second, the fragmentation of many larger states, and the rise of conflict, even mass rape, ethnic cleansing, and genocide.
- Third, the Americanization of the Holocaust and its growing importance as a symbol of secularized evil in the western world.
- Fourth, a generalized movement in Western countries to atone for past crimes; to recognize and apologize to those wronged by the state.

My work has involved exploring how these elements go together. I first became interested in the Holocaust's new role in group identity during the ethnic conflict in the former Yugoslavia. My first book, *Balkan Holocausts?*, examined how Serbian and Croatian nationalists abused the Holocaust during their federation's fratricidal collapse. Both nations worked to dismember Bosnia-Herzegovina, in the process initiating ethnic cleansing and mass rape, even establishing concentration camps. Yet both sought to compare themselves to Europe's Jewish populations during World War II, so much so that a 'Jewish trope' developed, where both sides cast themselves as victims to court domestic and international support.[6]

Yugoslavia features later, but I also throw much needed attention on the impact of Holocaust consciousness on indigenous struggles in America, Australia, and New Zealand. I then examine the role of the Holocaust in Armenian and Chinese Diaspora attempts to combat Turkish and Japanese denialism, while promoting collective memory. I have chosen my cases based on the extent to which the Holocaust has come to frame a group's representation of its past. My methodology involves using qualitative discourse analysis to gauge how important the Holocaust has become in framing group history and identity. I use qualitative methods to analyze primary material, isolating the most important themes and images. This is in line with Thomson's suggestion of paying attention to 'the more obvious pattern frequencies that come from a general view of contents'.[7] This implies being receptive not only to the vocabulary and imagery of the Holocaust, but also to how groups have copied the style by which the Holocaust has been represented.

My goals are as follows. First, I aim to explore how the Holocaust has attained its current status, through a discussion of its Americanization during the 1960s and 1970s. A central message throughout is that the Holocaust provides an unrivaled *moral clarity* in historical representation. As such it has a profound influence on how other ethnic and social groups choose to represent their collective histories. Yet, the Holocaust is unique for many reasons, and will continue to occupy a privileged place in genocide studies, and in Western consciousness more generally.

While the Holocaust might help other groups to structure and represent their own history, every atrocity should be understood first on its own merits, not in comparison with any other atrocity. Each group must find its own vocabulary and imagery for what happened to *them*. Basing our sympathy and understanding on derivative representations of the Holocaust will ultimately fail, if we are unconvinced that their tragedy is sufficiently like the Holocaust to merit our full attention.

Yet we need also to be careful about how remembering the Holocaust might lead to the forgetting of other atrocities. At the turn of the millennium, Sweden's Prime Minister, Goran Persson, launched the *Stockholm International Forum on the Holocaust*. Forty-eight countries sent delegates to discuss the universal impact of the Holocaust, and how to apply its lessons to prevent future atrocities. In January 2000 the *Forum* issued a *Declaration*, which stated: 'The Holocaust (Shoah) fundamentally challenged the foundations of civilization.'[8] Participants concluded that the Holocaust was 'unprecedented', and contained 'unique traits' which were to be recognized when comparing it with other genocides.[9] As then French Prime Minister Léonel Jospin made clear, the basic 'mystery' of the Holocaust was its Western origin: 'how, in the context of European civilization, could the organized massacre of millions of human beings ever have come about?'[10]

Sweden's *Forum* was one of many examples of nativization, where the Holocaust has been commemorated and institutionalized by Western countries, in part for their own purposes. Not only does the Holocaust define evil – it also sets out the nation's values by demonstrating in the starkest terms what the nation is not.[11] The *Forum* brought together most of the countries of Europe and North America, in addition to former Nazi havens like Uruguay and Argentina. Yet notable for their absence were several *continents* – Africa, Asia, the Middle East, and Oceania. While the Holocaust does have universal lessons, it often fails to resonate in non-Western contexts, especially when other historic crimes continue to go unpunished and unremembered.

The unrivalled status of the Holocaust imparts a number of different and sometimes contradictory lessons. First, Western governments should commemorate the Holocaust to forestall any such crimes occurring again. Second, the Holocaust is unique, unprecedented, and European; nothing that came before could prepare the world to expect it. And yet, the Holocaust is supposed to create an open, moral climate where Western governments will be obliged to recognize and commemorate the crimes of their own pasts, enabling apologies and reparations to groups *they* have wronged. The Holocaust should also engender a public space where victim groups can freely discuss and present *their* histories of victimization and abuse.

The first two points contradict the second pair. If we see the Holocaust as primarily a 'mystery', 'unique', 'unprecedented' and 'European', then the commonalities between this and other crimes are difficult to discern. How should non-Jewish groups, in an age of identity politics, understand it? To what extent is it morally permissible for them to employ that understanding when rewriting their own histories of persecution? Can one go too far in using the Holocaust; if so, how far is acceptable? Who does invoking (or even manipulating the imagery of) the Holocaust hurt, if anyone? If the Holocaust is unique and unprecedented, what sort of benchmark can it be for understanding less 'unique' tragedies? Does a tragedy have to be unique and unprecedented, or 'a mystery', to gain Western recognition? I devote this book to searching for these answers, ever aware that recognizing one genocide does not imply equal respect for all others. Indeed, since most countries to some extent practice a form of 'chosen amnesia', deliberately excluding unwanted or unsavory aspects of their national past, the Holocaust is sometimes remembered at the cost of ignoring other atrocities closer to home.[12]

How this book is structured

I have structured this book into three parts. I begin with two theoretical chapters, followed by Parts II and III, which group my cases together under similar themes. In Chapter 1, I understand the rise of the Holocaust as a gradual process, charting how its importance as a symbol evolved during the 1960s and 1970s, then still further in the 1980s and 1990s, when it became a part of mainstream American identity. I argue that the Holocaust's extrinsic importance accounts to some degree for its growth as a symbol of suffering. Some cosmopolitan theorists hold that the 'success' of Holocaust awareness has created a window of opportunity for other groups seeking to reframe their histories in a similar manner. However, if one assumes that passing through this 'window' delivers tangible benefits to non-Jewish groups, how should Jews and Holocaust historians respond? What do they stand to gain or lose in such a process? This chapter concludes by examining the debate about whether the imagery of the Holocaust should be used by other groups, and to what degree the Holocaust should serve as *the* standard of comparison for other atrocities.

Chapter 2 complements the first by examining the intrinsic importance, uniqueness, and unprecedented nature of the Holocaust. I focus on fifteen uniqueness claims, which suggest that the Holocaust must stand on its own as a landmark event despite the fact that its significance evolved over time. This is a new and innovative approach which has not been undertaken before in Holocaust scholarship. I divide this chapter into three sections. The first examines claims that the Jewish people and their contributions to the Western world are unique. I also engage with claims that anti-Semitism is a unique form of hatred. A second section examines the Holocaust as a unique and distinct horror, separate from the unique identity of its primary victims. This leads into the third section, which examines post-Holocaust events — unique legacies and lessons other groups might draw from Jewish experiences after 1945.

I feature an overview of the history of indigenous peoples in America, Australia, and New Zealand in Chapter 3. Here I focus on such issues as Western settlement, indigenous–settler relations, and whether genocide was committed in these countries. Chapter 4, on American Indians, pays particular attention to the work of David Stannard and Ward Churchill, who make widespread use of the Holocaust in their writings on the 'American Holocaust'. Both are ardent critics of Holocaust uniqueness scholars. While I endorse some of their objectives (i.e. gaining justice for indigenous peoples), I am critical of their methods. Attacking Holocaust historians detracts from the important message Native America needs to send to the American government.

Chapters 5 and 6 examine the legacies of the Stannard–Churchill thesis on indigenous historical representation in Australia and New Zealand. In Australia, we have proven cases of genocide and a government unwilling to acknowledge or apologize for the wrongs of the past. An Australian unfamiliarity with other genocides meant that only the Holocaust featured in public and academic discussions. While Australia's child-removal policies may well constitute genocide under the UN Genocide Convention, few of the nineteenth-century frontier wars or massacres fall within its ambit. A confusing (and ironic) situation arises where brutal massacres were not genocide (although perhaps 'genocidal acts'), while forced assimilation was. Attempts to compare the Australian genocide and the Holocaust can sometimes yield interesting insights into both cases. Yet overall, comparison decontextualizes and confuses an already divisive issue now at the heart of Australian national identity.

In New Zealand, some Maori activists and politicians began promoting a 'Maori Holocaust' in the mid-1990s. The discussion aroused national interest when the Waitangi Tribunal (tasked with resolving Maori–Crown grievances from the nineteenth century) used the term in 1996. Debate became more heated when Associate Minister Tariana Turia spoke of a 'Maori Holocaust' in 2000. This debate cut to the heart of Maori–settler relations, displaying very divergent perceptions of history.

In Chapter 7, I offer a historical background to the Armenian genocide and the importance of Diaspora activists and historians in continuing to keep memory alive in the face of active and pernicious denial by the Turkish government. I conclude by examining attempts at Armenian–Turkish dialogue. Chapter 8 then examines the role of the Holocaust in contemporary scholarship on the genocide. Works by Vahakn Dadrian, Richard Hovannisian, and others highlight similarities between Jews and Armenians. These scholars, like those writing from an indigenous perspective, rebut the uniqueness of the Holocaust, focus on commonalities, and highlight that *their* genocide came first. Some Armenian scholars accuse Holocaust historians of promoting uniqueness, while downplaying the moral or historical significance of other genocides. Nevertheless, many writers on the Holocaust actively support Armenian genocide research and memory, and oppose Turkish denialism.

The brutal siege of Nanking by Japanese forces in 1937 forms the basis of Chapter 9. I offer a historical overview, then problematize the 'Chinese Holocaust' and the imagery which surrounds it. I approach these issues through a reading of the late Iris Chang's *The Rape of Nanking* (1997) and the work of Diaspora Chinese activist groups based in the United States. Diaspora groups have created Chinese holocaust museums and Chinese holocaust curricula, in an effort to stimulate attention. However, direct comparisons have led to a series of false dichotomies which distort historical accuracy. The matter is further complicated by Japan's own myths of suffering based on Nagasaki and Hiroshima (known as 'atomic victim exceptionalism').

Chapters 10 and 11 examine civil conflict in the former Yugoslavia, and the use of Holocaust imagery in Serbian nationalism. Beginning with some essential background, I then move to discuss critically how the Holocaust and more general myths of victimization framed reinterpretations of national history. Here, Holocaust claims legitimated territorial aggrandizement, ethnic cleansing, rape, and the murder of over 240,000 people. Manipulating Holocaust imagery helped rally co-nationals together in a time of escalating hostilities, convincing many Serbs that the threat of genocide required decisive action. Internationally, the barrage of Holocaust imagery confused and obscured the conflict, giving Western countries a much-needed excuse not to intervene. Serbia, as well as Croatia, tried to gain Jewish sympathy and support, courting Israeli and American Jews.

Invoking the Holocaust

At the most basic level, my case studies have invoked the Holocaust's *vocabulary*. Terms such as Holocaust, pogrom, death camp, Final Solution, Wannsee Conference, Nuremberg Laws, Hitler, Nazi, SS, and Stormtrooper describe anything from the theft of ancestral land to ethnic cleansing. *Holocaust imagery* is also used, where basic vocabulary gives way to more detailed images, comparing Jews with group members. This might feature 'holocaust' museums, or educational curricula, leaflets, books or websites. *Direct comparisons* are then made, to buttress the similarities between the two groups, their common suffering, and the shared evil/hatred of the perpetrators involved.

What follows is *competition*, where aspects of the Holocaust are downplayed, although not denied. There is no real anti-Semitism, but a sense that other groups have been unfairly dealt with by history. There may be condemnation of Holocaust historians, or 'Holocaust consciousness'.[13] Common here is anger against a 'double standard', where the Holocaust is recognized as a unique genocide while other genocides are downplayed or denied. While the *facts* of the Holocaust are upheld, the motivations of Holocaust scholars are questioned, alongside the moral legacies and significance of the Holocaust itself. *Denigration*, even *Holocaust denial* represents the most extreme version of competition. Here, anti-Semitic or anti-Zionist groups with an overtly political agenda use Holocaust imagery against the Jews, trying to prove that Jews or Israelis are hypocritical in their treatment of Palestinians.

Why invoke a 'Holocaust'?

Underlying *academic* goals is the belief that some atrocities have been ignored or denied in academic literature, and should be made a stronger focus of study. When discussing the fate of peoples very different from white Westerners, invoking the Holocaust may help a Western audience better understand and engage with 'foreign' group experiences. A desire to *popularize* memory of group atrocities is also important. The success of the television series *Holocaust* (1978) and the film *Schindler's List* (1993) demonstrated how popular representations could greatly increase awareness of group tragedies, and stimulate interest and sympathy. Recent films like Atom Egoyan's *Ararat* (2002) and Terry George's *Hotel Rwanda* (2004) have similarly attempted to represent genocide by using Holocaust films as a template. Certainly, the ordeals of Paul Rusesabagina and Oskar Schindler are startlingly similar.

Activists sometimes invoke the Holocaust to bring about *social change*. The general public is likened to a Western bystander, who is enjoined symbolically to 'bomb the rail lines to Auschwitz' by joining or at least supporting the activist group. Sensationalist displays and imagery on Internet sites, campus promotions, television and radio ads can help gain the public's immediate attention. At another level, nations and ethnic groups also use Holocaust imagery to promote *self-determination* or *increased autonomy*. Bringing in the Holocaust can signal the persecution a minority population faces within a larger multi-ethnic state, arousing recognition and sympathy for the group's goals. Alternatively, governments or dominant national elites sometimes use the Holocaust as a means of legitimating *territorial expansion*. Other acts of statecraft, such as making war or introducing controversial domestic or foreign policies, can also lead to similar invocations.

Finally, *anti-Semitism* inspires some groups to use Holocaust imagery as a means of denigrating Jews or attacking Israel. An example is Michael Hoffman's 'Palestinian Holocaust' website and his online 'Palestinian Holocaust' museum, which exhorts web-surfers to 'Heil Sharon' the 'kosher war criminal'.[14] While I don't focus on what in my view is crude racism, its presence signals the apprehension many people feel when the Holocaust is used in contexts where it emphatically does not apply.

Genocide

Some but not all of my cases are examples of genocide. Genocide has been formally defined in international law, and codified (thanks to Raphael Lemkin's efforts) in the United Nations Genocide Convention (1948). Article 2 defines genocide as follows:

> Any of the following acts committed with intent to destroy, in whole or in part, a national, ethnical, racial or religious group, as such:
>
> a Killing members of the group;
> b Causing serious bodily or mental harm to members of the group;
> c Deliberately inflicting on the group conditions of life calculated to bring about its physical destruction in whole or in part;
> d Imposing measures intended to prevent births within the group;
> e Forcibly transferring children of the group to another group.[15]

In recent years, the International Criminal Tribunals for Rwanda and the former Yugoslavia (ICTR and ICTY) have further refined the UN definition. Among the contributions of recent case law, we have judicial interpretations of how large a 'part' of the target group must be killed for an act to be considered genocide.[16] Other issues concern how clearly 'intent' to commit genocide must be proven, and whether or not rape can be considered an act of genocide. It now can be.[17] While case law moves forward, this has not prevented acrimonious academic debate about whether the official definition is too broad, too narrow, or just about right.[18]

'Genocide' has long been overused to describe a diverse range of social problems. Jack Porter observed in 1982 that everything from 'race mixing' to the closing of Soviet synagogues was being labelled genocide. Helen Fein later noted a 'wave of misuse and rhetorical abuse'.[19] Chalk and Jonassohn, in their seminal work on genocide, also posit that, when improperly used, 'the term becomes devoid of all cognitive content and communicates nothing by the author's disapproval.'[20] Yet genocide is clearly defined in international law. This perhaps explains why 'Holocaust' has gained currency. It is emotive and attention-grabbing, while its definition can in the wrong hands seem vague and difficult to pin down.

The Holocaust: definitions and controversies

'Holocaust' comes from two Greek root words, *holos* and *kaustos*, meaning 'wholly burnt'. Early English translations of the Old Testament employed the term in a variety of ways, including Jacob's willingness to sacrifice his son Isaac, and, more generally, offerings consumed by fire.[21] From 1900 to 1959, Western media used 'holocaust' to describe a wide variety of events, including the genocide of the Armenians, the 1918 Minnesota forest fire, even the explosion of a cinema projector in May 1947.[22] Of course, we understand the term to refer to Hitler's Final Solution against the Jews. This usage was first publicly employed in 1956, when Yad Vashem introduced 'holocaust' in its journals, *Yad Vashem Bulletin* and *Yad Vashem Studies*. By 1965, in part popularized by Elie Wiesel's writing, 'Holocaust' was widely used in the United States, and figured as the title of a literature course offered at Brandeis University.[23]

Jon Petrie argues that Holocaust (complete with capital letter) was privileged because of its association with nuclear annihilation. It thus helped Americans 'associate emotionally the Nazi Judeocide with a feared nuclear mass death'.[24] By the 1970s and 1980s, Holocaust was widely used, especially after NBC launched its *Holocaust* mini-series in 1978, followed later by President Carter's commission on the Holocaust.

Obviously we know the Holocaust by other names. In Israel, *Sho'ah* (catastrophe) and *Hurban* (whirlwind) are more often used.[25] Shoah is originally of biblical origin, denoting an unforeseen or terrible disaster. The Books of Zephaniah and Isaiah both present Shoah as evidence of a wrathful God, while in the Proverbs and Psalms, Shoah figures primarily as punishment for an individual's evil deeds.[26] However, both imply an act of God – and give the Holocaust a sense of fatalism. Like a volcano, Omer Bartov argues, the Holocaust was impossible to prevent: 'The Event itself is taken therefore almost as a given, as a natural law, as being anything but surprising. If not ordained by God, it was at least an historical inevitability.'[27] However, one could flee to a 'safer location' (Israel) away from the danger. The term helps legitimate Israel's existence and its efforts to safeguard Jewish life.[28]

France, with its more ambiguous collaborationist legacy, prefers 'génocide'. This legalistic definition fails to identify the event as being as singularly unique as English writers describe.[29] Shoah is also widely used, especially since Claude Lanzmann popularized the term in his landmark documentary and later book of the same name.[30] In Germany, *Judenvernichtung* or 'destruction of the Jews' is common – a very literal, precise definition of what transpired. Germans call it what it is, using a 'detached, objective, reliable scholarly term'.[31] *Endlosung* or Final Solution is also employed in German publications, which echoes the Nazi-era terminology.[32]

Throughout this book, I use Holocaust to refer to the genocide of six million Jewish victims at the hands of the Nazi regime, a process consciously planned and executed between 1933 and 1945. I am fully aware of the debates about whether the mentally and hereditarily ill,[33] Roma, Slavs, Communists, and others should be included as part of the Holocaust. Simon Wiesenthal used to talk about a Holocaust of eleven million victims, including some five million non-Jews. Wiesenthal's definition has inspired a number of recent websites, devoted to 'the five million others' who are seemingly forgotten.[34] Yet after being challenged on his figures by historians, Wiesenthal eventually conceded that he invented the number.[35] This arbitrary figure, he felt, recognized non-Jews, while still highlighting the numerical superiority of Jewish victims.[36]

The total number of Nazi victims is closer to fifty million in Europe, including the horrific death tolls in the Soviet Union.[37] I focus on the significance of the 'narrow Holocaust' applied exclusively to European Jews, versus the 'broad Holocaust' which encompasses other groups.[38] My aim is not to exclude other victims, but rather to understand what the *Jewish* Holocaust represents as a universal symbol, and how *this* symbol has been used in other contexts.

Identity politics

Identity politics traces its roots to nineteenth century nationalist and ethnic movements, as well as to decolonization movements before and after World War II. However, identity politics came to prominence during the late 1960s when members of social 'groups' (however defined) began to identify themselves through shared experiences of injustice, and the belief that their group had been, or was continuing, to be oppressed.[39] At a general level, group members demand respect for and recognition of group rights by the dominant society. They want respect, not as members of a universal human community or as individuals, but as members of groups that have traditionally been marginalized or stigmatized.[40]

Groups sometimes perceive success in legal terms. As Hekman notes, they want to be 'legally recognized as a disadvantaged group, enabling [them] to seek legal redress. This can take the form of including the group on a census form, thus enabling the government to collect statistics on income, family makeup, and so on. Or it can take the form of judicial recognition as a protected group that is due special consideration under the law.'[41] Many groups also seek access to political or social power. They offer educational curricula on their group's experiences, organize protests, demonstrations, and campus exhibitions, or become active in political campaigns.

A new phase of identity politics has been the creation of museums devoted to promoting a group's perception of history and reality. As Stephen Weil of the Smithsonian Institution put it recently: 'There's been a big change in museums over the last 20 years.... They used to be primarily about things and defined by objects. Now they're often about processes, including historical processes. Almost every ethnic group has one.' While such museums were originally state-funded, private museums can freely advocate their own reality and can be as partial and polemical as they choose to be. As Weil cautions, museums are no longer just for education. Rather, some have become 'instruments or tools to carry out particular goals. People have agendas, and a museum is one way to advance an agenda.'[42] The United States Holocaust Memorial Museum is arguably the best-known museum of this kind (although it is partially government-funded and well-balanced), but museums to tragedies suffered by Japanese Americans, Chinese, American Indians, African Americans, and Armenians have also been created in recent years, with many more on the horizon.

At a general level, we can divide identity politics into two groups. The first encompasses ethnic, racial, and national groups; the second, gays, lesbians, and women. A key difference between these groups is that the second, as Zaretsky notes, 'has a special relation to what has previously been considered the private sphere of the family and personal life.'[43] I focus my attention primarily on ethnic and national groups, or 'historical communities': indigenous peoples, Armenians, Chinese, and Serbians.[44] These are coherent and bounded collective entities, with long continuous histories, able to make reasonable comparisons between themselves and Jews.

If we adopt Craig Calhoun's theory of how identity politics works, groups 'adopt a common frame of reference within which their unity is more salient'. As he writes further: 'struggle to achieve a "trump card" salience for a categorical identity – in the face of a modern world where there are always many possible salient identities – often encourages an ironic in-group essentialism'.[45]

Tosh is correct to observe that popular historical knowledge 'tends to a highly selective interest in the remains of the past, is shot through with present-day assumptions, and is only incidentally concerned to understand the past on its own terms.'[46] Identity politics also has a strong subaltern dimension. For example, women's history during the 1960s and after signaled the problems of patriarchy in suppressing female views of history and the role of women in history. Historical themes involving women were therefore 'hidden from history'. The same holds true of African American scholarship.[47] Such forms of history, Tosh notes,

> demonstrate historical experience of a predetermined kind ... to the exclusion of material that fits less neatly with the political programme of the writer. Thus the complicity of West African societies in the transatlantic slave trade may be omitted, or the sexual conservatism of much nineteenth-century feminism ... the differences between 'then' and 'now' may be downplayed in the cause of forging an identity across the ages, while no serious effort may be made to understand the experience of other groups with a part in the story...[48]

This lack of nuance is important to remember. As I demonstrate, while all the groups reviewed were certainly victims of brutal persecution and in some cases genocide, framing history through the Holocaust presents them as *only* victims. As constructivist accounts of International Relations make clear, there is a distinction between '"brute facts" about the world, which remain independent of human action, and "social facts" which depend for their existence on socially established conventions'.[49] My hope is to show how the Holocaust has acted as a means of framing the history of many groups, and in so doing highlight what has been left out of many historical accounts by this process.

I conclude this book by promoting the merits of using theories of individual, collective, and intergenerational trauma to highlight the commonalities at individual and family levels between Holocaust survivors and survivors of other historic atrocities. As I try to make clear, although there are a myriad of ways of remembering and representing the Holocaust, this does not mean that all forms of representation are equally valid. Rather, we need to think carefully about how memory of the Holocaust and other atrocities can be preserved and transmitted to future generations. While comparing historical atrocities can be academically fruitful, activists will do better to highlight the traumatic effects of atrocities on individuals and families, noting their intergenerational legacies. This may be a better way of representing history. It may help to build bridges between groups with quite different *collective* experiences, who at an individual *level*, share fears, suffering, and trauma that can readily connect all victims as fellow human beings.

Part I

The Holocaust in history and politics

1 Cosmopolitanizing the Holocaust

From the Eichmann trial to identity politics

When a few years ago I saw an episode of the hit science-fiction television show *X-Files*, in which the disappearance of amphibians from a rural lake was described as a 'frog holocaust', I realized a boundary had been crossed in American culture. From President Clinton's justification for the NATO bombing of Yugoslavia to the pop culture of television, the Holocaust has become the benchmark for universal suffering and victimhood ...

(Jonathan Tobin 'From Silence to Cacophony'(1999))[1]

[I]n an age of uncertainty and the absence of master ideological narratives ... [the Holocaust] has become a moral certainty that now stretches across national borders and unites Europe and other parts of the world.

(Daniel Levy and Natan Sznaider, 'Memory Unbound: The Holocaust and the Formation of Cosmopolitan Memory'(2002))[2]

As his contribution to the Jewish Museum's *Mirroring Evil* exhibition in 2002, Boaz Arad cut and remixed original film-clips of Adolph Hitler's speeches, to produce a short Hebrew greeting: 'Shalom, Jerusalem, I apologize'.[3] Many victimized peoples dream of such apologies, if not from the actual perpetrators, then at least from their descendents. Acknowledgement, compensation, reconciliation – these are but some of the goals persecuted groups seek as they grapple with their histories. Few, however, have come as far as the Jewish people in gaining acknowledgement of and reparations for their collective suffering. Of course, token amounts of money and an official apology may mean little to those who suffered horrendous loss. Nevertheless, the Holocaust has become the pre-eminent symbol of evil in the modern world, encouraging other groups to copy its vocabulary and imagery, while sometimes contesting its significance.

In this chapter I examine how and why the Holocaust has come to attain its current status. I also aim to highlight some of the positive and negative aspects of this status on the Jewish people, while further charting its impact on identity politics generally. I divide this chapter into two sections. In the first, I present a historicized account of the rise of the Holocaust, with reference to events in Israel, America, and, to a lesser extent, Europe. While public discussion of the Final Solution was suppressed in both America and Israel in the 1950s, it came to the forefront of Jewish identity during the 1960s and 1970s. In the context of the Six Day War (1967) and the emerging conflict between Blacks and Jews in America, the Holocaust helped Jews make sense of a seemingly anti-Semitic climate. By the 1970s, the death of survivors, coupled with the assimilation of American Jews, gave the Holocaust an important role in reanimating Jewish identity.

The 1970s and 1980s also marked an era when the Holocaust became Americanized – a part of mainstream American culture. The creation of the United States Holocaust Memorial Museum and the screening of *Schindler's List*, exemplified the Holocaust's growing significance not only in America, but also throughout the Western world. This process also fed into America's own national ideal of being a liberator of and haven for oppressed peoples. Americanizing the Holocaust further buttressed America's own feelings of uniqueness and exceptionalism.

The second section examines the Americanization and potential 'cosmopolitanization' of the Holocaust during the post-Cold War era. I argue that the institutionalization and nationalization of Holocaust memory helped reinforce Jewish loyalty to America. However, in an age of identity politics and globalization, other groups sought to undermine idealized narratives of the state, when national sovereignty seemed less salient than before. If, as Jeffrey Olick argues, 'we are all Germans now'[4] – every state needs to face up to its past transgressions and attempt to make amends. Adopting this model, however, requires not just apologizing for past crimes and compensating disadvantaged groups. It also requires assuming a level of national guilt that most countries are manifestly unwilling to do.

1 The Holocaust as emergent

Throughout this book, I adopt the stance that the Holocaust evolved over several decades and was hardly seen in the 1940s as the seminal event we now perceive it to be. Peter Novick, in *The Holocaust in American Life* (1999), gives clear voice to this argument:

> The murderous actions of the Nazi regime which killed between five and six million European Jews were all too real. But 'the Holocaust', as we speak of it today, was largely a retrospective construction, something which would not have been recognisable to most people at the time. To speak of 'the Holocaust' as a distinct entity ... is to introduce an anachronism that stands in the way of understanding contemporary responses.[5]

Mary Lagerwey, in *Reading Auschwitz* (1998), charts the progression of memory, from 'fragments of experience, perception and information' to today's current view of the Holocaust as 'a historically bounded phenomenon

... [a] coherent story'.[6] For Levi and Rothberg, too, the Holocaust 'took years to be perceived as distinctive and significant', going through a 'latency period' or 'cultural lag' before a 'broad, public Holocaust consciousness' arose in later decades.[7] Milchman and Rosenberg similarly describe a process of 'eventing', where the Holocaust was not a fixed 'event', and to term it as such, as with any other 'event', 'seems to belie the social construction of reality and its processual character'.[8]

These authors aim to account for both the lack of public discussion about the Final Solution during the 1950s, and its rapid emergence in public consciousness thereafter. Younger academics like myself, who grew up during the 1970s and 80s, take the Holocaust for granted as one of the twentieth century's most horrific events. Yet, the Holocaust took time to be seen as a separate and unique crime against the Jewish people. The 'special consciousness of the Holocaust' we now take for granted only emerged decades after the War was over.[9]

The Holocaust's Americanization has given hope to other groups, especially since the 1990s, that they too might achieve the same level of recognition and respect if they can provide solid proof of similar events in their collective past. If, however, such proof is unavailable, cloaking or framing their history in the vestments of the Holocaust has also proven to be effective. As I asserted in the Introduction, identity politics often makes use of 'trump cards' to advance group interests. As Joseph Nye wisely cautions, while 'morality is a powerful reality' that can shape conduct in positive ways, one needs also to be wary. Moral arguments 'can also be used rhetorically as propaganda to disguise less elevated motives, and those with more power are often able to ignore moral considerations'.[10] We also have to pay close attention to what Laslo Sekelj has dubbed the 'functionalization' of Jewish imagery, with 'the use of Jews, Jewish symbols, and the Holocaust for political manipulation'.[11] Occasionally, as in the former Yugoslavia, the rhetoric of victimization can disguise ethnic cleansing and genocide.

America, Israel, and the Holocaust

Scholarship on the Final Solution took several decades to develop. In the years following the War, two notable memoirs emerged from survivors: Primo Levi's *If This is a Man* (1946), and Robert Antelme's *The Human Race* (1947).[12] Leon Poliakov's *Breviaire de la haine* (1951) was perhaps the first general history of the Holocaust.[13] The forty-two volumes of the Nuremberg Trial also resulted in a number of books – such as Gerald Reitlinger's *The Final Solution* (1953) and Raul Hilberg's classic *The Destruction of the European Jews* (1961).[14] Elie Wiesel's *La Nuit* (1958), abridged from a longer Yiddish semi-autobiographical story, was a landmark contribution which helped cement his own iconic status. However, while discussion and commemoration of the Final Solution *did* take place in the 1950s and early 60s, these decades are more notable for their silence, for the inability or unwillingness of survivors to talk publicly about their experiences, a problem which Irving Louis Horowitz has ably documented.[15]

Part of this may be explained by tracing the motivations and experiences of Holocaust survivor immigrants in the United States. For many survivors, a key goal after leaving Europe was to suppress painful memories of the past, to merge into mainstream America and 'belong', abandoning overt displays of difference (especially victimization).[16] This was further encouraged by West Germany's transformation to America's newfound ally in the fight against Communism.[17]

Memory of Jewish suffering was certainly vividly discussed *within* the American Jewish community, as Hasia Diner reveals through a wide-ranging exploration of primary sources from that period.[18] However, 1950s America was hardly ready to listen. Henry Greenspan describes how survivors rarely felt comfortable speaking about their experiences. Seen in America as 'the refugees', the 'greenhorns', or 'the ones who were there', survivors encountered a mixture of 'pity, fear, revulsion and guilt'. Most were 'isolated and avoided', to the extent that one can speak of a 'conspiracy of silence' suppressing survivor testimonies and discussion.[19] Even when the Final Solution was discussed, representations tended to be diluted and universalized during a time when American Jews were afraid to publicize their experiences too loudly. An obvious example was the popularity of Anne Frank's *Diary*, whose widespread success can be explained ironically by its very distance from the actual horrors of the events themselves. The Holocaust was always present, but ñever in the foreground.[20]

As in America, Israel was marked by a period of avoidance. Survivors, building a new country, often looked forward, as Flora Lewis recalled in 1961:

> People speak of the present and the future, and only when pressed, do they turn to the past. For Israel now is, a self-assured, self-absorbed country, proud and expectant, too busy and eager for growth to feed on the bitter herbs of tragedy.[21]

Zvi Sternhell too recalls the need for survivors to transform themselves after reaching Israel, to become ' "new" people ... to become Israelis'.[22]

The period from 1948 to the late 1950s has commonly been referred to as the 'statist' era. Here, nation-building necessitated a focus on values such as the Yishuv (or 'the settlement'), heroic resistance, and toiling on the land.[23] Joseph Trumpeldor's heroic stand against invading Arabs (at the Tel Hai settlement in 1920) was celebrated,[24] alongside the collective suicide of Zealots and Sicarii at Masada in AD 70,[25] and the Warsaw Ghetto Uprising.[26] Positive myths of bravery and resistance were privileged; victimization was rejected as counterproductive to the new nationalism. As Yael Zerubavel cogently observed, Israel wanted to own the 'heroic' aspects of the Holocaust, while disowning the 'nonheroic' aspects. Ghetto fighters were thus praised as 'Zionists' and 'Hebrew youth', Holocaust victims more amorphously as 'Jews'.[27] There was a sharp contrast between the victimized European Jews and the hardy and brave 'Zionists' who emerged from the ashes of the Holocaust.

The Holocaust's emergence in the 1960s

It was only during what Liebman and Don-Yehiya call the 'second phase', beginning in the early 1960s, that the Holocaust assumed a central position within 'Israel's civil religion'.[28] The phase began with the trial of Adolf Eichmann in 1961. Held in Jerusalem, the trial brought together over 100 witnesses, vividly testifying on national television to the horrors they had endured.[29] Eichmann's conviction and execution inspired such works as Hannah Arendt's *Eichmann in Jerusalem*, and Arthur Morse's *While Six Million Died* (1967). A key objective of the trial, as Arendt argued in 1963, was to force Israelis to confront their own past. The trial would also, however, reify Israel's confrontation with a 'hostile world', exemplified by the 'daily incidents on Israel's unhappy borders'.[30] Holocaust memory and defense of the homeland were closely tied together.

Also crucial to Holocaust commemoration was the Six Day War in 1967, which further reinforced Israel's tenuous position in the Middle East. This was a rallying call for American Jews to come together in defence of the homeland, and the war marked a profound 'Israelization'.[31] Many saw 1967 as a wake-up call, proof that Israelis needed to be constantly vigilant against their hostile Arab neighbors. At the same time, the war ended in victory, proving once more that a cycle of 'Holocaust and Redemption' existed, where the Jewish people, due to their faith and cohesion, could count on divine protection.[32] Saul Friedlander concludes that the war 'formalized and ritualized' the Holocaust, which was then instrumentalized in Israeli politics in three ways. Arabs and Nazis were compared with one another, while Holocaust imagery was increasingly used to frame Israeli domestic and regional conflicts. Finally, the Holocaust helped emphasize the isolation of Israel and its vulnerability.[33]

As the Holocaust assumed a greater role in Israeli national identity, so too did it become influential amongst American Jews.[34] A flowering of counterculture narratives emphasized the vibrancy of marginalized groups, long submerged by dominant readings of national history and culture. African Americans, American Indians, and American Jews all found a new sense of ethnic pride. In each case, memory of past oppression or genocide bound individuals together, as it did for social groups defined by class, gender, or other attributes. In many cases, groups desired to 'maintain and perpetuate "difference" by ensuring the continued survival and flourishing of the distinct values and ways of life of particular groups'.[35]

Waves of decolonization in Africa and Asia gave formerly oppressed colonial peoples control over their own ancestral lands and resources. 1960 alone saw fourteen African nations gain their independence from France, while Belgium evacuated the Congo, and Britain announced that it too sensed that the 'winds of change' were coming.[36] In this era before dictatorship, corruption, and civil war ravaged the African continent, such countries were a model for African Americans and American Indians in their struggle to be freed from 'internal colonialism'.

This era also coincided with the work of hegemony theorists, who promoted class-based analyses of how official histories and national memories served the goals of dominant social groups. Eric Hobsbawm's *Invention of Tradition*, for example, demonstrated how national myths were largely manufactured by elites seeking political power.[37] An entire school of nationalism theory – Modernism – was premised on the belief that elites artificially manufactured nations to consolidate control over society.[38] Post-modernist theorists contributed their own radical (if sometimes indecipherable) challenge to established readings of everything from linear history, teleology, truth and identity, to prisons, families, and pop culture.[39] A key lesson American Jews drew from the Holocaust was the need to help bring about a more just society. Jews were active in the civil rights movement, through individual and communal activities. They campaigned and fundraised for better civil rights legislation, school desegregation, and many other initiatives.[40] Jews and Blacks marched on Washington in 1963, and the majority of White Freedom Riders were Jewish.[41]

Yet conflict also developed between Blacks and Jews, as Jews became socially mobile – moving to 'increasingly comfortable suburbs' and away from the inner-city communities they once inhabited.[42] Blacks moving to the North came to see Jews as landlords and shop owners. Originally, many poor neighborhoods were Jewish, with small businesses run by local Jewish residents. As Jews departed and Blacks moved in, many Jewish landlords and shop owners remained, leading to resentment.[43] A typical example was Lawndale, on Chicago's West Side, which went from being 13 percent Black in 1950 to 91 per cent by 1960. During this time, tension led inexorably to a 'web of conflicting interests, misrepresentations, and misunderstandings'.[44] In the 'long hot summer' of 1965, race riots in New York, Los Angeles, Philadelphia and other major cities saw Jewish neighborhood businesses attacked by angry African Americans. In Philadelphia, 80 per cent of damaged stores were Jewish-owned. The attacks were not anti-Semitic per se, but they did reinforce a sense of Jewish vulnerability.[45]

Added to this was the Six Day War, which brought home fears that Jews were safe neither in Israel nor in the Diaspora. Commentators describe a 'new consciousness of Israel's vulnerability and centrality to Jewish life and culture' which arose amongst American Jews.[46] After 1967, 'The hallmark of the good Jew became the depth of his or her commitment to Israel'.[47] Support was both financial and political. The United Jewish Appeal managed to raise $100 million in one month to send to Israel, and by the 1973 war, another $675 million had been raised. Active lobbying in Washington to maintain high levels of military aid to Israel also stems from this time, through the work of the American Israel Public Affairs Committee and other organizations.[48]

At the level of social protest, Novick rightly notes increasing competition between Blacks and Jews, with an escalating and unedifying 'discourse of competitive claims to victimization'. Here the Holocaust featured as 'a trump card, repeatedly slammed down on the table'.[49] Lucy Dawidowicz, less sympathetic to African Americans, would deride the use of Holocaust imagery by 'extremist blacks' who abused terms such as Holocaust, Auschwitz, and genocide, 'exploiting them in excesses of rhetorical overkill to describe conditions in urban slums'.[50]

Yet Jewish identity and Holocaust history were hardly 'normalized', and Jews continued to perceive themselves as outsiders in mainstream America, despite some socio-economic gains.[51] Second, as many American Jews identified themselves with Israel, they opened themselves up to a new form of attack. Alongside prominent UN member-states from the developing world, some African American organizations condemned Israel as a colonial entity in the Middle East, seeing Palestinians as persecuted indigenous peoples. When in 1967 the Six Day War was cast as an 'imperialist Zionist war', Jews seemed to be on the wrong side of the decolonization trend. This tension would only increase in later decades.[52]

The 1970s: a decade of survivors

During and after the Vietnam War, a sense of national victimization or 'national trauma' emerged. The trauma of being targeted with death, witnessing (and committing) atrocities, continued after the war, contributing to a psychiatric recognition of 'post-traumatic' stress disorder among returning veterans.[53] As Ball observes, 'Vietnam veterans' experiences in a variety of venues contributed to the medicalization of trauma in psychiatric terms while allotting it a social cogency it had hitherto lacked'.[54] We can also trace a more general idealization of the 'survivor' image in American life – be it survival in one's job, family life, or through struggles with addiction.[55] Christina Crawford's *Mommie Dearest* (1978), detailing decades of drunken abuse by Hollywood siren Joan Crawford, epitomized the view that everyone was a survivor. A culture of talk shows and radio programs made personalized stories of trauma and survival accessible to mass audiences.

The victim was now transformed from 'humiliated degradation to moral leadership and almost heroic pride'.[56] Holocaust survivors now took on a more prominent role. Organizations such as the American Federation of Jewish Fighters, Camp Inmates, and Nazi Victims (created during the 1970s) promoted Holocaust Remembrance Day, prepared educational materials, and lobbied to make the Holocaust a mandatory part of the curriculum in many schools, particularly in New York.[57]

Survivors were now increasingly seen as heroes, with stories to tell, and lessons for future generations. This was doubly the case as survivors began to pass on. A new phase of Holocaust consciousness began in the 1970s, moving from very personalized 'memory' to more general representations of 'history'.[58] The 'proliferation of movies, books, classes, and museums that tell the Holocaust story' must be understood, Amy Hungerford posits, as a means of keeping the past alive to be passed on to future generations.[59] The duty of commemorating the Holocaust shifted in part from survivors to the second generation, who 'witnessed through imagination'. The second generation would promote forms of 'postmemory', imagining and reinterpreting the events. The Holocaust was thus mythologized and re-scripted, as it was consciously preserved.[60]

The 1970s was also a decade when many Jews found themselves successfully assimilated in mainstream America. A dynamic and confident minority, Jews were at the forefront of popular culture – in literature, the media, and movie industries. Jewish studies and Jewish history as a subset of American history became fashionable. However, this self-confidence and assimilation brought with it a reduction in Jewish identity. Rates of intermarriage rose by 500 percent between 1955 and 1965, and attendance at synagogue declined precipitously.[61] Another feature of assimilation was the dramatic decline of anti-Semitism. The Holocaust became for many the 'most vivid and ethnically alive' aspect of their Jewishness. It was similarly 'the easiest and most accessible of Jewish themes to employ' at a time when parents became 'frightened at the evaporation of the Jewishness of their children'.[62]

Then we have the events of 1978, which are pivotal in the Americanization of the Holocaust. A Nazi march in the predominantly Jewish Chicago suburb of Skokie touched off a storm of public protest. Also in 1978, NBC's mini-series *Holocaust* attracted some 120 million viewers in America and Western Europe. As Judith Doneson writes, '*Holocaust*, with its uncomplicated historical narrative, did establish a framework of knowledge of the Final Solution for the viewing public'.[63] While from 1963 to 1978 Hollywood produced almost no films related directly to the Holocaust, the situation changed dramatically afterwards, and Holocaust movies became a noticeable part of American culture.[64] *Inside the Third Reich* (1982), *Sophie's Choice* (1982), and Lanzmann's *Shoah* (1985) made the events of the Holocaust even more accessible to the viewing public. Herman Wouk's two television mini-series, *Winds of War* (1983) and *War and Remembrance* (1988), further gave the Holocaust a feature role.

The Skokie march, together with the influence of *Holocaust* prompted President Carter to create a presidential commission on the Holocaust, which eventually paved the way for the creation of the United States Holocaust Memorial Museum.[65] As he launched his commission in April, 1978, he argued the following, firmly rooting the Holocaust in contemporary American history:

Although the Holocaust took place in Europe, the event is of fundamental significance to Americans for three reasons. First, it was American troops who liberated many of the death camps, and who helped to expose the horrible truth of what had been done there. Also, the United States became a homeland for many of those who were able to survive. Secondly, however, we must share the responsibility for not being willing to acknowledge forty years ago that this horrible event was occurring. Finally, because we are humane people, concerned with the human rights of all peoples, we feel compelled to study the systematic destruction of the Jews so that we may seek to learn how to prevent such enormities from occurring in the future.[66]

While a positive contribution to Holocaust memory, Carter was also seeking to appease Jewish voters at a time when he had openly declared support for a Palestinian state, and had sold aircraft to Saudi Arabia and Egypt.[67] Yet Carter's speech is revealing, and suggests that the Holocaust was indeed becoming a more mainstream part of American identity. First, the Holocaust ironically became a feel-good story for Americans. Americans had helped liberate the camps, and could reasonably claim some credit for ending the genocide of European Jews. This was certainly a source of pride for returning veterans.[68] Further, large numbers of survivors were granted asylum. The Jewish 'success story' was thus a story of American beneficence – their survival a testament to American kindness. Third, the Holocaust embodied all the things a democratic, pluralist, freedom-loving America was not. Traditional myths of American exceptionalism thus received a new boost in the wake of Vietnam and an economic downturn.

The Holocaust also had important moral lessons to convey. As a bystander nation which did little to prevent the Holocaust, America now had a special mission to spread democracy and freedom, in the name of other victims of totalitarian systems. While this sense of mission had always been there, it was reinterpreted and revitalized. America thus became a moral beacon, and Holocaust victims gave America a newfound moral stature at a time when African Americans, American Indians and other groups were challenging America's dominant myths of goodness and fair play.

The Reagan and Bush eras

By the early 1980s, centers devoted to the Holocaust were created in Los Angeles, New York, Philadelphia, and St Louis. Schools in twenty-five states offered courses or aspect of their curricula on the Holocaust, as did 140 higher academic institutions.[69] The rise of Ronald Reagan and his Christian Right support base also put the Holocaust and Israeli politics increasingly on the agenda. Jerry Falwell's *Moral Majority* (1979) pledged support for Israel and hostility to the Arab world. Jews were after all God's chosen people, and the return to Israel was a significant event heralding Christ's

Second Coming.[70] Falwell pushed for 'total military and financial support for Israel' in the early 1980s, and warmly praised Israel's invasion of Lebanon.[71]

Groups like the Christian Israel Public Affairs Committee, the National Christian Leadership Conference for Israel, and the Washington Institute for Near East Policy (1985) actively supported Likud's policies, especially Israeli settlement in the West Bank, which some groups like the CFIC helped fund.[72] Perko has noted: 'The Conservative Christian Zionists' literal interpretation of biblical texts, together with its resultant theology, makes them highly supportive of the most conservative elements in Israeli politics, as well as of the concept of a Greater Israel'.[73] This close alliance between Likud, the Republicans, and the Christian Right worried a great many American Jews, who saw themselves as lifelong Democrats and part of the liberal mainstream. After all, only 20–25 percent of Jews voted Republican. Many Jews also worried about the motives of the Christian Right, who saw the Jews mainly as 'an instrument in bringing about the second coming' and as targets for conversion. While Falwell was conciliatory, others, like Pat Robertson, had made worrying anti-Semitic remarks.[74] And despite Reagan's close affinity with Israel, he could not avoid the occasional blunder, such as his speech at a commemorative service for German soldiers (including Waffen SS) interred at Bitberg, West Germany.[75]

With the Americanization of memory, and closer US closer support for Israel, came the Holocaust's use as a rhetorical device in many non-Jewish contexts. This prompted Alain Finkielkraut in 1982 to remark that the Holocaust was being overused in popular discourse, leading invariably to a trivialization of its importance, and a 'growing lapse of memory'.[76] Nazism, Finkielkraut lamented, was being 'invoked almost religiously to represent civilization's Other', in the process becoming 'the reference for all accusatory discourse'.[77] That Jews had become 'the gold standard of oppression ... the paradigm of the victim' was a worrying phenomenon, leading to the rise of anti-Semitism and Holocaust 'negationism' in Europe.[78] By 1984, William Shawcross, in his study of America's lack of intervention in the Cambodian genocide, observed that only when events could be 'plausibly' compared with the Holocaust could they then assume 'truly disastrous proportions in our perceptions'.[79] Rescripting atrocities as 'holocausts' now became a useful means of gaining public attention.

There are a plethora of examples. Pol Pot's regime of terror was termed a Holocaust from the late 1970s. Once the Vietnamese invaded Cambodia in 1978, the infamous Khmer Rouge prison Tuol Sleng became a museum to the 'Asian Holocaust'. Its curator was promptly dispatched to former Nazi death camps to get the 'image' just right. In the early 1980s, Soviet atrocities in Afghanistan were often compared to the Holocaust, by journalists, Afghan mujahideen, and American government officials.[80] Social groups too made use of the Holocaust. Paradoxically, both gay and lesbian *and* Christian right movements cast themselves as victims (or 'moral actors') during the Nazi era, accusing the other of being a key perpetrator.[81] By 1990,

President George H.W. Bush glibly compared Saddam Hussein to Hitler, in the run-up to *Operation Desert Storm*. Kuwait was upheld as a Czech or Polish-like victim needing to be saved from an 'Arab Hitler'. Bush unsurprisingly adopted the role of a 'valiant appeasement-resisting Churchill'.[82]

As the Holocaust's significance was being diluted, West Germans were also trying to normalize their past. From 1986, the *Historikerstreit* or Historians' Debate inaugurated attempts to contextualize the Holocaust within German history. The debate pitted a number of right- and left-wing academics and journalists against each other. On the right, Michael Stürmer, Ernst Nolte, Andreas Hillgruber, Joachim Fest, and Klaus Hildebrand attacked the left for submerging German history and national identity under a guilt complex. Hitler, they argued, had committed atrocious excesses, but so had Stalin; even the Western Allies during their firebombing of German cities. On the left, Jurgen Habermas, Martin Broszat, Hans Mommsen, Jurgen Kocka, and Eberhard Jackel, attacked the right's attempts to revitalize national pride.[83] The 1980s finished with the sense that the Holocaust's significance was increasing, a necessary change in light of the very real dangers of German relativization, Holocaust denialism and universalization, and more general forms of anti-Semitism. All of this, needless to say, was occurring at a time when fewer and fewer survivors were alive to articulate their experiences.

2 America and the Holocaust in the post-Cold War era

At one level, an unprecedented level of Holocaust commemoration came forth in the 1990s. This was influenced in part by the events of 1989 and the rise of new forms of international morality (the focus of section 2). However, a number of specific factors came into play. These included the reunification of Germany, which spelled an end to its former 'punishment' (i.e. being split in half).[84] A united Germany now began to remember its own victimization (Soviet rape and killing, deaths on the Russian front, aerial bombing, etc.).[85] This involved a juggling act, commemorating both the 'unspeakable acts of barbarism' committed by Germany, as well as their 'enormous losses', while being careful not to draw false comparisons.[86] What was one to make of this newly rehabilitated Germany and its more ambiguous memories?[87] At another level, Eastern Europe opened up. Western Jews could more readily travel to the former sites of the Holocaust, from the villages where *Einsatzgruppen* carried out their massacres, to Auschwitz, Terezin, Warsaw, and Krakow. A reclaiming of 'lost Jewish spaces' began, triggering long-dormant memories amongst survivors, while prompting questions from the next generations.[88]

In 1993, Steven Spielberg's *Schindler's List* was screened, and the United States Holocaust Memorial Museum opened its doors in central Washington DC.[89] In Los Angeles, the Simon Wiesenthal Center (founded in 1977) opened its Museum of Tolerance-Beit Hashoah, also devoted to Holocaust remembrance. These events firmly anchored the Holocaust as a central part of American national identity. The USHMM proved to be far more popular than its planners had hoped, attracting two million visitors in the first year, a surprising 62 per cent of them non-Jewish. Some 150,000 people donated $200 million for the museum, both for its construction and for the collection of artifacts from around the world.[90]

The positioning of the Museum on the Mall highlighted how the Holocaust was now perceived 'less an actual historical event and more as an ideal of catastrophe against which all other past and future destruction might be measured ...'.[91] For Ball, the museum demonstrated that 'Jewish identity politics [had obtained] ... national recognition of the Holocaust as a singular trauma and of the Jews as the "world's greatest" historical victims'.[92] The proximity of the USHMM to major monuments to Washington, Jefferson, and Lincoln was no accident. Rather, as Miles Lerman, Chairman of the Museum Council, made clear, the horrors of Nazi Germany were deliberately contrasted to the 'great American monuments to democracy'. These would take on 'new meaning as will the ideals for which they stand' after a visit to the Museum.[93]

Further, the Council argued:

> This museum belongs in the center of American life because as a democratic civilization America is the enemy of racism and its ultimate expression, genocide. An event of universal significance, the Holocaust has special importance for Americans: in act and word the Nazis denied the deepest tenets of the American people.[94]

Thus the Museum positioned the Holocaust in stark contrast to American history and values. It became interpreted as 'the most un-American of crimes and the very antithesis of American values'.[95] The more evil the Holocaust, and the more its significance grew, the better America could seem by comparison. Further, Americans adopted a special and unique role in the family of nations, becoming the 'primary keepers of the flame of remembrance'.[96]

To this, *Schindler's List* added another dimension. By 1996, Spielberg's opus had grossed a respectable $96 million and secured seven Oscars. In February 1997, Ford Motors (perhaps in a public act of atonement for its founder's pro-Nazi views) screened the film on national television without commercials.[97] Funded from a modest budget of $23 million, Spielberg had never intended to make money from the film. Rather, it was the outcome of a long process of personal soul searching, and an 'increasing sense of Jewishness'. This Spielberg credits to the birth of his son, which he claims inaugurated a decade of self-reflection.[98]

Reparations

Yet another aspect of Holocaust Americanization was the campaign to compensate Jewish survivors and their families for slave labor they were forced to perform during the War. Another campaign focused on retrieving Holocaust-era assets from Swiss banks. In 1997, Swiss banks finally agree to create a $5 billion fund to compensate Jewish families whose relatives' deposits had disappeared after 1945.[99] Several German companies who used slave labor (including Volkswagen and Siemens) agreed to set up special funds to compensate survivors.[100] Here a number of different factors were at work, most notably the rise of a global culture of restitution for past crimes. Other key factors included the opening up of East European archives from World War II. The end of the Cold War also reduced Switzerland's significance as a 'neutral' country. Neutrality now smacked of appeasement, and Switzerland was now derided for having 'played both sides' during the War.[101]

America's role in securing reparations was crucial. First, America's principle of universal jurisdiction helped victims to file suit in US courts, even if the events happened in Germany or Poland.[102] In the Swiss case, the US Senate's Banking Committee worked closely with the World Jewish Congress, which in turn worked with the World Jewish Restitution Organization, and the Swiss Bankers Association. The three groups created the Independent Committee of Eminent Persons, chaired by former US Federal Reserve Chairman Paul Volker.[103] World Jewish Congress head Edgar Bronfman's good relations with the Clinton administration certainly helped smooth this process along.[104] America thus adopted a clear policy of aiding (and even cajoling) reparations from Swiss and German companies.

By the end of the Clinton years, Novick would describe a virtual 'flood of books, films, university courses, and docudramas',[105] while Levin noted the Holocaust's 'dramatization through the huge proliferation of literature, television programs, and films'.[106] Yet, there's hardly anything sinister about the Americanization process. As Doneson rightly concludes, it made perfect sense in the American context to 'revert to American symbols and language in order to convey a comprehensible, Americanized perception of the (European) Holocaust'.[107] Further, as America contained a large survivor community, it made more sense to locate monuments and memorials in the United States, where for decades 'serious efforts have been undertaken to forge some remembrance'.[108] While some might see American backing for Holocaust slave labor claims as proof of some sort of 'special status' for Jews, these amounts (often largely symbolic) came well over fifty years after Nazi crimes occurred. Those who organized the claims process took advantage of a 'small window of opportunity' and a 'unique combination of historical events'. They certainly were under no illusions about their chances for success.[109]

The Holocaust in a globalizing age

The end of the Cold War in 1989 played a major role in creating increased public space for identity politics. The collapse of European Communism ended the ideological division between East and West, and unblinking loyalty to one's country became less important. Old Cold War alliances broke down; states split off from larger entities. By the middle of the 1990s, there were thirty-five major conflicts with over 1,000 deaths each year, proving that Cold War stability had irrevocably broken down.[110] While criticism of one's government was formerly labeled pro-Communist or rightist, ideological distinctions largely disappeared. Regula Ludi rightly makes the point that after 1989, 'Wartime memories no longer served as a political metaphor.... The fall of communism hence freed political discourses from the cold war's ideological grip'.[111]

For many looking back on the twentieth century after the Cold War, the death tolls from various Utopian projects were too high to 'speak glibly about "striding over corpses" on the way to the good society'.[112] In the 1990s, works by Eric Hobsbawm and Zbigniew Brzezinski highlighted the 187 million people killed as a result of political violence in the twentieth century.[113]

What Nytagodien and Neal term 'the age of apologies'[114] or John Torpey calls 'reparations politics' began in many Western countries. Governments, churches, and private firms were increasingly being held to account for past actions against indigenous peoples and other disadvantaged groups.[115] The old 'heroic, forward-looking tales that underpinned the idea of progress for two centuries' were now replaced by 'narratives of injustice and crime...'.[116] Olick's analysis of the 'memory boom' which emerged after the Cold War is little different. Here too, national groups became caught up with 'new versions of the past rather than the future'. Olick notes the 'increase in redress claims, the rise of identity politics, a politics of victimization and regret, and an increased willingness of governments to acknowledge wrongdoing ... all part of the decline of the memory-nation as an unchallengeable hegemonic force'.[117]

Marginalized groups asserted themselves, and more significantly, states were actually willing to listen. New forms of history were developed where, as Elazar Barkan posits, 'victorious histories of the elite and rich are replaced by the lives of the conquered, the poor, and the victimized Other'. History and historical memory became more than ever 'the territory of injustice'.[118] With a conscientious objector from the Vietnam War in the White House, a left-leaning Labor government in Australia, and the decimation of Conservative rule in Canada, many Western societies now seemed more open to debating and discussing the past. Bill Clinton, Jacques Chirac, Gerhardt Schroeder, and Tony Blair all engaged in forms of 'self examination', apologizing to various groups for the 'gross historical crimes' committed in their own countries and to others.[119] The world was thus confronted with 'an unusual moment in human history in which grappling with the past is a priority issue on the agenda of dozens of contemporary states'.[120] This led to a process of 'democratizing the past' – where, as Allan Cairns describes, states now tried to give equal recognition to those who had been previously marginalized or victimized.[121]

For many groups, identity politics was not about breaking new ground, but reworking arguments and images that had already succeeded in practice for American Jews. Levy and Sznaider, in several recent articles and in their book *Memory in a Global Age: The Holocaust* (2004), argue forcefully that a new cosmopolitan morality emerged after the Cold War, based on the lessons and symbolism of the Holocaust.[122] The 'old, national narratives' which focused only on the nation-state were complemented by more universal concerns for human beings in whatever state they may reside. A 'new, global narrative' emerged, based on the cautionary lessons of the Holocaust.[123]

While the UN Conventions on Genocide and Human Rights both stemmed from the horrors of World War II and the Holocaust, international law and morality was suppressed when the UN became a creature of Cold War politics. With the end of the Cold War, and the putative decline of the nation-state, the Holocaust as a universal standard of good and evil properly came into its own.[124] Levy and Sznaider credit the Holocaust for creating the space for discussion of historical victimization, for bringing about the 'post-heroic' age.[125] While the authors decisively fail to make a case for the decline of the nation-state, they do rightly highlight the spread of a new Holocaust-based Western morality.

Holocaust survivors set the parameters for what other groups felt they could reasonably demand. These demands included 'transitional justice' (punishment of the perpetrators and reparations from the perpetrators); 'apologies and statements of regret'; then 'efforts to commemorate past suffering' through forms of 'communicative history' (involving school textbooks, memorials, and commemorative events).[126] In short, the Holocaust became the 'true emblem' of our age, a 'kind of gold standard against which to judge other cases of injustice'. Yet, rather than seeing this as a problematic phenomenon, a case of an 'established' genocide 'suck[ing] the juices out of alternative commemorative and reparations projects', Torpey posits that the opposite is true and the Holocaust began to function as a window of opportunity, giving hope to other groups by presenting a frame of reference and a model to follow.[127] Absent the Holocaust, 'other projects oriented to coming to terms with the past would not have been so successful'. Torpey continues that 'widespread Holocaust consciousness, in turn, has been the water in which reparations activists have swum, defining much of the discourse they use to enhance their aims'.[128]

Comparativists

Despite the potential usefulness of the Holocaust as a comparative device, there are obvious problems. Identity politics has always involved competition for recognition. John Mowitt's work on 'trauma envy' rightly signals that groups seek to display 'wounds' in order to legitimate themselves in a social climate dominated by identity politics. Proving trauma generates useful 'moral capital' for the group, even if its suffering is sometimes exaggerated.[129] Stein too notes that the Holocaust as an 'atrocity tale' *par excellence* possesses 'protagonist identify fields' (comparing oneself to the Jews) and 'antagonist identity fields' (accusing one's enemies of being Nazis). A series of binary opposites is created ('homologies') which help frame the protagonist's case. Since the media focuses on extremes, the more sensationalist one's rhetoric (so the argument goes), the better the chances of being heard.[130] Torpey has also noted the 'vigorous competition' that has emerged as a result of various groups seeking to claim that their experiences are 'Holocaust-like' or 'worse than the Holocaust'. The result, he argues, 'is an often unseemly contest for the status of the worst-victimized'.[131]

The cases in this book feature scholarship by Comparativists, those who consciously use Holocaust imagery and vocabulary to reinterpret the collective history of their group. Olick's view that 'we are all Germans now' is particularly attractive. They see the public space opened by 'The Holocaust' as a potential window of opportunity, allowing them to gain acknowledgement of past wrongs, and, potentially, reparations. Yet there is also competition, and sometimes resentment. Holocaust scholarship is often criticized by Comparativists, who, as Alan Rosenberg describes, are 'quite willing to see the Holocaust as an event of major importance, but they nevertheless agree that the claim of uniqueness cannot be sustained in any non-trivial form'.[132]

Comparativist historians often view Holocaust uniqueness claims as a double standard. While Western governments recognize the Holocaust, they often fail to recognize other genocides. Witness, for example, the unwillingness of any American administration officially to apologize for African slavery. President Clinton gave a personal apology in 1998, but any official version would surely have led to legal action against the government, and a groundswell of demands for reparations from some and anger from many others.[133] Further, 'Comparativists' reject the idea that Jews necessarily suffer from the use of the Holocaust, and that those who apply the term in non-Jewish contexts are somehow dishonest or malign. They also deny that the Jewish people actually own 'holocaust' to begin with. Stannard, for example, argues that while the Holocaust (with a large 'H') 'clearly applies exclusively to the genocide that was perpetrated by the Nazis against their various victims', holocaust with a small 'h' should 'belong to anyone who cares to use it'.[134]

Most Comparativists reject (at least some) claims of Holocaust uniqueness. Genocide and other mass horrors have occurred since Biblical times. To focus on the uniqueness of the Holocaust is inherently Eurocentric, and implies that the western world never committed genocide in its past. The Holocaust is hardly, Shelley Wright argues, 'a great chasm dividing us irrevocably from our brutal past. It is a very thin line. We have crossed it many times'. The difference between the pre and post-Holocaust world is not that the world has necessarily become any more violent or evil. Rather, the Holocaust has forced us to 'understand that the violence of ethnic tribalism is not confined to Africa, or Asia, or the Middle East, or the cities of Eastern Europe – it is here, at home – We are the Savage'.[135]

Competition between Comparativists and some Holocaust historians continues. Yet there is a great deal of recognition and respect between serious historians of the Holocaust and other serious and well-meaning historians seeking to represent their own group's suffering. In recent years, the *Porrajmos* ('Devouring' or genocide) of the Roma peoples has become recognized by many Holocaust historians as an integral part of the Holocaust, despite some notable exceptions.[136] Similarly, Black slavery and the Armenian genocide have also received recognition as horrific crimes. More recently, Japanese atrocities during World War II received top billing at the USHMM, even when terms such as 'forgotten Holocaust' and 'Pacific Holocaust' were used to describe them.[137]

Holocaust historians like David Moshman argue that since our contemporary understanding of genocide is based on the Holocaust, we have little choice but to invoke this 'prototype' as a symbol for comparison.[138] Michael Berenbaum also promotes comparison as a way of 'deepen[ing] our moral sensitivity while sharpening our perception'. 'Such inclusion', he feels, 'displays generosity of spirit and ethical integrity'.[139] Still others have noted how obviously every genocide will 'seem unique to those who identify with it'.[140] Scholars also adopt a cautionary note. Ismar Schorsch worries that uniqueness claims can 'impede dialogue' and 'alienate potential allies from among other victims of organized depravity'.[141] Israel Charny too condemns what he calls a 'fetishistic atmosphere in which the masses of bodies that are not to be qualified for the definition of genocide are dumped into a conceptual black hole, where they are forgotten'.[142]

Preserving uniqueness: Absolutists

As will be made obvious in the case studies that follow, attempts to invoke the Holocaust have met with sharp criticism from some Holocaust historians. As the next chapter outlines, the Holocaust is unique for many reasons. And the continuation of anti-Semitism throughout the world, as well as Holocaust denial, is real. Most Holocaust historians are well aware that Holocaust memory is being constantly challenged from all quarters, necessitating a spirited defense. Further, many feel both empowered *and* threatened by the fact that the Holocaust has been so Americanized. The fate of Jews, Holocaust memory, and Israel seems to rely heavily on America, and how it is perceived within and outside its own borders.

Absolutist and Relativist Holocaust historians work to promote Holocaust uniqueness. As Rosenberg argues, the first group sees the Holocaust as a unique and incomparable event.[143] Claude Lanzmann, for example, sees any attempt to explain the Holocaust as nothing more than an 'obscenity'.[144] Others more realistically fear that Holocaust trivialization will lead to increased anti-Semitism and Holocaust denial. Ronnie Landau has described a process of 'hijacking' and a 'grotesque competition in suffering' resulting from comparison.[145] Rosenbaum too notes the Holocaust's 'superficial' application 'to so many different types of calamities' resulting in 'inappropriate 'word-napping'.[146] Such Absolutist views negate the idea that the Holocaust can or should be compared to anything that preceded or followed it.[147]

Absolutists generally fear that invoking the Holocaust in non-Jewish contexts will reduce the significance of Jewish suffering and make Jews more vulnerable worldwide.[148] As Robert Melson rightly notes, this school does not necessarily rely on emotion or ethnocentrism. Rather, the belief in the extreme nature of the Holocaust leads to fears that careless comparison 'will diminish its moral force as an example and warning of radical evil in the world'.[149] For this school, using Holocaust imagery inappropriately trivializes Jewish suffering, demeaning survivors, their families, and the Jewish community at large. It may also threaten Israel. This leaves Jews open to the continued problems of anti-Semitism and Holocaust denial.[150]

Preserving uniqueness: Relativists

Relativist historians, by contrast, do engage in comparative work, although much of this is undertaken expressly to prove that the Holocaust is both unique and unprecedented.[151] Selective genocide denial is sometimes, but certainly not always, a hallmark of this approach. Many Relativists have seemingly internalized the lessons of the USHMM, namely that American history represents the very antithesis of the Holocaust. Steven Katz's assertions of Holocaust uniqueness have therefore sought to uphold Holocaust uniqueness *and* the integrity of America's historical identity. In his lengthy study *The Holocaust in Historical Context* (1994),[152] Katz begins with the supposition that the Holocaust *must* be unique and then sets out to prove it by comparing it with other tragedies of history.[153]

Its uniqueness, he posits, lies in that it was 'unmediated, intended, complete *physical* eradication of every Jewish man, woman and child'. This 'unconstrained, ideologically driven imperative that *every* Jew be murdered' makes the Holocaust an unprecedented and unique event.[154] The 'intentionality' of the Holocaust is central to its uniqueness,[155] and any other genocide which does not share the intent to exterminate all members of a target group thus falls short.[156] Unsurprisingly, the Holocaust stands alone, since, as Katz argues, 'There is, in fact, not one instance before the Holocaust that fits this description ...'.[157] Katz's definition essentially excludes all other cases of genocide, including the "genocide" of North America's indigenous peoples, and the Armenian genocide.[158] While Katz acknowledges that the word 'genocide' has 'enormous connotative force', 'prestige and emotive power', he seeks to deny the label to any historic tragedy save the Holocaust.[159]

Another Relativist is Guenther Lewy, in his study of the 'persecution' of the 'Gypsies'. Lewy, like Katz (who he uses uncritically to support his case) favors a narrow view of the Holocaust, one that not only excludes the Roma but also so compartmentalizes and fragments their experiences that he is able to posit that they did not even suffer from genocide. This descends to attacks on their culture and ways of life, implying that they brought much of their own misfortune on themselves.[160] Even at Auschwitz, Lewy argues that Roma had a relatively easy time, with some classes of privileged Roma listening to music, eating well, smoking, and drinking, while girls gave themselves freely to sexual escapades and 'orgies' with SS soldiers.[161]

In general, Relativists are more concerned with promoting Holocaust uniqueness than in submerging themselves deeply enough in other groups' history. As I explore a range of case studies, the constant battle between Comparativists and Relativists will become apparent. Absolutists generally refrain from becoming too involved (if at all) in such debates. The other two groups, by contrast, have engaged in sometimes vitriolic turf wars over which group has suffered worse in its history, and which historical events are more 'unique' than others. Both sides seem to believe that there is only a limited amount of moral capital available, which each needs to carefully guard against 'theft'.

Conclusions

Overall, Americanization has yielded a greater awareness of the horrors of the Holocaust and its devastating impact on those who endured it. This includes the official commemoration of the Holocaust through countless memorials, museums, and traveling exhibits. From movies and literature to academic conferences, tenured academic positions, and school curricula, the Holocaust has achieved an unparalleled level of public and scholarly attention. Equally positive has been American support for the State of Israel. While geopolitical concerns were often paramount, the Holocaust did help orient American policy-makers towards Israel, even if only (in some cases) to court Jewish and Christian Zionist votes. Further, intercession by the American government helped Jewish survivors and their families gain recompense from Nazi-era corporations and Swiss banks.

However, Americanization has a downside. This includes competition for recognition during the civil rights era between Blacks and Jews, and an increase in anti-Semitism and Holocaust denial. This was especially prevalent during the 1970s, when the Holocaust began to be commemorated at the national level. Jews as a 'successful' minority group were challenged by other minorities, who resented their sometimes upwardly mobile status and the institutionalization of Holocaust memory. As the Holocaust became a more universal symbol, and was pitted in stark opposition to the ideals of American history, Holocaust historians sometimes became defenders of an idealized version of America.

In the 1990s, this put many Jewish organizations in conflict with indigenous groups, African Americans, and, to a lesser extent, Diaspora Armenians and Chinese. America (like some other western nations) was willing to recognize the uniqueness of the Holocaust, in part because this helped deflect attention from its own historic crimes. As an increasing number of disadvantaged groups began to reframe their own group histories *through* the Holocaust, competition invariably arose. When many western governments in the 1990s tried to apologize and effect reparations for past wrongdoing, the use of Holocaust imagery increased.

I thus end this chapter on a cautionary note. The Americanization and 'cosmopolitanization' of the Holocaust is a reality, and a reality welcomed by many Jews, and many non-Jewish groups. The Holocaust can certainly be presented as a unique event in many respects, as the next chapter discusses in depth. However, the Holocaust is also seen as a window of opportunity. It provides hope that, in an era of identity politics, reframing history through the Holocaust may achieve tangible benefits. This might include increased awareness of their past victimization, and, potentially, some form of redress. Future cases engage with whether or not this assumption bears out in practice.

2 Considering Holocaust uniqueness

From Hebrew peoplehood to the Americanization of memory

> Every event, like every human being and even every dog, is unique. We would be condemned to be isolated monads if we didn't compare and generalize, for comparisons are the bridges from one unique life to another. In our hearts we all know that some aspects of the Shoah have been repeated elsewhere, today and yesterday, and will return in new guise tomorrow; and the camps too, were only imitations (unique imitations, to be sure) of what had occurred the day before yesterday.
>
> (Ruth Kluger, 'The Camps' (2003))[1]

'Is the Holocaust unique?' The question has been asked countless times since the 1960s, eliciting a wide variety of responses from academics, activists, and the general public. Alan Rosenbaum's courageous volume[2] in 1996 sketched the rough outlines of the debate, pitting Relativists and Comparativists against each other in an intellectual and emotive confrontation. No clear 'winner' emerged, nor could any one answer have satisfied everyone. Some posit that the Holocaust *is* intrinsically unique; others that it has been *made* unique by Holocaust historians and other interpreters. Some see all events as unique in some way. Others, like Gunnar Heinsohn, see the Holocaust as 'uniquely unique'. As Margalit and Motzkin succinctly phrase the basic problem:

> The question of historical uniqueness has two aspects. First, why is the Holocaust viewed as the preeminent atrocity in human history? Second, is this attribution of historical uniqueness a consequence of something about the Holocaust itself? It may be that the Holocaust is not unique, but that the reaction to it is unique, and it may be that this reaction is unique because the Holocaust is unique, and it may be that both the Holocaust and the reaction to it are independently unique.[3]

In this chapter I argue that the Holocaust does indeed possess many unique elements, elements which give the Holocaust an iconic status among genocides. However, every other genocide and historical atrocity can also claim elements all its own. So what then sets the Holocaust apart? What encourages scholars to focus on the uniqueness of one genocide, over and above all others? At one level, the Holocaust is significant because its imagery, vocabulary, and lessons have been Americanized, then subject to a process of cosmopolitanization. I echo Novick's conclusion that the Holocaust has achieved a unique 'floor', 'below which the level of Holocaust commemoration will not fall for the foreseeable future'.[4] Further, no other genocide has laid the basis for a new international morality. The belief amongst many non-Jewish groups that Jews have achieved media, cultural, economic, and geopolitical success, also makes Holocaust vocabulary and imagery worth of emulation. Thus, to echo the previous quotation, the Holocaust is both intrinsically and extrinsically unique. This chapter attempts to set out precisely how and why this is so.

Uniqueness claims abound in the literature, from the uniqueness of Jewish monotheism, to twentieth-century forms of redemption in a territorially bounded nation-state. From the onset, I should make clear that I don't agree with every claim reviewed here. All claims are *valid* – in so far as the events described did happen. However, not all of the events described were unique or unprecedented. World history encompasses much more than twentieth-century western European events, a point which is raised repeatedly by Comparativists.

This chapter attempts something new. I aim to offer a systematic analysis of fifteen major uniqueness claims. I do this for several reasons. First, no other study has attempted to pull all the scattered uniqueness claims together, to present an overall picture of how and why the Holocaust can be said to be unique. Second, no other study has joined together uniqueness claims covering the pre-Holocaust, Holocaust, and post-Holocaust periods.[5] Third, if we claim the Holocaust as a unique benchmark, we need to establish precisely what we're comparing – what aspects of the Holocaust are unique, and are subject to comparison and competition. The cases that follow my two theoretical inquiries, from American Indians to Serbian nationalists, clearly demonstrate how crucial the Holocaust has become as a frame of reference.

I have divided this chapter into three sections. The first examines claims that the Jewish people and their contributions to the Western world are unique. I also engage with claims that anti-Semitism is a unique form of hatred. This section asks whether there are attributes intrinsic to the Jewish people which make their fate of special significance to non-Jews. A second section explores whether the Holocaust (because of its many characteristics) stands out as a unique and distinct horror separate from the unique identity of its primary victims. This leads to the third section, which examines post-Holocaust events – the unique legacies of the Holocaust, and the lessons other groups might potentially draw from Jewish experiences after 1945.

1 Jewish contributions to the Western world

As Elie Wiesel has argued, encapsulating the first claim, the specifically *Jewish* nature of the Holocaust makes it unique. 'Remove the Jews from the Holocaust', he posits, 'and the Event loses its mystery'.[5] The Holocaust is unique because Jews as a people are unique. Their contributions to the West, and their longevity as a coherent people, contribute to this ideal. First, perennialist theorists of nationalism see the Hebrew people as the world's first proto-nation, exhibiting the world's first example of territorial nationalism. Adrian Hastings, for example, asserts that 'nations originally "imagined"... through the mirror of the Bible'.[6] Michael Walzer similarly traces how Biblical exodus history has shaped the 'civic-political aspirations of national liberation movements', a view also favoured by Sammy Smooha.[7]

Second, Hebrew collective identity bequeathed the ideal of a covenant to European nations. By this I mean a special agreement made between a people and their deity to deliver them in the midst of hardship, laying the basis for 'myths of divine election'.[8] The Hebrew covenant also created a cyclical reading of how history operated, in a cycle of 'rise, fall and rise again', or what Northrop Frye has dubbed a 'covenential cycle'. Here, negative events were followed by positive rewards. The chosen people were redeemed if they continued to adhere to their faith and their laws.[9] The ideal of a covenant between God and his people would make each person theoretically an equal member of the nation, creating a more 'democratic' collective without the need for 'high priests' to interpret national identity. For Hans Kohn, this distinction gave the Hebrews a 'national ideal and purpose' to history.[10]

Third, the expansive oral and written traditions of the Jewish people, as Yehuda Bauer recalls, 'decisively influenced modern civilization ... "Western" or "Northern" culture, from Chaucer, Shakespeare, and Dante to Polish and Russian literature, from the impact of the moral teachings of the prophets to legal concepts and the Rights of Man'.[11] This is followed by a fourth unique feature – Jewish longevity as a distinct people. While 'Athens and Rome' (the only other main pillar of Western tradition, according to Bauer) faded away, Jews have a unique continuity, making Jews 'and their culture ... if not the oldest', then at the very least 'one of the oldest continuing civilizations we know'.[12] Equally, Bernard Susser posits that Jews' 'very survival attests to the miraculous intervention of the Hand of God'. He concludes: 'we are part of an unbroken chain whose innumerable individual links go back directly to Sinai ... It is a record without historical parallel'.[13]

Some of these claims are intuitively appealing. Hebrew ideals of chosenness and covenant *were* certainly influential in other forms of national identity. Leah Greenfeld's work demonstrates the importance of Hebrew-style myths of chosenness in England, France, and America.[14] Others have investigated the widespread use of myths of chosenness, from Afrikaner nationalism to collective identity in the American South.[15] Generally, the ideal of being like the chosen people of the Bible has been attractive, from poet William Blake's dream of creating 'Jerusalem' in England, to earlier Puritan claims of America as 'God's Canaan' and the 'New Jerusalem'. Myths of exodus, persecution, and deliverance certainly influenced early forms of national identity, so much so that Hugh Trevor-Roper's definition of 'normal nationalism' (1962) was almost entirely based on the Hebrew example.[16] Jewish people *have* decisively and uniquely influenced Western culture.

However, claims of *unique* Jewish longevity and continuity seem untenable. First, Hebrew was hardly the dominant language of Jews in the Diaspora, even if it became popular after 1948 in Israel. Second, countless examples of ethnic longevity and continuity exist throughout the world. The Arabs, Persians, Hindus, Tibetans, and many cultures of the Asia-Pacific region, Africa, and South America (despite colonialism) have preserved their traditions, religions, and languages over thousands of years. Within Europe, ancient language groups, cultures, and civilizations remain after centuries – the examples are too numerous to list here. To claim that Jews are unique in this respect is in part the product of wishful thinking. While 'Athens and Rome' as we once knew them are gone, this does not mean that only the Jewish people possess forms of continuous culture and tradition.

The uniqueness of Christian anti-Semitism

Anti-Semitism's uniqueness is a popular topic which has been exhaustively covered since at least 1943, when Joshua Trachtenberg wrote his classic work *The Devil and the Jew* during the ravages of the Holocaust. Here, he traced the connections between medieval anti-Semitism and Nazi manifestations.[17] For Walter Laqueur, anti-Semitism has been an 'all pervasive and changing force throughout time and space',[18] while for Yehuda Gothelf it has been 'the companion of the people of Israel from the time it was exiled from its homeland ...'.[19] Elie Wiesel terms it 'the oldest group prejudice in recorded history', while similarly disdaining it for its lack of imagination, since: 'The arguments used by Pharoah in Egypt are exactly the same as those used by Haman in Sushan, by Nebuchadnezzar in Babylon, by Torquemada in Chmelnitski, and later on by Hitler and Stalin'.[20]

Anti-Semitism is also uniquely flexible, changing to suit social, political, cultural, economic, technological, and religious exigencies. Dan Cohn-Sherbok's *The Crucified Jew: Twenty Centuries of Christian Anti-Semitism* exemplifies the work of some authors who chart the evolving nature of anti-Semitism from Roman times to the Protestant Reformation, the Enlightenment, and the Industrial Revolution.[21] Alternatively, one can chart 'waves' of anti-Semitic anger, interspersed with periods of acceptance.[22] Tracing the precise era when anti-Semitism was born is contentious, and depends on how individual historians choose to read Jewish history. A number of historians chart anti-Jewish hatred back to Biblical times,[23] even a 'special Egyptian strain in anti-Semitism'.[24] Others locate anti-Semitism from the third century BCE, with Christianity and Judaism definitively parting ways by AD 70.[25] Still others trace the apogee of early anti-Semitism to the First Crusade in 1096,[26] or to the later medieval era, when the Catholic Church practiced a 'holy war of extermination' against Jews.[27] This era also featured anti-Jewish myths, including 'poisoning wells, murdering Christian children for their blood, and using Satanic magic to confound and gain supremacy over innocent Christians'.[28]

The overall conclusion from this growing literature is that anti-Semitism 'stands alone' among 'all other cases of collective antagonisms'. It does so because of its 'unprecedented systematicity, for its ideological intensity, for its supra-national and supra-territorial spread, for its unique mix of local and ecumenical sources and tributaries'.[29] And ultimately, the uniqueness of *Christian* anti-Semitism makes the Holocaust unique.[30] Rubenstein's uniqueness arguments stem from the ideal of the Jews as a special people. Thus:

> In no other instance of genocide in the twentieth century was the fate of the victims so profoundly linked to the religio-mythic inheritance of the perpetrators. In Christianity, the Jews are not simply one of many peoples of the world. They are the people in whose midst God himself deigned to be incarnated. ... Jews are depicted as the God-bearing and the God-murdering people par excellence. No other religion is as hideously defamed in the classic literature of the rival tradition as is Judaism by Christianity.[31]

Thus, Jews make the Holocaust a unique event with great religious significance for Christians, unlike Stalin's massacres, or Yugoslavia's ethnic cleansing.[32] Rubenstein hastens to add, however, that the Holocaust fails to resonate to the same extent in non-Western societies. His research indicates that for Japanese, Chinese, and Koreans, the Holocaust has 'very little meaning'. The event is purely secular and devoid of any 'distinctive importance in and of itself' – being but one of 'many bloody chapters in human history'.[33] This is an important point, but it needn't discount the Holocaust's significance within the Western Christian world. As my previous chapter made clear, the Holocaust does have special significance in Europe, North America, and Australasia, and is perceived to be much more than a secular event comparable to others.

Jewish ethics and Nazi religious anti-Semitism

Closely tied with Christian anti-Semitism was a Nazi form of anti-Semitism which otherized Judeo-Christian morality itself. Jews were not only blamed for 'killing Christ' or refusing to convert; they were also blamed for (indirectly) creating Christianity in the first place, thus imprisoning the West in a monotheistic morality. This argument has most forcefully been advanced by George Steiner, who posits that while there may be 'parallels in technique' and in the 'idiom of hatred', making the Holocaust comparable to other genocides, the event is ontologically different, since the intent behind it 'takes us to the heart of Western culture, in the relations between instinctual and religious life'. He begins from Hitler's jibe that 'conscience is a Jewish invention', and works to the conclusion that the invention of monotheism by the ancient Hebrews 'tore up the human psyche by its most ancient roots'.[34]

Steiner credits Judaism with the production of a 'summons to perfection' which imposed itself on the West, such that Jews became the 'bad conscience of Western history'.[35] The Jewish God was fundamentally different from anything that had preceded it, presenting a totalitistic, omniscient, and omnipotent being, a god who defied understanding, but who was all-seeing and wrathful.[36] By initiating the Final Solution, the Nazis try to destroy monotheism and its moral code. As he paraphrases Hitler's rationale: 'Kill the rememberer, the claim agent, and you have cancelled the whole debt'.[37]

Heinsohn's arguments, while distinct, also locate the Holocaust's uniqueness in Hitler's hatred of Jewish morality – particularly the fifth commandment, 'Thou shalt not kill'.[38] Hitler's Final Solution is explained as an attempt to destroy the Jewish principle of 'the sanctity of life', to escape from the 'Jewish code of ethics of Jewified Christianity'.[39] The Holocaust is therefore 'uniquely unique' for the simple reason that 'it was a genocide for the purpose of reinstalling the right of genocide'.[40] In Heinsohn's rather odd phraseology: 'In the cold language of the computer age one could say that Hitler smashed the hardware – Jewish men, women and children – to destroy the software – the Jewish code of ethics'.[41] That Nazism rejected equality and mercy in favor of hierarchy and destruction of the inferior is, rightly, very common in the literature. The Nazi ethical system was highly distinctive and unique in many ways.[42]

Nazi racial anti-Semitism and the 'biocracy'

For most academics studying the Holocaust, Nazi racial anti-Semitism is unique, by its nature and virulence. By extension, the Holocaust as a product of this radicalized hatred is also unique. Obviously, racism and racial anti-Semitism predate the Nazi era. Such musings can be traced back to the nineteenth-century work of Houston Stewart Chamberlain (amongst others), who identified an enduring history of deep racial antagonism between 'Aryans' and 'Semites'. That Christianity was a Semitic invention necessitated that its beliefs be rejected.[43] Joseph-Arthur Compte de Gobineau's theories were little different, as expressed in his well known *Inégalité des races humaines*.[44] Equally, forms of eugenic theory (promoting the sterilization of certain groups and the reproduction of others) were advanced by

Sir Francis Galton, his American disciple Charles Davenport, German theorist Wilhelm Schallmeyer, and many others.

However, the uniqueness of Nazi racial anti-Semitism lay in the state's unprecedented ability to 'redefine evil' – to re-conceptualize race relations by pitting one group in stark competition against another.[45] If Germans were the apogee of racial development, Jews were dangerous 'racial aliens'.[46] Ethics were so twisted in the Nazi era that good and evil assumed entirely new definitions. As Peter Haas posits, while the regime committed 'what we judge to be heinous crimes', this was not, he reveals, 'because they were quintessentially evil and brutal people, but because they were in fact ethically sensitive'. Simply put: 'vast numbers of people simply came to understand ethics in different terms'.[47] Claudia Koonz's more recent work on the 'Nazi conscience' explores how the regime rejected universal forms of morality. Instead the state promoted particularist ethical values, 'appropriate to their Aryan community'.[48] In their highly racialized view of the world, Nazis became 'ethnic fundamentalists'.[49]

The primary target of this fundamentalism was Jews, who were perceived as 'a race to undermine and poison all other races', with an agenda to destroy the entire 'racial order' itself. As Bauman avers, the Holocaust was then not so much a self-interested German strategy, but a war 'waged in the name of all races, a service rendered to racially organized humankind'.[50] In Leon Poliakov's work, the role of the Jews as an 'anti-people' or a 'pseudo-people' figures prominently.[51]

Herein lies the uniqueness of Nazi anti-Semitism and, by extension, the uniqueness of the Holocaust. Bauer sees the Nazi project as being 'the most radical attempt at changing the world that history has recorded to date: the most novel and the most revolutionary'. The Nazi regime's 'unprecedented quality' has much to do with 'explaining the unprecedented nature of the Holocaust'.[52] Even though Jews were not actually any sort of threat at all,[53] a racial ethic cast them in a demonic light – making their destruction inevitable. Thus: '... No genocide to date has been based so completely on myths, on hallucinations, on abstract, nonpragmatic, ideology – which then was executed by very rational, pragmatic means'.[54]

Part and parcel of this unique ethical system was the obsession with racial hygiene and biological purity. Robert Jay Lifton in his seminal (but sometimes maligned) *Nazi Doctors* provides a useful definition of what 'biocracy' meant within the Nazi system:

> The model here is a theocracy, a system of rule by priests of a sacred order under the claim of divine prerogative ... the divine prerogative was that of cure through purification and revitalization of the Aryan race ... Just as in a theocracy, the state itself was no more than a means to achieve 'a mission of the German people on earth': that of 'assembling and preserving the most valuable stocks of basic racial elements in this [Aryan] people ... [and] ... raising them to a dominant position'.[55]

The 'biocracy' was a world view unique to the Nazis, by extension making the Holocaust (a product of this world view) unique as well: '... only the Nazis have seen themselves as products and practitioners of the science of life and death processes – as biologically ordained guides to their own and the world's biological destiny'.[56] While not the first to hypothesize on the importance of racial purity, and the killing of those deemed to be inferior, the Nazis were the first to construct an entire *Weltanschauung* based on these concepts.[57] National Socialism was soon dubbed 'applied biology' – with biology figuring as 'one of the defining features of the Nazi world view'.[58]

The Holocaust derives some of its uniqueness from the Nazi racial world view – a perception of reality I argue *is* unique in world history. Of course Jews were certainly not the only victims of the biocracy. German mentally- and physically-handicapped persons were first killed in the T-4 program, and Roma were also slated for extermination. Nevertheless, Jews were the chief victims of Nazi biocratic principles, and the most obvious target of the state.[59]

Normality and assimilation of victims (fratricide)

Another aspect of uniqueness, one that seemingly contradicts others, was the uniquely assimilated nature of European Jews before the Holocaust. They were white, often middle-class, urban Europeans, well-educated, well represented in the professions, with great European artists, writers, and statesmen in their numbers.

While generally disparaging of uniqueness claims, Lilian Friedberg has outlined a case for the unique 'fratricidal' dimensions of the Holocaust. As she explains, the Holocaust 'represents the first incidence in history of geno-cidal assault directed against an assimilated, 'civilized' (and therefore human) population'. Friedberg uses the term 'fratricide' to describe the Holocaust, which was nothing less than the 'squabbling sons of the same God in a serial rerun of Cain and Abel'.[60] She revisits the idea of 'spiritual kinship' between Jews and Christians, arguing that unlike other genocides where the Other was seen as a 'savage' or wholly different, the genocide of Jews was in some respects more tragic, with special theological connotations over and above the contributions of the Jews themselves. 'Brothers killing brothers is classified as a mortal sin by the religious doctrines governing moral standards in both religions ...'.[61]

Inge Clendinnen too suggests that we in the Western world are better able to understand the sufferings of the Jews than Rwandans, Chinese peas-ants, or American Indians. 'We recognise ourselves as very like urban Euro-peans of five or six decades ago', she advances, 'people who looked like us, lived like us, who had like us come to assume the reliability of physical and emotional comfort, with death tamed to a distant prospect'.[62] This may fly in the face of the *otherness* which some Holocaust historians stress, but it does tap into one of the reasons why we are so revolted by the Holocaust. The wealth of personal memoirs, from Samuel Pisar's *Of Blood to Hope* to Art Spiegelman's *Maus*, forms the bedrock of a strong personal identification with the victims involved.[63] The diary of Anne Frank too allows us to enter the world of a young girl in a confined attic, as her country is overrun by Nazis. According to Anne Frank House: 'In confronting her story we are made acutely aware that the persecution of the Jews did not annihilate an *anonymous six million* ... it was the murder six million times over of unique individuals, of human beings'.[64]

Other memoirs, like the journal of Hannah Senesh, tell a similar story and reinforce the same point – that Jewish victims were educated, enlightened human beings, able to reflect on their experiences in meaningful ways we still find accessible.[65] Laurence Kutler has isolated approximately seventy memoirs for detailed study, concluding: 'The diaries humanize the numbers. Six million people become individuals with passions and agonies that we can understand'.[66] And more historical accounts are regularly discovered. A recent French publication features five recently unearthed memoirs excavated at Auschwitz, written by *Sonderkommando.*[67]

The uniqueness of the Nazi 'fratricide', however, is debatable. Peoples similar in culture, language, and religion have been killing each other for millennia. Cases reviewed in later chapters, like the Armenian genocide, carried out primarily by Turks and Kurds, and the Rape of Nanking, carried out by the Japanese, both have obvious fratricidal dimensions. In his dissection of ethnic nationalism in the 1990s, Michael Ignatieff made ample use of Sigmund Freud's 'narcissism of minor differences' to explain the relatively normal tendency for very similar peoples to slaughter one another. As he has explained: 'the smaller the real difference between two peoples, the larger it was bound to loom in their imagination ... Without hatred of the other, there would be no clearly defined national self to worship and adore'.[68] Fratricidal war has sadly been a normal part of human history.

As well, the fratricide argument counters more forceful claims of Jews being otherized throughout history. If Jews and Christians were brothers, as Friedberg alleges, they were not always thus. This image seems of relatively recent vintage. This does not discount the claim fully, because there were certainly fratricidal impulses at work here. Jews *were* a crucial part of German society, and were often assimilated, speaking German, even worshipping as Christians. Indeed, they were for all intents and purposes German in ways that mattered.

2 Bureaucracy, modernity, and mass death

Arguably, the Holocaust was the product of one of the most advanced Western countries in modern history. Uniquely, all the attributes of the organized Weberian state were directed to exterminating an entire race of people. The regime used every modern means at its disposal, including an enormous (if often highly fragmented) bureaucratic system. Work by

German theorists like Gotz Aly and Susan Hein helped pave the way for an analysis of the Holocaust, based on the methods by which Jews were killed.[69] For Aly and Hein, the Final Solution was dependent on large cadres of 'academically trained advisors' who planned and implemented a vast 'economy of the Final Solution'. These advisors included 'economists, agronomists, demographers, experts in labor deployment, geographers, historians, planners and statisticians'.[70] The Holocaust emerged as a rational undertaking. Jews were identified as a problem in bureaucratic terms, and then dealt with in the most efficient manner possible.

Reflecting Aly and Hein, Milchman and Rosenberg focus on how technology and rationality distinguish the Holocaust from other historical forms of mass murder. The Holocaust is the outcome of 'the ruthless application of the prodigious creations of twentieth-century science and technology'. 'Zyklon B, and the crematoria, as instruments of death', they advance, 'were far more technically sophisticated than the guns of the Einsatzgruppen, or the deliberate torture, starvation, or working to death of millions in the Gulag'.[71] The Holocaust's uniqueness is thus derived from the fact that 'perhaps for the first time in human history, science and technology, together with their bases in planetary technics, were joined in the effort to totally exterminate the Other …'.[72]

This argument has a number of supporters. Kren too describes a German 'industrial revolution in the manufacturing of death', leading to the creation of 'gigantic factories of death comparable to Detroit's River Rouge plant' – a view similar to that of Rubenstein and Roth, who describe killing 'on an assembly-line basis'.[73] These musings echo earlier reflections by Grossman, whose work in the early 1980s also focused on the rationality and efficiency of the killing process, complete with schedules, 'standards to be observed, monthly and quarterly deadlines…'.[74]

Technology and rational efficiency made Nazi mass murder more palatable for those tasked with carrying it out. As Bauman has argued in his classic study *Modernity and the Holocaust*, relatively normal people, even 'tepid anti-Semites', could be used to implement the genocide.[75] A 'routinization' of procedures, a 'distantiation', and the creation of 'multifinal' tasks (that could be 'combined and integrated into more than one meaning-determining totality') helped bureaucrats to absolve themselves from guilt. A complex process of dividing up tasks allowed for the 'substitution of technical for moral responsibility'.[76] The Holocaust was thus 'an outcome of the bureaucratic culture', including such mundane processes as 'means-end calculus, budget balancing, universal rule application'. Coldly rational bureaucratic procedures effectively distanced those who planned the Final Solution from its ultimate victims.[77] Evil became routine.

Added to this was the use of the latest advanced technology, as Edwin Black's groundbreaking *IBM and the Holocaust* recently revealed. Black has laid bare the intricate connections between the International Business Machine Company and Nazi Germany, describing how IBM Germany – and its Dehomag Hollerith punch-card machines – organized and systematized very detailed information on all German Jews from 1933 onwards.[78] Eventually, IBM became an enthusiastic collaborator in the Final Solution. It 'did not invent Germany's anti-Semitism', Black concludes, 'but when it volunteered solutions, the company virtually braided with Nazism. Like any technological evolution, each new solution powered a new level of sinister expectation and cruel capability'.[79]

This systematized, industrialized, bureaucratic dimension is unique to the Holocaust. Yet evil was not so banal and routinized. Expressing anti-Semitic beliefs did not hurt an engineer or bureaucrat's chance of promotion, as Burleigh and Wippermann have pointed out. Further, we should not assume that a bureaucrat hiding behind procedures and routines did not also operate out of malice.[80] Irrespective of the personal motivations of the perpetrators, however, the mechanization of death was a feature that the Holocaust shared with no other genocide before it, or to the same extent after it.

Universal and global dimensions

Hitler's world war was global and so too was the fight against the Jews, and eventually all Jews – men and women, children and the elderly, urban and rural, full and 'mischlinge' – were slated for extermination. Bauer holds that the Holocaust was 'unprecedented' for this reason. Since 'Nazi ideology saw in the Jews a universal devilish element', he argues, 'so the pursuit of Jews was to have been a global, quasi-religious affair...'.[81] It's thus clear in Bauer's mind that: 'Because the Germans fully intended to control not just Europe but the world, whether directly or through allies, this meant that Jews would ultimately be hunted down all over the world'.[82] Katz's view is similar, as we have seen, with the Nazi state's intention to commit 'all-inclusive, noncompromising, unmitigated murder' against Jews.[83] Roth too cites the Nazi desire to eliminate Jews 'root and branch',[84] while Gilbert refers to 'the fierce ideological determination of the Nazi machine to blot out Jewish life in its entirety'.[85]

Many adherents of this thesis point to the Wannsee Conference of 20 January 1942. Here, the Final Solution was meticulously planned and coordinated with the participation of a number of government agencies, although Reinhardt Heidrich was certainly in overall control.[86] Adolf Eichmann issued a proposal for the eventual extermination of Europe's Jewish population, which totaled over eleven million persons, including 330,000 in Britain and 4,000 in Ireland. Also included were Spain, Turkey, and Russia east of German-controlled areas.[87]

Those promoting the unique totalizing and universal intent of the Nazi extermination drive rely on a projection of what would have occurred had Nazis completed their plans for world conquest. Arguably, the strength of Nazi ideology, the amount of effort spent on systematically accounting for each and every Jew, and then creating and running the death camps, demonstrates a clear intention to kill at least all of *Europe's* Jews. However, it seems less clear that Hitler intended to control the entire world – to kill every Jewish person on the face of the earth. Irrespective of intent, he simply did not possess the means to do this, and was no doubt aware that allies such as Japan and Italy had different views and different policies concerning Jews residing in their conquered territory.

It's also clear that the intent to kill all members of a defined group was a historically unique occurrence. I am critical of Katz's assertion that no other groups were subject to forms of total genocide in the past. Certainly, cases in America and the Ottoman Empire appear to be attempts at total genocide, as I will argue in later chapters. Other cases of genocide differ from the Holocaust, in that perpetrators focused their gaze on a much smaller geographical area, and were certainly less organized and systematized in their killing operations. The Nazi state was technologically advanced, and had the military means to kill Jewish people in other countries. Other genocidal nations have had neither the technology nor the military means to go this far.

It is also relatively easy to claim that Jews were subject to a unique universal and global focus, because Jews were a Diasporic people. They were globally dispersed. Most victims of other genocides, before and after the Holocaust (even now in Darfur), were indigenous to the regions they inhabited. Their religion, culture, and heritage were confined to relatively traditional and fixed geographical locations. A global focus was less important, since the target group was already concentrated. This begs the question of whether universalization boils down to the uniqueness of Nazi intent and Nazi evil, or can be reduced to the fact that Jews were uniquely dispersed through the world as a people. Perhaps other perpetrators would not have gone through the laborious process of seeking out all members of the target group using the latest technology. Of this we can never be certain.

Jewish collaboration in their own destruction

Jews were not the only people unwittingly to collaborate in their own destruction. The British in India practiced forms of divide and rule which encouraged splits between 'Indians' (a highly diverse national group which really only came together under Mohandas Gandhi). Indian Sepoys from one part of the country were used to put down uprisings in another. White Australian settlers used Aboriginal trackers to hunt down Aboriginal children escaping from residential schools, well into the twentieth century. African Americans derided their 'uncle toms', American Indians their 'uncle tomahawks'. However, these are all cases of colonialism, where perpetrators aimed to control victim populations, not exterminate them. Collaborators gained long-term (even intergenerational) benefits from supporting the regimes which oppressed their fellows.

The Nazi ability to manipulate traditional forms of Jewish leadership in order to exterminate a people is unique. Equally unique is the cunning by which bureaucrats slowly narrowed the choices for death-camp inmates – forcing them to turn on each other and collaborate in their own humiliation and destruction. This arguably has no historical parallel. Traditionally, European Jewish communities exercised some degree of control over local affairs through 'Jewish communal affairs' committees (the *Kultusgemeinde*), which they maintained for centuries in Germany. These were similar to the Jewish councils (*kehal* or *kehilla*) in Poland and Eastern Europe. These forms of leadership were first manipulated during the process of ghettoization, when community elders were forced to organize and carry out Nazi policy. Nazis created Jewish Councils of Elders who were, in Haas' analysis, 'fully responsible (in the literal sense of the word)' for their actions and any 'mistakes' they could make in the running of the ghettos. While there were sometimes personal motives, many elders operated from altruistic motives, feeling they might in some way reduce suffering, by sparing their people from brutal Gestapo personnel. Still others may have hoped in vain to somehow influence German policy-making.[88]

The ghetto system was established in part to force Jews to destroy themselves. Collaboration was 'a crucial condition' in the Holocaust's success. Councils provided lists of inmates, controlled ghetto economies, and even printed money and maintained police forces. They kept their people alive until the Nazis ordered them to deliver them for transportation.[89] Uniquely, Bauman notes that

> quite untypical for a genocide, the total subjection of a population to the unconstrained will of their captors was achieved not through destruction, but by reinforcing the communal structure and the integrative role played by native elites. ... To some remarkable extent, the Jews were part of that social arrangement which was to destroy them....[90]

Once inmates were finally shipped to the death camps, another set of bureaucratic procedures took over. Tadeusz Borowski's *This Way for the Gas, Ladies and Gentlemen* describes a new type of society created at Auschwitz – one in which survival depended on either ignoring or helping to bring about the deaths of others.[91] As Rubenstein and Roth put the situation, starkly, 'living well depends on access to power that condemns others'.[92] A strong 'managerial design' was at work in the death camps, where coercion as well as force was used to control the inmate population. Illusions were important. Victims each had to believe that they could manipulate their environment sufficiently to save themselves from destruction.[93]

Jews had to believe that they were not being targeted as a homogenous people. Some would be targeted first, while others might survive. Thus religious Jews might be targeted over Christian converts, war veterans might survive, while assimilated West European Jews might be privileged over

Yiddish-speaking Central and East European Jews. Few had grasped – and the Nazis allowed few to grasp – that all Jews were slated for death, not just some classes or type.[94] Psychiatrist Viktor Frankl's account of his experiences in four camps also supports this view. Frankl describes how his 'inborn optimism' worked to keep him alive. However, he adds that this 'delusion of reprieve' also prevented he and his fellow prisoners from rebelling against the Nazi system, under the illusion that 'he would be reprieved, that everything would be yet be well'.[95]

In his now classic essay 'The gray zone', Primo Levi also observed how crucial Jewish collaboration was in maintaining the stability of the death-camp system. Levi describes three levels – the lowest rank, 'sweepers, kettle washers, night watchmen, bed smoothers', and then the reviled kapos – barrack leaders, clerks, administrators – who actively collaborated for power and small luxuries.[96] At the bottom were the *Sonderkommando* – those forced to remove the corpses from the gas chambers, and who had the horrific task of stripping them of any remaining 'valuables'. For Levi, the fact that *Sonderkommando* were overwhelmingly Jewish was no coincidence. Rather Nazi principles held: 'it must be the Jews who put the Jews into the ovens; it must be shown that the Jews, the subrace, the submen, bow to any and all humiliation, even to destroying themselves'. The entire edifice attempted to shift the blame and the guilt onto its victims, 'so that they were deprived of even the solace of innocence'.[97] Levi puts his finger on a central feature of the killing process – there was something intensely satisfying for Nazis in tricking the Jews, in dividing them up and pitting them against each other.

Brutality and horror

Ultimately, the Holocaust is unique because of its absolute horror. For Daniel Goldhagen, it is 'the most shocking event of the twentieth century'; Weiberg sees it as 'the most terrible even in modern history'.[98] Kren and Rappoport similarly see unprecedented horror in such features as 'the systematic dehumanization of the victims, the assembly-line process of mass murder, and the bureaucratic organization on a continental scale that brought people from every corner of Europe to be killed'.[99] For the general public, who possess only a basic knowledge of Holocaust history, the Auschwitz-Birkenau complex and its gas chambers function as shorthand for the Final Solution. The main watchtower at Auschwitz Birkenau II, and the *Arbeit Macht Frei* arch over the entrance to most death camps, have become highly recognizable symbols. The Holocaust is tied up with the images of Auschwitz and its symbols of destruction. Ball typifies this view when she describes being haunted by the 'mind-numbing enormity of the cattle cars, slave labor, gas chambers, crematoria, human experimentation, and the skeletal bodies of the murdered and liberated'.[100]

Clendinnen too argues that 'the idea of the gas chambers outrages our feelings in a way which the mass shootings, with all their brutality, do not'.

The horrors of the gas chamber lie for Clendennin in their rational, factory-like nature, 'designed by humans solely to produce human death swiftly, on a grand scale'.[101] Margalit and Motzkin, by contrast, see the Holocaust as unique by virtue of the combination of 'systematic humiliation' and 'systematic destruction'. Jews were to be humiliated and dehumanized, and then killed afterwards. Germans not only wanted the Jews dead, they also wanted to 'emphasize the *difference* of their eventual collective death over the common identity that death imposes on us all'.[102]

But the camps go further still, bringing into being visions of a medieval Christian Hell. As Steiner describes: 'The camp embodies, often down to the minutiae, the images and chronicles of Hell in European art and thought from the twelfth to the eighteenth centuries'.[103] Thus an aspect of Holocaust uniqueness lies in the unprecedented horror of the gas chambers and the impersonal and dehumanizing nature of the killings. Arguably, Auschwitz has a special resonance that *Einsatzgruppen* massacres or death by disease don't possess. Are the gas chambers the worse forms of killing in history? Historians of other genocides and atrocities question this assumption, as later chapters reveal. Should scientific, well planned forms of killing by 'professionals' worry us more than the rape and bludgeoning of Armenian civilians by their Kurdish and Turkish neighbors, or similar form of atrocity carried out by one warring Bosnian group against another? This claim of unique horror, like others, relies on a perception of what is worse and should be worse in Western sensibilities.

3 A rupture in civilization

Having established the ultimate horror of the Holocaust, it is a minor stretch to claim that the Holocaust has caused a rupture or break in Western civilization. The Holocaust represents a perversion and destruction of Enlightenment ideals by one of the most powerful and advanced Westernized states in existence. Only the Holocaust lays claim to fundamentally altering our belief in modernity, rationality, and technological progress. Theodore Adorno was perhaps the first to publicly articulate this perspective in his famous essay published in 1959.[104] By 1972, Steiner posited that the Holocaust had spawned a new age – a 'post-culture' which destroyed old concepts of good and evil, right and wrong. As he argued, again imbuing the Holocaust with theological significance:

> [T]he mutation of Hell into a metaphor left a formidable gap in the coordinates of location, of psychological recognition in the Western mind.... To have neither Heaven nor Hell is to be intolerably deprived and alone in a world gone flat.... Because we have it and are using it on ourselves, we are now in a post-culture. In locating Hell above ground, we have passed out of the major order and symmetries of Western civilisation.[105]

We now live in an age when the horrors of the death camps can be contemplated. Hell has been reified, brought to earth, where before we could only imagine how horrible it might be. From a similar standpoint, Dan Diner later described a *Zivilisationsbruch*, or a rupture in civilization, where the Holocaust figured as the 'ultimate or absolute genocide', eclipsing all other historical atrocities.[106]

Previous eras of optimism have passed, to be replaced in their stead by a new age of darkness. For Bauman, we now live in an age when 'the unimaginable ought to be imagined',[107] with Jurgen Habermas observing that the belief in a 'common layer' of humanity was shattered by the Holocaust: 'Auschwitz has changed the basis for the continuity of the conditions of life within history'.[108] Or to put it another way, we can conceptualize and imagine the worst forms of horror – we are no longer strangers to them. The unimagined has happened – and could thus happen again. The taboos on violence, cruelty, and depravity have all been broken at Auschwitz – now anything is possible.

Another aspect of the Holocaust is our loss of belief in science, technology, and the modern state. Mass death, rather than a proliferation of public goods, was the result of the Nazi experiment. The smokestack, formerly a 'prominent symbol for the idea of progress for humanity', now also represents Auschwitz.[109] The Holocaust, signaled by the absence of divine intervention, represents what Rubenstein and Roth term 'a season of the "death of God"' leading to a post-War era of 'radical secularity'. The result is an increasingly secular 'disenchanted' world, 'in which the credibility of traditional moral and religious norms has been threatened perhaps beyond repair'.[110]

Whether one accepts the Holocaust as a rupture is a matter of how one reads history before and after the Holocaust, and how one locates the events of Holocaust within that history. Arguably, the Holocaust might have been a civilizational rupture in *Europe*, introducing the concept of unspeakable horrors committed by Europeans against Europeans. However, as I argued in the previous chapter, it was hardly seen as such at the time, and other European events of the twentieth century certainly provide competition.

Jonathan Glover highlights the profound changes wrought in Europe by the carnage of World War I, a conflict that destroyed Europe's 'innocence' and led it on a downward spiral into World War II. Then we have the Russian Revolution and the horrors of Lenin and Stalin's Gulags, the purges and the Ukrainian famine genocide of the 1930s. Glover, in his first chapter, 'Never Such Innocence Again', contrasts European faith in progress at the end of the nineteenth century with the gloom and depression after 1918, as states scrambled to find solutions to their own readily apparent self-destructive tendencies. History for early twentieth-century Europeans, he argues, was an 'unpleasant surprise'.[111]

This rupture can also be problematized from other perspectives. Genocide and subjugation in the non-Western world were hardly uncommon before the Holocaust. Wright, as we have already seen, criticizes the view that the

Holocaust was a 'great chasm dividing us irrevocably from our brutal past'.[112] Future chapters support Wright's claim that we crossed the border between civilization and barbarism many times before 1933. And, to reiterate Rubenstein's comments, the Holocaust's Jewish/Christian symbolism fails to resonate in Asia. It tends to be viewed more along the lines of Flanzbaum's 'fratricide' than Diner's *Zivilizationsbruch*. Writers discussed in later chapters of this book negate the belief that the Holocaust was a uniquely singular event, signaling the death of faith in God or reason. Most argue that such faith was lost long before Hitler – from the beginnings of European colonization and Europe's first confrontations with the 'other' during the age of exploration and colonization, or at the very least during World War I and the Armenian genocide.

International legal legacies

Another uniqueness claim concerns the international legal legacies that follow in the wake of the Holocaust. Commonly cited are the United Nations Charter, the UN Conventions on Genocide and Human Rights (1948), and the principle of 'universal jurisdiction' which contests earlier notions of near-unlimited state sovereignty. Further, the Holocaust helped popularize such concepts as 'human rights', 'crimes against humanity', and 'genocide'. Additionally, one also has international war crimes tribunals, the Nuremberg and (later) Tokyo trials. While largely absent during the Cold War, the International Criminal Tribunals for Yugoslavia and Rwanda are also based on the Nuremberg legacy, as is the International Criminal Court from 2002. Robertson argues that before World War II: 'It dawned on no political leader, even after the carnage of the First World War, that international institutions might tell states how to treat their nationals'. 'Human rights' seemingly mattered little until 'Hitler made them irrelevant'.[113]

For Richard Goldstone, these legacies help demarcate the Holocaust as a unique horror: 'the most permanent, important and unique feature of the Holocaust is that it gave birth to the international human rights movement and the recognition of an international jurisdiction for the prosecution of war criminals'. He elaborates, reflecting Robertson: 'The shock to the conscience of humankind triggered by the Holocaust gave rise to the realization that it was necessary for the law of nations to protect individual members of the human race'. The UN Charter and other humanitarian aspects of international law are, he concludes, in consequence of the Holocaust.[114] The questioning of the 'inviolability of national sovereignty' as well as universal jurisdiction 'in respect of certain grave war crimes' also flows from the lessons of the Holocaust.[115]

Robertson and Goldstone's arguments reflect Sznaider and Levy in their emphasis on the role of the Holocaust as both inspiration and warning for generations after 1945. Implicit here is an assumption that the Holocaust was a rupture, whose unique horrors finally led to unique legislation against war crimes and genocide. Certainly the Holocaust made explicit the dangers of unlimited territorial sovereignty and the consequences of having no international mechanisms for protecting minority groups and civilians. Yet the Holocaust was not as strong a rupture as some assume it to be. International law *did* exist before 1945, and to draw a stark contrast between the post-War and pre-War eras is misleading.

Thus 1918 rather than 1945 seems a more plausible beginning for European conceptions of human rights. After all, the horrors of World War I did serve as a catalyst for the birth of 'liberal internationalism'. Crude 'balance of power' politics were abandoned in principle, and emphasis was placed on promoting democracy and national self-determination domestically. Western leaders advocated the creation of international institutional structures to bind states together to prevent war. The League of Nations was one outgrowth of this new type of thinking, as was the Treaty of Paris or Kellogg-Briand Pact of 1928, a highly ambitious (but ultimately futile) attempt to abolish war.[116]

It seems short-sighted to ignore the impact that eight and a half million deaths had in Europe by 1918. After all, the concept of 'crimes against humanity' goes back to 1919, when the Commission of Responsibilities of the Paris Peace Conference condemned the 'new crimes ... against humanity and civilization' committed by the Turkish Committee of Union and Progress against the Armenians.[117] Even genocide is partially based on the Armenian precedent, as anyone familiar with Raphael Lemkin's work would know well.[118] Earlier wars, while certainly not international ruptures, also helped promote conceptions of human rights and morality. Horrified by the bloodshed at the Battle of Solferino in 1859, Henri Dunant founded the Red Cross and later helped formulate the Geneva Conventions in 1864.[119] Francis Lieber, whose Lieber Code was central to the Conventions, was himself traumatized by the carnage of the American Civil War.

While the international community was shocked by the events of the Holocaust in 1945, these did not have the distinctive significance they do today. Ignatieff has referred to a 'revolution in the modern moral imagination' after 1945, but also notes that 'aggressive war itself, rather than the extermination of the Jews' was the subject of Nuremberg. While 'genocide' was certainly under discussion, it was not designated until much later as 'the unique abomination that most contemporary reflection believes it to be'.[120]

The Holocaust has been significant in the formation of international law and morality. However, Goldstone and Robertson's view suggests that there was no real conception of international law and morality before Hitler, and something of a groundswell afterwards. This is inaccurate, and sadly, despite the Holocaust and Stalin's Great Terror, Mao's Great Leap Forward, the Cambodian genocide, and the Rwandan genocide, we still have little interest in intervening to stop genocide. The United Nations still does not possess adequate deterrent and enforcement mechanisms. We can perhaps find solace in the fact that these Declarations and Conventions have at least empowered the general public to bring forth what Ignatieff has called an 'advocacy revolution' comprising, among other things, 'a network of non-governmental human rights organizations' – such as Amnesty International and Human Rights Watch.[121]

Redemption in the states of Israel

Another aspect of the Holocaust's uniqueness is derived from the creation of the State of Israel in 1948. The Holocaust thus has a redemptive legacy that few other crimes can claim – the chance for surviving victims to start again in a new land, and very soon after having suffering such a traumatic calamity. From 1949, the conception that Israel was 'the inheritance of those who perished' became increasingly common.[122] For post-Holocaust Zionists struggling with the genocide of six million Jewish people, the return to Zion would take on new and more urgent meaning. As Menachem Rosensaft describes, the 'ultimate historically unparalleled implementation of anti-semitism' necessitated the creation of the State of Israel.[123] Israel was thus, as Yaakov Herzog argues, the 'immediate recompense and revival' after the 'greatest crime in history'.[124]

Friedlander too has stressed the significant links between the Holocaust and Israel: 'The short period of time that elapsed between the catastrophe of European Jewry and the creation of the Jewish state presented the official discourse with a framework both natural and deeply embedded in Jewish tradition, that of "catastrophe and redemption"'.[125] In token of this reality in Israel, *Yom Hashoah* is followed by a commemoration day for fallen Israeli soldiers, to be then followed by Israel's Independence Day celebrations.[126]

Certainly such a rapid national salvation after such a horrific genocide is unique, and the links between Holocaust and redemption have formed an important aspect of Israeli identity. There are, however, detractors. Yaffa Eliach worries that reducing Jewish history to little more than 'a record of futility and frustration' omits the 'rich Jewish intellectual and communal activities which here based on traditional values as well as on positive inter-actions between Judaism and European society'.[127]

Israel's 'new historians' or 'post-Zionist historians' have more recently problematized Israeli's use of the Holocaust to legitimate territorial expansion and mistreatment of the Palestinians.[128] The Lebanon War and the second *Intifadah* have led to new public debate about how Israeli history should be presented. Benny Morris, for example, attacks 'Zionist historians' for being ethnocentric and self-righteous. He looks sympathetically at the Palestinian cause, and even sees Israel's formation as a colonial project against a pre-existing indigenous population.[129] 'New historians' even criti-cize the axiomatic links between the Holocaust and Israel. They draw com-parisons between Israeli settlement and the French in Algeria, and White populations in West and Southern Africa. Further, they dismiss the claim that Israel was actually in a dangerous or tenuous position after 1948.[130]

Yet despite criticisms of early Zionist scholarship, Israel is unique in many ways. No other victim people have so quickly gained a homeland after centuries without one. Certainly other nations did gain a national home after a major war. The creation of Poland, Czechoslovakia, Albania, and Yugoslavia after World War I come to mind. However, none of these groups suffered from genocide, and none were Diaspora peoples who had to immigrate to a national homeland and then fight to liberate it. At the same time, a new *homeland* cannot always replace a centuries old *home*. Israel was a haven, but for many German, Austrian, Polish, and other Jews Europe had been their home for centuries. Thus while Jews gained a homeland, they lost their equally important cultural, linguistic, territorial, and other ties to Europe. Many European countries implicated in the Holocaust displayed a marked reluctance to welcome back surviving Jews, who had a very difficult time after 1945.[131]

Acknowledgement, commemoration, restitution by the former perpetrator

Related to the creation of Israel has been the restitution and assumption of guilt (however imperfect) by West Germany after 1945. Through the DENKMAL and other forms of commemoration, this guilt plays an important role in contemporary German identity. Another aspect of uniqueness concerns the compensation given to victims and their families. Goldstone notes the 'very substantial political and material acknowledgement which victims of the Holocaust have received'. This adds to our appreciation of Holocaust uniqueness, as 'victims of no other genocide have received this kind of acknowledgement. Neither have the Romani or the other non-Jewish victims of the Holocaust'.[132] Kurt Jonassohn too locates West Germany as 'the first country to admit that a genocide was committed and to agree to a modest form of reimbursement to some of the survivors ... the only case in which a perpetrator has admitted guilt'.[133]

And yet, anti-Semitism continued well into the 1950s.[134] Nazism too remained popular. As Hans Kung argues, dismissing the notion that Hitler was some sort of accident or aberration of history: 'Adolf Hitler came to power with the broad assent of the German people, and for all the hidden criticism was supported to the bitter end by the majority of the population with a loyalty which is terrifying even today'.[135] The lack of full German repentance was obvious even in 1959 with Adorno's famous lecture 'What does it mean to come to terms with the past?' in which he accused the Federal Republic of trying to get beyond the Nazi past rather than trying to fully engage with it.[136]

Nevertheless, the post-War German government did endeavor to take some responsibility for the actions of the Nazi state. As we have already seen, the Adnauer government accepted responsibility for Nazism, and agreed to pay reparations. By September 1952, German officials agreed to

$867 million for 'reparation for the material damage to the Jews at the hands of the Nazis'.[137] Germany also acknowledged that it had perpetrated 'unspeakable criminal acts' against the Jewish people.[138] For Israeli government minister Pinhas Lavon: 'The people who wanted to exterminate us is forced to bear some of the burden involved in creating a new Jewish centre of strength and a place of rebirth'.[139] By 1972, Willy Brandt knelt at the memorial to the Warsaw Ghetto Uprising, inaugurating a new era of commemoration.[140]

Of course, acknowledgement and memory in Germany was far from perfect, and Hitler and his henchmen were demonized while the people themselves were absolved.[141] During most of the Cold War, West Germany continued to normalize its history, proceeding through three different phases or 'major legitimation profiles' in order to 'normalize' its past.[142] By the 1980s, Germans were trying to distance themselves from the Holocaust. Helmut Kohl's comments in 1981 that German sovereignty should no longer be held hostage to Auschwitz were followed later in 1985 by the Bitburg controversy.[143] The view that Germans were also victims of Nazism became increasingly popular during the 1980s.[144] In Communist East Germany, memory was even more problematic.

Implicit in claims that Germans were uniquely repentant is the notion that Germany is a model of what a good genocidal nation should do to atone for the crimes it has perpetrated. Implicit also is that the Holocaust was so singularly unique and so uniquely horrible that German crimes could by no means be ignored. Yet the German case is unique. With their leader dead, their armies defeated, and their country occupied and divided, Germany had little choice but to come to terms with its past. There was no way to avoid responsibility for Nazi crimes. Other genocidal nations have been able to evade justice. Even Japan, while humiliated, defeated, and occupied until 1952, managed to keep its emperor, its bureaucracies, and most of its major family-owned industries intact.

Uniqueness of Holocaust denialism

A final aspect of Holocaust uniqueness concerns the organized and seemingly irrational (i.e. non-political or economic) movement to deny the Holocaust. Argues Bennett, promoting Holocaust denial's uniqueness: 'No other historical event as recent and well documented – nor many far more distant and ethereal – is subject to a similar dispute ...'.[145] In response, from the mid-1980s, over a dozen countries have passed legislation prohibiting at least some variety of hate propaganda – largely as a reaction to the problems of Holocaust denial.[146]

At some level, denial by the *perpetrators* of genocide is expected. The Turkish government denies the Armenian genocide, while Japanese atrocities during the Asia-Pacific War are elided in history books. Nevertheless, Holocaust denial is a more pervasive and irrational phenomenon – because denialism is not promoted by the perpetrator nation. Instead, individuals around the world, from widely diverse economic, social, religious, linguistic, and cultural backgrounds, have united in their desire to 'debate' and deny the facts of the Holocaust.

Deniers can be found in almost every country. Hidden behind the façade of defending civil liberties we have the Australian League of Rights, whose leader has called the Holocaust a 'gigantic lie'. Saudi Arabia has financed numerous publications accusing the Jews of inventing the Holocaust in order to gain support for the State of Israel.[147] Iran's denialist conference is but the latest public gathering of the international denialist community. French denial largely began in the late 1940s, with such deniers as fascist writer Maurice Bardèche, and socialist Paul Rassinier, followed later by protégé Robert Faurisson.[148]

American denialism, as epitomized by the extreme ranting of ultra-right wingers such as Benjamin Freedman and George Lincoln Rockwell, was rarely taken seriously, when it first appeared in the 1950s.[149] However, in the 1960s and 1970s denialism took on a pseudo-scholarly gloss, as academics like Harry Elmer Barnes, Austin J. App, and Arthur R. Butz manipulated their scholarly credentials to promote denialism.[150] Organizations such as the *Institute for Historical Review* continue to hold 'Revisionist Conferences', even publishing their *Journal of Historical Review*, which purports (falsely) to advance legitimate scholarship.[151] In 1987, Bradley Smith and Mark Weber founded the Committee on Open Debate on the Holocaust (CODOH), which began advertising their 'open' point of view in university newspapers.[152]

Denialism also spread to Canada, with German denier Ernst Zundel distributing denialist and Nazi material through his Samisdat Publications.[153] A series of Canadian court cases against Zundel brought to light a whole new scientific aspect to denial, epitomized by Fred Leuchter's now infamous *Leuchter Report*, which alleged that the gas chambers at Auschwitz and Maidenek had never been used on human victims.[154] British historian David Irving was one of the latest to promote Luechter's denialist views, claiming to have been swayed during the Zundel trials.[155] Irving later unsuccessfully sued academic Deborah Lipstadt for arguing in her book, *Denying the Holocaust*, that Irving was a Holocaust denier.[156] He has subsequently been jailed in Austria for denying the Holocaust.

Deniers have a number of key arguments. They seek to rehabilitate Hitler as a man of peace who was pushed into war by the Allies, or who alternatively went to war only because of the dangers of Soviet expansion. When Germany and its wartime leaders admitted their guilt, deniers explain this as a strategy by Germans to seek re-admittance to 'the family of nations', even though they were 'innocent' of any wrongdoing. The claim that 'Jews are not victims but victimizers' is also crucial, with the Holocaust presented as a means of gaining international sympathy and support for the State of Israel.[157]

Other key issues concern the gas chambers, which are frequently denied as a means of killing Jews. Anne Frank's diary is also dismissed as a forgery. What is the end goal for deniers? Edward Alexander, among others, sees the denialist project as one of rehabilitating Nazism. Removing the Holocaust from the equation allows deniers to comment on the 'positive' aspects of National Socialism.[158] Yet much of this also has to do with discrediting Israel. Asserting that Israel was built on a lie helps some Middle Eastern leaders justify strong anti-Israel policies which help deflect public attention away from their own despotic practices, and ensure domestic support for their continued rule.

Conclusions

So – is the Holocaust unique? I have argued that it is, although many of the uniqueness claims on closer reflection are a matter of opinion. Some claims rest on how we choose to interpret history, and on what historical events we include or exclude in our analysis. As I will demonstrate, many of the ethnic groups and social activists who invoke 'holocausts' use a variety of comparative elements from the Holocaust. Often included as comparative devices are the following: methods of destruction; nature of hatred and ethics; bureaucratic means and methods of killing; the impersonal nature of the killing; and denialism after the fact.

Several aspects of uniqueness are rarely challenged, however. Few challenge Jewish contributions to Western traditions and to the development of Christianity. However, many nations have adopted myths of chosenness, covenant, and divine election, which, while first used by Jews, became crucial building blocks of national identity. Few operationalize the uniqueness of forced collaboration in their approaches to history. Equally, few claim that their group was fundamentally like the perpetrator group, in its assimilation into mainstream culture and society. Most other groups view themselves as having been targeted explicitly because of their otherness.

Most groups covered in this book seek acknowledgement, recognition, apology, compensation, and increased rights. Jewish commemoration of the Holocaust is seen as successful because Jews have gained a state, as well as American support for the defense of that state, and a sense of legitimacy even when the state engages in questionable acts of foreign or domestic policy. They have also received some reparations from the perpetrators. The feeling that Jews are somehow a model of success allows Holocaust imagery to be seen as a formula or guide for action, a door through which aspiring groups must pass in order to gain increased rights and recognition for themselves. This view is perhaps most strongly iterated in the case of North American indigenous scholarship, which is the subject of my first case study.

Part II

Colonialism and indigenous identity

3 Colonialism, genocide, and indigenous rights

America, Australia, and New Zealand

Indigenous peoples, sometimes known collectively as the 'fourth world', have undergone profound hardship during centuries of Western colonialism. Currently, 40 percent of the world's countries contain indigenous populations, who collectively comprise 350 million people, divided into 5,250 distinct nations or tribal groups.[1] This chapter explores in brief the struggles encountered by indigenous groups in three Western settler countries – the United States, Australia, and New Zealand. This background chapter lays the basis for the three chapters which follow. First, I outline the case for or against genocide having been committed in the course of Western settlement. I argue that genocide *has* been committed in both America and Australia, but not in New Zealand. However, this hardly means that race relations are ideal, or that Maori do not have legitimate historical grievances with the government.

Many historians have noted the frequent use of 'vanishing' as a trope.[2] The romantic ideal of 'vanishing' or 'melting away' suggests that the 'disappearance' of indigenous peoples, while sad, was really no one's fault. One might abstractly blame historical inevitability and a Darwinian belief in evolution and 'progress'.[3] The presence (or lack) of perpetrator intent is often flagged in cases of indigenous genocide. Did the perpetrator intend to kill the victims 'as such', intend to kill the group in its entirety, or were perpetrator goals more focused on gaining land for settlement? Were the victims an existential threat, or 'merely' a political and territorial impediment to colonization? Were the deaths of the victims actively sought, or just 'allowed' to happen through benign neglect? In the American and Australian cases, there may not have been any intention to exterminate *all* indigenous peoples in a given territory, and many deaths by disease and starvation were not intentional. Nevertheless, I argue, consistent with the work of a number of prominent genocide scholars, that even if there was no overarching intent to kill all indigenous peoples in a given area, if the end result had genocidal consequences that could have been foreseen but were not prevented, then genocide can be understood to have occurred.

For example, in the American case, Bischoping and Fingerhut focus on 'relations of destruction' – the outcome of colonization for the victims rather than the ideology or the specific intent.[4] From an Australian perspective, Tony Barta also asserts that a lack of intent need not detract from the reality of genocide. He argues for 'a conception of genocide which embraces relations of destruction and removes from the word the emphasis on policy and intention which brought it into being'.[5] For Helen Fein, genocide can be the result of 'sustained purposeful action by a perpetrator to physically destroy a collectivity directly or indirectly'.[6] To this Roger Smith adds the cogent point that even if there is no genocidal intent at the beginning, once a colonial government recognizes that its policies are genocidal, and does nothing, genocidal intent can be proven to exist. After all, 'to persist is to intend the death of a people'.[7] At the same time, these scholars call for revisions to the understanding of genocide under international law. The UN Genocide Convention is clear that intent to commit genocide must be proven. In practice, this is often difficult to prove.

Readers may feel that I am unfairly picking on Anglo-Protestant settler societies while avoiding discussion of other perpetrators. This is not the case. Rather, I focus on cases where the Holocaust has been used as a means of repackaging indigenous history. This has proven to be far more prevalent in Western countries than in Africa or Asia. I am well aware that colonial atrocities were committed throughout the world, and there is a growing body of literature on this topic. In *Late Victorian Holocausts*, Mike Davis reveals that almost thirty million Indians were killed during British rule in India as a consequence of largely man-made famines at the turn of the nineteenth century.[8] Adam Hochschild's *King Leopold's Ghost* posits that Belgian colonialism in the Congo resulted in some ten million African deaths. This 50 percent rate of decimation is starkly similar to the death tolls in French Equatorial Africa, suggesting the Belgians were not the only offenders.[9] The Germans too perfected techniques of total war in Africa before applying them to Europe. From 1904–07, colonial authorities in German Southwest Africa (now Namibia) brutally crushed a Herero rebellion, reducing their population from 80,000 to 15,000 in three years. This genocidal crime seems to have inspired the Holocaust.[10]

In this chapter, I do not aim to cover every feature of indigenous genocide. Nor do I have sufficient space adequately to elaborate the myriad of social and economic problems indigenous peoples have faced since the nineteenth century, or how these problems have been addressed (or not) by Western governments. My primary goal is to provide essential background for the next three case-study chapters. Readers wishing fuller information will find suggestions for further reading in the endnotes.

The United States of America

I have limited my focus to the post-revolutionary era in America. Organized forms of ethnic cleansing and massacre occurred primarily after the War of 1812. Before that time, the British Empire armed and trained its Indian allies, in an effort to create an 'Indian barrier state'.[11] Much of the nineteenth century was consumed with efforts to remove Indians from their land, often by force, to encourage White settlement. A variety of highly questionable court rulings underpinned America's 'right' to take control of indigenous territory.[12] Historians note the use of bribery, trickery, and other manipulation to gain land without bloodshed.[13]

However, when cajoling failed, massacre, deliberate spreading of disease, and other brutal means were employed. Ethnocide was a major part of US policy, with the government also willing and able to engage in outright genocide.[14] Stiffarm and Lane describe a widespread genocidal mentality in nineteenth-century America, with policy-makers and military planners talking openly of the need for 'complete extermination' of any indigenous peoples who refused to be uprooted from their ancestral lands. Genocide was to a high degree privatized, with bounties put on Indian scalps – men, women, or children.[15] Prucha too notes that crimes against Indians 'were so numerous and widespread that their control by judicial means proved impossible'.[16]

By the early nineteenth century, the US Army distributed blankets infested with smallpox to the Mandan in present-day North Dakota, which resulted (at least in part) in a pandemic that raged through the region from 1836 to 1840, with a death toll of 100,000.[17] Eliminating traditional food and game supplies also decimated populations. In the 1870s, General Phillip Sheridan killed at least sixty million buffalo in a successful effort to deny the Cheyenne, Lakota and other people the basis for their centuries-old subsistence. Sitting Bull described the killings as 'a cold wind ... across the prairie, a death wind for my people'.[18]

Forced marches similarly reduced indigenous numbers while freeing land for further colonization. In the well known 'Trail of Tears', in 1838, some 17,000 Cherokee were rounded up at bayonet point by US troops and forced to walk up to 1,500 miles. The purpose of this campaign was to clear land for White settlement east of the Mississippi River. Malnutrition, disease, and exposure resulted in a death rate of 50 percent. In a similar manner the Choctaws, Chickasaws, Creeks, and Seminoles were herded from Oklahoma between 1836 and 1837, with death rates ranging between 15 and 50 percent. The Navajo also suffered a similar fate (roughly 30 percent killed) during 'The Long Walk' (1864–68).[19]

In 1849, the Bureau of Indian Affairs assumed control of indigenous issues from the War Department. Fleras and Elliot note the 'continuation of greed, incompetence and exploitation' that was extant under the previous department.[20] Attempts to assimilate indigenous peoples into Western society often resulted in legislation designed to outlaw indigenous languages, cultures, and religions. Reservations were created to clearly demarcate Indian land (which was often barren) from the rest of the country.[21]

The 'General Allotment Act' (or 'Dawes Act') was a particularly noxious piece of legislation. Seen by Theodore Roosevelt as a 'mighty pulverising

engine to break up the tribal mass', the Act destroyed collective land hold-
ings and freed up farmland for White settlers. Any tribe considered to be
sufficiently 'advanced' could have their tribal lands split into 160-acre
blocks, each to be allocated to a nuclear family. The remaining land (often
desirable farm land) was 'restored to the public domain'. The first thirteen
years of the Act saw some 33,000 allotments being created with a total loss
of some 28.5 million acres of 'surplus land'.[22]

The residential school system as a means of assimilating indigenous children was another facet of American policy. While such schools were often
created for the 'altruistic' motive of bringing indigenous peoples closer to
White society, such schools often stripped indigenous children of their language and culture, while ill-preparing them to enter a xenophobic and
racialized society.[23] By 1899 there were 148 boarding and 225 day schools
funded by the government, with over 22,000 students, representing some
10 percent of the total indigenous population at the time.[24] We know now
too, thanks to works such as Adams' *Education for Extinction* (1995), that the
rates of sexual and physical abuse, as well as death, were inordinately high in
these schools.[25] As Lisa Poupart advanced recently:

> it is estimated that 60 to 70 percent of all students attending the board-
> ing schools were beaten or raped ... children were also forced to admin-
> ister assaults upon one another.... For many, violence became a way of
> life as entire childhoods were spent in the boarding schools.[26]

The interwar period was marked by a certain degree of progress under
Roosevelt's New Deal reforms. Citizenship rights were granted in 1924, followed later by the legalization of traditional religious practices.[27] In 1925,
the BIA conceded that the Indian death rate was double that for Whites.[28]
The 'Meriam Report' (1928) highlighted the deplorable status of indigenous
peoples, recommending a wide variety of proposals, which culminated in
more liberal government policy and a great increase in funding for
reserves.[29]

Under Truman, the government admitted to 'unfortunate and tragic
errors' and offered token compensation for lands 'bought' from Indians. The
Indian Claims Commission (1946) would create a veneer of legality over
Indian Affairs.[30] However, the post-war era also heralded a new type of
assimilationist policy, stemming from a philosophy of 'termination'. Republicans under Eisenhower argued against New Deal policies, which had
expanded health and welfare services on reservations and tried to improve
reserve economies. 'Operation Relocation' (1952) and other such programs
targeted specific tribes for elimination, supposedly to encourage urbanization. In total, some 108 indigenous nations were dissolved during this
period.[31]

Social and economic legacies of cultural and physical destruction remain.
While the pre-conquest population numbered in the millions, by 1920

there were less than 250,000 indigenous peoples living in the United States. Fortunately, the population has been growing, and has greatly increased over the past two decades.[32] American Indians now account for roughly 1.5 percent of the population, with another twenty-five million Americans in possession of some indigenous ancestry. Collectively, American indigenous peoples are divided into 554 legally recognized tribes, with 60 percent living in urban areas.[33] There is still much to be done. Land claims have not been fully resolved, despite some cash settlements and land hand-backs. America today only guarantees the right to 'internal self-determination [that] does not include rights of independence or permanent sovereignty over natural resources'.[34]

Indigenous people in America remain at the bottom of most social indicators for malnutrition, disease, infant mortality, teen suicide, and life expectancy. The unemployment rate often hovers between 40 and 70 percent on and near many reserves.[35] Social commentators often blame 'internal colonialism' for the continued trauma faced by American Indians. Having internalized the 'dominant culture's codes', Poupart argues starkly that American Indians now view themselves 'within and through the constructs that defined us as racially and culturally subhuman, deficient, and vile'. This has led invariably to a plethora of social problems: 'Turned upon ourselves, American Indian people express rage, pain, and grief in depression, anxiety ... drug abuse, alcohol abuse, and suicide'.[36] While the situation is slowly improving, there remain very serious intergenerational problems that will take considerable time and effort to resolve.

Australia

For most of Australia's history Aborigines have been treated as third-class peoples, and were not even recognized as citizens and hence had no official right to vote or carry a passport until the mid twentieth century. On average, Aboriginal peoples die twenty years before White Australians, and are fifteen times more likely to end up in prison. They fall prey to a host of other alarming social statistics.[37] At the same time, more people are finding out about their often hidden Aboriginal ancestry. The 2001 census lists some 410,003 people as being Aboriginal and Torres Strait Islanders, up from approximately 265,000 in 1991.[38]

Aboriginal peoples have been in Australia for 40,000–70,000 years, and were divided into at least 250–300 different language and cultural groups.[39] In 1788, the first British colony at Sydney Harbour was established, and Aborigines became subjects of the British sovereign. Aboriginal traditions of equality, rejection of hierarchy, and strong spiritual ties to the land were treated with disdain.[40] Aborigines were seen, according to eighteenth-century accounts, as 'one degree above brute creation', 'the lowest race in the scale of humanity', 'the connecting link between man and monkey tribe', 'a species of ... tail-less monkeys', and so on.[41] As Aboriginal lands were not cultivated, nor used for grazing or for urban development, the British declared Australia *Terra Nullius* as 'belonging to no one, empty, a wasteland that could be claimed without having to acknowledge the native title of the Aborigines'.[42]

In recent years, a significant body of research has developed around the theme of Aboriginal genocide. Colin Tatz argued recently that genocide of Aboriginal peoples occurred in the eighteenth and nineteenth centuries, which reduced the Aboriginal population from between 250,000 and 750,000 in 1788, to less than 31,000 by 1911.[43] Initially Aborigines maintained non-violent relations with settlers, either avoiding them or engaging in friendly relations. This changed when settlers began claiming lands for themselves and fencing off areas of importance to Aborigines, such as watering holes.[44] Initial contact soon gave way to 'competition for land'. Priorities underwent a shift from 'assimilation to extermination' as Aborigines resisted.[45] Henry Reynolds describes a gun-toting culture on the frontier, where settlers feared the Aborigines and heavily armed themselves, even in urban areas. Retaliation, when meted out, was often disproportionately severe, even aiming at extermination.[46]

Massacres began in the eighteenth century and were recorded until 1928. By the 1930s, commentators argued that all Australia could do was 'to smooth the dying pillow' of the Aborigines – they were seemingly doomed to extinction.[47] Prevalent throughout the Australian colonies was a firmly-held belief that the Aborigines were dying out. This perception traces its origin to the 1820s, and only grew stronger as the century progressed. However, attitudes to this were not uniform. Some were horrified, others accepted it as inevitable but mildly regrettable, while others welcomed it 'and sought to hasten the predetermined result'.[48]

Reynolds argues that at least some 20,000 Aborigines were directly killed through massacre in the nineteenth century, with roughly 3,000 settler casualties from Aboriginal attacks.[49] Knightley adds that once one factors in wars, and looks also at the twentieth century, then a figure of between 50,000 and 100,000 becomes more realistic, although he offers no source for these numbers.[50] The use of poisoned flour was also said to be 'almost a common occurrence' during the same period.[51]

Tasmania and Queensland are commonly cited as two examples of colonies where genocidal atrocities took place in the nineteenth century. From the 1820s, Tasmania was engaged in frontier wars. Settlers were attacked by Aborigines, who then retaliated. Governor Arthur first resisted calls by settlers to exterminate or expulse the Aborigines. He initially attempted to settle them on plots of farmland. However, by 1828 the plan was unsuccessful, and he ordered Aborigines to leave settled areas to be placed on a reserve. A famous 'black line' was created in 1830, where the island was swept from one side to the other to capture any remaining Tasmanians.[52] Despite some arguably good intentions on the part of colonial authorities to keep the Tasmanians alive, the 200 survivors were placed on

Flinder's Island, where they died, primarily from pneumonia and respiratory diseases.[53] In 1839 the last Tasmanian expired, at the age of thirty-four.[54]

In Queensland, intent to commit genocide seems easier to prove. Here the state seems to have engaged in genocidal aggression from the 1830s and 40s against the Dharug people, with Governor Macquarie proclaiming that any unarmed group of more than six Aborigines could be legally killed, as well as any Aborigine coming within a mile of a White habitation.[55] A Native Police force led by White officers was used as the primary instrument for the killings. While it would have been impossible for this small force to kill all of the 100,000 Aborigines in Queensland, Moses notes the state's 'explicit approval' of what were in essence 'mobile death squads aimed at eradicating Aborigines'.[56] The use of euphemisms for killing, such as 'dispersal', 'customary chastisement', 'shooting a snipe', etc., became common on the frontier.[57] Reynolds too highlights official and public approval for the 'dispersals', reproducing a large number of letters, newspapers articles, and speeches.[58] Roughly 10,000 Aborigines were killed in Queensland between 1824 and 1908, a clear sign of genocidal destruction, as Tatz has concluded. Further proof of genocide can be adduced, he argues, by the fact that the world's first 'anti-genocide statute – the *Aboriginals Protection and Restriction of the Sale of Opium Act 1897*' was passed after the worst of the massacres.[59]

The 'stolen generations'

A clearer instance of genocide involving state policy was the removal of 'half-caste' Aboriginal children from their parents. The intention was to assimilate these children into the White communities, through adoption in White families, or through networks of church-run schools and foster homes. Eventually they would enter the workforce as laborers, and would be further interbred with the rest of the settler population. We must be clear that genocide does not only imply the intentional killing of a target population. Intentionally restricting births within a group and transferring children from the group can also qualify as genocide under the UN Convention; death need not be involved.[60]

Australian officials did try to prevent Aboriginal births, and did transfer 'half-caste' Aboriginal children out of their family groups. One of the chief instigators of this policy was A.O. Neville, the Chief Protector of Aboriginals in Western Australia. He addressed the first national governmental conference on Aborigines in 1938, and managed to unanimously pass a resolution entitled 'The Destiny of the Race', calling for the total absorption of all part-Aboriginal children into White society.[61] Reynolds sees Neville's objectives as openly genocidal.[62] Between 20,000 and 25,000 Aboriginal children, now known as the 'stolen generations' (a term first coined by Peter Read in 1981), were separated from their parents between 1910 and 1970.[63] Another aspect of this campaign was the active prevention of marriage between 'full-bloods' and 'half-castes', in favor of 'half-caste'/White marriages as a means of 'breeding out the colour'. Sterilization of all 'half castes' was also proposed by one leading Queensland politician.[64]

The term 'genocide' certainly had no mainstream appeal until 1997, when the Australian Human Rights Commission's report *Bringing Them Home: the report of the National Inquiry into the Separation of Aboriginal and Torres Strait Islander Children from their Families* argued that Aboriginal child removals did in fact qualify as genocide.[65] The report advanced that around 10–30 percent of Aboriginal children had been forcibly separated from their families between 1910 and 1970.[66] The forcible transfer of children, under Article II (e) of the Genocide Convention, does qualify as genocide, even if removal policies were primarily targeted at only one part of a group. Manne argues, supporting Tatz and others:

C. Tatz

> On the foundation of a variety of legal authorities it is argued that the crime of genocide can be committed even where the intention to destroy the group fails; where the destructive intent focuses only on a part of the targeted group; and where the motives of those carrying out the plans are 'mixed', for example when plans to destroy the group are not driven solely by 'animosity or hatred'.[67]

Paul Bartrop too sees this as genocide and backs it up with Neville's statements on the necessity to 'separate any half-caste from its aboriginal mother, no matter how frantic her momentary grief might be....'.[68] Knightley adopts Hannah Arendt's definition of genocide that it was 'the desire to make a distinct people disappear from the earth'. 'That', he argues, 'was the shameful desire of the Australian government for at least sixty years'.[69] In so far as the stolen generations are concerned, the case for genocide seems relatively straightforward. Nevertheless, the debate over what is (and should be) considered genocide remains heated.

New Zealand

Maori are the indigenous inhabitants of New Zealand and, with Pacific Islanders, comprise almost 25 percent of the country's population. The first Maori settlements date back to AD 850, and by AD 1200 there were over twenty tribes in the North Island and some three or four in the South Island, each possessing its own territory, government, and self-sustaining economy.[70] Initial contact between British explorers and Maori took place in the eighteenth century, followed soon after by slow colonization, which rapidly increased in the nineteenth century. While Maori were devastated by almost two centuries of British colonization, their hierarchical and structured society helped them fare comparatively better than other indigenous groups. Maori were often cast as a model or superior indigenous people. For novelist Anthony Trollope, they were 'the most civilised' of all 'savages', and in racial hierarchies Maori were usually placed just under Europeans, well above Aborigines and southern Africans. Imagery of Maori as 'selected stock' who had braved long voyages to reach New Zealand prompted such epithets as 'Vikings of the Sunrise' and 'Aryan Maori'.[71]

The 1840 *Treaty of Waitangi* is considered New Zealand's founding document, and the basis of an enduring myth of equality between Maori and White New Zealanders. In return for loyalty to the British Crown, Maori were to receive sovereignty over their lands and resources, and legal protection. The Treaty was signed between British Governor Hobson and over 500 North Island Maori chiefs, formally making the North Island a British colony, while paving the way for the direct annexation of the South Island. Views of the Treaty vary, from a positive protection for Maori, to a sham document designed to steal Maori land and destroy their culture.[72] Misunderstanding would develop over the differences in wording in the English and Maori translations. An ambiguous promise of 'governance' (kawanatanga) was inexplicably substituted for the more common term for 'sovereignty' (mana).[73]

Whether or not the Treaty was just (or its vocabulary accurate) soon became irrelevant when the British by and large refused to honor it.[74] In the litany of abuses, Chief Justice Prendergast rejected the Treaty as a 'nullity' in 1877, and dismissed Maori as being 'incapable of performing the duties and therefore assuming the rights of a civilised community'.[75] While Maori possessed comparatively more rights than other colonized people in the British Empire: 'British settlement was taken by the Crown as a given, and Maori were expected to make way for it. If they did not, the Treaty guarantees were watered down or set aside'.[76] The biggest threat to Maori in the long term was massive land theft, which resulted in the destruction of traditional culture and modes of living. Between 1840 and 1990, over 100 pieces of legislation were introduced in breach of the Treaty, which afforded little of the protection promised to Maori.[77] The 1863 New Zealand Settlements Act and the creation of the Native Land Courts in 1865 paved the way for the alienation of Maori from their lands. By 1900, 95 percent of Maori land had been taken away.[78] War, disease, cultural destruction, and a declining birth rate also took their toll. From an estimated Maori population of 300,000 in 1840, by the turn of the century Maori numbers had declined to 30,000.[79]

However bleak their plight appears, Maori have a long history of resistance to European colonization.[80] The Maori 'Declaration of Independence' in 1835 was designed to create a Maori nation-state.[81] The 1853 movement for Maori unity, a Maori King movement in 1858, and resistance to British expansion during a series of Land Wars in the nineteenth century would demonstrate both organization and resolve.[82] Maori also received political representation – four seats in the colonial assembly – while Section 4 of the Australian Commonwealth Franchise Act of 1902 entitled Maori to vote, a privilege not extended to Aborigines, Asians, Africans, or Pacific Islanders.[83]

Despite these relative advantages, loss of land, culture, and language, together with religious conversion and cultural assimilation, took their toll. By the 1940s, Maori had turned their back on many traditional practices, including the Maori language, resulting in a Maori 'non-culture which existed in a sort of limbo'.[84] Things worsened after 1945 with increased urbanization, to the extent that by the 1970s scarcely 10 percent of Maori were making a living from the land. The use of machine power during the 1940s destroyed small-scale farming, leading to increased draining of the rural environment.[85]

Were Maori the victims of genocide? The charge is difficult to sustain. There is little evidence that colonial authorities set about deliberately and systematically to destroy the Maori as a people, even in the sense of ethnocide or cultural genocide. Historian Ranginui Walker notes his people's 'success in maintaining cultural continuity in the face of tremendous assimilative pressures'.[86] For Irihapeti Ramsden: 'Maori have utilised the material culture of the Pakeha [settlers] and have retained what has been possible under the severe impact of colonisation and built upon it to create the people of today'.[87] Tony Simpson similarly argues that the temptation to see Maori as a 'dying race should be avoided'. Rather: 'the Maori people who emerged from the disorganisation and demoralisation of the wars and land-grabs were not ... a people destroyed. On the contrary, they exhibited a quite remarkable resilience'.[88]

While attempts at cultural assimilation and suppression are undeniable, colonial authorities never envisioned completely destroying Maori identity, nor was there much societal support for this either. There were no residential schools, and parliamentary representation and Waitangi militated against complete cultural destruction. This may not necessarily show good-will – it certainly (at least partially) reflects the numerical and cultural strength of Maori.

Conclusions

Colonialism impacted negatively on indigenous populations, restricting their ability to practice their centuries-old religious and cultural practices, while depriving them of ancestral lands. Massacres took place in all three countries, and in America and Australia genocidal crimes were also carried out, although not systematically or uniformly across each country. In each case governments had a paternalistic interest in 'helping' indigenous peoples, but on terms that were designed permanently to place them at a lower social and economic level. Possibly well-meaning initiatives, like residential schooling, had a corrosive impact on the physical and emotional well-being of indigenous peoples. The profoundly negative legacies have created forms of intergenerational trauma which have yet to be resolved.

The 1960s and 70s paved the way for an increased privileging of difference, leading to group activism. While there has clearly been some interest in redressing some of the outstanding grievances of indigenous peoples, there has been a marked reluctance in all three cases to operate pro-actively. Activists often need to push the limits to have their grievances addressed, and reparations or other forms of redress are often token. In the next three chapters, I attempt to grapple with how the Holocaust has increasingly come to frame indigenous history. The Americanization process is perceived by many indigenous activists to have brought tangible benefits to the Jewish people, at least in the sense that their tragedy is acknowledged by the perpetrator, apologized for, and to some extent compensated. For many activists, then, the indigenization of the Holocaust promises to bring about similar benefits to American Indians, Aborigines, and Maori. To what extent this belief is true remains unclear, and I devote the next three chapters to a discussion of the appropriateness of using the Holocaust within indigenous rights movements.

4 Uncle Sam's willing executioners?

Indigenous genocide and representation in the United States

Nobody got it worse than the American Indians. Indians got it bad. Indians got it the worst. You know how bad the Indians got it? When was the last time you met two Indians? You ain't never met two Indians. I have seen a polar bear ride a tricycle in my lifetime. I have never seen an Indian family just chillin' out at Red Lobster.

(Chris Rock, 'Bigger and Blacker' (1999))

I would like to see a red stone wall like the black stone wall of the Vietnam War Memorial. ... It would be hundreds of times longer than the Vietnam Memorial ... The number of our brave souls reaches into the many millions, and every one of them remains unquiet until this day. Just as effective might be a Holocaust Museum to the American Indian to recall the voices of those who were slaughtered.

(Leonard Peltier, *Prison Writings* (1999))[1]

I begin this chapter by juxtaposing how two very different genocides have been represented in the United States. I start with the Holocaust, and then turn to the genocide of America's indigenous populations. Anyone entering the USHMM through Wallenberg Place, located near the Jefferson and Lincoln Memorials, will be immediately confronted with symbols of American history. On one wall is the Declaration of Independence, followed by the text of a speech delivered by George Washington to the Hebrew congregation in Newport, to whom he assured: 'the government of the United States ... gives bigotry no sanction, to persecution no assistance'. Visitors entering from 14th Street are welcomed by the flags of American army units who helped liberate the death camps. When visitors begin their tour of the Museum, they are treated to the horrified recollections of American servicemen.[2]

The use of American liberators as witnesses is no accident. We, the visitors, relate to the American soldiers as they go through the camps. We share their shock and revulsion, and feel that the horrors committed here were wholly alien to the American experience. Here are quintessentially 'un-American' crimes. Yet since President Carter's 1978 speech, the image of

America as the Holocaust's other has been controversial. Yes, America helped liberate the death camps, but it also committed genocide against its own indigenous peoples, killing mass numbers through the spread of disease, forced marches, massacres, destruction of food supplies, and a host of other means. The horrors soldiers encountered at Auschwitz were certainly *different* (and in most respects worse) from the ones their predecessors committed on American soil, or in the Philippines, or elsewhere. Yet American troops *did* participate in the massacre and mutilation of indigenous peoples. This is historical fact, even if it is not widely discussed in America.[3]

Now the second genocide: In 2004, the National Museum of the American Indian opened its doors. Located between the Capitol and the National Air and Space Museum, this impressive edifice was built at a cost of $219 million, funded in part from private donations. Unlike the USHMM, this Museum was designed to remember (and forget) very different peoples and events. Director W. Richard West's summary of his Museum's message is as follows:

> [Indians] are at present cultural phenomena, a set of communities, a set of peoples. We want people to understand that, because for much of American history, until rather recently, native communities were relatively invisible. We are still here and making vital contributions to contemporary American culture and art.[4]

In addition to the *usefulness* of American Indians, West also makes clear that his people will not be challenging America's established view of itself anytime soon. Reviewing the Museum in the entertainment section of the *Washington Post*, we sense palpable relief when Jacqueline Trescott reveals:

> The displays don't wallow in the genocide, broken promises and bloody wars of the 19th century, West says. Planners didn't want Native Americans viewed as victims, but as fully dimensional people. Yes, there have been horrors, West says, but they are presented through native voices and treated as part of a long history.[5]

While victimization takes center stage in the USHMM, and forms a part of American national identity, precisely the opposite development is at work at the NMAI. Genocide is downplayed in the search for indigenous 'vital contributions'. While remembering the Holocaust functions as a warning and to some extent a story of American goodness, forgetting indigenous genocide (versus 'wallowing') promotes patriotism and well-being.

Sadly, American representations of indigenous genocide have been described as a 'flawless mirror image' of the situation in Germany. If Holocaust denial is seen as a deliberate affront to the victims of Nazi terror, 'In America', Lilian Friedberg describes, 'the situation is the reverse: victims seeking recovery are seen as assaulting American ideals'.[6] This problem was present well before the opening of either museum. As Jonathan Boyarin cogently observed in 1992 of America's attraction to the Holocaust: 'One effect of this displaced eulogization is to encourage amnesia about domination closer to home'.[7] As he expressed the issue clearly, raising a poignant question to which there is no easy answer:

> [S]ince remembering the Holocaust is hardly a central project to all American Jews, let alone the majority of U.S. citizens – by advertising that America has the space in its heart and in its capital to commemorate genocide committed elsewhere, the genocidal origins of the United States will be further occluded. How, then, could or should Native Americans react to the fact that there is a U.S. Holocaust Museum but no U.S. Memorial to the Slaughtered Native Americans – especially if they want to avoid offending Jews in the process of expressing any opinion whatsoever?[8]

This important question forms the root of this chapter. Why has the Holocaust been Americanized, while America's own genocidal past has not? Can both be properly commemorated in America, or is there space for only one? To what extent does Holocaust Americanization compete with indigenous representations of genocide? Or, conversely, can we see the Holocaust here (as in some other cases) as the sort of 'window of opportunity' so vividly described by Torpey? Finally, what roles do America's own myths of exceptionalism play in demarcating which genocides will be enshrined, or be denied? I attempt to grapple with these questions as this chapter unfolds, through a dissection and discussion of the debate between Comparativists and Relativists over American indigenous history, and how it should be remembered and represented.

The comparativist critique in America

Many Comparativists, like David Stannard and Ward Churchill, see the Americanization of the Holocaust as inherently destructive to indigenous interests. Indeed, so important is this putative threat that Churchill cites Relativists as the 'negative inspiration' for his work.[9] Claims of Holocaust uniqueness steamroll attempts to put American genocide on the agenda. If America is a fundamentally good society – the antithesis of Nazi Germany – it follows that it cannot *by definition* have committed genocide.

Both Stannard and Churchill have a number of goals. First, they seek to present indigenous victims anew as innocent human beings to whom we can all relate. Like the Jews, indigenous peoples were civilized and rational, deserving of life and cultural autonomy. Second, not unlike the Nazis, American perpetrators were inspired by forms of eliminationist racism to commit genocide. Both authors seek to horrify the reader with what was done in America's past. This is necessary, they argue, to push for a necessary level of reparations, while ending the genocide denial that has become a pervasive part of American national identity.

Comparativists struggle to gain moral capital. For them, the small amount of it that exists in America has been literally 'stolen' by Jews. Comparativists endeavor to get it 'back'. This is problematic, because the fight between Jews and American Indians is largely (but not entirely) a product of the Comparativist imagination. Jewish Holocaust scholarship has been brought into American genocide scholarship as a means of gaining public attention, and packaging history in a provocative way. In light of the general American ignorance of genocide, this is understandable. However, Jews are being used as straw-men to bolster American Indian claims. I find this problematic, and my stance on the Stannard–Churchill thesis is critical.

Ultimately, I conclude that while the Holocaust and its associated vocabulary and imagery works well as an attention-grabbing device, there is no need (academically) to bring it in. Nor is there any justifiable reason to target Absolutists and Relativists. The Holocaust has been Americanized because it helps buttress traditional myths of American exceptionalism and goodness. Claims of domestic genocide have the reverse effect. In short, American Indian academics face an uphill battle to get their genocide(s) recognized. While comparisons with the Holocaust might promote knowledge, they will not bring about the type of soul-searching or reparations that Stannard and Churchill desire, especially as America's 'War on Terror' continues.

A new look for indigenous history

The 1980s saw a flourishing of writing on indigenous genocide, which in part coincided with the coming of the 500th anniversary of Columbus' arrival in America in 1492.[10] Of the writings to emerge from this period, Richard Drinnon's *Facing West: The Metaphysics of Indian-Hating and Empire Building* (1980) is arguably one of the most important. It clearly laid out many of the themes and arguments which Stannard and Churchill later used. Masterfully researched using a wealth of primary sources, Drinnon traces an almost direct link in racist mentality from the early Pilgrims, through to the founding of the Republic, the nineteenth-century expansion of America, and its twentieth-century forays into new 'frontiers' like the Philippines and Vietnam. Adopting Herman Melville's term 'the metaphysics of Indian-hating', Drinnon's analysis is based on a simple proposition: 'Societies are known by their victims'.[11]

For Drinnon, 'Indian-hating' and 'nation-building' were 'twin metaphysics'. In the history of conquest, the pre-modern Other needed to be destroyed or displaced to make way for civilization. Progress could and did often imply genocide.[12] His reading of American history reflects this view of reality. The age of the early pilgrim is filled with puritanical sexual repression. John Endicott exemplifies the 'suppressed sexuality' which delighted in 'whipping pagans', such as the Pequot of Block Island.[13] American literature too demonstrates a widespread level of 'Indian-hating', even the encouragement of what novelist Robert Bird called the 'emptying' of the eastern states.[14]

Presidents like Thomas Jefferson were similarly seen as exemplary Indian-haters. In 1792, a diplomat accused Jefferson of wanting to 'exterminate the Indians and take their land', an impolitic sentiment Drinnon saw as perfectly accurate.[15] As for John Adams, his hatred was based on 'timeworn virtues: "industry, frugality, regularity, and religion"', while Andrew Jackson took a more active role in massacring indigenous peoples – seeing them as 'ruthless savages'.[16] James Monroe seemed little different in his attitudes, while the BIA's first head in 1824, Colonel Thomas McKenney, would also promote similar views.[17] Such candour, needless to say, was rare in the literature on indigenous peoples, as was the ascription of genocidal intent to the entire history of the colonization of North America.

Most works hitherto stressed the benevolence of America's founders. Ronald Satz's 1975 study of the Jacksonian era, for example, exonerated 'Old Hickory'. Dismissing charges that he was a 'merciless Indian-hater', Satz tells us that he was a worthy leader who showed 'overwhelming concern for the nation's growth, unity, and security'.[18] Similarly, Brian Dippie, in *The Vanishing American*, rejects that 'modish word "genocide"', refusing to acknowledge any 'deliberate program of extermination'.[19] Drinnon, the son of Norwegian immigrants living on the frontier, helped pave the way for more activist critiques of US history. However, Drinnon's work appeared as the Americanization process was beginning. By the 1990s, terms such as 'genocide' and 'genocidal' were insufficient to garner the necessary public attention. Academics now turned to the Holocaust instead.

In 1992, Stannard published his *American Holocaust*, to coincide with the quincentennial of Columbus' arrival. Drinnon is credited with 'carefully and pointedly' commenting on an entire earlier draft of Stannard's book, which explains why many of his ideas seem to flow naturally from *Facing West*.[20] Stannard followed this with a chapter in Rosenbaum's edited volume *Is The Holocaust Unique?* (1996). Churchill's *A Little Matter of Genocide* was published in 1997. His work is heavily reliant on Stannard, and even features a preface by him, lauding the book for its audaciousness, and its 'extraordinarily compassionate and humanitarian goals'.[21] While Stannard is selective in his use of the Holocaust, it is omnipresent in Churchill's telling of American history, and by design. His book 'seeks to contextualize the American holocaust through direct comparison with other genocides – most especially to the nazi Holocaust – *to an extent not previously undertaken on such a scale*'.[22]

Dimensions of the 'American holocaust'

One of the more controversial aspects of Stannard and Churchill's work is their demographic statistics. Arguing that the pre-conquest population of the Americas was well over 100 million people, both see the decimation of indigenous nations as the largest genocide in history. The higher the numbers, the worse the genocides naturally appear. According to Stannard, between 90 and 98 percent of indigenous peoples were killed in the five centuries following Columbus, making it 'far and away, the most massive act of genocide in the history of the world'.[23] Churchill, echoing Stannard, also sees the 'American holocaust' as 'unparalleled, both in terms of its magnitude and the degree to which its goals were met, and in terms of the extent to which its ferocity was sustained over time by not one but several participating groups'.[24] His numbers and percentages are similar to those of Stannard, which should not surprise us, since many of his sources are identical.[25]

An important objective of Stannard and Churchill's work has been to re-humanize indigenous victims of genocide, stressing their innocence and sophistication.[26] Stannard casts the victims as civilized people, with well-proportioned cities, well-organized economies, manufacturing, and agricultural industries, as well as advanced religious and philosophical beliefs.[27] In North America, too, Stannard notes the sophisticated religious and cultural practices of indigenous peoples, 'their fairness and dignity and self-control', and the ritualized, often non-lethal, forms of warfare they practiced.[28] Central to Stannard's message is that indigenous peoples were innocent victims of unprovoked aggression. In keeping with the political motivations of their work, neither Stannard nor Churchill are concerned with shades of gray. Kindly colonizers are certainly not mentioned, nor are genocidal indigenous peoples, like the Iroquois, the topic of Geoffrey Blick's extensive research.[29]

The image of the innocent Jew being led to the gas chamber is constantly in the background, with any suggestion of moral ambiguity scrupulously avoided. In order to make the strongest possible case, the starkest contrasts are required. Indeed, we are enjoined to *like* the indigenous peoples, and relate to them, just as we are to relate to Jewish Holocaust victims. And so as to make the case more strongly, Stannard performs an academic sleight of hand. In Rosenbaum's edited collection, he takes a previously published passage from *American Holocaust* and substitutes Jews for Indians:

> After the total population of Jews on this immense island – plus the hundreds of thousands of Jews on neighboring islands in the Caribbean had finally been exterminated in a matter of decades, the horrifying violence then spread to the entire continent. And now still more Jews, numbering in the *tens* of millions, died from the Spanish onslaught. Scores of Jewish cities were reduced to rubble. Synagogues beyond counting were crushed. All the religious books that could be found were burned. Jewish women and children were enslaved and branded on the face with their owners' initials.... When all the dust had settled, throughout the entire North American continent approximately 95 percent of the original Jewish population had been exterminated – from the combined violence, torture, removal, disease, exhaustion, exposure and other factors that snatched their lives away.[30]

This is but a small portion of the quotation, which continues over several pages. The horrors recounted are bleak, and leave little to the imagination. Here, quite clearly for the author, Jews and Indians are interchangeable. Stannard invites us to consider how horrible we'd think it was if Jews suffered in these ways. Then he reminds us that indigenous peoples are human too, and deserving of the same respect.

Demonizing the perpetrators

At another level, Spanish and American perpetrators are fully demonized to make the dichotomy function properly. Stannard devotes a lengthy section to the cruelty and brutality of the Spanish, who killed, raped, and mutilated with abandon, alongside other horrors such as the sport of 'dogging'.[31] The conquistadors were little more than brutal, degenerate savages, 'the equivalent of a horde of ravenous locusts'.[32] If indigenous peoples were in some respects like us, Europeans were not. They and not the Indians were the other. Contra indigenous sophistication, Europe featured open sewers, open-pit graves with rotting corpses, and 'other noxious habits'. As for the people themselves, they were truly repulsive. Stannard describes 'the vile aromas given off by the living … the scabs, running sores, and other nauseating skin diseases'.[33] He thus reverses the traditional imagery associated with Spanish conquest, and brings in elements of tragedy.[34]

Tarring American leaders with a genocidal brush is crucial in constructing a case for genocide. America's founding fathers, including Washington,[35] Jefferson,[36] and Jackson, are presented as genocidal figures, bent on the extermination of the Indians.[37] Early leaders, Churchill argues, were infused with a 'virulent Anglo-Saxon supremacism' little different from 'nazi Aryanist ideology'.[38] Of all colonizers, he concludes, the English were the most 'overtly genocidal'.[39] Colonel John Chivington, who instigated the massacre of Sand Creek Indians in 1864, constitutes a fine example of the genocidal characters that dot American history. Chivington famously argued 'kill all and scalp all – little and big', then coined the popular phrase 'Nits make lice' – encouraging settlers to massacre children as well as adults. Stannard remarks wryly that Chivington was a man ahead of his time: 'It would be more than half a century, after all, before Heinrich Himmler would think to describe the extermination of another people as "the same thing as delousing"'.[40]

Churchill, too, cannot resist Nazi comparisons when examining how American history has been framed as a conflict between warlike Indians (and their 'Indian wars') and peaceful, hard-working settlers. Had the Nazis won World War II, one could have expected a similar narrative: 'When the Poles, led by sullen Jewish chiefs, savagely attacked our innocent troops west of Warsaw in 1939, murdering thousands, we were forced to respond by …'.[41] Spanish and Nazi cruelty are also compared, further imparting the view that the 'American Holocaust' is in some ways a seamless 500-year genocidal project. Colonization and *Lebensraum* 'bear more than a casual resemblance to one another', and the rapid decimation of colonial American populations can certainly be compared with 'Himmler's slaughter mills'. The conquistadors were as unrelentingly vicious as any 'SS trooper'.[42] His conclusions here are stark:

> all practical distinctions between Columbus and Himmler ... evaporate upon close inspection. They are cut of the same cloth, fulfilling precisely the same function and for exactly the same reasons, each in his own time and place. If there is one differentiation which may be valid, it is that while the specific enterprise Himmler represented ultimately failed and is now universally condemned, that represented by Columbus did not and is not.[43]

Similarly, those Spanish who denied the atrocities, accusing others of inventing a 'Black Legend' against them, are little different from Nazis who complained of 'zionist propaganda'. Tales of 'Aztec sacrifice' and cannibalism are little more than American versions of the myths of 'Jewish ritual murder'. Both should be treated with scepticism, instead of 'hearty self-congratulation'.[44] In these cases, any ambiguity about what the perpetrators intended is stripped away. Seen through the Nazi lens, the 'American Holocaust' is a continual killing process that covers over five centuries.

American genocide as precedent for the Holocaust

Comparativists often claim that the Holocaust is derivative. That is, Hitler was inspired by earlier genocides when he embarked on his crusade to kill the Jews. This is a not uncommon view amongst some Maori, Australian Aboriginal, Armenian, and other activists and historians, who see their genocides/colonial experiences as precedents for the Holocaust.

Through this optic, anti-Semitism also emerges as a typical (rather than aberrant) form of group hatred. Stannard effectively rebuts the uniqueness of Christian anti-Semitism by focusing on Christian cruelty towards the *Other* more generally. If Jews were hated by Christians, this paled in comparison to Christian hatred of indigenous peoples. Thus: '[the] characteristics of Christian tradition ... [that] prophesized, prepared for, and brought to maturity a frame of mind that would allow to take place the genocide that was carried out against the native people of the Americas were in many cases the same religio-cultural traits that buttressed justifications for the Holocaust'.[45] For Churchill, too, the Nazi regime was hardly unique or unprecedented. The Third Reich was more a 'crystallisation' of Columbus era themes such as 'racial supremacism, conquest, and genocide'. Nothing ever really changes. 'Nazism was never unique: it was instead only one of an endless succession of "New World Orders" set in motion by "the Discovery"'.[46]

Concretely, America's success at killing its indigenous peoples showed the Nazis how genocide could be carried out. Hitler biographer John Toland notes the Fuhrer's admiration for the 'efficiency' of America's genocide campaign, seeing it as 'a forerunner for his own plans and programs'.[47] This leads Stannard to conclude: 'on the way to Auschwitz the road's pathway led straight through the heart of the Indians and of North and South America'.[48] Churchill contributes his unsurprisingly similar claim that that Hitler's *lebensraumpolitik* and 'many of his more repugnant policies' were derived from 'earlier U.S. conduct against Native America'. Manifest Destiny was little different from Hitler's conception of 'living space', which in any event was inspired by America's 1830 Indian Removal Act and the military campaigns directed against indigenous peoples in the 'Great Plains, Great Basin and Sonora Dessert Regions'.[49] In short, there's little we can learn from the Holocaust that could not already have been observed from the American experience.

Disease, slavery, and genocide

While pushing for a high percentage of dead as well as a high absolute number of deaths is an important goal of his work, Stannard has also attempted to prove intent to commit genocide. He seeks to refute the long-held belief that disease was but an 'inadvertent' or 'unintended consequence' of colonialism. For Stannard, disease was deliberately used as a means of killing, alongside massacre. Both, he argues, 'were interdependent forces acting dynamically – whipsawing their victims between plague and violence'.[50] Genocide, he posits, was the result of 'intertwined and interacting *combinations* of lethal agents ... direct slaughter, disease and forced labor – combined, as in the Nazi concentration and death camps, with the consequential reduction of live birth rates to far below replacement levels...'.[51]

Stannard focuses on forms of killing shared by both the Holocaust and the American genocide: disease, forced labor, forced marches, and other conditions calculated to bring about the deaths of a target group. Crucial to his case is that (just like the Holocaust) indigenous deaths by disease must be counted as genocide. We thus read that projected deaths by illness accounted for 60 percent of annual deaths at Auschwitz-Birkenau, while for Buchenwald 'disease and malnutrition' were the highest causes of death. Overall, some 2.4 million Jews died of 'natural' causes and what Raul Hilberg has called 'ghettoization and general privation'.[52] Thus, if disease is part of the Holocaust, Stannard reasons, it must also be included as part of the 'American Holocaust'. Deaths by slave labor too must be added to the total. If Jewish slave laborers were victims of the Holocaust, so too were indigenous slave laborers under the Spanish. At three four months life expectancy, he sees this as 'about the same as that of someone working at slave labor in the synthetic rubber manufacturing plant at Auschwitz in the 1940s'.[53] Churchill too is in no doubt that forced labor in the Americas was a 'holocaustal ... prototype for nazi policies in eastern Europe'.[54]

'Orthodox denial' and the holocaust

Is Holocaust denial unique? Stannard and Churchill argue that it isn't, and refer to two pernicious and destructive forms of genocide denial at work in America. The first is promoted by the American establishment, the other primarily by Relativists. Stannard sees the first type as traditional, fairly common amongst those whose forefathers committed the genocide. The need to protect the 'moral reputation' of the perpetrators and their country seems obvious enough, as does the desire, in some cases, to continue mistreating and persecuting the target group. The perpetrator's reputation is saved, while legacies of the genocide continue. Stannard sees the first type as 'common ... even readily understandable, if contemptible'.[55]

Churchill is more cutting about this 'orthodox scholarship', which he sees as 'among the most well developed of any genocide'. He describes an entire industry of denial, 'substantially reinforced on television ... in popular literature, and in the well over 2,000 films Hollywood and its Canadian counterparts have produced ...'.[56] This includes established cultural and scientific centres like the Smithsonian Institution, whose estimate of the pre-conquest population north of Mexico was 'not more than one million', an estimate which it has had to revise upwards several times since the real total was 'about *fifteen times*' higher.[57] Nevertheless, like Stannard, he muses that this is little different from what 'might have been expected of ... German counterparts with regard to Jews, Gypsies, Slavs, and others in the aftermath of nazi victory ...'.[58]

For both writers, the Americanization of the Holocaust has been crucial in deflecting attention from indigenous genocide, while allowing the United States to appear sympathetic and morally upright – 'quite an intellectual pirouette'.[59] If Nazi Germany is 'the very idea of evil', Jews become by extension 'the ultimate "worthy" victim'. However, the Americanization process buttresses America's image as a model of democracy, multiculturalism, and enlightenment. Indigenous peoples are thus the 'the ultimate "unworthy" victims'.[60] Churchill too sees a focus on the Holocaust as problematic. Any other genocide is devalued, 'unless it was done in precisely the fashion the Nazis did it'. The destruction of indigenous groups becomes acceptable when their internal displacement and extermination can be successfully distanced from what the Nazis did: 'technical differentiation is then magnified and used as a sort of all purpose veil behind which almost anything can be hidden, so long as it is not openly adorned with a swastika'.[61]

Clearly, there are problems with memory of Western atrocities. Recognizing the Holocaust has contributed to amnesia in some cases. Yet I am troubled by the fact that 'orthodox' denial seems inseparable from the Holocaust. Neither man considers how the US government might recognize the Holocaust *and* the American Indian genocide at the same time. Indeed, they buy into a dichotomy which pits Jews against American Indian interests.

They then seek to undermine the Jewish 'side' by attacking Holocaust scholarship in an effort to bolster their own position.

'Exclusivist' denial

Since Jews and not the US government are the primary focus of attack, it should not surprise us that Holocaust 'exclusivism' is presented as a morally worse form of denial. If orthodox denial is somehow expected, Absolutist and Relativist scholars seem to be engaged in a much more cynical game. These, Stannard argues, are 'denying recognition to others who also have suffered massive genocidal brutality ... play[ing] into the hands of the brutalizers'.[62] Yet presumably these 'brutalizers' are the 'orthodox deniers', who he claims are not as bad. Stannard has angrily insisted that the elevation of the Holocaust has been little more than 'the hegemonic product of many years of strenuous intellectual labor by a handful of Jewish scholars and writers who have dedicated much if not all of their professional lives to the advancement of this exclusivist idea'.[63]

Stannard's problem with uniqueness theories is the following: that 'advocates *begin* by defining genocide (or the Holocaust or the Shoah) in terms of what they already believe to be experiences undergone only by Jews. After much laborious research it is then "discovered" – *mirabile dictu* – that the Jewish experience was unique'.[64] The Holocaust as benchmark denies other genocides the right to be recognized and appreciated on their own terms. This double standard is even worse, Stannard argues, in light of Israel's 'ongoing genocidal actions' against the Palestinians.[65] This differs little from Churchill's view that Jews have cynically used their 'moral capital' to 'political advantage, particularly in garnering support for the Israeli state'.[66] However, neither Stannard nor Churchill can offer any convincing proof that Israel has committed genocide or is continuing to do so. Such a charge, needless to say, is groundless.

Relativists like Deborah Lipstadt and Steven Katz receive the brunt of the attack. They lump Comparativists with Holocaust deniers and neo-Nazis.[67] Churchill covers the same ground, similarly taking aim at Holocaust historians and 'a substantial component of Zionism' for promoting an 'exclusivist' interpretation of the Holocaust. He echoes Stannard in lambasting Lipstadt and Katz for 'holocaust denial', with Lipstadt 'a firm denier of the American holocaust'. The small 'h' is significant here. All other genocides are termed 'holocaust', including the genocide of America's indigenous peoples. For Churchill, exclusivists 'have contributed to the invisibility of the victims' and are indeed worse than Holocaust deniers. 'Those who would deny the Holocaust after all, focus their distortions on one target. Those who deny all holocausts other than that of the Jews have the same effect upon many'.[68]

What precise crimes have these Relativists committed? First, Lipstadt comes under fire for her assertions, in *Denying the Holocaust*, that Comparativists are the equivalent of 'David Duke without his robes'. While they may not be 'crypto-deniers, the results of their work are the same: the blurring of boundaries between fact and fiction'.[69] She is also accused of denying the genocides of the Armenians, the Cambodians, and the Ukrainians. These for Churchill are 'genuine' holocausts deserving of full recognition, deserving of being 'exhumed' from the 'black hole' where they now reside thanks to Jewish 'exclusivists' and 'neonazis'.[70] Much of this attack parrots Stannard's earlier critiques.[71]

Katz is similarly accused of 'minimisation and denial of the first order' by arguing that the maximum number of Indians killed in wars with Europeans from 1775 and 1890 was 45,000.[72] Then, Yehuda Bauer is attacked for framing the Holocaust as a separate and unprecedented form of genocide. He is accused of denial for not recognizing that the Roma were fellow victims of the Nazis, nor that Poles and other Slavs were also slated to be victims of 'physical eradication every bit as complete as that intended for the Jews ...'.[73]

In keeping with the focus on Jewish Holocaust historians, 'holocaust deniers' are denounced as considerably more dangerous than those who deny the Jewish Holocaust. While Holocaust deniers exist on the margins of society, Lipstadt, Katz, and others are established academics, with the legitimacy to accuse anyone who attacks them of being an 'anti-Semite' or 'neonazi'. Further, Jewish 'exclusivists' and the 'mythology' they 'peddle' forms a perfect fit with the 'institutionalised denials of genocides' promoted by countries who have committed genocide. Their list includes the United States, the United Kingdom, France, Turkey, and Indonesia.[74]

Reflections on the Stannard–Churchill thesis

In making their case, Stannard and Churchill rely on a widespread Nazi-like intent to exterminate indigenous peoples. Yet the case is not as clear-cut as the authors would have it. First, we have disease. Elazar Barkan, in his critique of Stannard, rightly takes him to task for including the majority of deaths by disease as part of an intentional genocide. Stannard *does* prove that disease was spread intentionally in some cases. However, in cases where disease raged ahead of the explorers and colonizers, Stannard counts the dead here too as victims of intentional genocide, though this runs counter to the thesis of assigning 'blame for intentional action'. Stannard, argues Barkan, 'overstates his case'. There must be distinctions made between intentional and 'collateral' killings.[75] This is a typical Relativist critique, and certainly one of the strongest.

Both Katz and Lewy have produced works denying genocide in America on the basis that disease was 'unintended', while the colonizers did their best to keep indigenous peoples alive.[76] European colonizers did lay the conditions for the spread of disease. However, not all disease was spread intentionally, and, despite their questionable motives, Katz and Lewy do highlight some mitigating factors. Stannard somewhat undermines his thesis by noting that in European cities of the fifteenth century, it was not unknown for 10–20 percent of a population to die 'at a single stroke' from diseases such as plague, smallpox, typhus, and typhoid fever.[77]

Henry Dobyns, in his exploration of disease in European history, has chronicled no less that forty-one smallpox epidemics and pandemics from 1520 to 1899, seventeen measles epidemics, and ten major influenza epidemics and pandemics in roughly the same timeframe, not to mention four plague epidemics (1545–1707), five diphtheria epidemics (1601–1890), four typhus epidemics, four scarlet fever epidemics, and six epidemics of other diseases including typhoid from the sixteenth to the early nineteenth centuries.[78] If *European* plagues were not intentional, and if they don't count as genocide or 'holocaust', is Stannard engaging in a double standard by suggesting that the *North American* ones were? He seems to combine intentional and unintentional diseases to achieve the mammoth totals and percentages he feels necessary to claim a 'holocaust'.

In Stannard's case (and Churchill's), the Holocaust usefully makes disease appear sometimes to be what it is not. Nazi-era ghettoes, concentration, work, and death camps were all created within a short time by Nazi planners. They were specifically designed to kill, and disease was one instrument of deliberate genocide. Jews and others were concentrated and isolated in order to make the killing faster and easier. While some comparisons could be made between the forced marches, forced labor, and the herding of indigenous peoples onto reservations, Indians were never ghettoized and concentrated to the same extent. Reserves were not concentration camps, whatever Stannard and Churchill infer in their accounts. Indeed, the reserve system seems less a tool of genocide than part of its aftermath.

Obsessed with 'exclusivists'

I also feel it necessary to follow up on some of the Stannard–Churchill attacks on 'exclusivists', demonstrating that, at least in Lipstadt's case, these attacks are overblown. However, they offer a more solid critique of Katz which bears further discussion. As we have already seen, Lipstadt in Churchill's account seems to be accusing other genocide historians of anti-Semitism.[79] This is disingenuous. A closer examination of her book reveals that her comments were largely in reference to *Historikerstreit* historian Ernst Nolte's contention in *The European Civil War 1917–1945*, that 'more "Aryans" than Jews were murdered at Auschwitz'. Nolte further claimed that the arguments used by deniers were not 'without foundation', while their motives were 'often honourable'.[80] Placed in context, Lipstadt is justifiably concerned about deniers accessing the work of serious historians and using it for their own purposes.

Nevertheless, Lipstadt's approach is wanting. She does trivialize other genocides, such as the Armenian 'tragedy', and Stalin's 'arbitrary' terror (contrasted to Hitler's 'targeted' variety). She then lumps these genocides together with conflicts like 'the disastrous U.S. policies in Vietnam', labeling any exercise in comparison 'historical distortion'.[81] While disturbing, Lipstadt does not deny that these other killings were genocide. She makes no attacks on scholars like Stannard or Churchill. Her criticism is largely reserved for German historians, and denier David Irving, who have used other crimes in world history to relativize the Holocaust.[82] Churchill makes some useful illustrative points about what Lipstadt might represent in terms of a certain style of Holocaust scholarship. Nevertheless, he is nit-picking. It is hard to agree that her 'splatters extend without nuance or distinction'.[83] She has some very clear targets in mind, and most if not all of them are German.

With Katz, both Stannard and Churchill are on more solid ground, although they exaggerate any potential danger he might pose.[84] Katz, as we have seen, promotes a form of 'phenomenological uniqueness' based on the universal and total dimensions of Nazi goals.[85] This claim is questioned and to some extent dismissed due to lack of evidence.[86] But Katz does promote forms of genocide denial. He refuses to recognize any 'Indian-hating' aspects of American history, including intent to kill Indians, or to eradicate their cultures, languages, religious beliefs, and ways of living. In his selection of 'experts' on American history, Katz deliberately excludes Drinnon, Stannard, and others, dismissing them as 'revisionist' (those who commit 'abuses of the "Holocaust paradigm"'), with Katz commenting 'I am not alas, fabricating this argument'.[87]

Katz's longer denial of American genocide in the Rosenbaum volume is more pointedly critical of Stannard and Churchill. In the entire history of American colonization, he concedes a tiny casualty figure of 106,000, 'due to war and conflict situations'. Since this total is but 'some fraction of 1 percent' of the rate of population decline, genocide cannot be proven statistically.[88] Finally, while he admits of some massacres, he also notes American restraint. By the end of the nineteenth century, 'the U.S. Army had subdued the great western tribes on the field of battle'. While they could have slaughtered the remaining tribal members, as their plans were not genocidal (he avers), they did not.[89] Since the Army missed such a fine opportunity, Katz concludes: 'perhaps surprisingly though undeniably, the U.S. government never undertook a general campaign, never articulated a comprehensive policy, aimed at the wholesale eradication of the Indian'.[90] US actions are thus presented as acceptable. Since it's not genocide under his very narrow definition, it's not really anything at all.

Another claim concerns the money and energy spent on converting indigenous populations to Christianity, with churches and missionary schools, funded by government and private individuals, a process 'contragenocidal in its intent'.[91] He couples this with discussion of the 141 managed reservations in place by 1880, an obvious 'alternative to extinction'. As for the 'Indian wars', these were designed not to exterminate Indians but to 'break their serious and continued resistance to removal to reservations'.

While 'paternalistic and imperialistic', such actions saved Indian lives. There was never any 'Hitlerian conclusion' because, despite any 'ethical and existential transgressions', reservations were a 'concession to survival'.[92]

Note that most of Katz's historical examples come from the post-Civil War era, a time when most Indians were already dead. They no longer represented a military threat, and had been divested of their ancestral lands. By focusing on this later era and eliding discussion of earlier periods, Katz is able to present late nineteenth-century Americans as 'well-intended ethnocentric men' trying to advance the 'Indians' and make them progress. These he sees as comparable to European liberals who tried to eradicate Jewish identity in order to emancipate Jews and give them 'civic equality'.[93] The two situations are very different. Indigenous peoples were not to be emancipated, nor were they to gain civic equality. Furthermore, there was an obvious trade-off for indigenous peoples not present for Jews. Indians had not only to give up their culture and religion, but also their lands, many of their worldly possessions and their means of subsistence, even if we accept Katz's argument that no genocide was committed. Jews were generally not required to make such trade-offs in order to fit into European society, nor were they forced to attend residential schools under threat of imprisonment.

While he accepts a pre-conquest population of 112 million and a death rate of 96 percent, Katz is unwilling to draw any lessons from the deaths of 100 million people.[94] If this isn't genocide, then what, under international law, should we call it? Crimes against humanity, perhaps? Katz provides no answer for the reader, nor does he seem remotely concerned with finding one. There may not have been the 'Hilterian conclusion' that Stannard and Churchill are at pains to prove, but there is certainly proof enough of genocide to cast doubt on Katz's scholarship – and his motives. Katz's work (and that of Lewy) clearly demonstrates that American Indian academics do have enemies among some Holocaust historians. Yet there are not many Relativists interested in denying America's genocidal past. The attacks on Lipstadt lack substance, while neither Lewy nor Katz express any overt antipathy towards American Indians. There is little of the knee-jerk racism we find with the 'orthodox' type of denial, and I find it impossible to conclude, as Stannard does, that uniqueness and denial are but 'two sides of the same debased coin'.[95]

My main concern in this chapter has been Stannard and Churchill's unwarranted attack on Jewish Relativist historians. Denial of indigenous genocide seems to be very much a status quo and widespread phenomenon on the United States. Yet the brunt of their attack focuses primarily on one ethnic/religious group, whose scholarship differs little from that of other American historians like Satz or Dippie. Holocaust historians need only be responsible for how they promote their own collective tragedy, not for the reasons why their genocide has been magnified in public consciousness. Can they really be 'blamed' for the fact that the US government chooses to commemorate one genocide while refusing to recognize another?

An attack too far

Shortly after September 11 2001, Churchill penned an essay in which he controversially called workers in the World Trade Center a 'technocratic corps at the very heart of America's global financial empire'. These, he posited, helped create the infrastructure that made American foreign policy (including war crimes) possible. It was therefore defensible to call them 'little Eichmanns', for 'willingly and knowingly' supporting US military policy. Further, the al Qaeda attacks could be seen as justifiable (from a Middle Eastern perspective) in light of the horrific death tolls inflicted by America on Iraq. The number of US victims pales in comparison to the 500,000 children who died as a result of US-led sanctions. This Churchill also called a 'holocaust'.[96]

Churchill's attack was nonsensical. First, it contributed, however unwittingly, to the assumption that Iraq and al Qaeda were somehow linked. The view that bin Laden had responded to Iraqi victimization at American hands was demonstrably false. Second, Churchill seemed to see the Middle East as an amorphous whole, full of Arab victims and American persecutors. Such a black-and-white image of regional politics is a near-perfect mirror image of Bush's own Manichean perceptions. While this type of posturing was vintage Churchill, the backlash from a public unfamiliar with his work was severe. In 2005 Churchill was invited to Hamilton College, to a forum on September 11. A Hamilton student found Churchill's article on the Internet, and the conflict began thereafter. In the aftermath Churchill became a *cause célèbre*, and cast himself as a martyr for free speech. He was forced to step down as Chair of the Ethnic Studies department at the University of Colorado, and a full-scale investigation into his academic career began.[97] Colorado's Republican governor, Bill Owens, demanded his dismissal, and joined a litany of other high-profile figures calling for Churchill's head.[98]

Churchill was also accused of plagiarism,[99] and, curiously, with not being an American Indian at all. A number of leading organizations, including the American Indian Movement, dismissed Churchill's claims of indigenous ancestry, calling him a 'wannabe' and a 'pseudo Indian', using a false identity to seek career advancement.[100] The loss of this legitimacy could be damning for Churchill, since his indigenous ancestry is crucial to his message, featuring prominently on his book titles *From a Native Son* (1996) and *Indians Are Us?* (1994). This scandal has yet to be resolved, and may indeed result in Churchill's dismissal or suspension from his academic position.[101]

A Denkmal for America?

In light of the strengthening of exceptionalist rhetoric after 9/11, it seems clear that the window of opportunity opened during the Clinton era is now at least partially closed. It now seems even less certain that American leaders will be willing to adopt Olick's 'German' identity and finally admit to their sins against indigenous peoples. In 2000, the Department of Indian Affairs did accept 'moral responsibility' for waging 'war on Indian people ... by threat, deceit and force', committing 'acts so terrible that they infect, diminish and destroy the lives of Indian people decades later, generations later ...'.[102] However, this stark admission, which still did not admit to genocide, failed to reflect official government or administration policy, nor was it consistent with the general thrust of American policies.

J. Angelo Corlett has noted the profound lack of remorse for crimes undertaken by the US government. There have been 'few, if any, apologies or reparations'.[103] He prescribes as part of the healing process (in addition to reparations) the development of 'a national sense of shame-based guilt and collective remorse' for past crimes. Yet while such shame will require 'a higher-level self-consciousness', this is precisely what may be lacking in US society.[104]

Churchill's hurtful comments about victims of 9/11 will also do the American Indian cause no favors. In a recent editorial, *Indian Country Today* emphatically rejected Churchill's position, arguing 'In no way does his insult reflect the views of Indian country'. Further, they saw Churchill's comments as politically dangerous for Indians: 'To call the people who were murdered on Sept. 11 "little Eichmanns" is a hideous expression that when combined [with] Churchill's mistaken Native identity can only poison the public discourse concerning American Indians'.[105]

Overall, both Stannard and Churchill are right to criticize the hypocrisy of the American establishment. The genocide of indigenous peoples *should* be a central part of American identity, and Native America's new museum *should* offer discussion of genocide and its effects. This trauma is very real, and continues still. As such, 'wallowing' in the genocide should be promoted. However, bringing in the Holocaust to promote memory of another genocide can lead to confusion. First, the audience/reader must obviously have sympathy for Jewish victims of the Holocaust. They must be able to relate to Jewish suffering, or else the rhetorical thrust of the Stannard–Churchill thesis accomplishes little. Our sympathy for indigenous people is conditional on our sympathy for the Jews, and conditional on Stannard and Churchill's ability to make the links between the two groups very clear.

Yet Stannard and Churchill also ask us to be open to some other ideas. First, we are to believe that the Holocaust consciousness and sympathy we need to relate to indigenous experiences is a cheat. It is a double standard, and the work of cynical 'deniers' who are manipulating history. At first we are enjoined to sympathize with indigenous peoples because we can relate to Jews. The focus then changes. We are then asked to relate to indigenous peoples and condemn Jewish Holocaust historians. We must accept that we have been manipulated into feeling as bad as we have for victims of the Holocaust. We must then *transfer* this feeling of kinship with a victimized people from the Jews to the indigenous peoples. The reader is put in an uncomfortable and compromising position.

Stannard and Churchill do much better to make us sympathize with indigenous people on their own terms and in light of their own history. Both academics give us more than enough detail to fully understand and relate to indigenous experiences. They have suffered horribly in the past, and continue to suffer in the present. Justice is long overdue. However, tying memory of indigenous genocide to the Holocaust fails to help Americans confront their own history. Indeed, as the public reaction against Churchill clearly demonstrates, it will most likely have the opposite effect.

5   Australia

Aboriginal genocide and the Holocaust

It remains one of the mysteries of history that Australia was able to get away with a racist policy that included segregation and dispossession and bordered on slavery and genocide, practices unknown in the civilised world in the first half of the twentieth century until Nazi Germany turned on the Jews in the 1930s.

(Phillip Knightley, *Australia: A Biography of a Nation* (2000))[1]

Like the *National Museum of the American Indian* in Washington DC, the *First Australians Gallery* at Australia's *National Museum* in Canberra avoids discussion of domestic genocide. While the Gallery promises to 'deal frankly with contact history', there is a paucity of information on the genocide claims arising from twentieth-century assimilation policies and nineteenth-century massacres.[2] At one level, memory and forgetfulness in Australia parallels the American experience. However, Gallery architect Howard Raggat was deliberately subversive. His design featured a not-so-subtle condemnation of Australia's turbulent past – another salvo in the 'History Wars' that so dominated the 1990s. The design was based on the Jewish extension to the Berlin Museum, which was commissioned by the German government as a memorial to the Holocaust. As Raggat argued of the Gallery's shape:

> This was the mark of the Jewish Museum in Berlin just completed, designed a decade ago, that mark of a jagged break in the star of David, of Jewish history in Berlin, broken by the Holocaust. A mark becoming as if the object of that terrible gap, the object of that unnamable void.[3]

Such architectural statements have not sat well with the Australian right. Revisionist historian Keith Windschuttle's view was a typical if somewhat exaggerated response. In 2003, he took aim at the Gallery in an open letter. Lamenting the copying of the German design, he saw it as 'signif[ying] that the Aborigines suffered the equivalent of the Holocaust'. His immodest suggestion was to 'reconstruct that part of the building that provides the lightning bolt symbol. This would remove the current connection between the fate of the Aborigines and the fate of the Jews of Europe'. Simply put, 'Aborigines did not suffer a Holocaust', and to compare the two events was 'not only conceptually odious but wildly anachronistic'. Colonization in his view was primarily a charitable and benign affair.[4]

Windschuttle lost this particular battle, and Aboriginal history slowly moves forward. The Gallery has yet to be 'reconstructed'. Yet misunderstanding and confusion over Aboriginal genocide and, indeed, genocide in general, continues to persist. This chapter considers the appropriateness of using Holocaust vocabulary and imagery in coming to terms with Aboriginal genocide. In this chapter I reflect Dirk Moses' conclusion that Australian 'liberals and leftists' have had their views of history 'transformed by the Holocaust', which has played an important role by its 'seepage into popular cultural memory'.[5] However, bringing in the Holocaust as a unit of comparison, while alerting the public to the plight of Aborigines, has also established a standard of evil which makes real comparison more difficult. As Moses again argues, 'the uniqueness of the Holocaust can mean that events that do not resemble it are not genocidal at all'.[6] This is precisely the problem in the Australian case.

The use of the Holocaust has become problematic due to the very different nature of the Australian genocide. While Australia's child removal policies qualify for II(e) of the UNGC, few of the frontier wars or massacres fall within the ambit of the Convention. The possible exceptions are Tasmania and Queensland, although even historians who recognize the 'stolen generations' as victims of genocide debate these other events. Attempts to compare the Australian genocide and the Holocaust can sometimes yield interesting insights into both cases, but overall they serve to decontextualize and confuse an already divisive issue, now at the heart of Australian national identity.

Genocide denial and the Aboriginal 'Holocaust'

Genocide denial in Australia enjoys support from the current Howard government. Many right-wing historians, journalists, and activists deny that genocide occurred in the nineteenth and twentieth centuries, while the left often promotes comparison between Jewish and Aboriginal experiences. It's worthwhile before proceeding further to grapple with the significance of the Australian denialist movement, which exalts settler history while demonizing Aboriginal peoples and the academic left. The history of the journal *Quadrant* illustrates well some of the deeply entrenched conflict that has taken place over collective memory since the 1990s. Formerly edited by Robert Manne, *Quadrant* became one of the vanguard publications advancing the case for an Australian genocide. *Quadrant* had actually been one of the first publications to invoke the term. In 1975, Peter Kerr lamented the 'inability of Australians to come to terms with their genocidal past'[7], a theme picked up by later writers like Raymond Gaita in his seminal articles published in 1997.[8]

However, a right-wing backlash ensued, and by December 1997 Manne was forced out as editor. New editor Padriac McGuinness dismissed Manne's 'mawkish sentimentality'. A large numbers of articles defending and/or denying government policies towards the Aborigines appeared, treating purveyors of much-hated 'political correctness' with a large dose of 'common sense'.[9] Prime Minister Howard was reported in 2000 to have read *Quadrant* 'religiously', and attended a *Quadrant* conference as well.[10] The journal has become a flagship publication for the right, and a vehicle for many of their denialist arguments.

What does *Quadrant* argue? First, 'half caste' victims are denied their status as a separate victimized people. A key point raised by Ron Brunton and others is that the stolen generations were half European.[11] Being partial members of the European 'group' to which they were being transferred, they could not possibly be afforded protection under the UNGC, which was intended to save distinct and authentic groups from extermination.[12] Brunton's arguments ignore that half-Aborigines *were* objectified as a separate group, and were never seen as part of a White Australia group. Chief Protector Neville was very clear that while the full-blooded Aborigines were dying out, a new and dangerous race was increasing prolifically. As he argued in 1937: 'Are we going to have a population of one million Blacks ... or are we going to merge them into our White community and eventually forget that there were any Aborigines in Australia?'[13]

Another favorite argument of the right is the relative 'backwardness' of Aboriginal peoples, victims of an unfortunate clash of civilizations. Kenneth Minogue, for example, has scorned any notion of 'cultural relativity'. In his work, White Europeans were clearly superior to Aborigines, who 'often seemed lost in their dream world'.[14] Aborigines, through the eyes of the average 'surfer on the beach', he posits, seem to be 'a pretty incompetent lot, who are difficult to help'. Minogue chooses to blame the victims for their plight. '[T]he drunkenness of many, the incapacity to manage income and the squalor in public housing from kinship reciprocities amongst Aboriginal tribes' all lead (in his view) to understandably high levels of discrimination.[15]

Doubtless the most active purveyor of denialism has been Windshuttle. A regular contributor to *Quadrant*, his lengthy tome *The Fabrication of Aboriginal History* (2000) attacked claims of genocide and even ill intent on the part of White settlers. His purpose has been to examine and disprove the Tasmanian genocide by a critical examination and refutation of many of the leading historians writing on Aboriginal history.[16] Windschuttle has dismissed claims of frontier massacres as being exaggerated or manufactured, first of all by 'neurotic Christian missionaries searching for souls and careers', then by 'ideologically-driven twentieth-century leftist historians intent upon denying the legitimacy of the British settlement and denigrating Australia's good name'.[17] He concludes that Australian history represents 'the least violent of all Europe's encounters with the New World'. He goes on to prove his case by radically reducing the pre-conquest population of Tasmania, and then promotes the theory that Tasmanians were primitive and dysfunctional. Due to their brutal treatment of women, their civilization was on the verge of collapse anyway. They were lucky to have lived as long as they did.[18]

The impact of such scholarship is not simply local. Minogue is a well-respected professor in the Government Department at the London School of Economics, and has a wide audience for his views. Windschuttle's popularity is growing, as fellow right-wingers endorse his work and promote it internationally. Another seemingly respectable purveyor of genocide denial is William Rubenstein, Professor of History at the University of Wales, Aberystwyth, who lived for almost twenty years in Australia. In his *Genocide: A History* (2004), Rubenstein tells us simply that there was no genocide of Aboriginal peoples. He acknowledges that there was a 'sharp decline in Aboriginal numbers', but blames disease and 'the usual highly negative indirect effects' of White settlement. He acknowledges some killing, but attributes it to 'former convicts' operating in opposition to the wishes of their central governments.[19]

As for the 'stolen generations', Rubenstein scoffs at the idea, since 'probably hundreds of children are taken from their mothers everyday in the democratic world, often following a custody battle, without any claims of "genocide" being made'.[20] At any rate, he excuses the policies as benign, to save the children from being raised as 'illiterate hunter-gatherers among a race who were, in a frequently heard view at the time, doomed to die out'. Echoing Brunton, he argues that since the children were half-European, there was no genocide. Europeans were merely trying to raise 'part-Europeans in a European society'.[21]

Rubenstein relies heavily on Windschuttle's 'important research', as it represents 'everything that a critical historian should be doing'.[22] Genocide claims are dismissed as the last gasp of Marxist historians, searching for 'new ways of undermining the legitimacy of established society'.[23] As for the Aborigines, he is scathing. Only 'political correctness' prevents historians from seeing Aborigines as the genocidal people they are, lacking '*any* abstract notion of human rights in the modern Western sense'. Based on nineteenth-century accounts, he reasons that 30 percent of Aboriginal children were killed at birth, with widespread 'cannibalism of a murdered baby'. The roasting and eating of infants is presented as a common occurrence.[24]

To add further insult to injury, Rubenstein tries to calculate how many children Aboriginal peoples must have killed in Australia's pre-colonial history. Taking a base population figure of 300,000 people in 1788, he reasons that if the population increased by 4 percent annually and Aborigines killed 20 percent of their offspring every year, in the 40,000 years in which they inhabited Australia they would have 'deliberately murdered' 100 million infants. Of course, this does not include 'other horrors such as tribal wars, often apparently ending in massacre'.[25] This conjecture is based entirely on Windschuttle's work and the author's own tentative speculations. I am amazed that Pearson Education saw fit to publish this overtly racist tract as a textbook, billed as 'the definitive account of genocide'.

The Holocaust in Australia

Clearly the right has engaged in polemics to advance its side in the growing 'History Wars'. Yet invoking the Holocaust is perceived in some quarters to be equally polemical. The Holocaust has made an appearance in discussions of Aboriginal history for two divergent reasons: ignorance on the one hand, and detailed knowledge on the other. First, the Holocaust is used as an attention-seeking device by those who know little of genocide. Australians are generally unfamiliar with other genocides, especially *indigenous* genocides. This has made the Holocaust attractive as a means of focusing public opinion. The moral clarity introduced by the Holocaust is also seen as a robust defence against genocide denial. If it is immoral and even illegal in some countries to deny the Holocaust, then denying the Aboriginal genocide should invoke an equal amount of condemnation from Australian society. An 'Australian holocaust' cements the facts of the genocide and gives them an additional emotional charge.

While the right scorns claims of genocide, those on the left have promoted it. Both sides see genocide as a taint on Australia's dominant historical narratives. The left seeks to re-evaluate Australia's history in light of its past atrocities. The right wants to uphold its pristine image of the 'lucky country'. There seems no *modus vivendi* between the two sides.

At another level, Holocaust comparisons are sometimes promoted by academics from Jewish backgrounds, who understand both genocides well and have obvious sympathy for both victim people. For example, Colin Tatz is a Jewish South African who, as former Chair of the Political Science Department at Macquarie (Sydney), focused on comparisons between South Africa, Australia, and Nazi Germany. Paul Bartrop is a professor in the Jewish Studies Department at Bialik College (Melbourne), while Andrew Markus is Professor of Jewish civilization at Monash University. Historian Robert Manne's interest in Aboriginal genocide and the Holocaust stems in part from the fact that his parents were Holocaust survivors.[26]

Part of the interest in comparing the two genocides may have to do with the belief that Jews and Aborigines were both subject to similar forms of discrimination by the Australian government. Aborigines were targeted because they were deemed inferior, and Jews because they were seen as an alien race, impossible to assimilate. Bartrop for example, decries early Australian efforts to produce a '"pure' population of blond-haired, blue-eyed Anglo-Australians' by forcing Aboriginal assimilation and capping Jewish immigration to only 10 percent of all applicants, even during the Holocaust.[27] Both groups, he avers, were targeted in an Australian 'quest for racial and cultural assimilation'.[28]

In general, the Jewish community in Australia contains the largest number of Holocaust survivors outside Israel,[29] and Jewish–Aboriginal relations have a long and positive history. Gary Foley has popularized the story of William Cooper, an Aboriginal activist who led a deputation from the Australian Aborigines League, one month after *Kristallnacht* in November 1938, to the German Consulate in Melbourne. Here he tried to lodge a formal complaint, presenting a resolution 'condemning the persecution of Jews and Christians in Germany'.[30] For Foley, the story demonstrates the compassion of Aboriginal people, and the similarities between what both groups had suffered or would soon suffer.[31] In 2004, the Melbourne Jewish Holocaust Museum dedicated a plaque to commemorate Cooper's protest.[32]

Australia's Jewish community has been supportive of Aboriginal efforts to achieve recognition and justice. In 2003, the New South Wales Jewish Board of Deputies made clear the long-standing Jewish support for the Aboriginal community, releasing a list of notable individuals who have contributed to Aboriginal rights. These include Aboriginal activist Eddie Mabo's lawyer, Ron Castan, and Chief Justice Jim Spigelman of the Supreme Court of New South Wales.[33] Barrister Jack Fajgenbaum, who worked with Castan on the Mabo case, describes a 'special relationship between Jews and Aborigines', premised on 'a shared understanding, a sense of lost culture and the importance of memory'.[34] In 1997, Board of Deputies leader Peter Wertheim delivered a powerful address appealing to all Australians 'not to repeat the mistakes of the past by committing the "crime of silence" in the light of overwhelming evidence of acts of genocide faced by the Aboriginal community in the past'.[35] Rabbi Raymond Apple even proposed a plan for national reconciliation at the Grand Synagogue in Sydney, based on traditional Jewish teachings.[36]

B'nai Brith, the Australasian Union of Jewish Students, and other organizations have all played a role in 'the Jewish community's efforts to support the Reconciliation process and to combat racism and intolerance in Australian society'.[37] As Aboriginal Senator Aden Ridgeway argued recently: 'We've always enjoyed the support of the Jewish community ... There have been very close relationships at the personal and professional level'. Australian Jews are generally seen to have a 'clean slate' in their history with Aboriginal peoples. Jews played a disproportionately large role in the 1960s 'freedom rides', and mirrored Jewish participation in the American civil rights movement.[38]

Aboriginal genocide and the Holocaust

Many Jewish organizations and individuals have supported Aboriginal interests for decades, and have been generally sympathetic to Aboriginal claims of genocide. But how has the general public responded? As many genocide historians record, public perceptions have been negative. The Holocaust,

Cambodia, and Rwanda have spawned stereotypes of what 'real' genocide is like. Genocide must be inspired by totalizing ideologies, corrupt governments, and irrational, blood-thirsty individuals. Genocide without Nazi-like symbols and images seems difficult to understand.[39] As Tatz explains:

> Australians understand only the stereotypical or traditional scenes of historical or present-day slaughter. For them, genocide connotes either the bulldozed corpses at Belsen or the serried rows of Cambodian skulls, the panga-wielding Hutu in pursuit of Tutsi victims or the ethnic cleansing in the former Yugoslavia. As Australians see it, patently we cannot be connected to, or with, the stereotypes of Swastika-wearing SS psychopaths, or crazed Black tribal Africans.[40]

Curthoys and Docker, in their edited work on Aboriginal genocide, also note the conceptual problems Australians have had when confronting a genocidal past. The idea that genocide could only mean the Holocaust is common, with the view put forth that 'any comparison with the Holocaust was insensitive to the latter's uniquely terrible nature as well as wildly exaggerating the negative aspects of Australia's history of colonisation, dispossession, institutionalisation, and cultural imposition'.[41] Bartrop too notes a public rejection of genocide claims. Australia as a 'land of mateship' and the 'fair go' could not possibly have committed genocide.[42]

Nevertheless, the Holocaust *has* helped make a case for restitution and justice. Important attempts have been made by Aboriginal activists to show kinship with Jews as fellow victims of suffering, while also casting parallels between early Australian governments and Nazi Germany. One of the earliest examples of this type of rhetoric was in the 'Platform and Programme' (1970) of the Black Panthers of Australia. Crucial to their message was a comparison with Jews during and after the Holocaust. If post-War Germany was willing to 'aid the Jews in Israel for the genocide [of] the Jewish people', it made sense for the Australian government to compensate Aborigines. This was especially so since the murder of six million Jews 'represented only a small portion of the Jewish population as compared with the significant attempted genocide of the Black people of this country'. The Black Panthers cited the total extermination of the Tasmanian Aborigines, and the 75 percent death rate of Aborigines in Australia.[43]

The Holocaust would emerge in the 1990s as a more sophisticated rhetorical device and unit of comparison. In their submissions to the *Bringing Them Home* report, Link-Up New South Wales (which works to reunite Aboriginal families) advocated establishing an Aboriginal Oral History Archive, 'modelled on the Shoah Foundation set up to record the oral histories of Jewish victims of the Nazi holocaust'. This would 'fund and facilitate the collection of oral histories of Aboriginal survivors of our holocaust'.[44] ATSIC, in their submission, saw European colonization in Australia as genocide and, further, that 'Their impacts were akin to the Jewish Holocaust.

The fallout from these policies will continue for many generations to come'.[45] These rather general comments reflect the work of a growing number of scholars in the 1990s who were trying to understand Aboriginal history through and in relation to the Holocaust.

Eliminationist racism

Similar to the work of Richard Drinnon, but more influenced by Goldhagen's *Hitler's Willing Executioners*, a number of Australian academics have looked for the links between German anti-Semitism and settler hatred of the Aborigines. These types of comparisons help highlight the similarities between two very different cases, in an attempt to elicit sympathy. For Barta, both cases feature forms of deep-rooted hatred and a 'discourse of genocide' inhabiting 'ideas and assumptions' that led to climates wherein genocide could be contemplated. An anti-Aboriginal equivalent of 'eliminationist anti-Semitism' was at work in nineteenth-century Australia, where, he argues, 'an Australia without Aborigines was both imagined and canvassed . . .'.[46]

Yet Goldhagen (in Barta's account) distorts history by seeing eliminationist hatred as being peculiar to German history. Rather, he echoes Hannah Arendt's conclusion that anti-Semitism was but a 'subset of the imperialist obsession' where the 'colonizing impulse to possess the world as the birthright of European superiority could become a genocidal one wherever the assumption of superiority was threatened by resistance or competition'. Jews as 'foreigners' could be targeted during attempts to cleanse or create a new nation within Europe. Similar views of other peoples in 'foreign parts' colonized by Europeans were little different.[47]

The missing link between indigenous genocide and the Holocaust is Germany's genocide of the Herero in the early twentieth century, which was briefly discussed in Chapter 3. The Herero genocide, argues Barta, inspired Hitler in his war against the Jews. Barta teases out the connections between both genocides, obliquely suggesting an international network of social Darwinists who aimed to destroy indigenous peoples and Jews.[48] In both cases, Barta posits that the mere existence of the 'Other' was an affront to the nation. In both cases 'their being had to be eradicated, as one eradicates a pest . . .'.[49] Colonial regimes throughout the world committed genocide, inspiring Nazi Germany to carry out its war against the Jews.

Markus's work also isolates similarities between the two people. In both cases the victims were 'the despised racial "other", both defined in pseudo-racial terms, and subject to special exclusionary laws. Both peoples were denied citizenship rights (although ambiguous in Australia), welfare benefits, freedom of mobility, etc., and both were eventually separated from the general population – in reserves or ghettoes.[50] As both groups were expected to die out, little effort was made to ensure that adequate food and medical supplies were available to the populations, resulting in high rates of mortality. Markus here compares the fourth stage of the Holocaust, the 'ghetto period', to Australia's policies of 'calculated neglect' in the late nineteenth and early twentieth centuries.[51]

Foley, who is Senior Curator for Southeastern Australia, at Museum Victoria, has also drawn links between Australia and Germany in their obsessions with Social Darwinism: 'This Australian fascination with racial theories, phrenology and eugenics, closely mirrors a similar obsession with identical notions by German society of the same period in relation to the Jews'.[52] As with Barta, Foley has recourse to Goldhagen's theories, with 'British settlers in Australia ... imbued with a similar fear and loathing of Aborigines ...'. Such loathing, Foley argues, led to 'numerous resultant "punitive expeditions", which differ little from German *Einstatzgruppen* activities in Eastern Europe.[53] In both cases, 'lebensraum' was the crucial goal of state policy, and mass murder was the preferred means of implementing policy. Foley's work also features demographic and other comparisons. Both groups comprised about 1 percent of each country's total population, and both groups suffered much higher death rates in geographic areas where the perpetrator regime wanted to settle its own people.[54]

An important difference between the two cases, however, lies in the 'necessity' of *actively* demonizing Jews in Nazi Germany. Reflecting Freidberg, Barta acknowledges uniqueness in the fact that Jewish victims were 'people like you and me'. The fratricidal nature of the killings gives the Holocaust 'a unique power to shock'.[55] However, as Stannard and Churchill have both argued, indigenous peoples did not need to be dehumanized, and their elimination or disappearance was neither unique nor shocking. For Barta, 'their humanity was already blurred in the minds of the settlers' as they were being forced from their lands.[56] Because dehumanization was not a particular problem, genocide and plans for it were more open; even resistance to it was public. Genocide could be carried out openly, unapologetically. It became the '*effectual* policy' of the state, 'because so little was done to restrain settlers'.[57] In Nazi Germany genocide was secret, because the dehumanization process, despite heavy-handed propaganda, had not fully succeeded.[58]

The bystander

Another aspect of comparative research is the role of the bystander as genocide unfolds. Anna Haebich's work compares Nazi Germany and Australia, tackling the concept of societal knowledge and guilt. She ably disproves the 'claims of ignorance' made by Germans about Nazi atrocities, claims which were increasingly challenged by survivor testimony during the 1960s. A crucial ingredient in the Holocaust, Haebich argues, was the passive bystander, who normalized the increasing dehumanization of Jews to the point where it became 'unremarkable and increasingly invisible to them'.[59] While she notes that Germans grudgingly admired the Jews while

Australians disdained Aborigines, a growing 'racialist 'mind set' in both nations promoted acceptance, tolerance, even active encouragement of actions that dehumanized and distanced the Other'.[60]

This sense of dehumanization allowed overtly racist and destructive policies to be promoted without any real public backlash. What worries Haebich is the 'understated normalcy' in the public documents, newspaper reports, church bulletins, and parliamentary debates over child removal policies, suggesting, she posits, 'a high level of acceptance for these policies'.[61] She then makes comparisons between Aboriginal residential schools and the 'concentration camp in Germany'. Both became 'part of the local landscape, linked to town through its reliance on the services of police, doctors, employers and businesses and townspeople's prurient interest in events there'.[62]

Aspects of Haebich's work are useful. In both cases there does seem to have been a public indifference to the fate of each targeted population, and there were public statements issued in both cases which gave a foretaste of the strategies to be pursued. Yet there are obvious differences which make her research seem over-reaching. Residential schools were not designed to kill, slowly or quickly, victim populations. Death was not commodified – prisoners were not quickly 'processed' through gas chambers. Major Australian industries did not set up factories to profit from Aboriginal slave labor, with the slaves seen as expendable as they were worked to death. This puts a different level of moral responsibility on the bystanders in both cases.

In the context of war and totalitarian rule, it was harder for the German or Polish bystander (because, in the case of concentration and death camps, we are talking more about Poles than Germans) to stop a worse form of genocide from taking place. It was easier perhaps to stop the residential school system, but was it as bad in the context of the time as a concentration camp? Can we retroactively put the same level of blame on the Australian 'bystander'? I am critical of attempts to do so, to push these comparisons too far.

An Australian *Historikerstreit*?

A more fruitful avenue of comparison is to examine the politics of the past in both cases – the role genocide has played in the collective memories of both Australia and post-War West Germany. Bonnell and Crotty have both questioned whether a German-style *Historikerstreit* is currently taking place in Australia. The authors rightly note that there has been 'considerable debate over whether the destruction of Aboriginal society, and the forcible dispossession of indigenous people, constituted an act of genocide'. Both see Australia's 'History Wars' as part of a larger 'culture war' over issues of political correctness between 'a loose alliance of conservatives and neo-conservatives against a supposedly hegemonic left-liberal academic and media establishment'.[63]

However, they see the Australian scene as somewhat different, if not worse than post-War Germany. First, while no one denied that 'Germany was a 'post-genocidal' society' and even 'right-wing and conservative historians in the German debate did not dispute the facts of the Holocaust', most of Australian history seems open to debate.[64] This seems fair, in light of the fact that Australia was never occupied after its campaigns against Aboriginal people. Nor were there any Nuremberg-like trials to apportion blame to the perpetrators. At another level, Australia has never had to face the fact that it did something wrong. There was no external pressure for the country to deal with the implications of its past crimes.

A second difference concerns the role of the genocide in the context of Australian and German society, which, while crucially important in German history, is actually even more important in Australian history. Since Australia is a settler society, 'the implications of the debate are profound, in that the displacement and destruction of Aboriginal society, with its potentially or actually genocidal dimensions, was an inextricable part of the very founding of the nation'. Conservative German historians could argue plausibly that the Holocaust was 'an aberration in the national history, caused by a variety of contingent factors'. However, Australian historians 'who represent the beneficiaries of the European usurpation of the continent' clearly cannot make the same argument.[65]

Germany has repented – Australia has made no attempt to do so. If Australia is indeed recognized to be 'post-genocidal', the authors argue, some 'act of refoundation, at least symbolically' would be required, 'just as Germany needed to be democratically reconstituted after 1945 …'.[66] Australia's claims to be a modern democratic society might have to be rethought, its founders scrutinized under a new lens. Moses reflects the same view, that 'the very existence of the nation state and the nationalised subject is predicated on the dispossession, expulsion, and where necessary, extermination of the Indigenous peoples'. Australian identity through this lens is more 'precarious' than German history.[67] This 'precarious' situation was rendered even more difficult when Australia moved further to the left in the early 1990s under Keating than German politicians were ever willing to go. Moses seems to feel that, for a short time, Australia was more progressive than Germany. However, the response from the right in both countries was similar. Helmut Kohl tried to restore some sense of German pride when he came to power in 1982, a situation similar to Howard's victory in 1996.[68]

Yet, Moses' prognosis aside, the Australia right has proven to be far more cutting than German conservatives in the 1980s ever dared to be. As Marcia Langton has rightly observed, Aboriginal peoples are confronted with 'pornographic and trivialising revisions … the accusations of cannibalism, infanticide and the litany of charges made against Jews and the "Elders of Zion" in medieval pamphlets, repeated in the hateful diatribes against Aborigines …'.[69] Unlike West Germans, who at least felt the need to pay lip service to the Jewish victims of the Holocaust, rightist historians like

Minogue and Rubinstein revel in blaming the victim, displaying overtly racist views of Aboriginal people, their history, and their current social condition.

As for the impact of denial on the victim people, it seems very much the same. Manne has argued: 'the term "stolen generations" had become for Aboriginal Australians what the term Holocaust was for the Jews – a way of referring, in a kind of moral shorthand, to a common and collective tragedy'. Discussing the Howard government's denial, he adds:

> To be informed by a government that there was no 'stolen generation' because some children had been removed because of neglect or voluntarily given up, or because 10 per cent did not constitute, according to a dictionary definition, a generation was rather like telling the Jews that there had been no Holocaust (literally a burnt sacrifice) because Hitler's victims had died by gas and gun and not by fire.[70]

Again, the Holocaust provides moral clarity in this case, and sharpens the reader's condemnation of the government.

Total extermination

Despite some similarities in hatred for the target group, both genocides were very different – it seems almost trite to say so. The most obvious difference is that the Jews were slated for total extermination, while the Aborigines were not. The parallels can only safely be taken so far before the different objectives of Australian settlers and governments become obvious. Historians like Barta argue that total extermination was not required – 'the final solution to the Aboriginal "problem" advocated by frontier propagandists was never put into effect as policy'. The settlers were ensconced in large cities, had taken the rich farmlands, and were securely separated from the Aborigines who remained. No longer threatening, fears of contamination were directed towards the Asian 'Yellow Peril'.[71] Barta tacitly accepts that Nazi hatred must have been worse. After all, 'Germany proceeded from eugenic preoccupations to radical genocide, while Australia progressed from genocide to eugenics'.[72] The Australians might have killed most of their Aboriginal populations – they chose not to.

Markus also makes the point that controlling land and achieving overall stability and security at the lowest possible cost were the primary goals of early Australian settler governments. Total physical annihilation of Aborigines was never the intention of the government.[73] As well, he concedes that while child removal policies were horrific in many cases, assimilation policies were not always effective in 'obliterating an individual's identity'. Bureaucratic inefficiencies account to some degree for the gap between intent and reality. Also, some Aborigines were 'placed in the care of loving people'.[74] Of course, this does not excuse the massive harm done.

In his analysis of the nineteenth century, Moses too concedes that many of the earlier massacres were 'sporadic and unsystematic'. Government intent to commit genocide is difficult to prove. There were laws punishing settlers who killed Aborigines, unless it was in self-defence. While states did try to prosecute, their actions were often frustrated by settler solidarity. Moses suggests that the colonization of Australia was not genocide although genocide did occur in Tasmania and Queensland.[75] What we are left with, then, is a very different sort of genocide, a result of very different perpetrator motivations and activities, different levels of coordination and planning, different political and social structures, different geopolitical dynamics – and, not unimportantly, very different kinds of victims.

Conclusions

In his seminal article in *Quadrant* (before it surged to the right), Raymond Gaita cautioned fellow academics about using the Holocaust willy-nilly. It was, he averred, a unique and extreme version of genocide. Indeed, 'it transcends genocide', possessing 'a distinctive evil' that stretches beyond the 'conceptual and moral reach' of the term genocide.[76] He later argued, and rightly, that the Holocaust would serve as a 'bad paradigm for our sense of the evil of genocide'. Genocide would be much harder to sell to the Australian people with the shadow of Auschwitz in the background. It would be far better, he mused, to 'disentangle' the Holocaust from genocide – thus allowing Australia to suffer from genocide without Nazis and Jews clouding the debate.[77]

I agree with Gaita's observations, just as I share Tatz's conclusion that 'no other event has matched the Nazi's messianic achievement'. Writing four years after Gaita, he rightly observed that Australians had a difficult time equating 'gas chambers with removal of children'. Yet he was also correct to observe that while we might not see colonial Australia as a Nazi-like state, this does not mean that one can deny that 'any killing took place in this country, or to assert that children were never moved unilaterally'.[78] Yet, Australia has largely been denied the ability to reflect on the bad points of its history in isolation, without the Holocaust clouding these debates.

Overt comparisons to the Holocaust help feed into the genocide denial movement, and makes any apologies, compensation or healing that much more difficult. The average Australian may concede to apologizing for the wrongs of settler massacres and misguided child removal policies. They may accept that under international law Australia committed genocide, but few will be willing to see themselves as Nazis. After all, part of Windschuttle's anger (or so he claims) stems from the 'charge that the British colonization of this country was a process comparable to the Nazi destruction of the Jews in Europe'.[79] Comparisons such as these are not helpful. They help the rightist establishment trivialize many well-meaning historians whose main purpose is to promote a better future for Aboriginal peoples.

Much better parallels might be made with American Indians, whose rates of decimation and disease were starkly similar to those in Australia. Settler motivations were also remarkably similar – gaining as much land as possible by pushing back, and then if necessary killing, indigenous peoples who were perceived to be in the way. The use of poisoned food, intentional spread of disease, settler militias, and other aspects of frontier life seem to parallel each other. America also pursued residential schooling, forced sterilization, and various other policies which comfortably fit under the heading of cultural genocide.

The same holds true of German *lebensraum* policies against Slavic populations, particularly Poles, or of Stalin's ethnic cleansing and killing of Ukrainians, Chechens, and other subject peoples. Yet there is a paucity of such comparative work in Australian literature. The Holocaust is better known and far more emotive. Curthoys and Docker quote Ward Churchill in their special issue on Aboriginal genocide: '...we need far more, not fewer, serious comparative studies'.[80] Yet when the opportunity arises for expanding the circle of comparison, the Holocaust sadly stands alone, and other genocides are largely ignored.

Graeme Davidson, in his *The Use and (Ab)use of Australian History*, approvingly quotes Charles Maier's conclusion that 'insofar as a collection of people wishes to claim existence as a society or a nation, it must thereby acknowledge that acts committed by earlier agents still bind or burden the contemporary community'.[81] Unfortunately, the issue is rarely so simple. The Australian government is unlikely officially to apologize for the genocide anytime soon. For a government and a generation that wish to profit from all the benefits of their ancestors, while paying for none of their crimes, there is little justice for a people robbed of their culture, history, and land.

6 Indigenous history through the prism of the Holocaust

New Zealand Maori

Inevitably, in students' minds, antisemitism loses out to the plight of the underprivileged: Jews in these particular contexts are always seen as privileged. It is the underprivileged who struggle for human rights, for freedom, citizenship and land rights; it is they who have to find, or 'we' who sometimes try to help them find, ways of attaining civil rights, slum clearance, equal opportunities, affirmative action mechanisms and anti-discriminatory legislation.

(Colin Tatz, *With Intent to Destroy: Reflecting on Genocide* (1998))

Maori were not the victims of genocide, although they were certainly the target of concerted efforts to assimilate them into settler society. Successful attempts were also made to severely limit their political power, while stealing much of their ancestral lands. Maori have fared relatively well compared with Australian Aborigines, although their level of cultural destruction exceeds that of other Pacific Islanders – a better regional standard of comparison. Further, Maori adopted many of the trappings of identity politics and civil rights activism from the 1960s, casting their plight as being similar to that of African Americans, American Indians, and Palestinians.

This short chapter examines how Maori have been drawn into an emerging comparative genocide debate, using the Holocaust as a means of articulating their own experiences of victimization, in the quest for some form of justice, restitution, and healing. As Tatz has argued above, in cases of indigenous protest, Jews are often perceived as a privileged minority: White, Western, and relatively affluent. Indigenous activists often have a difficult time sympathizing with the past victimization of Jews when they feel their people continue to suffer gross economic and social inequality.[1]

In New Zealand, the Holocaust has functioned as a new way of interpreting Maori experiences, although the invocation of the Holocaust demonstrates a lack of knowledge of the events of the Holocaust and a conflation of 'holocaust' with 'genocide'. Some Maori activists have been strongly influenced by North-American indigenous activists such as Stannard and Churchill, whose arguments and style have been borrowed to advance Maori interests. This follows a pattern of incorporating the protest styles and images of other marginalized groups, from North America and elsewhere. In New Zealand, where genocide was not committed, anger against colonization, theft of land, and cultural assimilation has meant that the Holocaust parallels are rather weak. While this case might at first appear to have only regional significance, it demonstrates clearly how widespread the globalization of the Holocaust has become. In most Western settler societies, many indigenous people seem aware of the power the Holocaust can exert in contemporary debates about historical restitution and justice.

Waitangi: Holocaust as a new frame of reference

In 1975, decades of concerted Maori protest against the government led to the 'Treaty of Waitangi Act', allowing Maori to lodge grievances and losses under section 2 of the Treaty of Waitangi with a newly formed Waitangi Tribunal.[2] As discussed in Chapter 3, Waitangi was New Zealand's founding legal document, and was putatively designed to foster equality between Maori leaders and the British colonial government. Over 150 tribal claims were initially lodged, and by 2001 some 884 claims had been advanced, claiming 70 percent of New Zealand's land and most of its off-shore fisheries.[3] It was in the context of settling Treaty claims that the first uses of 'holocaust' appeared as a descriptor for Maori history. This represented a new form of protest discourse, and one that tapped into the growing importance of the Holocaust as a frame of reference.

Before 1996, individual Maori tribes used charged vocabulary in their claims before the Tribunal, but the Tribunal itself had refrained from doing so. The Orakei tribe, for example, claimed to have suffered one of the 'worst cases of cultural genocide this country has known' when their people were dispersed by the government in the nineteenth century and some of their lands were seized.[4] The Ngati Paoa alleged a 'holocaust', but cited another tribe (the Nga puhi) as the instigators of 'dreadful massacres' in 1821 to invade and conquer their territory.[5]

It was only in 1996 that the Tribunal itself invoked a 'holocaust', when examining the history of Taranaki and the tribe based at Parihaka in the North Island. In 1881, colonial authorities dispersed some 2,000 Maori from their ancestral lands, instigating frightful massacres in the process.[6] Claiming an uprising against the government, colonial forces confiscated almost two million acres of land, giving the bulk of it over to British settlement.[7] The subsequent 'Taranaki Report' described the dispersal of the Parihaka settlement as 'the holocaust of Taranaki history ... rank[ing] with the most heinous actions of any government, in any country, in the last century'.[8] Despite the use of 'holocaust', its meaning was ambiguous. 'Taranaki history' suffered from a holocaust, not the Taranaki peoples themselves. While the Tribunal suggested that more Maori had died than quoted in the official statistics (534 Maori killed and 161 wounded), there was no accusation of genocide here.[9] I agree with Margaret Kewley that these were 'political rather than evidence-based findings'.[10]

Tariana Turia and the 'Maori Holocaust'

If these claims seem rather tame by American or Australian standards, more was to come. In August 2000, Associate Maori Affairs Minister Tariana Turia provoked much controversy during a speech delivered to the New Zealand Psychological Society Conference. She began by describing European colonization as a 'home invasion', which had led inexorably to what she termed 'Post-Colonial Traumatic Stress Disorder'. She then equated Maori experiences with those of European Jews. Both, she argued, had suffered from a 'holocaust'. Healing would come once there was 'acknowledgement of the holocaust suffered by many Maori tribes during the Land Wars ...'.[11]

While not claiming that Maori suffered from genocide, Turia's comments were unique. This was the first time a high-ranking political leader in a Western government had accused her predecessors of committing a 'holocaust', especially when her immediate superior (the Minister of Maori Affairs) was also the Prime Minister. While the Tribunal and its petitioners made oblique arguments in favour of cultural genocide in specific cases, Turia was the first to refer to a generalized 'Maori holocaust'. Implicit in Turia's speech was the assumption that European colonialism could be every bit as devastating for survivors and their families as Hitler's Final Solution and the Vietnam War.[12]

Like these two categories of survivor, Turia reported that Maori internalized the suffering of their forefathers, a suffering which was now 'culturally integrated into the psyche and soul of Maori'.[13] Yet Maori suffering was seen to be worse, because 'Post-Colonial Traumatic Stress Disorder' had been passed on from Maori in the nineteenth century to their descendants in the twenty-first. Accounting for the relatively high levels of domestic abuse and violence in some Maori homes, Turia blamed the effects of 'colonisation and subsequent theft of land', 'culturally endemic ... inter-generational systemic abuse', and 'numerous assimilationist policies and laws to alienate Maori from their social structures' for leading to 'internalisation by Maori of the images the oppressor has of them'; 'a despair leading to self hatred and for many, suicide' as well as 'externalisation of self hatred [in the form of] crimes of violence'.[14]

The historical suffering of Maori gave them moral equivalence with European Jews, and Turia used 'holocaust' to denote the genocide of European Jews, and the colonization of Maori and theft of their land. In both cases (contrary to what many alleged after the fact), Turia used a small 'h' to describe Hitler's Final Solution and the colonization of New Zealand.[15]

Initial criticism came from three main sources: concerned members of the general public, including members of the Jewish community; MPs from most political parties; and the media. Prime Minister Helen Clark was soon obliged to respond. There was also support for Turia, which will be examined in the next section. Criticism of Turia's methodology and use of spurious comparisons came soon after her speech. Barry Parsonson, Chairman of the New Zealand Psychological Society, described Turia's speech being greeted with 'astonishment, even disappointment, from some psychologists present' – largely due to her intergenerational analysis of the effects of colonialism on Maori.[16] 'Post-colonial traumatic stress disorder' is not a recognized psychiatric condition, and is not found in any medical book.

By using this newly minted term to explain (or even excuse) high rates of child abuse and violence, Turia raised concerns in the Jewish community. They found it doubly offensive – first because of the use of 'holocaust' with reference to colonialism, and second because it implied that Jews and Maori shared similar problems of domestic violence. While Wendy Ross, Chair of the Auckland Jewish Council, agreed that New Zealanders should better understand the painful legacies of colonialism, she rejected any comparisons between the two peoples: 'I personally know many, many Jewish people who lost everything ... Yet they have nurtured their children ... It hasn't caused them to bash their children, and I just don't accept that that is cause and effect'.[17] One Holocaust survivor, who lost sixty members of his family, noted: 'What happened in New Zealand may have been an injustice, but it cannot be compared'.[18]

Political reaction soon followed. Former Labour Cabinet Minister Dover Samuels called Turia's speech 'political and cultural correctness gone porangi [mad]'.[19] National Party MP Nick Smith denounced her 'separatist' objectives.[20] His colleague Roger Sowry described it as 'the most off-the-planet speech by a politician in living memory'. For New Zealand First Leader Winston Peters, it was little more than 'psychobabble'.[21] Seeking to avoid 'all sorts of alarm bells' ringing in 'middle New Zealand', Helen Clark issued an edict prohibiting her MPs from using 'holocaust' in relation to colonization. Her comments were very clear on the matter: 'I don't accept that the word holocaust can be validly used about the New Zealand experience'. While acknowledging the mistakes of the past, she argued against using a term with 'a specific and very tragic meaning'.[22]

Turia was told to keep her opinions to herself. She was also to have future speeches vetted by one of the Prime Minister's staffers, but her offer to resign was refused.[23] While Turia did apologize, this half-hearted effort was neutralized by her public support for the use of 'holocaust' in the 'Taranaki Report'.[24] The controversy continued when Conservation Minister Sandra Lee similarly invoked a Maori holocaust at a national conference on child abuse some weeks after Turia's speech.[25]

Paralleling this was an accompanying round of unfavorable articles and reports in the media. *The Press* found Turia's 'colonial analogies' to the 'Nazi nightmare' to be 'demeaning and obscene'.[26] The *Nelson Mail* traced the term holocaust back to biblical history, advancing that it 'is almost exclusively used to describe the mass destruction of human beings', but excused

Turia on the basis that 'it still has occasional uses in other contexts'.[27] Colin James, while arguing that multiple meanings for holocaust now exist, maintained that the 'connecting thread' linking holocausts together 'is total destruction (usually by fire) and systematic destruction.... Colonisation ... falls short of those criteria'.[28] Hugh Laracy slighted Turia for her 'reprehensibly careless generalisation', while noting what should be a truism amongst serious historians: 'Not only was the loss of life in New Zealand not comparable with that in the Jewish Holocaust, but Nazi policy was deliberately aimed at the extermination of the Jewish people'.[29]

Other criticisms slated Maori themselves for instigating their own 'holocausts' against other groups, and each other. Ammunition was derived from the plight of the Chatham Island-based Moriori. King's seminal study (1989, 2000) demonstrated how the non-violent Moriori were exterminated after their islands were invaded by Maori tribes in the 1830s.[30] For Peters, the only real 'holocaust' was perpetrated by Taranaki Maori against the Moriori, a people 'invaded, enslaved and annihilated'.[31] Journalist Keith Rankin concurred, seeing this as 'every bit a holocaust to the Moriori ... pure conquest and genocide for the purpose of colonisation'.[32] Rankin did nuance his remarks by noting the cultural dislocation of Maori, now living 'in an alien social environment; in a society whose expectations reduce to a kind of multi-choice test in which all of the answers are wrong'.[33]

On the critical side of the debate, we thus have a number of key themes – Turia invented false disorders and conflated Maori and Jewish suffering. Similarly, she was culturally insensitive to Jews, while abusing her position as a Minister of the Crown to engage in inflammatory discourse. At the same time, she obscured the 'real' 'holocausts' that occurred in New Zealand's colonial history – 'holocausts' inflicted on Moriori and other Maori tribal groups.

Turia's supporters

The official fallout from Turia's comments was minor. Turia did not incite racial hostility when referring to a Maori holocaust – this the Race Relations Conciliator ruled a few weeks later. While he did note that her comments were not 'helpful and they did not help promote understanding' of Maori–settler relations, this did little to harm Turia's career.[34] In the 2002 elections, Turia retained her seat in Parliament and continued to operate as a Minister outside Cabinet. By August 2001, Turia's 'holocaust' moved from a disputed term to something of an established fact among some mainstream commentators. In *The Press*, Wellwood wrote on 'the controversial Tariana Turia, who was in trouble last year for referring to the Maori holocaust'.[35] In her later exposé of Turia, whom she refers to as 'a tiny, cuddly grandmother with grey hair and eyes as bright and curious as a sparrow', Wellwood lambasted the Labor government for censoring her, 'however true her descriptions'.[36] More recently, in 2005, Turia left the government to found the Maori Party, of which she became co-leader.

While shouldering criticism, Turia received praise and support, primarily from Maori academics, activists, and the extreme left. Generally, there was a conflation of holocaust with genocide, and a debate about whether Jews had the moral right to exclusive use of the term. Those refusing to recognize a Maori holocaust were labeled racists and deniers, while arguments were advanced for a broader definition of holocaust. The refusal of Helen Clark to have 'holocaust' used with reference to Maori provoked accusations of denial. Clark was condemned as a latter-day Nazi by Maanu Paul, Chief Executive of the New Zealand Maori Council, for undermining Turia's freedom of speech. Hers was 'a violent act', bringing to mind Hitler's supposed practice of 'gagging the Jews and burning them off'. Paul continued: 'Jews talk about concentration camps but we were the first victims. Holocaust is an apt description of what happened'.[37]

Corso, New Zealand's leading NGO for international aid and development, lamented how the 'furor' raised by Turia was 'totally predictable, given the denial of the violence of colonization so prevalent in colonial societies such as NZ'. For coordinator Suzanne Menzies-Cullen, not allowing indigenous groups to use 'holocaust' was tantamount to denial. In view of indigenous genocides in world history – here she noted the Spanish conquest, as well as the Atlantic slave trade – she reflected ironically: 'Maybe a Holocaust only reflects genocide of white people by white people'.[38] Denialism of past atrocities was thus linked to the denial of the right to indigenous groups (or non-Whites) to use 'holocaust' to describe their experiences.

Maori academic John Mitchell went further, alleging that there was little difference between colonialism and the Holocaust. Differences, where they existed, were 'in degree, not in kind'. Referring to his own people, Ngai Tahu, Mitchell argued:

> To excuse New Zealand's colonial oppressors and the commercial/political/military masters they served as 'angels by comparison with Hitler and his henchmen' ... is to show an appalling lack of sensitivity to those who suffered; such oppressors on the New Zealand scene were guilty of actions every bit as evil and depraved as Hitler's excesses.[39]

How do Maori and Jewish suffering converge? For Mitchell, both groups were both targeted by evil, all-powerful states, bent on their destruction: 'A common factor ... was to have the juggernaut of the state arrayed against them – legislative machinery, military might, and a determination to annihilate every last vestige of opposition ...'.[40]

This, for Mitchell, included 'devious ruses', such as the imprisonment of Maori chiefs, and a 'number of incidents' provoked by the Crown as a pretext to seize land. In the course of these 'incidents' some 200 members of his iwi were arrested and never returned home, prompting Mitchell to ask: 'Was this their holocaust, or merely their unfortunate deaths at the hands of "angels"?'[41] 'Holocaust' thus became a personal but also universally applicable term. It could be used for the Jews of Europe, but also for local Maori communities, applying to arrests, land seizures, or, in the extreme case, massacres.[42]

While journalist Huw Turner did not acknowledge a holocaust 'in the strictest sense of the word', he did take aim at New Zealand's 'Jewish lobby' for trying to reserve the term exclusively for their use. They were accused of 'jealously attempting to hang on to the word holocaust for itself and spite-fully denigrating the experience of any other people seeking to find an expression sufficiently headline-grabbing to describe the effects of their colo-nial experience, and its aftermath'.[43] Turner also took issue with 'the descen-dants of the colonizers themselves', who, he argued, were 'appalled that the wholesomeness and philanthropy of their ancestors' pioneering intentions could be likened to the worst SS-induced nightmares'. Turia's comments were a wake-up call, forcing them to snap out of their 'ignorance of their own colonial history'.[44] Turia was perhaps stretching the truth – he seemed to argue – but not by much.

The far-left in New Zealand also contributed to this growing debate. The Communist Worker's Group, in their journal *Class Struggle*, began their class-based analysis with the contention that 'capitalism has visited "holo-causts" on indigenous peoples long before it discovered the Jews to persecute and it is still visiting holocausts on oppressed peoples ...'.[45] Again, reflect-ing the arguments of some Maori activists and groups, denying Maori the right to use the term holocaust amounts to a denial of the atrocities themselves:

> ... many Jews have taken ownership of 'holocaust' to describe the extreme horror of their oppression, their suffering, and their genocide. These are all very real events but to claim exclusive rights to the term holocaust serves to demean and belittle suffering by other peoples, in particular that of indigenous peoples largely wiped out by the spread of capitalism or the oppression of other peoples today.[46]

Such arguments had at their core the belief that 'holocaust' should be a more universally applicable term – morally Jewish 'ownership' of holocaust was wrong. The argument that the Holocaust was simply an internal matter (Whites killing Whites) was another theme found on many occasions. To deny Maori the 'right' to commemorate their own holocaust was an exercise in denial perpetrated by White Europeans – whether Jewish, German, or British. An International Workshop on indigenous peoples held shortly after Turia's speech produced a position paper, calling for the broadening of the term 'holocaust' to encompass indigenous experiences. As they argued: 'Lim-iting definitions such as "holocaust" is a manifestation of racism. Whether murder, slaughter and dispossession was achieved indiscriminately through a musket, cannon, sword, legislation or a gas chamber is irrelevant in defin-ing the term "holocaust"'.[47]

For this Conference, 'holocaust' was too narrow – it excluded indigenous suffering, and was racist by design. Speaking for their delegates, conference organizers stressed that 'Indigenous Peoples claim the right to define "holocaust" in a broad sense, encompassing the oppression and systematic extermination of Indigenous Peoples by any means engaged by the Colonial Governments'.[48] How they arrogate for themselves the 'right' to reinterpret holocaust is not explained, nor do they explain why claiming 'genocide' would not be sufficient.

Abusing 'holocaust'

Generally, New Zealand is not considered to be an anti-Semitic society. A 1997 study by the Institute for Jewish Policy Research gives the country a relatively good report, with anti-Semitism playing 'a minor role in political and cultural life ...'.[49] Maori groups receive no mention, nor does the Waitangi Tribunal. In light of the reaction to a Maori holocaust and to claims of Jewish exclusiveness and Pakeha denial, should we rethink the above analysis? I would argue no. Much of this debate – the anti-Semitic undertones included – can be traced to Stannard and Churchill's work. None of the statements by Maori leaders and activists are new in academic terms, or in relation to indigenous struggles in North America.[50]

In the New Zealand context, 'Jews' were denounced for their exclusive ownership of holocaust, while anyone not recognizing a Maori holocaust was denounced as a racist and a 'denier'. The difference in the New Zealand case was that few activists spelled out what denial actually implied. For Churchill, denial referred to deliberately misquoting sources, omitting and suppressing any data contrary to one's conclusions, while 'orchestrat[ing] fabricated "facts"'.[51] In the Maori holocaust, activists offered no proof that facts were being distorted or denied – nor were there any Bauers, Lipstadts, or Katzs to specifically attack. Their primary contention was that by refusing to use the *label* holocaust, some form of denial was being practiced.

What emerges from Stannard and Churchill is the equation holocaust = genocide (the two here are interchangeable terms). Similarly, covering up indigenous genocides is morally equivalent to Jewish Holocaust denial. Both authors are specific – they deal with proven and extremely well-documented cases of genocide in America, featuring photos, journals, newspaper articles, and biographies, as well as oral and written testimonies by both surviving victims and (often proud) killers. While one might justify using such extreme vocabulary and imagery in the case of such horrific genocide and such deplorable denial, transferring such theories and methods of argumentation to New Zealand has resulted in spurious generalizations. These generalizations are further conflated when they are not used in the manner the authors intended. While much violence, land theft, trickery, and forced assimilation can indeed be proven in the case of Maori, there is no record of genocide being committed, and certainly no proof of intent to exterminate

Maori as a people (or peoples). The fit between Stannard and Churchill on one side and Maori activism on the other is, to say the least, an imperfect one.

Conclusions

While New Zealand is not marked by any overt anti-Semitism, there is a general lack of sensitivity to the Holocaust and its significance. The Jewish population is relatively small, and government ties with Israel are minimal although cordial. In April 2005, Labour government MP John Tamahere provoked another storm of controversy by confiding to a reporter how 'sick and tired' he was of 'hearing how many Jews got gassed'. He blamed the Wiesenthal Center for promoting memory of the Holocaust: 'How many times do I have to be told and made to feel guilty?' he asked.[52] He was censured by the Prime Minister, but remained in the Labour Party to contest the next election. Tamahere's comments followed on the heels of a number of other incidents. In 2004, tombstones in a Jewish cemetery in Wellington were desecrated, perhaps in reaction to a scandal involving two Mossad agents trying to obtain false New Zealand passports.[53] Holocaust denier David Irving entered the fray, blaming Mossad agents for the desecration and offering a $10,000 reward for information.[54] Parliament soon issued a resolution condemning anti-Semitism, which smoothed tensions some-what.[55]

I would not suggest that New Zealand race relations are ideal – much work is needed to redress social, economic, and other forms of inequality. A 2004 survey published in the *National Business Review* recorded that 59 percent of New Zealanders believed race relations between Maori and White New Zealanders were getting worse.[56] Turia was right to point out the very real problems Maori face. However, despite the vague assertions of the *Taranaki Report*, and the ambiguous claims of Turia, Mitchell, and others, no coherent proof of a Maori genocide exists at present, unlike the cases of Australia and the United States. Invoking a holocaust acts to obscure the real injustices perpetrated against Maori by successive New Zealand governments, and promotes neither healing nor understanding.

Part III

War, genocide, and nationalism

7 The Armenian genocide

The politics of recognition and denial

It is not true that the Turkish authorities are unwilling to state their position on the so-called Armenian issue. Our position is very clear. It is evident today that the Armenian claims are unfounded and illusory in light of historical facts. Armenians were not subjected to genocide in any way.

(Turkish Prime Minister Tanzu Ciller (September, 1994))[1]

I think that the tabooing of the Armenian Genocide in a republic whose foundation was created this way is 'understandable'. The devastation that would ensue if we had to now stigmatize those whom we regarded as 'great saviours' and 'people who created a nation from nothing, as 'murderers and thieves' is palpable. It seems so much simpler to completely deny the genocide than to seize the initiative and face the obliteration of the ingrained notions about the Republic and our own national identity.

(Dissident Turkish historian Taner Akçam (1999))[2]

The international network of fanatics who deny the Holocaust has slowly grown in recent years, gathering some degree of momentum in the wake of the Iraq invasion and Iran's recent conference on denialism. However, few atrocities are as perniciously and as systematically denied as the Armenian genocide. Turkey is a democracy, a European Union aspirant, and a long-time member of NATO. Despite these accomplishments, it continues to hold that the Armenian genocide is a fiction perpetrated by Armenian terrorists and nationalist zealots. The government continues to persecute individuals and countries who oppose its view of events.

In 2005, the Turkish Ministry of Foreign Affairs (through their Center for Strategic Research) released a booklet entitled *Armenian Claims and Historical Facts*. This work, an updated version of a twenty-year-old Foreign Ministry position paper, denies the Armenian genocide, provides a lengthy list of 'Armenian terrorist' acts in the 1970s and 1980s, and features a declaration made by American academics in 1985 denying the genocide.[3] In April 2005, the Turkish State Archive released a list of some 523,000 Turks purportedly killed by Armenians between 1910 and 1922. The release was timed to coincide with ninetieth anniversary of the Armenian genocide, proving to some that this is a 'debate' with two sides.[4]

Today there is an impressive and growing literature on the Armenian genocide, one that may someday rival that of the Holocaust. I begin by outlining the trajectory of the Armenian genocide, including the role of Turkey's founder, Mustafa Kemal Ataturk, in its continuation after World War I. I then highlight some salient features of Diaspora commemoration before and after the independence of Armenia in 1991, before turning to a discussion of Turkish denialism. This also includes a discussion of Israel's surprising contribution to denial, and some of the conflicts over memory and representation that have developed between Diaspora Armenian and Jewish organizations in the United States.

I conclude by examining attempts at Armenian–Turkish dialogue and the potential for future agreement. While relations between Turkey and Armenia may normalize if their common border is opened, recognition of the genocide will continue to be a serious sticking point. Turkey should, and eventually will have to, come to terms with its genocidal past, not only to promote good foreign relations but also to create a healthy civil society able to engage comfortably with its own past.

The context of genocide

The Armenian people have an ancient history, stretching back to at least the ninth century BC. In the fourth century AD, Armenians embraced Christianity, and lived under a succession of Armenian kings, nobles and patriarchs. In the fourteenth century, most of Armenia came under the sway of the Moslem Ottoman Empire. As Christians, Armenians were considered 'tolerated infidels' under the *Akdi Zimmet* system.[5] Sizable Armenian communities were also located in neighboring Russia and Persia.[6] Historically, the multinational, multi-confessional Ottoman Empire allowed some degree of autonomy for the Armenians and, until the Empire began to collapse in the eighteenth century, Armenian life was relatively stable and peaceful. However, by the eighteenth century, rival empires such as Russia, covetous of Ottoman territory, began to assert themselves. The nineteenth century saw many Christian regions of the Empire gain their autonomy or independence with European support. Serbia gained a high degree of autonomy after 1829, and Greece its independence in 1830. Lebanon, with its Maronite Christian population, achieved independence in 1860, while Bosnia-Herzegovina, Montenegro, Serbia, and Bulgaria erupted in anti-Ottoman fighting by the 1870s.[7]

By the 1870s, Armenian demands for reform and increased autonomy, together with their suspected 'cross-border ties to conationals' in Russia, led many Ottoman officials to see the Armenians as a 'serious security danger'.[8] While the danger posed by Armenians was minimal,[9] a number of massacres were carried out under the rule of Sultan Abdul Hamid II. First, the 1894

Sassoun Massacres, instigated by local Kurds loosely allied with Ottoman military forces, led to an Armenian uprising, followed by lengthy massacres, which lasted twenty-four days.[10] This was followed in late 1895 by a series of demonstrations in Constantinople, organized by two Armenian parties (the Hunchaks and Armenakans). The largely peaceful demonstrations provoked massacres in the capital, and 4,000 were attacked, primarily by Kurdish mobs armed by the government.[11] From 1895–96, there was a series of Ottoman provocations, Armenian responses, and massacres in Zeitoun, Van, Istanbul, and elsewhere. The total killed between 1895 and 1908 has been estimated at between 100,000 and 200,000 people.[12]

The Ittihadists and genocide

In 1908, Hamid II was overthrown by the leaders of the Young Turk Movement, known also as the Committee for Union and Progress, or *Ittihad ve Terakki Teshkilati*. At first there was cooperation between Young Turks and Armenians, both seeking common cause against the despotism of the old order.[13] Amongst exiled Young Turks, pan-Turkish ideas had not yet taken root, and there was much optimism about the revolution. There was even a form of parliamentary democracy.[14] However, the liberal era did not last long. Soon after the revolution, the Empire began to deteriorate further. Bosnia-Herzegovina was annexed by Austria-Hungary, Crete united with Greece, Bulgaria won full independence, and Italy pushed for control of Tripoli and parts of the Libyan heartland. In the turmoil that followed, a series of massacres began against Armenians, promoted primarily by people loyal to the Sultan.[15] This included a massacre in Adana in April 1909 which led to the deaths of 25,000 Armenians. Around the same time some 200 villages were destroyed, with their Armenian inhabitants slaughtered.[16]

By 1910 the CUP had became more radicalized, and discussions were under way for the 'complete Ottomanization of all Turkish subjects'. In practice, this meant imposing Turkish culture, language, and Islam on ethnic, national, and religious minorities.[17] Under a slogan of 'Freedom, Justice, Equality, Fraternity', the CUP attempted to transform the Empire into a unitary, European style nation-state, with Islam and the Turkish nation as supreme.[18]

During the Balkan Wars of 1912–13 the Empire was further weakened, and lost 70 percent of its European population and 85 percent of its European territory.[19] The wars also gave rise to a short-lived coup, led by a group of army officers known as the 'Saviour Officers'. In 1912 they compelled the CUP to relinquish its power. However, by January 1913 the CUP was back in power in a countercoup launched by the ultranationalist wing of the CUP. Enver was Minister of War, Talaat was Minister of Internal Affairs, and Jemal was the military governor of Constantinople. By June, a military dictatorship had been imposed.[20] These leaders remained in power until 1918, and played a key role in the genocide that followed.

A network of party offices and branches was created across the Empire, which helped fuel a climate of anti-Armenian sentiments. In 1914, Enver and his colleagues created the 'Special Organization' (*Teshkilat-I Makhususiye*), tasked with preparing for the conquest of lands in the Caucasus and Iran.[21] The Security Office of the Interior Ministry set up a special department of surveillance and intelligence where files on influential Armenians were assembled and studied.[22]

The genocide unfolded in a series of stages, aimed quite simply at the 'extermination of Ottoman Armenians in Armenia'.[23] Stage One began in February 1915, when the CUP issued an order that all Armenians were to be disarmed. Serving members of the armed forces were put into 'labor battalions', and stripped of their rank and their weapons. Many were shot in groups of 50–100 men, while others were worked to death.[24]

Stage Two began on April 8, 1915, when the CUP issued its first deportation order, with more to follow. Able-bodied men from towns and villages were ordered to present themselves at the *konak* (government office) for compulsory military service. Most were imprisoned, and a short while later marched out of town and shot. Some remaining men, as well as women and children, were sent on forced marches to Iraq and Syria, where many died from starvation, beatings, and murder. As the Armenians were forced out, some 750,000 Turkish *muhajir* refugees were resettled in Armenian lands – proof, argues Christopher Walker, that the process of killing, expulsion, and resettlement was part of a centrally controlled and premeditated plan.[25]

Stage Three began on April 24, when the Interior Ministry called for all political and community leaders suspected of nationalist or anti-government sentiments to be rounded up and arrested. In Constantinople, some 2,345 leaders were arrested. The Ministry also issued a Memorandum (later implemented as the 'Temporary Law of Deportation') empowering authorities to order deportations if they had 'a feel or sense of the offense or danger'.[26] 'Deportation' was often a euphemism for mass murder. Members of the Special Organization were dispatched to remote areas of the Empire to ambush and kill Armenian deportees. The majority of these killers were convicted criminals who had been released from prison and armed by the military.[27] Kurdish and Circassian tribesmen were encouraged to rape, loot, and kill.[28]

Cities, towns, and villages were systematically cleansed and their inhabitants killed or forced out. While it seemed at first that only those in militarily sensitive areas were to be 'deported', this proved to be false. Those far from any battle zone, in Sivas, Mersifun, Angora, Kharput, and elsewhere, were targeted just the same.[29] The CUP also did its best in a country of limited technological resources to control and organize the genocide. CUP leaders had telegraphic equipment installed in their homes in order to better coordinate the massacres.[30] A series of concentration camps was also established, to deal with the 870,000 Armenians who did manage to reach the deserts of Mesopotamia and Syria alive.[31] Many of the survivors were

rounded up and held in camps along the Euphrates. Of the surviving deportees, recent estimates indicate that 630,000 were killed.[32]

On October 30, 1918, Turkey and the Allies signed an armistice agreement which contained provisions for the release of Armenian detainees and
the return of survivors to their homes.[33] In 1919, Britain, which occupied
Turkey, arrested key members of the CUP leadership, and established a tribunal to try offenders for crimes 'against humanity and civilization'. Talaat
and his co-conspirators were sentenced to death *in absentia.* Under the *Treaty
of Sevres* (1920), Turkey was to surrender all suspects to the tribunal. The
Treaty, however, was short-lived and ineffectual, and by 1923 (under the
Treaty of Lausanne) no further mention was made of prosecution. At this
stage Mustafa Kemal Ataturk created a new Turkish Republic, and the old
order seemed to have been laid to rest.[34]

However, in some respects Ataturk's regime was no break from the past.
Killing continued after the War, partially because of Ataturk's need to find
allies amongst CUP supporters. And the genocide continued. Under
Ataturk, Ankara ordered General Kiazim Karabekir to 'physically annihilate
Armenians'.[35] Karabekir, as Walker recalls, was a 'fanatical anti-Armenian
extremist', although Ataturk was more moderate.[36] Fortunately, intervention by the 11th Red Army stationed nearby saved Russian Armenians
from what Dadrian terms 'miniature genocide'.[37] And while there is no
precise tally of the numbers killed, most scholars give a range of between
600,000 and two million, although 800,000–1.5 million dead is seen as a
reliable estimate.[38]

Armenian commemoration and remembrance

From the 1920s, commemoration of the genocide within Soviet Armenia
was banned by Soviet authorities, and after 1945 the genocide was dwarfed
by the Holocaust and other German horrors. The events became virtually a
'forgotten genocide' until the mid-1960s. Modern Armenian protest began
during this time, signally in April 24, 1965, when the Opera House in
Yerevan hosted an official commemoration of the fiftieth anniversary of the
genocide. The pro-independence National Unification Party was formed in
1966, as were a number of other organizations.[39] Despite such activities,
Armenians, in their Soviet-dominated country, had little power to influence
commemoration of the genocide outside their own borders.

During the Soviet era, the Diaspora came to represent Armenian national
interests worldwide. Indeed, the Armenian Dashnak Party became a sort of
'government in exile'.[40] At the top of their agenda was combating Turkish
denialism, while promoting memory of the genocide in America, Europe,
and elsewhere. In 1973, an elderly genocide survivor assassinated two
Turkish consular officers in California. The resultant trial and press coverage
encouraged further discussion around the world. In the 1970s and 1980s,
French and American Armenians began lobbying their governments to gain

affirmation and acknowledgement of the genocide.[41] By 1986 the United Nations Commission on Human Rights recognized the genocide, although the UN as such has taken no official position.[42] The following year the European Parliament adopted a resolution recognizing the genocide, followed later by individual European member states.[43]

In 1988, fears of another Armenian genocide were stoked when Armenians in the Karabagh region of Azerbaijan (an Armenian region awarded to Azerbaijan by Stalin) began to agitate for self-determination and incorporation into Soviet Armenia.[44] Armenians formed about 80 percent of the population in Karabakh, yet complained bitterly about ethnic discrimination and economic underdevelopment.[45] Their calls for the region to be administered by Armenia were swiftly put down, and by mid-1989 some 180,000 Armenian refugees had fled.[46] Armenia entered the conflict in 1989, and sent over paramilitary forces, weapons and equipment.[47]

In September 1991 Armenia achieved its independence from Soviet rule, with Levon Ter-Petrossian as President.[48] The following year, after a referendum, an independent Republic of Nagorno-Karabakh was proclaimed, which exacerbated civil conflict. From 1992 to 1994, fighting continued between Karabakh Armenian and Azeri forces before a cease-fire was declared. This left Armenia in control of Nagorno-Karabakh and roughly 11 percent of Azerbaijan.[49] Sadly, democracy has not flourished in either region. The ruling ANM became increasingly dictatorial and corrupt as the 1990s progressed.[50] Ter-Petrossian won handily in fraudulent elections held in 1996, although he eventually stepped aside in favor of Robert Kocharian in 1998, who was then re-elected in another dubious election in 2003.[51]

In this messy geopolitical situation, the influence of the Diaspora in agenda-setting has been profound. As Yossi Shain observes, 'Diaspora hardliners are said to care less about the homeland's present and future than about the past's dead'.[52] Indeed, the Diaspora has come to identify itself first with commemoration of the genocide. Other issues, like the economic well-being of the homeland, are seen as secondary.[53]

Since taking power, Kocharian has put the genocide at the top of the agenda, and has also allowed peace negotiations with Azerbaijan to taper off.[54] The weakness and corruption of Armenia has meant that the Diaspora continues to exert a great deal of influence. Their $50–75 million in annual contributions goes a long way.[55] In addition to aid, the Diaspora has been able to promote US economic support for their homeland, while ensuring that Armenia's rival, Azerbaijan, has been cut off.[56] Armenia, however, is neither secure nor prosperous. While Israel is a strategic asset to the United States, Armenia's role is far less geopolitically significant than that of Turkey or Azerbaijan.[57] This helps explain why Turkish genocide denial has been tacitly accepted by successive American administrations, despite decades of acrimonious debate within the media and Congress.

Denying the Armenian genocide

Currently, the Turkish Foreign Ministry alleges that 'The Armenian deaths do not constitute genocide' since 'Their violent political aims, not their race, ethnicity or religion, rendered them subject to relocation'.[58] As dissident Turkish historian Taner Akçam has argued, this continued hard-line stance has much to do with the fact that the founders of the current Republic were themselves implicated in the genocide. There was no clean break between the old regime and the new.[59] To admit to genocide is not to concede the actions of a crumbling Ottoman dictatorship, but to acknowledge that the modern Republic is founded on mass murder and cover-up.[60]

As with Holocaust denial, Armenian genocide denial progressed in a series of stages. After 1918, the general carnage of war, Kurdish hatred of Armenians, and the predations of common criminals were blamed for any massacres. Other strategies were later pursued: blaming Armenians for provoking Turkish responses, while submerging artificially-low Armenian death tolls within a larger casualty total for all Ottoman subjects.[61] Another strategy was to remove historical references to Armenians in Turkish publications, including Armenian city and town names, the names of churches and other public buildings, and monuments. In such a way, 'Armenians [could] be made to vanish from their homeland'.[62] By the 1950s, Armenians were divested in Turkish literature from any indicia of nationhood. They were denied recognition as a coherent people on a given territory, and denied any racial, linguistic, or religious attributes.[63]

In the 1980s, the Turkish government was able to pressure successive Reagan and Bush administrations into defeating Congressional resolutions calling for 24 April to become a national day of commemoration for the genocide. They also tried to disrupt conferences covering the genocide. In 1982, Turkish officials tried to shut down a genocide conference in Tel Aviv through intimidation and threats. The United States Holocaust Memorial Museum also encountered threats when it wanted to include references to the genocide in one of its exhibitions.[64]

To legitimate its view of history, the Turkish government began to found a series of chairs in Turkish studies at major American universities (including the Ataturk Chair in Turkish Studies at Princeton), and research centers such as the Institute of Turkish Studies, founded in Washington DC in 1982. These academic endeavors were designed to give a respectable gloss to genocide denial.[65] Some key deniers include Stanford Shaw, Heath Lowry, and Justin McCarthy.[66] In 1985, Lowry was instrumental in getting a letter against the Genocide signed by sixty-nine American academics. The letter was then printed in the *New York Times* and the *Washington Post*.[67]

Turkey, as a key NATO ally, continues to rely on its alliance with America to prevent any official recognition of the genocide. When a non-binding resolution recognizing the genocide went before the US House of Representatives in 2000, Turkey threatened to stop all US military flights from its Incirlik airbase, which America was using to enforce Iraq's no-fly zone.[68] It also threatened to pull out of NATO. President Clinton personally intervened to challenge the resolution.[69] Another unsuccessful attempt was made in 2003.[70] Countries who recognize the genocide are penalized. After French recognition, in January 2001, the Turkish Defence Ministry stopped a $149 million deal with Alcatel to build and launch a remote-sensing spy satellite. France's Giat Industries was also excluded from a $7 billion contract to furnish the Turkish army with 250 tanks.[71] Nevertheless, fifteen countries, including Argentina, Italy, Russia, and Switzerland have officially recognized the genocide through resolutions in their legislatures, as has the European Union.[72]

While America has not officially recognized the genocide, some of its presidents have done so unofficially. President Reagan recognized the genocide in 1981, while Presidents George H.W. Bush and Clinton recognized the genocide as Presidential candidates, even if they did not do so in office.[73] Most American Holocaust and genocide scholars have also joined forces to condemn denialism. In June 2000, a petition signed by 126 scholars was published in the *New York Times*. It affirmed that 'the World War I Armenian Genocide is an incontestable historical fact and accordingly urge the governments of Western democracies to likewise recognize it as such...'.[74]

Israel, Turkey, and genocide denial

It might seem counterintuitive to imagine that Israel would support Turkey's efforts to deny the Armenian genocide, yet this is precisely what has happened. Turkey has been particularly skillful in acknowledging the Holocaust while denigrating Armenian claims, forging good relations with Israel while going to 'extraordinary lengths ... to prevent Jews from learning about the Armenian Genocide'.[75] In 2001, Israeli Foreign Minister and Nobel laureate Shimon Peres made the astounding claim that the Armenians had never suffered from genocide, provoking negative reactions from Holocaust and genocide scholars.[76] Armenian genocide deniers are quick to distance themselves from Holocaust denial. Justin McCarthy, for example, sees Holocaust denial as the preserve of a 'fringe group'. While no 'reasonable historian of Germany' would ever question the Holocaust, the so-called '69 Scholars' questioning the Armenian genocide are billed as 'the foremost experts on the history of Turkey in the United States'.[77]

In *The Banality of Denial*, Israeli historian Yair Auron has traced the cementing of bilateral relations between Turkey and Israel to the first Gulf War. While Iran and Ethiopia were the sort of 'strong, stable, pro-Western peripheral states' Israel supported in the 1970s, the post-Cold War world necessitated new regional allies.[78] At the same time, Turkey has seen good relations with Israel as a means of strengthening ties to Washington, and indeed Turkey has 'grown to appreciate how useful an ally the American Jewish lobby can be against the Greek- and Armenian-American lobbies'.[79]

This mixture of historical, emotional, and pragmatic reasons for the alliance has muddied the relationship between Armenian Americans and Jews. Armenians remain frustrated that, despite the perniciousness of denial, many American Jewish organizations actively pursue good relations with Turkey. In December 2004, Anti-Defamation League officials met with Turkish leaders in Istanbul and Ankara, promising Prime Minister Erdogan that 'ADL strongly supports Turkey's bid for full membership in the European Union'.[80] Organizations like the Jewish Institute for National Security Affairs (JINSA) and the Center for Security Policy (CSP) have been pushing for a deeper Israeli–Turkish alliance for years.[81] Turkey also maintains good relations with the American Jewish Committee, B'nai B'rith, the American Jewish Congress, and the Conference of Presidents of Major Jewish Organizations.[82]

Auron's work clearly articulates a deep-set mentality in the Israeli establishment to foster good relations with Turkey, whatever the cost to historical truth. The view that Israel must safeguard its self-preservation above all other considerations is palpable in its constant attempts (albeit sometimes reluctantly) to uphold Turkish denial. One senses from Auron a deep frustration about the extent to which Israeli leaders are afraid of reprisals if they don't toe the line on this sensitive issue. The Israeli–Turkish relationship obviously adds a further antagonistic dimension to Armenian–Jewish relations in the United States. This has sadly been played out at the domestic level over how the Armenian genocide should be represented (or not) in museums dealing with twentieth-century genocide.

Museums and the politics of memory

Commemorating genocide in the 1990s and after has necessitated the creation of large, publicly accessible museums. Unsurprisingly, after independence in 1991, the Armenian government drafted plans for its own museum. In 1995, the Armenian Genocide Institute-Museum was founded in Yerevan.[83] France is arguably the most progressive Western country in recognizing and promoting memory of the genocide. Paris' Louvre Museum, at the request of President Chirac, hosted a year-long exhibition on Armenian history and civilization, which began in the autumn of 2006.[84]

America has been served for decades by a wide variety of Armenian institutes and organizations devoted to promoting memory of the genocide. In 1982 the Zoryan Institute was founded in Cambridge, Massachusetts, with a Canadian chapter created in Toronto two years later.[85] The Gomidas Institute and other organizations like the Armenian National Institute, the Armenian Assembly of America, and the Armenian National Committee of America also promote memory of the Armenian genocide. Equally important for public agenda-setting has been Atom Egoyan's recent film *Ararat* (2002), which explored the genocide in a new way, through modern Canadian–Armenian engagements with the past.[86]

In 1993, a number of Armenian organizations began lobbying to have their genocide included alongside the Holocaust. Jeshajahu Weinberg, the USHMM's founding director, has described an intense lobbying campaign by Armenian Americans in 1993 to have their genocide included in the museum. This was countered by Turkish lobbying and further lobbying on Turkey's behalf by the Israeli embassy.[87] While the museum has featured guest lectures by notable Armenian historians like Richard Hovannisian, there is little mention of the genocide even now.[88]

The Armenian National Institute and the Armenian National Committee of America have also pushed for inclusion of their genocide at the Simon Wiesenthal Center's Museum of Tolerance. The Museum, some Armenian organizations charge, promised to feature the Armenian genocide when it opened in 1993. However, despite touching on the topic in an introductory film and in temporary exhibits, mention of the genocide was practically non-existent. Indeed, after the museum's introductory film was changed in 1997, references to the Armenian genocide were omitted. In 2003, after ten years of operation, Armenian groups began aggressively lobbying for inclusion of the genocide. This included a hunger strike by the Armenian Youth Federation.[89]

Perhaps as a result of these setbacks and the rise of Turkish denialism, or perhaps because of the increasing affluence of the Armenian Diaspora, an Armenian Genocide Museum and Memorial is now being planned for Washington DC. This is to be located in the old National Bank of Washington building, two blocks east of the White House. The Museum will, unsurprisingly, be used as a vehicle to promote memory of the genocide.[90] The museum's Director of Planning, Ross Vartian, argued in a 2002 memo that its construction was a 'sacred mission'. While only one-quarter the size of the USHMM, planners anticipate attracting about 250,000 visitors annually when it is completed. According to Vartian, the museum will also honor 'Righteous Turks' who saved Armenians – a not-so-subtle copying of Yad Vashem's recognition of 'Righteous Gentiles'. This inclusion may also be designed to open a much-needed dialogue with Turkey.[91]

Dialogue

In recent years, dialogue between Armenian and Turkish scholars has begun in earnest. Most Armenians ultimately want Turkey to recognize that it committed genocide, to apologize, and to pay some form of reparations. Some even demand that Turkey returns Armenian territory. Many Armenians, however, recognize that Armenia's poverty and isolation could be greatly helped by Turkish trade and other forms of assistance.

Historian Ronald Suny was one of the first to begin a process of academic dialogue. In 1998, he agreed to become the first Armenian scholar to deliver a lecture in Turkey on the genocide.[92] Suny, Fatma Müge Göçek, and Gerard Libaridian later organized a workshop at the University of Chicago in 2000 which brought Turkish and Armenian scholars together to tackle common research interests.[93] Further workshops were held in the United States and Europe.[94] More ambitious but equally controversial was a Turkish–Armenian Reconciliation Commission. This was created in July 2001, largely initiated and funded by the US government. Meetings were held in Istanbul, London, and Moscow.[95] The ten-member Commission was composed of Turkish and Armenian representatives, and mediated by David Phillips, a senior adviser in the US State Department. The TARC was not mandated to investigate the genocide, but to promote goodwill by looking at avenues of educational and cultural cooperation.[96]

The TARC soon became mired by an internal dispute over the genocide 'issue'. Armenian representatives argued that they could go no further with negotiations until the matter of the genocide was resolved. In December 2001, the Committee met in New York and asked the International Center for Transitional Justice to independently investigate whether or not the 'Events' of 1915 constituted genocide under the 1948 UNGC.[97] By mid-December, the four Armenian members announced that they would no longer participate in the dialogue. They argued that Turkish members, pressured by their government, had unilaterally instructed the ICTJ not to proceed with the genocide study.[98]

After a great deal of discussion and mistrust on both sides, the Commission reconvened in mid-July 2002.[99] The genocide report went ahead as planned, and findings were released in January 2003 as a seventeen-page Memorandum.[100] The conclusions were unambiguous: 'the Events, viewed collectively, can thus be said to include all of the elements of the crime of genocide as defined in the Convention, and legal scholars as well as historians, politicians, journalists and other people would be justified in continuing to so describe them'.[101] Predictably, the Turkish government largely ignored the findings, and indeed tried to scuttle the genocide study before it even began, as Philips relates in his recent book, *Unsilencing the Past* (2005).[102] Philips feels that increased dialogue may one day bring about Turkish recognition of the genocide, yet he makes it clear that the government is currently unready for such an admission: 'Turks refuse to acknowledge the genocide because acknowledgement contradicts their noble self-image. ... In addition, the government of Turkey fears that the campaign is laying the legal groundwork for reparations or territorial claims'.[103]

Conclusions

In 2005, in yet another attempt to deny any Armenian role in Turkish history, the government decided to change the Latin names of several local animals. The *Ovis Armeniana* (wild sheep) is now the *Ovis Orientalis Anatolicus*, while the roe deer, formerly known as *Capreolus Capreolus Armenus*, has become *Capreolus Cuprelus Capreolus*. These previous names have disappeared thanks to the Turkish Environment Ministry, who deemed them 'contrary to Turkish unity'.[104] Other attempts to suppress the past are much in evidence. The year 2005 ended with Turkish novelist Orhan Pamuk potentially facing three years in prison for 'insulting Turkey's national character' under Article 301 of the Turkish Penal Code. He had done this by arguing, during an interview with a Swiss magazine, that Turkey had killed 30,000 Kurds and a million Armenians.[105] With European MEPs watching the trial and Turkey's membership in the EU in the balance, the charges against Pamuk were eventually dismissed. He received the Nobel Prize for literature in 2006, in what can be interpreted as a stinging rebuke against Turkey. In 2006, over sixty writers and publishers continued to face similar charges for their desire to exercise freedom of expression.[106] Ironically, as Pamuk prepared to stand trial, a suit was filed by a Swiss court against Yusuf Halaçoğlu, head of the Turkish History Foundation. Doğu Perincek, head of Turkey's Workers Party, was also arrested, and both were charged with denying the Armenian genocide. Switzerland sees this act as a criminal offense.[107]

Turkey seeks admission to the EU and this might be facilitated if the Armenian issue can be resolved. Armenia seeks an open border and trade with Turkey; its economy could improve immeasurably with normalized relations. A 2005 Turkish–Armenian survey indicates that a majority of Turks and Armenians want the border opened and diplomatic relations established between their two countries.[108] Yet the study also reveals that discussion of the past has raised two opposing reactions in Turkey. On one hand, the survey reveals 'spurred initiatives for a re-evaluation of Turkey's accepted history' which helps promote Turkish–Armenian dialogue. On the other, the debate about the Armenian genocide has also 'triggered reactionary tendencies feeding into a reaffirmation of national identity and the formation of an inward-looking national policy'.[109]

As Akçam astutely observes, civil actors on both sides have been hiding behind Turkey's official policy of denial, refusing to engage in much-needed forms of informal cooperation and dialogue. Both sides are imprisoned by long-held collective stereotypes. 'Instead of thinking about ways towards an eventual solution', concludes Akçam, 'each side makes "deposits" into a kind of World Bank of trauma and guilt'.[110] Akçam rather optimistically argues for a process of detachment, of stepping back from the past and trying, as he has done, to examine it impartially. Past and present must be viewed as separate entities. Yet he also rightly observes that no reconciliation is possible without Turkey acknowledging the truth of what its predecessors did.[111] Civil dialogue, joint surveys, and other means may help normalize relations, but ultimately the Turkish government will have to make the decision to recognize the genocide. Only then can history, and Turkish–Armenian relations, properly move forward.

8   The Armenian genocide and contemporary Holocaust scholarship

> Several weeks ago I was in Galicia, says the Major, at the Austrian front.
> And do you know, Mudir Bey, what I noticed there? No, says the Mudir.
> There are too many Jews there. And do you know how they act when they
> barter? No, says the Mudir. Like Armenians, says the Major. These two
> peoples are so similar, one can barely tell them apart. It is unbelievable. May
> be, says the Mudir. Do you have problems with the Jews here? No, says the
> Mudir. Here we have problems with the Armenians.
>
> (Edgar Hilsenrath, *Das Marchen vom letzten Gedanken* (1989))[1]

The Armenian Diaspora is about seven million strong.[2] Armenian Americans number about one million and, with their relative wealth and political influence in Washington, have proven to be influential in agenda-setting.[3] They, and not their brethren in Armenia, have been at the forefront of keeping memory of the genocide alive. Invoking the Holocaust actively keeps the Armenian genocide and the struggle with Turkey at the top of the agenda. Desires for Turkish recognition of the genocide, for apology, and for compensation will only come when sufficient pressure is put on them by American and Western European governments to force them to buckle. And Western governments will only be persuaded to push if the Armenian genocide is sufficiently like the Holocaust to elicit a sense of moral outrage against continued denial – so the thinking goes.

Much of this chapter puts Vahakn Dadrian's scholarship at center stage. Dadrian is a towering figure in the field of Armenian genocide history. After two decades as a professor of Sociology at the State University of New York, Dadrian began full-time research into the genocide as part of a major project funded by the Guggenheim Foundation. His voluminous list of publications includes *The History of the Armenian Genocide* (1995), as well as more recent works such as *German Responsibility in the Armenian Genocide* (1996), *Warrant for Genocide* (1999), and *Key Elements in the Turkish Denial of the Armenian Genocide* (1999). Dadrian currently serves as Director of Genocide Research for the Zoryan Institute.[4]

Dadrian's views are amongst the strongest of Armenian genocide historians, in that he believes in a Nazi-like hatred of Armenians. This emerges from the Ottoman era and continues through to the Turkish Republic – a hatred little different from Goldhagen's eliminationist anti-Semitism. His views differ notably from some other Armenian historians, like Ronald Suny.[5] Dadrian is perhaps the closest equivalent to Stannard or Churchill, in that he attempts to read the Armenian genocide *through* the Holocaust. Dadrian's goal, in addition to exploring the genocide to its fullest possible extent, is to make the history of the genocide so unimpeachable that it cannot successfully be denied by the Turkish government or their Western supporters.

In this chapter I outline the Armenian case for comparison of their genocide with the Holocaust, engaging with the host of similarities and differences Comparativists unveil in the course of their growing scholarship. As discussed in the previous chapter, the problems of memory and representation are complex. Turkey remains an ally of Israel and America, and the debate about Jewish commemoration of the Armenian genocide, either at the USHMM or the Wiesenthal Center Museum of Tolerance, has become overtly political, involving public confrontation between Armenian and Turkish lobbyists, and protests and hunger strikes.

While some Holocaust historians promote reasoned discussion and support Armenian efforts to commemorate their genocide and combat denial, others do not. Some Relativist historians have sought to downplay the similarities of the two genocides while promoting Holocaust uniqueness. Some fear that aggressive Armenian lobbying might reduce the significance of the Holocaust in America and elsewhere. Still others, like Guenther Lewy, seem to have been inordinately swayed by Turkish arguments, and actively peddle denial.

Finally, I argue that despite all of the similarities between the two genocides, the full 'Americanization' of the tragedy is most likely impossible. This has little to do with Dadrian's scholarship or that of his colleagues. It has rather more to do with the special role that Jews and Israel have in American life, which (perhaps maddeningly for Dadrian) means that while the Armenian genocide may be recognized and commemorated in America, it will never have the same social resonance, nor make the same contribution to national memory, as the Holocaust.

Comparisons: Armenian perspectives

The term 'Armenian holocaust' is not new. Holocaust historians like Israel Charny have been using it for some time, even deriding those who don't for their 'snobbism and elitism'.[6] Well before Charny, American missionary Corinna Shattuck used it in 1895 to describe the deaths of 3,000 Armenians 'burnt alive in their cathedral at Urfa'. Journalist Bernard Lazare also used it in 1898 with reference to anti-Armenian massacres.[7] The Armenian genocide itself has placed a key role in our understanding of what genocide is. Raphael Lemkin was motivated by the genocide (and the rise of Nazism) to initiate an international convention against genocide in 1933. Jewish-Austrian writer Franz Werfel's *The Forty Days of Musa Dagh* depicts an episode from the genocide, making implicit comparisons with Jews during the 1930s.[8]

Adolf Hitler, in an oft-quoted statement to his officers, argued 'Who, after all, speaks today about the annihilation of the Armenians?' Hitler invoked this not to justify the genocide of Jews, but also in speaking of the upcoming invasion of Poland in 1939, and the need ruthlessly to destroy any resistance to German expansion.[9] Comparing the two genocides helps put the Armenian genocide in a twentieth-century context as the first modern genocide, as well as a precursor to the Holocaust. Many Armenian academics advance strong similarities, dismissing claims that the Holocaust is unique or incomparable. For Dadrian, 'the sense of uniqueness belongs to the domain of emotive self-images intruding into the functions of analysis'.[10] The elision of that uniqueness theoretically opens an academic and emotional space that can be filled with the Armenian genocide.

Many Armenian Comparativists have internalized the lessons of Holocaust Americanization, and seek Americanization for their tragedy too. The most effective way might be to stretch comparisons as far as they will go. For Dadrian and his colleagues there is a large number of similarities between Armenians and Jews, which should help us to sympathize with each. First, both Jews and Armenians were subject to a 'vulnerability syndrome', and were both seen as 'disdained minorities' and 'ideal objects of persecution'.[11] As a result, both groups 'learned to be submissive externally while developing an inner toughness', resulting in resistance to assimilation, and the continued perpetuation of an ethnic identity which could act to 'disconcert, irritate, or even provoke their potential victimizer groups'.[12]

Because both groups were 'politically impotent', they had little choice but to seek economic mobility as a substitute for other forms of advancement. Economic ascendancy for some members of the community led to the perpetuation of stereotypes against everyone, which equally discriminated against poorer members.[13] Further, as Libaridian adds: 'Armenians believed in progress and in change at the expense of the traditional because, to paraphrase what was been said of German Jews, these attitudes facilitated emancipation from the political and social disabilities that has oppressed them for centuries ...'.[14] Others too see the Armenians carving out a role as a 'middlemen minority group'. The belief that the Armenians hoarded wealth and were richer than the average Turk inspired envy, contributing to a climate of distrust.[15]

Then we have similarities in the victim groups' links with foreign governments and political movements. In both cases, victims 'developed and fostered pools of support groups abroad'. Such support meant that perpetrators had to proceed slowly, 'cautiously rather than carelessly'.[16] However, once it became clear that outside countries would not intervene to halt mass atrocities, genocide progressed unabated.[17] The lack of any external deterrence 'considerably emboldened the Nazis'. They had been 'testing the waters' without result, just like the CUP before them had also 'tested the waters and released trial balloons' without resistance.[18]

Comparing the perpetrators

At another level, the perpetrators are compared – and the CUP hierarchy is forced into a Nazi mold. In both cases, Dadrian posits that the genocides were orchestrated from the top, by small cabals of elites working very closely with one another. The Wannsee Conference was similar in nature to a conference convened in Constantinople in 1914. In both cases, high-ranking party leaders met with security and military officials to draw up 'blueprints' for genocide. Both genocides resulted from the 'exercise of informal authority by political parties that held the levers of power of a state but also had covert genocidal agendas'.[19]

Dekmejian too notes the similarities in ideology, with the '*raison d'etre* to perform genocide' present in both Pan-Turanist and National Socialist ideologies. Moreover, both leaderships profited from 'intense crises – social, political and economic' at the 'pregenocidal stage', related to 'deeper psychological disorientations' in both societies.[20] To this Walker observes that the genocide was 'truly a twentieth-century phenomenon in its blend of racism and rationalism'. Yet there were darker, medieval forces at work: 'Both ideologies despise conventional religion, and hark back to pagan mythologies in order to justify deeds that pagan man himself would have shuddered to accomplish. Both propound the notion of a master race, with the implication of legitimised terror towards those who do not belong to it'.[21]

Similarities of methods

One can also compare the various stages the perpetrators employed to carry out their respective genocides. Both victimizers assumed power in a step-by-step process, stripping victims of their rights as they gained control. The Ittihad takeover began with the suspension of Parliament, then the issuing of 'Temporary Laws', massive arrests, deportations, and massacres, together with the rounding up of leaders and the conscription of able-bodied adult males. The Nazi procedures were similar – the 1933 Enabling Act, the Nuremberg Laws, and a further 250 decrees between 1935 and 1943 which reduced Jews to 'outlaws'. In both cases, a new legal climate allowed for the relentless persecution of the victims.[22]

At another level, both genocides involved 'security forces' who possessed a wide range of arbitrary powers, 'with levels of authority that in most cases bordered on license for criminal abuse'.[23] Both regimes also employed common criminals to carry out some of the dirty work. Dadrian highlights the *Special Organization*'s use of convicted criminals, a process similar to the SS strategy of arming and mobilizing convicts.[24] Dekmejian's work highlights the role of railway systems in transporting victims to the sites where killings would take place. While Nazi Germany was more advanced in its use of transportation, the Turkish authorities used available technology to the maximum. Completed sections of the Berlin–Baghdad Railway in Anatolia were used to ship Armenians in cattle cars to join convoys of deportees forcibly marched to the Syrian desert.[25]

Additionally, war was an important expedient to both genocides. War, as Dadrian argues, 'allows legislative authority to subside, if not vanish entirely, with the executive branch of government as the main beneficiary of "emergency powers" accruing to it'. 'It is', he argues, 'no accident that the destruction of the Armenians and the Jews was consummated in the vortex of two global wars'. Moreover: 'In both cases the perpetrator groups had precipitated the respective wars'.[26]

An inspiration for Germany

Like the indigenous cases already explored, Armenian Comparativists bill their genocide as *the* crucial precedent for the Final Solution. The Holocaust is stripped of its unique and unprecedented status, but indigenous genocides are forgotten too. At a very basic level, we have Libaridian's assertion that the Armenian genocide was 'the earliest case of a documented modern day extermination'. The systematic and planned nature of the genocide may also made it 'a paradigm for a type of "political" genocide likely to become the pattern of twentieth century genocide'.[27] The Holocaust as another 'political' genocide, planned and executed by a revolutionary regime, falls into a pattern established by the Ittihadists decades before Hitler came onto the scene.

Dadrian's arguments are somewhat more detailed.[28] That the CUP escaped justice encouraged Hitler when he was contemplating the Holocaust. He writes: 'There are many indications that Hitler and his cohorts were fully aware of the Armenian cataclysm and that they drew from it lessons suitable for wanted to emulate the Turkish model of enacting a "final solution"'.[29] The Turks set the prototype for what a final solution should look like, and Hitler 'emulated' a pre-existing model. Dadrian later cites the 'relative ease' with which the genocide was carried out as an instructive precedent for Hitler.[30]

At another level, both Genghis Khan and Kemal Ataturk are role models for the German Fuhrer. Dadrian argues that the concept of *Lebensraum* or 'living space' was at least in part derived from Hitler's appreciation of Genghis, who 'sent millions of women and children into death knowingly and cheerfully ... Yet history sees in him only the great founder of states'. Hitler, in Dadrian's work, also saw Ataturk as a role model, as a 'true statesman, as the founder of modern Turkey'.[31] Both men shared a cynical view of *raison d'état* which allowed them to carry out genocide in pursuit of state expansion, even if Ataturk's was but a continuation of a much nastier process at work before he assumed office.[32]

German complicity in genocide

Another aspect of Dadrian's case is to prove that the Armenians were Germany's first victims of genocide (He does not engage with the Hereroes). Dadrian refutes the long-held stereotypes advanced by Johannes Lepsius, that the Germans were neutral (if horrified) observers of the events in Turkey at the time. Lepsius was both pro-Armenian and a German patriot, so his views of the situation need some clarification.[33] The Germans were a key ally of Turkey during the war, and a number of high-ranking officials seem to have known and approved of the Armenian massacres. Indeed: 'Without the steady infusion of massive German material help, involving military, economic and fiscal resources, Turkey's ability to survive, let alone wage a comprehensive war, was practically nil'.[34]

Dadrian lists evidence of German complicity, which ranges from the Kaiser's instructions not to interfere in Turkey's domestic affairs (while suppressing news of the massacres and bribing German media correspondents to keep quiet), to actual involvement in and incitement to genocide. This includes using German diplomatic and civilian personnel to collect information for the CUP on the Armenians,[35] as well as the role of certain key officials in inciting the deportations, even killings. Dadrian's lengthy analysis includes such military figures such as Colonel Sievert,[36] General von der Goltz,[37] General Major Fritz Bronsart von Schellendorf, and others.[38] Germans seem to have been particular advocates of pan-Turanism, and saw themselves as enemies of Tsarist expansion. The 'Ottoman Armenians', Dadrian tells us, 'were considered to be a subsidiary part of the overall Russian threat', and therefore had to be eliminated as part of the war against Russia.[39]

Anecdotally, Hitler seems to have known of the links between Germany and the Genocide. But how does one genocide connect to the other? Here, Max Erwin von Scheubner Richter is instrumental as a sort of 'missing link'. Scheubner Richter was Vice Consul of Erzurum and, later, Co-Commander of a Turkish–German Expeditionary force that witnessed massacres of Armenians in 1915. In one report, he concluded that 'except for a few hundred thousand survivors, the Armenians of Turkey, for all practical purposes have been exterminated'. In 1920, Scheubner Richter was introduced to Hitler, after which he and his wife joined the Nazi party. He soon became a close collaborator and advisor to the future German leader, later becoming the general manager of the Nazi *Fighting League* in Bavaria.[40]

Scheubner Richter is imbued, in Dadrian's account, with no love for either Jews or Armenians. On one occasion he referred to urban Armenians as 'these Jews of the orient, these wily businessmen'. By 1920 he was railing against an 'international-Jewish plot of world domination' against which 'a ruthless and relentless campaign' should be undertaken.[41] Scheubner Richter thus creates a direct link between the two genocides, proving that Hitler was not just influenced by the Armenian genocide – he was also directly inspired by one of its perpetrators to propose an *Armenian* solution to the Jewish question.

Denial: Armenians and the Holocaust

Unsurprisingly, denial is often compared. While Holocaust deniers are a lunatic fringe, Armenian-genocide deniers have the backing of Turkey and the tacit acquiescence of Israel. It is difficult to disagree with Hovannisian that, in the case of the Armenians, 'denial is far more advanced and has gained a foothold in the mainstream of the historical profession'. Both groups of deniers appeal to a university audience with their desire for 'fair play' – that both 'sides' have a right to be heard in the 'historical debate'.[42] Yet the Armenian case is far more troubling, as 'denial has become institutionalized by a government, its supportive agencies, its influential political and academic collaborators, and by extension, its powerful military allies and trading partners'.[43] This seems a fair statement in light of Germany's almost full repentance for its crimes.[44]

Hovannisian has highlighted eight points common to both Holocaust and Armenian-genocide deniers. This includes blaming genocide claims on wartime propaganda, blaming the target groups as 'very real security threats', denying any intent to annihilate, submerging the group's losses within the general carnage of war, reducing the group's losses, alleging that the 'myth' of genocide was created merely to profit the group, alleging Communist or Soviet involvement in any 'myth', and, finally, alleging that powerful lobbying interests are at work to prevent the denier's 'truth' from coming forth.[45] Both denier groups work hard to discount survivor testimony, while pushing the view that the victims actually provoked attacks against themselves.[46]

Differences: promoting the Armenian Holocaust

Most of the similarities advanced by Comparitivists demonstrate that, in ways that count, the Armenian genocide and the Holocaust share so much that they should receive similar if not equal coverage in America. Dadrian also notes differences, however. Most of these are designed to give the Armenian genocide an edge over the Holocaust – to make an additional case for increased recognition. First, Dadrian presents the Armenian genocide as a more tragic event than the Holocaust in that more was lost. Armenians were destroyed on their own ancestral lands, so not only the people but their 'social, religious, and cultural institutions' stretching back to antiquity were also destroyed. This is contrasted to the Jews, with their 'treasures of a diasporan subculture' – a tragedy certainly, but with a loss of less material culture.[47]

A second difference concerns the relative safety of the Jews in pre-Nazi Germany, versus the more precarious Armenian existence during the late nineteenth century. Dadrian recalls: '[t]otal helplessness rendered the Armenians exceedingly vulnerable', which made them stockpile weapons for self defense.[48] German Jews had no need for arms, and could therefore not be accused of plotting against the state. This seems a tacit rebuttal of the Turkish charge that Armenians were violent agitators against the regime, while Jews were not against theirs. Jews were 'innocent' because they seemingly had an easier time before Hitler's genocidal program began. Armenians had suffered for far longer, and were under no illusions.

Third, there are differences in the way brutalities were carried out. 'Given the primitive conditions and the level of technology in Turkey in World War I', Dadrian tells us, 'the operations of mass murder were particularly harrowing, as dying was made a prolonged and agonizing experience for most of the victims, especially the old, the women and the children ...'. He also refers to the frequent use of 'drowning operations' and the burning of people alive, particularly children, which 'underscores the holocaustal dimension to the Armenian experience'.[49] This is contrasted with the Holocaust, where most of the killing took place in death camps 'where the killing operations were streamlined, mechanized, and systematic through the use of advanced technology'.[50] In order to make this point more explicit, later Dadrian argues: 'if one disregards the operations of the *Einsatzgruppem*, the mobile killer bands, there were mostly the death camps'.[51] The subtext here is that Nazi killers used technology to spare their victims from many of the brutalities Armenians endured.

Tied to the methods of killing were differences between those actually carrying out the killing. In the Holocaust there was a 'division of labor' and the use of 'special cadres', while the general public was not involved. Dadrian contrasts this with the Armenian case, where 'large segments of the provincial population in particular willingly participated in regional and local massacres'.[52] Implicit here is that localized killings were more cruel and personalized, and therefore worse for their individual victims. While the Holocaust was secret, Turkish and Kurdish killers operated in public and seemed proud of their work.

Fourth, Dadrian refutes the idea that the Holocaust was conceived and planned in advance. Adopting a functionalist view, he believes there was no clear genocidal intent towards the Jews at first, and a number of options were considered, including deportation, and social and economic alienation. Claims Dadrian: 'evidence demonstrates that the Nazis *eventually* opted for the Holocaust, *largely by default*' [Italics mine].[53] He later argues: 'Notwithstanding the sporadic pronouncements of Hitler ... it is clear that Nazi antisemitic activities were not necessarily on a genocidal track'. This is contrasted with the Armenian situation, where 'at the very onset the genocidal intent was there'. Government documents and, wartime reports, all 'unmistakably attest to this fact'. If the Holocaust was 'emergent', the Armenian genocide was planned from the beginning in 'firm and implacable' terms.[54]

Fifth, the CUP let fewer of its victims escape. Dadrian dismisses claims that the Armenian populations of Istanbul and Smyrna were spared and survived – a fate not available to Jews in any German city. Those who survived only did so because of 'military setbacks and ancillary handicaps' in the case of Istanbul, and the personal intervention of a key German commander in the case of Smyrna. He then compares this to the Holocaust, where he estimates that of 515,000 German Jews 165,000 were allowed or obliged to leave, while in France only 80,000 Jews of a total population of 330,000 perished in the Final Solution.[55] Again, he implies that the Nazis were far more lax in their persecution than the Ittihadist regime.

Finally, the perpetrators of the Armenian genocide were never punished, while those of the Holocaust were.[56] While Jews gained from forms of retributive justice after the war, including 'German contrition, the payment of indemnities on a massive scale, and correlative atonement', Armenians received nothing. Equally, while Jews gained Israel, Armenians lost their homeland. Those who survived were dispersed to other countries, or endured seven decades of harsh Soviet rule. Their fate was thus different and worse than that of the Jews.[57]

Overall, Dadrian presents a convincing case for why at some levels the Armenian genocide might be both similar to and worse than the Holocaust. As he argues in his book, the differences between the genocides 'are of little significance'; they 'simply collapse into an abyss of irrelevance as they are leveled by the mechanisms and claws of a mammoth engine of destruction'.[58] Here there is an obvious recognition that the Holocaust functions as an archetype. There is a need to stress the similarities between the two events, to perhaps elevate the Armenian genocide by tying it closely to the Holocaust. The role of the genocide as a precedent for the Holocaust also becomes crucial. However, once it has been established to his satisfaction that enough commonalities exist, a form of competition ensues. He elevates the Armenian genocide above the Holocaust and implies that Armenian suffering was worse. All the differences he notes are marshaled in order to prove this point.

The international genocide community is generally very supportive of Armenian genocide scholarship. As discussed in the previous chapter, 126 prominent genocide scholars published an 'International Affirmation of the Armenian Genocide' in 2000, condemning Turkish denial. More recently, the International Association of Genocide Scholars (IAGS) held its biennial conference in 2005 on the theme 'Ninety Years after the Armenian Genocide and Sixty Years after the Holocaust'. The event foregrounded both genocides, and featured Richard Hovannisian as a keynote speaker, with Taner Akçam, Yair Auron, Simon Payaslian, and Rubina Peroomian as additional panelists. The IAGS' 'Lemkin Award' for 2005 went to Peter Balakian for his book on the Armenian genocide, *The Burning Tigris* (2003). Further, IAGS President Robert Melson presented Dadrian with a Lifetime Achievement Award.[59] Dadrian's influence on American genocide scholarship has been considerable. A number of Holocaust historians have also undertaken detailed study of the links between the two genocides, many of which echo the work of Dadrian and his colleagues. We can include Helen Fein, Irving Louis Horowitz, and Robert Jay Lifton here.[60]

Relativists and the Armenian *Historikerstreit*

Despite Dadrian's towering presence, not all genocide scholars are comfortable with the close connections between the Holocaust and the Armenian genocide. The most extreme Relativist views within the genocide community are found in the works of Steven Katz and Guenther Lewy, the only major figures who actually try to withhold the label 'genocide' from the Armenians. At another level, Yehuda Bauer, Robert Melson, and Michael Marrus acknowledge that genocide occurred, yet do not see it as of the same order as the Holocaust, which they perceive as unique. Bauer's views on this matter have changed somewhat in recent years, and I cover this briefly in the conclusion. In what follows, I want to sketch the general contours of the Relativist critique of Armenian genocide scholarship. I argue here that Relativists are attempting to trivialize the Armenian genocide, to normalize it within Turkish history, in a similar manner to what conservative German historians attempted to do during the *Historikerstreit*. We can see some parallels here with Australian genocide deniers. The Relativist goal, however, is arguably not to normalize Turkish history, but to preserve the uniqueness of the Holocaust against a possible 'competitor'.

Genocide or tragedy?

Unlike the Turkish government and their supporters, Katz does not dispute the numbers killed, although his figures are certainly towards the low end of the accepted range. His is a definitional objection – if not all Armenians were slated for extermination, it isn't genocide. Katz' lengthy tome *The Holocaust in Historical Context* devotes a minuscule section to a discussion of the 'Armenian tragedy'. He gives a death toll of between 550,000 and 800,000 individuals, which translates into between 35 to 60 percent of the total Armenian population of 1.5–1.7 million people.[61] Katz's understanding of Armenian history 'does not support a fully genocidal reading of the event'. He argues, rather disingenuously: 'The fact that I choose for specific reasons of definition to deny the term genocide to the Armenian case is not meant to entail any diminishment of Armenian suffering and death'.[62] At the same time, he rails against 'fraudulent, deceitful efforts of Turkish apologists to deny the Armenian tragedy'. And, while he claims his work should not be perceived as supporting denial and should not play into their hands, it obviously does. After all, Turkish deniers have been fighting the label 'genocide' for decades. Doubtless any new 'methodological and phenomenological' reason would be most welcome.[63]

Nationalism versus Anti-semitism

The Relativist critique further attempts to draw stark differences between Nazism and the various Turkish ideologies which inspired the Armenian genocide. This, on the surface, seems reasonable, as neither Ottoman nor CUP ideology are markedly similar to Nazism. However, Relativists go further than simply noticing the differences – they also seek to deny that the genocide was motivated by racism. Rather, genocide is largely imputed to a side-effect of an almost justifiable Turkish fear of Armenian separatism and nationalism.

For Katz, CUP ideology was little more than 'a most primitive jingoism'. It was also very broadly focused, not specifically on Armenians per se, but aiming at 'the elimination of (not the murder of) *all* non-Turkish elements – and most especially and specifically the eradication of the Armenian community – from the national context'.[64] The 'anti-Armenian crusade' was a 'delimited political crusade'. There were never any 'ornate ontological' or other far-reaching, 'primordial', 'biological' or 'noumenological' goals in the Armenian 'tragedy'. Rather, the CUP was acting against a 'political' threat: 'The Armenians were secessionists, Russian spies, fifth-columnists, and divisive nationalists who would subvert the Turkish people's revolution and destroy Turkish national and political integrity'.[65] Anti-Semitism retains its uniqueness.

Alex Grobman, influenced strongly by Katz, is also conceptually vague on whether the Armenians actually suffered genocide. The Turks, after all, did not see the Armenians as a 'satanic or biological threat', they did not kill all of them (sparing the Istanbul Armenians), and the conflict was nationalist in nature: 'Once the Armenian nationalist threat had been thwarted, the Turks no longer felt a need to kill them'.[66]

We have a similar perspective from Robert Melson. While Melson is an Armenian genocide historian in his own right and a close collaborator of Dadrian at the IAGS, his views are quite different. First, he sees the Armenians as a legitimate threat – a 'territorial ethnic group that had sought autonomy'. Downplaying CUP ideology, he observes that the killers were motivated by 'a variant of nationalist ideology'. Nazi killings, by contrast, were motivated by 'racism and anti-Semitism, ideologies of global scope'. Jews as a 'pariah caste' were 'hated and feared in a manner than the Armenians in the Ottoman Empire were not'.[67] In his *Revolution and Genocide*, Melson takes thirteen pages to examine the uniqueness of Christian anti-Semitism in Europe, but concludes that anti-Armenian sentiments were not comparable. There were no specifically anti-Armenian political parties or ideologies in the Ottoman Empire, and genocide was a result of Turkish nationalism, which excluded Armenians but did not specifically target them.[68]

Yehuda Bauer too has charted the 'nonpragmatic and irrational' goals of the Holocaust. Jews 'did not possess territories, nor did they command military might, nor did they control any national economy ...'. However, in a climate of 'redemptive anti-Semitism', facts were largely irrelevant.[69] The Armenians, though, were singled out for 'pragmatic' reasons; there was a 'nationalistic motivation for their murder'.[70] While horrific, the genocide seems rational. It 'served the pragmatic purposes of political expansion, acquisition of land, confiscation of riches, elimination of economic competition, and the satisfaction of chauvinistic impulses ... exacerbated by feelings of utter frustration and humiliation in a crisis-ridden and disintegrating empire'.[71]

Michael Marrus' portrayal of genocide is little different. Here, too, genocide occurred 'in the absence of the kind of all-consuming ideological obsession associated with the Nazis' detestation of the Jews'. Bernard Lewis, a favorite of genocide deniers, is quoted as saying that the genocide was about 'real issues', and never associated with 'demonic beliefs or the almost physical hatred'.[72] The point of much of this is to downplay or even deny Turkish hatred, especially if it should approach the virulence of anti-Semitism. This leads Relativists to normalize Turkish goals and objectives – presenting them as understandable reactions to the collapse of an empire during wartime and the secessionist demands of a troublesome minority.

Intent and scope

The genocide's universal dimensions and global scope are rejected in the Relativist critique. Since the Armenians were a *political* threat primarily, there was no need to kill *all* of them. Typically, Katz argues that the killings 'entailed limits'. National goals could be accomplished without a global and universal attack on all Armenians. There was no Nazi-like 'biocentric war' – the *community* and its *political* threat was to be eliminated, rather than the race itself.[73] Bauer adds that if the Holocaust was 'global' and 'universal', the Armenian genocide was not designed to kill everyone: 'The Turks targeted Armenians in ethnically Turkish areas; they did not care about Armenians elsewhere; even the Armenians in Jerusalem ...'. Also, some Armenian women and children were spared.[74] Marrus' view is little different, and he adds: 'I have seen no indication, for example that the Turks felt the killing ended prematurely or considered that their plans for the Armenians had *failed*'.[75]

This aspect of the Relativist critique rejects Dadrian's overwhelming body of evidence that the killings continued well after the CUP had fallen from power. Obviously the Kemalist regime felt that the CUP *had not* done enough, and thus continued. Akçam also points out that Turkish forces only stopped their forays into Russian Armenia when confronted by Soviet force, an obvious example of military failure fully to carry out a genocidal operation. Contrary to Marrus' account, the Turks did feel they had failed in Russia. They certainly did not succeed in entirely wiping out the perceived Armenian threat.

Islamic conversion

The 'mediating role of conversion to Islam' is promoted by some Relativists, with the claim that 200,000 people were 'saved' by abandoning Christianity. This escape route proves to Relativists that CUP ideology was devoid of 'a racist ideology'. According to Katz, cultural and not biological purity was the primary objective.[76] Melson's point is virtually identical. While Jews (as an 'alien race') could not convert to Christianity, 'even Pan-Turkish left the door open to conversion and assimilation of minorities, something that racism and anti-Semitism explicitly rejected'.[77]

Overall, the key thrust of most Relativist accounts is that the Holocaust was unique and unprecedented. The Armenian genocide is certainly horrific, but seems rational, politically-motivated, and limited in scope. Melson, for example, can highlight similarities between the two victim groups, genocides, and perpetrators, focusing on such issues as the 'ancient provenance' of the victims,[78] the key role of 'revolutionary movements',[79] war as a catalyst,[80] and the presence of Russia as a enemy supposedly allied to the victims.[81] Yet the death camps ('an extraordinary organization, not seen before or since') give the Holocaust its unique edge.[82] Again, one is confronted with the uniqueness of hatred and the uniquely systematized killing operations. No matter what other similarities Dadrian can marshal, Auschwitz continues to be the standard by which to appraise the uniqueness of one case against the other.

Lewy's denialism

Very much in a class by himself is Guenther Lewy, who actually *denies* the Armenian genocide in a manner similar to his denial of the American Indian and Roma genocides. In a recent article in *The Middle East Quarterly*, Lewy begins by contextualizing the history of the genocide as a 'debate over what happened to Armenians in the Ottoman Empire during World War I'. He notes that 'many historians, both in Turkey and the West, have questioned the appropriateness of the genocide label'. While the sources he uses are either Turkish or overtly pro-Turkish, Lewy insists that the 'debate' is ongoing and there has been no resolution.[83] Just how long this 'historical debate' is meant to drag on without resolution is unclear. Lewy, it appears, would like it to continue until any proof of the Armenian genocide has been successfully quashed.

Having in typical denialist fashion presented the 'debate' as an equal and open-ended affair, Lewy then proceeds to argue that while the numbers claimed by both sides are roughly the same (they aren't), the heart of the debate concerns premeditation. Lewy sees the Armenian genocide scholarship resting on three wobbly pillars. These are first, 'the actions of Turkish military courts of 1919–20, which convicted officials of the Young Turk government of organizing massacres of Armenians'; second, 'the role of the so-called 'Special Organization' accused of carrying out the massacres'; and third; 'the Memoirs of Naim Bey ... which contain alleged telegrams of Interior Minister Talât Pasha conveying the orders for the destruction of the Armenians'.[84] We soon discover that these pillars are straw men which Lewy proposes to knock down.[85]

First, Lewy attempts to discredit the Courts-Martial of 1919–20 which were designed to punish the perpetrators of the genocide. The trials, he posits, were created because of Allied pressure. They usefully allowed enemies of the CUP to discredit the old regime and move forward. Lewy criticizes both the 'procedures of the trials' and the 'reliability of their findings'.[86] The second 'pillar' is the Special Organization, which Lewy denies was an instrument in the 'genocide'. He argues that: 'Many of the allegations linking the Special Organization to massacres are based not directly on documents but rather on the sometimes questionable assumptions of those reading them'. Key witnesses like the German Colonel Stange are distanced from the activities of the Special Organization.[87]

As for the third 'pillar', this too is refuted: 'There are many doubts as to the authenticity of the documents reproduced in [key CUP official] Naim Bey's memoirs'.[88] Lewy is content to rely on the work of Turkish deniers Şinasi Orel and Süreyya Yuca, who accuse 'the Armenians' of having 'purposely destroyed the "originals", in order to avoid the chance that one day the spuriousness of the "documents" would be revealed'. This accusation seems reasonable to Lewy, as does the further accusation that Turkish documents used to prove the genocide are little more than 'crude forgeries'.[89] Lewy's conception of shaky pillars echoes the work of Holocaust deniers, who also see Holocaust history resting on pillars, such as the gas chambers, the authenticity of Anne Frank's *Diary*, a Führer order, and so on.[90] This is a dangerous proposition, because it assumes from the start that genocide scholarship rests on lies which can easily be disproved once a deeper examination of the historical 'truth' is undertaken. As such, consulting 'authentic' documents and exposing 'forgeries' brings one closer to the truth.

Dadrian is correct to note Lewy's misunderstanding of sources and his obvious sympathy for Turkish denial. Indeed, he puts overtly Turkish denial material on a par with that of serious Armenian historians.[91] Lewy's 'pillars' are then rebuilt one by one. Dadrian proves that the German Colonel Stange *did* play a role in the Special Organization. He also upholds the authenticity of the documents produced at the post-war Tribunal, while disproving Lewy's contention that the Special Organization did not carry out atrocities. The notion that the Special Organization was not involved is 'flatly contradicted by first-hand Turkish evidence'. He goes on to provide that evidence.[92] The Armenian genocide is Lewy's third attempt at genocide denial, and, while he has since retired from teaching at the University of Massachusetts, he seems unwilling to allow any other genocide to compete with the Holocaust.

Conclusions: the problems of Americanization

Crucially, what categorizes the Comparativist–Relativist debate is a search for connections and similarities on one side, and stark differences on the other. Dadrian, for example, rarely engages with why the Holocaust *might* be unique, nor do the very real differences between the two cases interest him. He searches primarily for elements that will help him better package *his* genocide. Yet it remains the case that the two genocides *were* markedly different. While the Armenians were the victims of a brutal genocide, the Holocaust was centrally planned and coordinated to a much greater extent.

Anti-Semitism also traces its roots further back into the ancient past. Nazism provided an extreme radicalization of anti-Jewish racism, but this hatred was to be found in Christian Europe for centuries. *National* hatred of the Armenians seems to be of a newer vintage, although local Kurdish–Armenian ethnic grievances were of longer standing. This should not diminish its significance for the victims who suffered from it, but it should alert us to be more cautious when drawing analogies with different forms of hatred.

However, I am also deeply critical of charges that the CUP was not a racist organization or that there were not cruelly irrational aspects of the Armenian genocide. Melson uses the amorphous term 'nationalism' for the CUP, while adopting the more value-laden 'racism' for Nazism.[93] The CUP was certainly a racist organization, and its genocide was neither a rational nor an understandable undertaking. Additionally, Armenians were hardly the security threat many Relativists purport them to be. The war against the Armenians did not end after Turkey's defeat, as Dadrian has ably shown. While the intended scope of the genocide was not as universal or global as the Holocaust, it certainly was not limited to Ottoman territory.

An interesting aside are the 'conversions' of some Relativists, whose approaches seem to be softening. In 1993, Deborah Lipstadt argued in *Denying the Holocaust* that the 'brutal Armenian tragedy' was not 'part of a process of total annihilation of an entire people'. She implied that no genocidal aggression had taken place outside of Turkey, and that there was no totalistic intent. However, Hovannisian observes that, when confronted with the evidence of massacres in northern Iran and in the Caucasus, Lipstadt came to accept the facts and now 'speak[s] out boldly against denial of the genocide'.[94]

Similarly, in his *Rethinking the Holocaust*, Bauer almost made the genocide seem logical: 'The Armenians, an "alien" nation, occupied stretches of Anatolia, the heartland of Turkey. They had to be done away with'. He also took their purported collaboration with Russians for granted. It was natural for them to 'seek support from the Russians, the bitter enemies of the Ottoman Empire'.[95] More recently, Bauer has taken a firmer stand, noting:

Many of these denials say, 'Yes, there was terrible suffering on both sides, the Turkish vs. the Armenian, these things happen in war,' ... But that's nonsense. This was a definite, planned attack on a civilian minority, and whatever Armenian resistance there was came in response to the imminent danger of mass murder.[96]

Ultimately, and tragically, Armenian desires for their genocide to be placed on equal footing with the Holocaust will not succeed. The Holocaust emerged in Western consciousness at a particular time in America's history. Despite the many similarities between these two cases, the Holocaust remains unique because of the Americanization process. This has had to do in part with the influence of the American Jewish Diaspora and Israel's geopolitical importance in the Middle East, but there are other crucial factors at work too.

One of these is the sheer weight of documentation about the Holocaust. Captured Allied documents, testimony during the Nuremberg trials, confessions of the Nazi hierarchy, and memoirs by survivors have all added to the undeniability of the Holocaust. Germany was forced into admitting its crimes. It really had no choice. The country was occupied and split in half, its leaders put on trial. This can be contrasted with Turkey, where Ataturk's government buried the past. Not forced to admit to it, they chose not to. National soul-searching was avoided, repentance rejected. Most traces of Armenian life and history were scrupulously erased.

Armenian genocide scholarship remains locked in a position of debating whether or not the events occurred; whether or not certain facts are accurate, or exaggerated, or forgeries. It has moved forward, but far more slowly than Holocaust history. While more than enough evidence of the genocide exists, one cannot underestimate the importance of a perpetrator government continuing to actively and perniciously deny the genocide after ninety years. Cynical attempts to dilute Armenian lobbying efforts, like the Armenian–Turkish Reconciliation Commission, will also make a genuine admission of Turkish guilt impossible.

Equally, Israel's pro-Turkish position in this matter adds another layer of difficulty, especially when the USHMM and the Museum of Tolerance seem reluctant to take a strong stand on the issue. As the Wiesenthal Center's Abraham Cooper has explained the situation:

We try to take a stand that is true to history, but which is also true to our friends, and hopefully our Armenian and Turkish friends understand. That a genocide of the Armenian people took place is a fact, and that for hundreds of years, the Turkish people [aided Jews in danger], when Christian and Muslim nations did not is also a fact, and that Israel needs close relations with Turkey is also a fact. That's not an easy triangulation, but it's our responsibility to make it.[97]

Another issue concerns the significance of the Jews in Western consciousness. As already discussed in Chapter 2, Jews *are* a unique people. Their uniqueness contribution to the Judeo-Christian faith, and Western morality makes them unlike other victim groups. Israel has special significance for the Christian Right in the United States, who support Israel for largely selfish reasons – to bring about Christ's second coming. Armenians are an ancient Christian people. They may be a vulnerable minority; they may have been 'middlemen'; they may have had connections with Russia and other national enemies. They may have represented for the Turks what Jews represented for Nazi Germans. Yet neither the Armenians nor Armenia has special religious, geopolitical, or cultural significance for *Americans*. While the tragedy resonates as *something very bad* that happened in the twentieth century, it possesses no larger ontological or spiritual significance for most Americans, other than a warning that genocide has long and terrible roots in the modern world. This really is the fundamental problem for historians like Dadrian who so wish to have the Armenian genocide put on par with the Holocaust. I salute his efforts, but am pessimistic about the extent to which his ambitious goals will succeed.

9 Nanking, the Chinese Holocaust, and Japanese atomic victim exceptionalism

On November 8, 2004, a thirty-six-year-old journalist and author left her husband and two-year-old son at home. She drove her car to a rural road in Los Gatos, near Los Angeles, where she subsequently committed suicide by shooting herself in the head. Iris Chang had been suffering from depression. Her hair was falling out; she had recently been hospitalized in Louisville, Kentucky, following a nervous breakdown. For her fifth book, Chang had been interviewing former victims of the Bataan Death march, while immersing herself in graphic pictures and documents from the war.[1] Chang's breakdown and suicide stands as a warning to those who contemplate plunging too deeply into the very depths of human depravity.

Chang's best-known work is *The Rape of Nanking* (1997), which used the Holocaust as a frame through which to highlight Japanese atrocities during the siege of Nanking in 1937. The book became an almost instant bestseller, and has been heralded as the most accessible resource on Nanking in the English language. While I am sympathetic to Chang's motives, and agree that the impact of her work has been immeasurably positive for the Chinese American community, I also have reservations.[2] In this chapter I problematize claims of a 'Chinese Holocaust', through a reading of *The Rape of Nanking* and the work of Diaspora Chinese activist groups. Framing Chinese victimization through the Holocaust, as in some other cases, leads to problems of misrepresentation. Direct comparisons have led to a series of misleading dichotomies, which distort historical accuracy.

Yet accuracy is precisely what is required when presenting the history of Nanking. Japan continues to elide its own belligerent past. Its own myths of suffering, based on Nagasaki and Hiroshima, have allowed Japan to portray itself as a peaceful, anti-nuclear society. Japan's leaders pay homage to the Yasukuni Shrine (where many war criminals are buried). Unlike Germany, there is no Japanese Denkmal to its murdered victims, nor is there likely to be one in the near future.

In March 2005, violent riots erupted in China over Japan's attempts to once more gloss over World War II-era atrocities like Nanking as an 'incident', and the war as one of 'self preservation'. Chinese and Koreans objected to right-wing publisher Fusosha's new history textbooks, which were approved by the Japanese Ministry of Education. They seemingly reflected the Minister's own desire, expressed in late 2004, to overcome 'self-torturing' accounts of Japanese history.[3] The People's Republic continues to rail against Japanese denialism. While trade between the two countries is worth over $200 billion annually, the Chinese remain distrustful of Japan. A recent poll conducted in several Asian countries indicates that the Japanese continue to be viewed negatively.[4]

I begin this chapter with an overview of Japanese crimes in Nanking, followed by a brief introduction to Japanese atrocity denial. I follow this with a detailed engagement with Chang's work, as well as numerous Chinese Diaspora publications about the 'Chinese Holocaust'. I will argue that while the use of Jewish Holocaust imagery may initially attract public interest in the historic plight of Chinese victims, framing Chinese victimization within a template created by the Holocaust leads to serious problems of misrepresentation. Direct comparisons have led to a series of false dichotomies which distort historical accuracy and reduce the authentic significance of Chinese victimization. Chang's work specifically encounters problems in this regard, as does the work of many of her fellow activists in the United States.

Japanese atrocities in China

The precise number of Chinese victims of Japanese aggression is impossible to establish with certainty. From 1931 to 1945, between 1,578,000 and 6,325,000 people are said to have died directly as a consequence of Japanese crimes against humanity. When one factors in Chinese deaths as a result of looting, medical experimentation, starvation, bombing, and battle deaths, the total may be as high as nineteen million people.[5] Some provide lower estimates, of ten million or less.[6] Chinese activists routinely use a much higher figure of thirty-five million deaths, a figure also advanced by the People's Republic of China.[7]

Within the accepted overall totals for Japanese atrocities, certain events stand out as particularly horrendous. The siege and brutal occupation of Nanking in December 1937 has figured as a key Japanese atrocity, which for some possesses 'the same resonance as Auschwitz had in Nuremberg'.[8] Generally, Nanking can be contextualized within a larger war of Japanese aggression in China. Signposts on the way to Nanking include the 'Manchurian Incident' of 1931, the 'Shanghai Incident' and the formation of Manchukuo in 1932, and the 'Marco Polo Bridge Incident' of 1937.[9] In some respects, Nanking was hardly unique.[10]

Yet it does possess unique features. Nanking, as Eastman reminds us, 'stands out because of its scale and intensity', but also because the horrors were witnessed by 'neutral observers'.[11] The presence of Westerners, and the fact that they were able to document the atrocities, makes Nanking an extremely well-known crime. That Nanking was the capital of Chiang Kai-Shek's Nationalist government also gives it special significance. By the end of 1937, much of Northern China and Inner Mongolia were in Japanese hands. Nanking was one of the few cities remaining.[12] As the Japanese approached, the rich and middle classes fled, making their way to Hong Kong or the foreign concessions in Shanghai. Most of the victims were in lower socio-economic groups.[13]

On August 15, Japanese forces began air raids; these continued until December 13, after which time Japanese troops entered the city.[14] Following the siege were six weeks of mass brutality, rape, and murder. Chang argues that massacres of civilians 'in every section of the city' led to 'moaning and screaming', 'rivers of blood' – unimagined horrors.[15] A figure of 20,000 rape victims is commonly noted.[16] Ian Buruma similarly notes the brutal games played by the Japanese during this time, including head-chopping contests, which were eagerly chronicled by Japanese newspapers.[17] As Morton recounts, the city degenerated into 'such horrible rape, murder and looting that even the Japanese High Command was alarmed ...', while Boyle describes an 'orgy of raping and looting'.[18] Others, however, dismiss the random nature of the violence. Eykholt cites the orderly disciplined seige: atrocities followed 'organized patterns', while rapes and robberies were rarely random: 'discipline and order continued amid the murder and mayhem'.[19]

The total number of deaths is contested. Beigbeder puts the number at somewhere between 42,000 and 100,000, but this is rather low.[20] Most put the death toll considerably higher. Bagish and Conroy advance approximately 200,000; Williamsen and Dreyer, a range of 200,000 to 300,000 killed; Freidman '200,000 or more'; Eastman 250,000, possibly more.[21] Chang quotes the official figures from the IMTFE at 260,000, while arguing that some experts put the death toll for Nanking at well over 350,000.[22] Is this an example of genocide? Certainly the Japanese did not mean to kill all Chinese, but they did intend to kill as many *Nanking* Chinese as possible. The 'part' of the Chinese people represented by Nanking Chinese was certainly slated for death. And if the killing of 8,000 Bosnian Moslem men and boys in Srebrenica in 1995 by Bosnian Serb forces constitutes genocide, then so (under international law) should Nanking.[23] This should be doubly true when one considers the overall death tolls wrought by the Japanese.

The 'second rape': denying Nanking

Added to Japanese crimes has been an active effort to deny or distort the history of these atrocities. As Chang argues in *The Rape of Nanking*: 'Sixty years later the Japanese as a nation are still trying to bury the victims of Nanking, not under the soil, as in 1937, but into historical oblivion'.[24] She has spoken of a 'double rape' – the first rape being Nanking, the second being the act of forgetting and/or denying the atrocities after the fact.[25]

This has consequences for memory and identity outside of Asia. Japanese denial has relegated Nanking to 'an obscure incident', 'neglected in most of the historical literature published in the United States'. Compared with the

Holocaust and the atomic bombing of Hiroshima and Nagasaki, 'the horrors of the massacre at Nanking remain virtually unknown to people outside Asia'.[26] This view is shared by other Diaspora Chinese, who have used the forgotten nature of the tragedy to highlight the injustice of historical scholarship. The notion that the Jewish Holocaust is remembered while the 'Chinese Holocaust' is not provides a point of departure for many activists.

Japanese atrocity denial can be traced back to the pioneering work of Hayashi Fusao, who contextualized the Japanese 'war of liberation' within a century-long struggle against Western imperialism.[27] Deniers in the 1970s, like Schichihei and Akira, dismissed Japanese crimes as exaggerated, particularly those in Nanking.[28] Later works, such as Manabu's *Japan Was Not an Aggressive Nation* (1983) and Masaaki's *The Fabrication of the 'Nanking Massacre'* (1984), denied any 'instance of planned, systematic murder in the entire history of Japan'.[29]

Better known in the West is the 'textbook controversy', which erupted in 1982 when the Ministry of Education began asking for revisions to school history textbooks.[30] 'Japanese aggression in China' was to become 'Japanese occupation of Manchuria'; 'Japan's aggression in the three eastern provinces' was to be 'the Manchurian Incident and the Shanghai Incident'.[31] Whether or not the Ministry was merely 'suggesting' changes rather than forcing them through, the revision issue raised a furore on mainland Asia which has yet to fully die down.[32]

Denial has often been promoted by the Japanese political and intellectual establishment, particularly conservative factions of the ruling Liberal Democratic Party, which has held political power almost continuously since 1955. The LDP has included many 'die hard nationalists' who have traditionally seen the Pacific War as a legitimate defense against Communism's 'Red Peril' and Western colonialism's 'White Peril' in Asia.[33] This type of conservatism was tolerated by America, even encouraged, during the Cold War, as long as Japan remained a staunch anti-Communist ally.[34] Dower and Hicks both locate denial in Japanese preoccupations with advancing a 'correct' national history – one which instilled pride in the nation. Not unlike the situation in America, Australia, and Turkey, nationalist writers see their role as helping Japan to avoid national humiliation and needless soul-searching.[35]

In 1985, Prime Minister Nakasone would use the term 'masochistic' to describe Japanese historians and activists who insisted on highlighting Japanese crimes, and he and his colleagues promoted denial during the 1980s.[36] More recently, in July 2003, former cabinet minister Takami Eto echoed the view that Nanking was a 'big lie', criticizing political leaders who apologized for Japan's wartime past.[37] The Japanese right also condemned Chang's *oeuvre*, arguing that it was little more than anti-Japanese propaganda, while criticizing 'errors', including the death totals.[38]

As a further twist in the tale, forms of Japanese anti-Semitism would also emerge in the 1980s and 1990s, although anti-Semitism was largely absent in Japanese history, even during the War.[39] Rotem Kowner locates anti-Semitism in Japan's feelings of vulnerability during the debates about its own wartime responsibility. For Kowner – logical conclusions were drawn from the work of American Holocaust deniers – if the Holocaust, 'the most notorious war crime ever, was a hoax, as some uninformed Japanese may have believed, Japan's war crime too could be a fabrication'.[40]

Despite this history of denial, Nanking scholarship has grown tremendously in Japan since the 1980s, when the veterans' association Kaikosha effectively proved that Nanking had taken place. Since this time, denial of the massacre itself has been on the decline, although there is still much debate about the number of dead, with Chinese historians often accused of exaggeration.[41]

The diaspora and the 'Chinese Holocaust'

America is now home to over one-third of overseas Chinese living outside of Asia. Approximately 70 percent are foreign born; the majority immigrated to America after 1980. In 2000, almost 98 percent lived in urban areas, with New York, Los Angeles, and San Francisco the preferred ports of entry. California and New York contain the largest numbers of Chinese Americans, with 40 percent residing in California alone.[42] Like the Jewish and Armenian Diasporas, the rising economic and political influence of Chinese Americans has helped promote Nanking in contemporary consciousness. It was not always this way.

Chinese have been in America since at least the eighteenth century. Over 100,000 Chinese immigrated during the mid-nineteenth century, as miners, railroad workers, and laborers. This period of 'unrestricted immigration' was curtailed in 1882 with the Chinese Exclusion Act, and further buttressed by the 1924 Immigration Act, which virtually stopped Chinese entry. A period of 'restricted immigration' followed from 1943 to 1965.[43] While racism has been a constant hallmark of early Chinese life in America, the situation improved markedly during the 1960s, especially after the passage of more liberal immigration laws in 1965.

However, Chinese Americans have remained on the margins of society, neither socially and politically established like Whites, nor a recognizable underclass like Blacks, Hispanics, or American Indians.[44] Chinese-American writers still maintain that they still do not quite fit into American society. As Henry Yu passionately argues, 'Asians are still exotic, still bearers of an authentic otherness that they cannot shake. Like other nonwhites, Asian Americans remain both American and examples through their existence of non-America ...'.[45] Frank Wu takes a somewhat different tack, and sees his people assuming a social and economic position once occupied by Jews: 'Asian Americans have superseded American Jews in the imagination of ethnicity' as those who work hard and strive for success in the establishment. Chinese Americans suffer from what Wu calls 'the model minority myth'.[46]

Like some American Jews, many Chinese Americans *have* worked hard to excel in America. Regarding the cultural and educational aspects, Asian-American study programs have been promoted since the 1960s, especially in California. Organizations like 'Chinese for Affirmative Action' (1969), the 'Organization of Chinese Americans' (1973), and the more recent 'The 80–20 Initiative' have given Asian-Americans political clout, while Chinese-American authors like Amy Tan, Ang Lee, and Wayne Wang have become increasingly popular amongst mainstream Americans. Chinese Americans have increasingly joined the media, television, performing arts, and other fields, in addition to their high standing in many white-collar professions. In 1990, almost 40 percent of Chinese Americans over the age of twenty-five had a BA or higher degree – double the national average.[47]

Chinese Americans now have more freedom of expression and more coercive power than at any time in their history. They also have access to the Internet, which has become a key means of promoting memory of Chinese victimization. Indeed, *The New York Times* recently identified a 'cottage industry' of remembrance, with 'dozens of groups working the Internet to publicize it, as well as recent documentaries, novels and exhibits'.[48] While long divided between support for the Taiwan and the People's Republic, in the 1990s, the Diaspora began to speak with a more united voice, joining together a 'multiplicity of voices'.[49]

Several key factors triggered Diaspora commemoration. One was a reaction to Japan's claim of sovereignty over the Diao-yu-tai islets (contested by the PRC during the 1970s), the other was a reaction to the textbook controversy in 1982.[50] The goal of Diaspora groups has since been to highlight the plight of the Chinese, through public lectures, scholarly seminars, art exhibitions, and other events.[51] Activism increased after the Tiananmen Square massacre in 1989, when pro-democracy groups began working increasingly to document and commemorate Chinese history.[52]

Diaspora groups such as the 'Global Alliance for Preserving the History of World War II in Asia'; the 'Alliance for Preserving the Truth of the Sino-Japanese War'; and the 'Rape of Nanking Redress Coalition' emerged during the 1980s and 1990s, and played key roles in promoting remembrance. The 'Global Alliance', formed in 1992, is the largest, comprising some fifty-two groups.[53] Chang was inspired to write her book after attending an Alliance conference in 1994. Ignatius Ding, one of the Alliance's leaders, notes that new generations of Chinese immigrants to America have been more sophisticated in their organizing and political skills: 'Chinese-American intellectuals have reached a "maturity" in this country [America] whose roots are secure, allowing them to turn their attention to issues such as Nanking'.[54] This sense of rootedness in the West, and the development of media skills and techniques partially explains why now, more than sixty years later, this 'Forgotten Holocaust' is slowly being remembered.

Teaching about Nanking

A key aspect of commemoration has been a copying of Jewish Holocaust educational curricula at the secondary school level in the United States. For school-teacher Poland Hung, the paucity of information on the Sino-Japanese War in World War II educational curricula is a deplorable omission, especially since 'the Chinese Holocaust created by the Japanese ... was more horrific and devastating than the Jewish Holocaust'.[55] Hung's program features sections on all aspects of the 'Chinese Holocaust' or 'Forgotten Holocaust of Asia', including the Rape of Nanking, germ warfare, and 'comfort women'.[56]

Written assignments include constructing narratives from the point of view of a Nanking victim 'whose family has suffered atrocities and home destroyed by the Japanese soldiers'. Another topic is more grounded in the present, requiring students to write to the UN, 'demanding that the Japanese military be tried for war crimes, showing the ways in which they violated the Hague Conventions'. An optional assignment includes creating a mock trial composed of three groups – the Japanese, a 'World Court', and a jury.[57] Curiously, the curriculum includes a section on Japanese denial, based on a handout – 'Nanking Massacre – The Japanese Version'. The curriculum prompts students to debate the handout, while seeking to understand why governments might seek to 'rewrite history'.[58]

Priscilla Chan's curriculum also presents Japanese atrocities as a 'Forgotten Holocaust', seeing the European and Asian conflicts as 'very similar', with a 'domineering group spreading its power' on one side and 'a prime group suffering from the take-over of the domineering group' on the other.[59] For both teachers, the 'other side' is crucial to the debate. Chan further notes that she 'tried to contact Japanese organizations in hopes to create a more balanced, "unbiased" unit. However, my attempts were unsuccessful'.[60]

Such courses have been implemented in several American states. This type of curriculum structure is interesting, as it differs substantially from Jewish Holocaust education, which refutes the idea that there is a debate with two sides. Lipstadt, for example, rejects the idea of denialism as 'the other side', or a 'different perspective'. To debate with deniers is to elevate denial 'to the level of responsible historiography – which it is not'.[61] Chinese atrocity scholarship has pursued a different approach, perhaps because Japanese denial is a more mainstream perspective which cannot so easily be marginalized as a fringe or lunatic movement.

Chinese 'Holocaust' museums

Supplementing curricula are public venues designed to highlight the suffering of the Chinese and their links with the Jews as fellow victims. This has from the 1990s included the creation of 'Chinese Holocaust' museums, directly inspired by Jewish lobbying and commemorative efforts. As one

Chinese community newsletter stressed: 'In recent years, Jewish-Americans have built Holocaust Museums in Washington, Los Angeles and Toronto.... These models inspired a group of Chinese Americans to develop and begin implementing a plan for building a Chinese Holocaust museum in America'.[62] A temporary 'Chinese Holocaust Museum of the United States' was constructed in Oakland, California in 2000.[63] A permanent museum for the Bay area was to be followed by another in Washington, DC, based on the Jewish USHMM.[64] The project was and is ambitious, including the formation of exhibition halls, libraries, workshops, and conferences, with publication of newsletters, journals, and books.[65]

By 2001, public exhibitions of some 918 artifacts from Japan's imperial forays and atrocities began touring a number of major American cities.[66] An exhibition on the Nanking Massacre, called 'Never Forget', was organized in Nanking, with help from the Chinese Holocaust Museum. For Chen Jiabao, the Vice-Mayor of Nanking: 'The Nanjing Massacre was no less a crime than the Holocaust ...'.[67] Following the Oakland-based museum was another in Falls Creek, Pennsylvania. The 'American Museum of Asian Holocaust WWII (1931–1945)' was opened in 2002 by Congressman Mike Honda, featuring many similar exhibits. The Alliance's contributions here were glowingly noted.[68]

The role of denying

Part and parcel of establishing a 'Chinese Holocaust' have been linkages and comparisons between what Jews and Chinese have endured at the hands of their respective aggressors. While many Jewish groups find invocations of other 'holocausts' unacceptable, Nanking is an exception. Part of this has to do with the vast scale of the atrocities. Another aspect of accepting a second 'holocaust' has to do with the very real problems of denial in Japan. Shermer and Grobman's analysis of Jewish Holocaust denial features a chapter entitled 'The Rape of History', devoted largely to Chang's book. They compare and contrast both forms of denial and express solidarity with the author:

> Nanking Denial is part and parcel with Holocaust denial in methodologies, arguments, and motivations, and reflects the larger pseudohistorical trends seen in other claims. Since Nanking denial evolved independently from Holocaust denial, it seems safe to assume that Japanese deniers have not been reading the literature of Holocaust deniers and purposefully mirroring their methodologies and arguments. Rather, we contend that such historical denial is a form of ideologically driven pseudohistory, which adopts techniques designed to undermine historical claims that do not fit with present ideologies and beliefs.[69]

Thus there is solidarity between Holocaust historians and Chinese scholars, partially because both are fellow victims of past atrocities, but equally because of shared struggles to promote truth and remembering in the face of active and pernicious denial movements. Some Holocaust historians see a powerful antagonist in the Japanese establishment, one which they problematize and compare with post-War Germany and the international network of Holocaust deniers. In many respects, the problems of Japanese atrocity denial are real. The Japanese political, cultural, and intellectual establishment has certainly downplayed and even denied many of the atrocities committed by Japanese Imperial forces during their occupation of China.

Packaging the 'Chinese Holocaust'

While forgetfulness and denialism are real, there are several key problems with representing the Rape of Nanking as a 'Chinese Holocaust' – problems which in some ways minimize atrocities and dehumanize the victims.

- First, Japan is stigmatized for its denial, while China's rather inconstant memory is generally excused or elided.
- Second, many of the direct comparisons between Nanking and the Holocaust, or Nanking and Auschwitz, do not measure up.
- Third, there is a false dichotomization of Germany and Japan as 'good' and 'bad' genocidal nations, blindly using a 'rehabilitated' Germany as a model for how Japan could and should behave.
- Fourth, there is a static view of the Jewish Holocaust and Holocaust scholarship presented in many Chinese Holocaust publications. The reality of the Holocaust as an emergent symbol of suffering is largely ignored in Chinese accounts.
- Fifth, there is an over-emphasis on Japanese perpetrators and Western bystanders, particularly in Chang's work, which diminishes the identities and importance of the victims themselves.

Japanese versus Chinese

The ideal of a 'double rape' *à la* Chang has entered the mainstream. In Chang's work, the Japanese become a cohesive other – they are the antagonists – deniers actively deny, while the public participates by actively forgetting. This dichotomy between suffering Chinese and denying Japanese can obscure two factors: first, those Japanese who have not denied the at-times heated debate in Japan over wartime memory, and second, the role of the Chinese Communist government itself in promoting forgetfulness. For the most part, Chang's analysis of Japanese denial is correct – there has been little on Nanking and other atrocities in Japanese history books. She briefly but ably documents some of the controversy in Japan about commemoration and denial, covering the textbook controversy and the struggles of historians Saburo Ienaga, Honda Katsuichi, and others.[70]

However, the other side of the coin privileges the Chinese, making them victims only. Comparing Jews and Chinese offers the implicit suggestion that the Chinese have been as active and as diligent in promoting their own tragedy, and that the Japanese bear the lion's share of the blame for the West's lack of knowledge. While Japanese historians and officials have denied Nanking in their own country, neither Taiwan nor the People's Republic of China have done a stellar job of keeping the memory alive. Chang makes cursory reference to a 'curtain of silence' and 'historical neglect' in the cases of the People's Republic and the United States, but offers no detailed analysis, preferring to save her condemnation for the Japanese.[71]

However, Buruma suggests convincingly that China's Communist government too had a part to play in suppressing the symbolic and emotive value of the Nanking massacres. After all, Buruma reminds us, Nanking was the Nationalist capital – a political force actively opposed to Mao's Communists. The fact that there was little if any official Chinese commemoration of the past until 1982 must also be factored into the equation, at least a mitigating factor in making Nanking's 'holocaust' a 'forgotten' one.[72] Maier's analysis is similar, but he cites the 'pride and determined self-reliance of the government in Beijing' as a more likely cause. China's 'self esteem' refused to allow it to admit failings or ask for foreign aid or pity in the case of disasters, man-made or natural.[73]

Eykholt, by contrast, traces talk of Nanking increasing during periods of diplomatic hostility between China and Japan, while ebbing during periods of strong economic cooperation – a trend also noted by Shambaugh.[74] Whether or not one adheres to this interpretation, it is clear that the PRC did not actively and consistently promote the massacre as a key determining factor in Chinese identity, nor did they push the issue too far if it might affect trade and economic relations between the two countries.

It was only in the 1980s that Nanking was officially commemorated. In Jiangdongmen, a long, low building known as the Memorial Hall of the Victims in the Nanjing Massacre was built in 1985 to house some excavated bodies. This hall, according to its website, is built atop just one of many '*wan ren keng*' (pits of ten thousand corpses) found in many of the areas occupied by the Japanese.[75] While large in size, the Nanking Massacre Museum was not a particularly impressive site. Made of concrete and surrounded by a rock garden, it features rocks inscribed with names of locations where people were massacred. Long, glassed-in sandboxes display the skulls and bones of a portion of Nanking's victims.[76]

Many have noted the half-hearted nature of Chinese commemoration, with the overarching message to 'move beyond the Massacre and hold out a hand of friendship to Japan in the name of China's development'. This is exemplified by a 'homily on brotherly love and international cooperation, specifically between China and Japan'.[77] Visiting Nanking soon after the Tiananmen Square massacres in 1989, Buruma noted with distaste the 'clichéd language of self-righteousness' exhibited by the Chinese authorities, so soon after they had cavalierly mown their own people down with such impunity.[78] In understanding the recent interest in Nanking, Schwarcz couples this with the 'enforced amnesia about 1989' that lingers still in China today. She argues that interest in Nanking only reached the forefront when the CCP chose to deflect criticism away from itself and onto a more historical enemy.[79]

The Memorial has improved somewhat since Buruma's reflections. It was renovated in 1995, and extensions were added to the Museum. Buildings are fashioned of black and white granite blocks. The new exhibition hall is better organized, and displays a large numbers of photographs and artifacts. The Memorial is now billed by its organizers as a 'national demonstrative educational base for patriotism', in addition to functioning as a symbol for peace.[80] A further expansion of the Memorial Hall began in December 2005, to be completed by 2007. The new premises includes a square large enough to accommodate 30,000 people.[81] These changes are of recent vintage. Memorial services only began in 1994, and take place annually on December 13. A bronze statue of John Rabe and an exhibition of his documents were both made part of the memorial in 1997.[82] Still, the pressure for commemoration and reparations has come primarily from Diaspora activists and individual citizens. The Chinese government has been quiet, even repressive. When Chinese university lecturer Tong Zeng gathered signatures to petition the government to push for reparations, he was stripped of his position.[83]

Nanking versus Auschwitz

While the term 'Holocaust' seems to be frequently used by museums and educational programs, more direct comparisons are often made, again to highlight the tragedy of Nanking's forgotten nature. Chang's introduction features a comparative dimension. Nanking is quantitatively worse than the sacking of Carthage, the Christian armies during the Spanish Inquisition, and some of the horrors inflicted by Timur Lenk. More people died at Nanking in 1937 than British, French, Belgian, and Dutch civilians during World War II. Arial attacks on Dresden and Tokyo likewise produced fewer casualties. Hitler and Stalin killed more 'it is certainly true', but their crimes were 'brought about over some few years', while Nanking has the demerit of being 'concentrated within a few weeks'.[84] While she does offer tacit comparisons between the Nanking massacres and the Holocaust, Chang has asserted that 'her book is not about winning popularity votes over the Jewish atrocities at the hands of the Nazis'.[85] Nevertheless, her view of Nanking being somehow worse because of its 'concentrated' killings belies this claim somewhat. Her claims are nevertheless more nuanced when compared to other Alliance members, like Hung, who argues simply that 'the Chinese Holocaust created by the Japanese during the war is so unprecedented in history that it was more horrific and devastating than the Jewish Holocaust'.[86]

Reactions against Chang's reference to a Holocaust were swift. Jacob Heilbrunn, associate editor of *The New Republic*, found Chang's use of the term 'unfortunate', 'since the massacre was not – for all its murderous horror – an attempt to wipe out the Chinese as a race'. David Kennedy, in the *Atlantic Monthly*, praised Chang's work but found little evidence of the 'systematic killing of the Holocaust'. If Nanking resulted from 'individual cruelty or the result of a poorly disciplined army run amok', the Holocaust 'entailed a methodical application of all the apparatus of the modern bureaucratic state and all the most advanced technologies of killing to the cold-blooded business of mass murder'.[87] Buruma has equally noted the problems of false equivalences. If the Holocaust was clearly about exterminating every last European Jew, it had no equivalent in Asia, where '[e]ven the most ferocious Japanese ideologue wanted Japan to subjugate China, not kill ever last Chinese man, woman and child'.[88] He blames the Tokyo trials for elevating Nanking in order to create an Asian parallel for the Holocaust, an error in judgment perhaps which has warped our interpretation of the facts.[89]

Chang's own arguments for why she used 'holocaust' were not particularly clear. In an interview in 1996, before her book's release, she was asked why she was using 'holocaust' when there was 'Never this sort of gas-chamber, mechanized attempt to kill all the Chinese as there was to kill all the Jews'. To this she replied:

> Obviously the Japanese could never be able to exterminate all of the Chinese people. There's so many of them. But they wanted to make an example of Nanking, and I would say the method of execution was quite systematic. Of course, it wasn't as systematic as what the Germans did to the Jews. The Japanese used swords and knives. They used machine guns and fire. But the results were horrifying. It wasn't as systematic, it wasn't as 'clean'. What happened in Nanking was actually quite messy.[90]

While the interview cleared up little of the confusion surrounding her use of the term, Chang's primary point was that none of her Jewish friends seemed to have problems with her use of the term.[91] This belief was further borne out when Chang gave two talks at the United States Holocaust Memorial Museum at their invitation, one a public lecture and one for a scholarly audience. At no time was her use of the term 'holocaust' in this context challenged or condemned.[92] Indeed, Chang has received much support from many Jewish Holocaust historians, suggesting that other well-documented tragedies can be commemorated using similar language, if they bear in mind the sensitivities of Jewish survivors.[93] However, some residual fuzziness remains about this issue.

The Jewish Holocaust versus Nanking

The argument that the Chinese Holocaust has been forgotten while the Jewish one has achieved great prominence is misleading. This dichotomization assumes that little if anything has been traditionally known about Nanking, while everyone knows today about the Jewish Final Solution. Yet citing Holocaust scholarship as a model ignores the fact that the Holocaust has achieved such importance only in recent years, and largely as a result of the very hard work of Holocaust historians and activists. It is important to view Nanking scholarship teleologically, to note that its importance will grow as time progresses, as has the Holocaust.

The Holocaust, after all, has not always been so prominent. Its pre-eminence was not instant, and evolved over time. Novick's argument that '"the Holocaust", as we speak of it today, was largely a retrospective construction, something which would not have been recognizable to most people at the time', provides hope for Chinese 'holocaust' scholarship in the future.[94] During her lectures at the USHMM, Chang found support in the audience for her work – even the belief among some that, while representations and scholarly study of the 'Pacific Holocaust' were some twenty-five years behind that of the Jewish Holocaust, a 'similar kind of flowering of literature on the Sino-Japanese war' would be forthcoming.[95]

Japanese versus Germans

Tied in with issues of remembrance, forgetting, and denial is a contrast of atonement versus unrepentance – the goodness of the Germans who remember, versus the evils of the Japanese who forget. This argument is advanced by various Chinese Diaspora organizations, who often pit a venal, unfeeling Japan against a seemingly good Germany. Chang's work typically juxtaposes and contrasts German with Japanese responses:

> What baffled and saddened me ... was the persistent Japanese refusal to come to terms with its own past. It is not just that Japan has doled out less than 1 percent of the amount that Germany has paid in war reparations to its victims. It is not just that, unlike most Nazis ... many Japanese war criminals continued to occupy powerful positions in industry and government after the war. And it is not just the fact that while Germans have made repeated apologies to their Holocaust victims, the Japanese have enshrined their war criminals in Tokyo – an act that one American wartime victim of the Japanese has labeled politically equivalent to 'erecting a cathedral for Hitler in the middle of Berlin'.[96]

She later argues from the same position in the book's conclusions. Germany has accepted both individual and collective guilt for the horrors of Auschwitz, something Japan has not been willing to do in Nanking.[97] For

Chang, knowing more is not just about advancing Chinese interests, but also helping Japan to grow: 'Japanese culture will not move forward until it too admits not only to the world but to itself how improper were its actions of just half a century ago'. To deny is to have an unbalanced and stunted culture – one which is historically inaccurate and perhaps contains the seeds of future conflicts.[98]

Slave labor is often a key point of comparison. The Chinese Holocaust Museum notes the payments made to Germany's surviving slave-workers by German companies. The 2.3 million survivors (of some twelve million slaves) have received 5.4 billion dollars. By contrast, the Museum advances of the thirty million Chinese slave laborers under the Japanese: 'They suffered far more in the hands of the Japanese than their counterparts in those of the Nazis. Certainly they deserve the same human rights and sympathy as bestowed upon the Nazi slave laborers'.[99] But activists like Tien-Wei Wu have wondered whether it is even possible for 'pagan Confucians like the Japanese war criminals who do not believe in Jesus the Christ' to demonstrate 'true remorse like the Germans did'.[100] For Wu, showing true remorse demonstrates some measure of repentance and transformation, something not evident in Japan. He even sees the possibilities of new conspiracies unless Japan is willing to repent:

> Unlike her wartime ally Germany ... Japan has persistently followed the 'three-nos policy' – no admitting of aggression, no apology, and no compensation. ... Without true repentance, the Japanese government can only continue to distort historical facts, deny truth and justice, and cheat the young, all of which naturally will redound to the revival of militarism and cherish the spirit of revanche. How could we know that the Japanese are not racking their brains and working hard for developing some new weapons more dreadful than the plague germs of Unit 731, which might be used to subjugate China and the United States![101]

This fear of hard-core militarists in Japan plotting World War III is not uncommon. As Zhang writes in his edited collection of missionary accounts of the Nanking massacre, while most Japanese are against the revival of militarism, a small 'very active minority' have 'never given up their wishful thinking of reviving an old dream of ruling the roost of Asia and contending for hegemony of the world'. This is why Nanking must not be forgotten, lest its lessons too be forgotten in the present. For Zhang, a very real danger thus exists which memory serves to combat.[102]

The Alliance's own site has used Germany as the benchmark for comparing treatment of Jews with Japan's treatment of the Chinese. On eleven separate issues, the Germans emerge as superior. This includes a formal apology, restitution, opening of wartime archives, admission of atrocities, discussion of actual wartime activities in school texts and educational materials, the identification and punishment of war criminals, restitution for slave labor, and return of looted property. Issues such as a tribute to the victims are particularly controversial – Germany has built a National Holocaust Memorial Museum in Berlin, while Japan's War Memorial Museum 'contains not a single trace of its wartime brutality in occupied or colonized nations'. While German war criminals have either been punished or rejected by society (for the most part), the Alliance notes how war criminals are 'openly worshipped' in shrines 'by government high officials and society at large. Most War Criminal[s] became key government, business, and academic leaders'.[103]

While Japan undeniably committed atrocities, Germany as a positive example is troubling, running counter to much of German post-war history. Maier's work reveals that the process of acknowledgement and justice in post-War Germany was hardly smooth. Comparisons between 'forthright Germans and prevaricating Japanese is to obscure much of the postwar history of both countries'. The Japanese debate over memory has been more vigorous than commonly assumed. Both countries have had an 'uneven and turbulent' evolution of their respective collective memories.[104] Such comparisons, while highlighting obvious Japanese hypocrisy, seem to clear Germany of any wrongdoing, which becomes a model of what a 'good' genocidal nation should do to shoulder its full share of responsibilities. Good genocidal nations must admit their mistakes, compensate their victims, feel guilty, and commemorate the evil they have committed.

Certainly, Japanese denial has been more pronounced than that of Germany. Germany has paid compensation to its surviving victims, and has publicly acknowledged its atrocities. Goldstone, as discussed in Chapter 3, notes the 'very substantial political and material acknowledgement which victims of the Holocaust have received'.[105] However, Germany's track record has not been as stellar as Chinese Diaspora publications allege.

When West Germany did compensate victims and recognize its past aggression, much of this has had to do with left-wing politics in the FRG. When right-wing historians tried to normalize the Holocaust during the *Historikerstreit*, the Marxist Left 'provided an important base for those intellectuals trying to control their countries' authoritarian histories ...'. The Left in Japan, however, was much weaker. Their attempts to offer critiques of wartime history soon after the War were shot down in the 1950s.[106] Thus while Germany has been 'better' than Japan, the reasons behind it, including popular support in the 1950s and 1960s, remain suspect. One must be careful about overplaying the German model of a 'good' genocidal aggressor.

Chinese victims versus Jewish victims

A serious problem in repackaging the rape of Nanking as a 'holocaust' is that by emphasizing the forgotten aspects of the genocide, by playing up the Chinese–Jewish comparisons, the victims of Nanking lose their stories and their identity. Chang's work focuses almost entirely on the Japanese aggressors and the Western bystanders, with little detail of the victims themselves. Some have argued that Nanking resonates so strongly because of the presence of Western observers, many of whom helped create the International Safety Zone.[107] As such, Nanking resonates partially because of its horrors but also because it could be observed by non-Chinese and non-Japanese witnesses.

Chang's account features German businessman and Nazi party member John Rabe, 'the living Buddha of Nanking' to many, and for Chang 'the Oskar Schindler of China'. His work in the Nanking Safety Zone makes him '[p]erhaps the most fascinating character to emerge from the history of the Rape of Nanking'. Rabe was a true believer in Nazism, but largely the *socialist* aspects of its program, according to Chang and Rabe's granddaughter. He worked for Siemens in China, and was a pillar of the Nanking German community. His rather naïve optimism about the good of Nazism even prompted him to pen a note to the Führer in November 1937, demanding help. He also petitioned the Japanese for mercy on behalf of the Chinese, and went out himself to scare off would-be rapists and murderers, sheltering victims and taking them to the safety zone.[108] As a result of his work, his tombstone was moved from Berlin to the Nanking memorial in 1987.[109] Other Westerners included surgeon Robert Wilson, Minnie Vautrin, missionary James McCallum, and other members of the International Committee for the Nanking Safety Zone. In total, there were fifteen members of the Committee who managed between them to save an impressive 250,000 people. Chang features character sketches and short biographies of many of these people.[110] The horrors of Nanking are seen largely through their eyes, not those of the victims themselves.

Who are the victims? Chang begins with a discussion of the Japanese, complete with interviews and profiles of some of the perpetrators, including Matsui Iwane, the Commander of Japan's Central China Expeditionary Force during the massacre. A cavalry photograph of Iwane inspecting troops can be found in the middle of the book. By Chapter 3, she offers details of Chinese Nationalist leaders and their decision to abandon the city. Chapter 5 focuses on Western bystanders and helpers. Even Chapter 9, on 'The Fate of the Survivors', focuses primarily on Rabe, Vautrin, and Wilson. A Chapter entitled 'What the World Knew' reveals what people knew of events at the time in Japan and in the West. The sinking of the *Panay* became big news around the world, while the smuggling of YMCA representative George Fitch's diaries out of Nanking alerted the world to the full extent of the horrors.[111]

Chang's family survived the War. Although they never witnessed Nanking, the tales of Japanese horror stayed with them throughout their lives, influencing the young Chang to take an interest in Nanking. Yet strangely the victims remain largely anonymous, their stories still untold. This is an odd aspect to the book which places more emphasis on perpetrators and Western bystanders than on victims. The massacre is in some respects still 'forgotten'. In the picture section of the book, perpetrators and bystanders receive captions and biographical notes, with an almost Victorian portrayal of the organizers of the Nanking Safety Zone, complete with oval black-and-white photos. The victims, by contrast, are depicted as rows of heads; blindfolded and bayoneted bodies; naked, raped women; beaten, bruised, and battered corpses; and, lastly, a pile of bones and skulls. We get little sense of the victims' humanity other than their broken and mutilated status.

For a book on Chinese suffering, there is surprisingly little on the actual victims. By the middle of the book, there are some personal stories of Chinese civilians and their suffering. Tang Shunsan, who survived a Japanese killing contest, is discussed, as is the sad case of the Hsai family.[112] The tragic but ultimately heroic tale of Li Xouying, a young eighteen-year-old bride during the siege, is a sadly uncommon example in this book.[113] There are very few personal stories here, although the author writes of interviews she conducted with survivors.[114] Moreover, there is little follow-up. What of the psychological scars left on the survivors after the conflict? What happened to those who did survive? Chang writes three paragraphs on the survivors today, their cramped squalid conditions, and their physical injuries.[115] Yet we have little insight.

For those studying the Holocaust, the victims of Nazi horror take center stage – certainly far more so than perpetrators or observers. Their humanness makes the tragedy both more accessible and more horrible. Memoirs such as *The Diary of Anne Frank* humanize the victims and make suffering real. An ability to understand and relate to the victims is crucial in keeping their memory alive. The paucity of survivor testimony is a serious problem of Chang's narrative. A further problem of an over-reliance on Rabe and other Westerners should be noted. As Novick has argued of *Schindler's List*, a common Jewish complaint was that it 'distorted the lesson and meaning of the Holocaust by focusing on a Christian rescuer'.[116] An over-reliance on Schindler gave the Holocaust a happy ending, thanks to a kindly German, casting Jews in a subordinate position. Novick's criticism of Schindler rings true for Chang's depictions of Rabe, who gains star billing while the identities of the victims are reduced.

In fairness to Chang, she discovered Rabe's diaries and made them public to the world, after convincing Rabe's granddaughter to release them.[117] However, marketing Rabe as 'the Oscar Schindler of China' is problematic. It relies on comparisons between Rabe as revealed through his memoirs, and the largely fictional Schindler as presented in *Schindler's List*. Henry Huttenbach contrasts the 'artificial "Schindler,"' with the '*actual* Schindler of the Final Solution' – two very different people, since of the real Schindler '*very* little of substance is known. So little in fact, that anything definitive said about this shadow Schindler of yesteryear is, at best, conjecture ... a paradise for a fertile imagination'. Huttenbach points out, and rightly, that we must be careful of allowing 'pure entertainment' to teach us moral and ethical lessons – 'trouble begins, when the *false* images are taken at face value'.[118] Thus we must be careful about making comparisons between reality and entertainment – between actual events and packaging.

Japan: defeat and transformation?

Not discussed in Chang but nevertheless pertinent to the discussion of memory and forgetfulness are Japan's own myths of victimization. If the Chinese invoke the Holocaust, so too do the Japanese. The Holocaust can be used by both groups for the same objectives – to tragedize their respective pasts. Japan too has used myths of victimization to re-order its society after 1945. This makes Japanese acknowledgement of any Chinese 'Holocaust' exceedingly difficult.

At one level, myths of victimization concern the numbers of Japanese soldiers and civilians killed during the course of the War. Over two million soldiers and sailors died in the War fighting for Japan, alongside one million civilians. All major cities with the exception of Kyoto were razed – some sixty-six cities in total.[119] As Dower recalls: 'It became commonplace to speak of the war dead themselves – and, indeed, of virtually all ordinary Japanese – as being "victims" and "sacrifices"'.[120] Orr similarly notes a 'mythologizing of war victimhood ... manifested in a tendency to privilege the facts of Japanese victimhood over considerations of what occasioned that victimhood'.[121]

Perhaps a more persuasive form of victimization for those outside Japan is the legacy of Hiroshima and Nagasaki. Atomic devastation has produced what Dower calls a 'victim consciousness' (*higaisha ishiki*) or, for Orr, 'atomic victim exceptionalism'.[122] As Dower describes the instrumental uses of bomb victim mentality: 'Hiroshima and Nagasaki became icons of Japanese suffering ... blotting out recollection of the Japanese victimization of others'.[123] To this, Buruma adds: 'Hiroshima is a symbol of absolute evil, often compared to Auschwitz'. To this end he documents such efforts at joint suffering commemoration as a Hiroshima–Auschwitz Committee in Hiroshima, novels which single out both Japanese and Jews as fellow victims of White racism, as well as a plan in the late 1980s to construct an Auschwitz memorial in a small town near Hiroshima.[124]

The view that Japan was transformed by its victimization would lead to the anti-nuclear 'peace movement' (*heiwa undo*) in the 1950s.[125] The ideal of Japan as a peace-loving society emerges clearly in the Hiroshima monuments, museums, fountains, domes, and statements issued. The Hiroshima Peace Memorial's Genbaku Dome epitomizes the suffering of Hiroshima, but also the striving for peace that has come after it.[126] The Hiroshima Peace Memorial Museum, which has seen over five million visitors since 1955, is designed to promote peace, while advancing Hiroshima's special significance as a martyred city. As the directors of the museum argue: 'Hiroshima's ultimate goal [is] a world of genuine peace free from nuclear weapons'.[127] The websites and declarations are totally free of any soul-searching, any sense of Japanese wartime guilt, repentance, or reconciliation. What is promoted is the victimized nature of the city and its people, the transformative power of suffering and destruction. From this destruction and humiliation emerges a Hiroshima and, by extension, a Japan which symbolizes peace and security for the modern world.[128]

The Peace Memorial becomes all the more interesting when one realizes that Kenzo Tange, the architect who designed the Peace Memorial Park, originally planned it back in 1942 as a grandiose imperial vision: 'the Commemorative Building Project for the Construction of Greater East Asia'. The original memorial zone was to be at the base of Mount Fuji, a grand Shinto memorial. The original plans, while abandoned, reappeared in 1949 in a new form, and the project was completed by 1954.[129] The portrayal of Hiroshima and its people as victim people is nowhere more apparent than in the recent 'Hiroshima National Peace Memorial Hall for the Atomic Bomb Victims', which was opened in 2002.

Not unlike the 'Hall of Remembrance' at the USHMM, the 'Hall for the Atomic Bomb Victims' features its own Hall of Remembrance, an underground cylindrical room with a vaulted ceiling. Perhaps the name is a coincidence – or perhaps not. Hiroshima's Hall is described as 'a space in which to reverently mourn the victims and contemplate peace. The walls of this room display a panorama depicting Hiroshima after the atomic bombing as seen from the Shima Hospital, which stood at the hypocenter. The picture is a mosaic of about 140,000 tiles, the number of victims said to have died due to the bombing by the end of December 1945'.[130] The professed aim of this Hall is to mourn the victims while 'praying for peace' – a not dissimilar aim to that of the Holocaust Memorial Museum's Hall: 'a solemn, simple space designed for public ceremonies and individual reflection. Epitaphs are set onto the limestone walls that encircle an eternal flame'.[131]

The need for Japan to ape the USHMM's use of memory-triggering symbols and monuments is somewhat disturbing, especially when one compares German professions of guilt through the Denkmal and other monuments. This is perhaps less surprising when we're confronted with the writings of such authors as Nanking denier Uno Masami, who wrote a series of popular books in the 1980s enjoining the Japanese to learn from the Jews. In a well-known chapter of *The Day the Dollar Becomes Paper*, Uno advanced that Hiroshima should have been left in ruins, like Auschwitz. Auschwitz allowed the Jews to remind the world of their martyrdom while restoring their vitality. It was the Japanese people's bad fortune to have been duped by the Americans into rebuilding Hiroshima so quickly. This has acted only to reduce Japanese identity and 'racial virility'.[132]

Nevertheless, American 'evil' is not the key determinant in the Hiroshima myth which has developed over the past five decades. The myth is based primarily, Buruma recalls, 'on the image of martyred innocence and visions of the apocalypse'. One is thus confronted with 'normal life – laughing children, young girls singing, house wives cleaning, good men working – then, in an instant, all was turned to ash'. Hiroshima and the Auschwitz become joined together symbolically by their existence outside of time and outside of the war itself. Both have apocalyptic overtones – both come to represent a form of absolute evil.[133] The inherent danger of turning Hiroshima into Auschwitz, and the Japanese into victims only, is that it masks the real atrocities committed during the war. Japan is seemingly absolved of its sins by the martyrdom of Hiroshima's 140,000 victims, with its Hall of Remembrance and mosaics, and so on.

The images continue in Hiroshima art – some of which reflects apocalyptic and Biblical themes. The husband and wife team, Maruki Iri and Toshi, depict the horrors. Araki Takako's ceramic book *Atomic Bomb Bible* features a scorched text in Hebrew – again stressing the links between Japanese and Jews as fellow victims of World War II.[134] Nagasaki bomb victim Takashi Nagai's writings were infused with Christian apocalyptic visions, with the city a 'chosen victim'. Was not Nagasaki, he asked, 'the lamb without blemish, slain as a whole-burnt offering on an altar of sacrifice, atoning for the sins of all the nations during World War II?'.[135] This idea of Japan as a peaceful country now – even one with a moral monopoly – is evident in surveys of the younger generations. Hiroshima and Nagasaki have given Japan the aura of being 'the unique moral nation of peace'.[136]

Conclusions

The Jewish Holocaust has performed an important role in helping Chinese, at least in the Diaspora, to come to terms with the history of Japanese atrocities and Japanese atrocity denial. Many Chinese face problems, however, stemming from the fact that the government of Japan at least tacitly condones 'forgetfulness', although admittedly things have improved since 1997. Nevertheless, the belief that to deny is inherently patriotic has not been refuted on a wholesale basis. The situation is further complicated by Japan's own competing myths of victimization, which have arguably conferred a transformative status on those who suffered from atomic and other forms of bombing, followed by several years of occupation.

What of the comparisons between Japan and Germany? True, Germany was 'better' at reconciling itself with the Holocaust. It has indeed paid compensation to Holocaust survivors. Yet West Germany was hardly ideal in the first decades after 1945, and East Germany had virtually no de-Nazification program, no apology, and no compensation. In Nanking, the Holocaust and its elements helps to 'sell' and package the atrocity, and here we have Nazi-like persecutors, Jewish-like victims, and Schindler-like bystanders. The Holocaust also provides a useful template for educating children and the general public about Nanking and other Japanese atrocities.

Nanking scholarship presents the Holocaust as a useful frame of reference – a window of opportunity for exploring further instances of victimization and atrocity. Thus the creation of Holocaust museums for Nanking and other instances of Chinese victimization are no coincidence; nor are school curriculum for studying about the atrocities. The Holocaust also helps to make sense of denialism. Jewish and other well-meaning scholars have mounted powerful cases against Holocaust denialism for decades, while Japanese atrocity denial continued to be a serious concern. At one level, the invocation of a 'Chinese Holocaust' performs a useful role in marketing and packaging the tragedy for a Western audience. Yet, as I have tried to show, applying these comparisons too widely is itself historical distortion. Ultimately, there is a need for a certain degree of caution and sensitivity in deciding how events are packaged and why.

10 Serbs, Croats, and the dismemberment of Yugoslavia

War and genocide in the twentieth century

> I can see that the situation is far more complicated and more difficult than other problems I have seen, even Cambodia. It is the peculiar three-sided nature of the struggle here that makes it so difficult. Everyone says that most people do not want this to happen. Yet it does. Everybody says it must stop. Yet it doesn't.
>
> (Chief US Negotiation Richard Holbrooke, *To End a War* (1998))[1]

In retrospect, Yugoslavia's meltdown seems sadly typical of the 'new wars' that characterized the 1990s. Yet, unlike Somalia, Chechnya, or Rwanda, this conflict was set in 'Europe's backyard', and was Europe's first example of major ethnic conflict since World War II. The participants were White, affluent, and well educated, reinforcing the sad reality that Europeans could still, in the wrong circumstances, initiate mass murder, while other Europeans pitifully stood by and did little to prevent it.

Contrary to the musings of some journalists, such as Robert Kaplan, the Yugoslav wars were not the result of 'ancient ethnic hatreds' but very much a product of the twentieth century.[2] Of the four main belligerent groups in the war (Serbs, Croats, Bosnian Moslems, and Kosovar Albanians), which lasted from roughly 1990 to 1999, only Serbian perpetrators have been found guilty of committing genocide at the ICTY. In August 2001, Bosnian Serb General Radislav Krstic was found guilty for the killing of some 8,000 men and boys in Srebrenica in 1995.[3] Before his death in March 2006, Former Serbian President Slobodan Milosevic was indicted with sixty-six counts of genocide.[4] Ironically, while Serbs were the perpetrators of genocide in the 1990s, many Serbs were victims of similar crimes in the 1940s at the hands of Croatian fascists. Indeed, the USHMM has featured a special exhibition on the Croatian concentration camp, Jasenovac, and its Serbian, Jewish, and Roma victims. Yet Croats too have their own myths of suffering at the hands of the Communist Partisans in 1945, when retreating collaborators and their families were massacred.

My goal is to provide some essential background to the successor wars in Yugoslavia, which I hope will correct some misperceptions about the

conflict. This will lay the basis for a detailed study of how Serbian ideologues reinterpreted their national history during the war. I scan the twentieth-century history of Yugoslavia, first as a unitary post-World War I
creation, then as a Communist federation after World War II. What follows
is the slow and steady collapse of Yugoslavia during the 1980s, as nationalism arose in Kosovo, Serbia, Slovenia, Croatia, and Bosnia-Herzegovina.

The conflict also provides insight into how collective memory can be
manipulated in order to justify ethnic cleansing, mass rape, and genocide.
National identity, at least in Serbia, remains locked in the past, even a
decade after the conflict's end. For example, the recent Serbian elections saw
the ultranationalist Serbian Radical Party gain the most seats in Parliament.
Under the slogan 'Serbia votes for the past', the public showed their
approval for war criminal and SRP leader Vojislav Seselj, now awaiting trial
at The Hague.[5]

A brief history of the Yugoslav conflict

Milica Bakic-Hayden rightly noted the tendency in the 1990s for Serbs and
Croats to forget decades of peaceful coexistence and cooperation. A history of
ethnic antagonism was played up as the country was dismembered. As she
explains:

> The explanatory slogan 'ancient hatreds' of the South Slavic peoples ...
> is but a rhetorical screen obscuring the modernity of conflict based on
> contested notions of state, nation, national identity, and sovereignty ...
> all Serbs are identified with Chetniks, all Croats with Ustashas and all
> Muslims with Islamic fundamentalists, or fascist collaborators.[6]

Such views were advanced by both sides, who argued that the contemporary
conflict was merely the latest instalment in an ongoing story of genocide and
terror, of which World War II was one of its most violent periods. Michael
Ignatieff, during his travels in the region, described the 'monstrous fable'
cooked up by nationalist leaders, 'according to which their own side appears
as blameless victims, the other side as genocidal killers. All Croats become
Ustashe assassins, all Serbs become Chetnik beasts'.[7]

Historically, the majority of Serbs and Croats had lived under different
empires, although their religious and national identities were relatively fluid
until the nineteenth century. Orthodox Serbs were subject to Ottoman rule
until the nineteenth century, when Serbia achieved its independence in
1878. Catholic Croatia and parts of multi-confessional Bosnia-Herzegovina
were under the rule of Austria-Hungary until the end of World War I. It
was only in 1918 that Serbs, Croats, Slovenes, Bosnian Moslems, and several
other ethnic groups came together for the first time in a common state – the
Kingdom of the Serbs, Croats and Slovenes (renamed Yugoslavia in 1929).[8]

The conflict over what form this state should take began in 1918 and continued into the 1990s. Croats desired a federal arrangement, where they would gain increased autonomy and cultural rights. Serbs saw Yugoslavia ideally as an expanded version of their pre-existing unitary state. This conflict between Serbian centralizers and Croatian sovereignty-seekers led to bitter political struggles in the 1920s and 1930s. While most Croatians supported the moderate autonomy-seeking Croatian Peasants Party, a radical Italian-trained guerrilla movement known as the Ustasha emerged during the violence of this period. The 1920s and 1930s were marked by widespread unrest and political assassinations, including the killing of CPP leader Stjepan Radic and Yugoslav King Aleksander.[9] While there were some attempts to placate Croatia, most Croatians were dissatisfied with what they saw as Serbian domination, while many Serbs saw the Croatians as ungrateful and duplicitous.[10]

On 5 April 1941, Yugoslavia was invaded by Italian and German forces, and split into different spheres of influence.[11] In Serbia, General Milan Nedic formed a quisling 'Government of National Salvation'.[12] The regime was unpopular, and most Serbs divided their loyalty between the fledgling Communist Partisans (whose ranks Croats also joined), and the Serbian Chetniks under General Draza Mihailovic. These were paramilitary bands loyal to the Yugoslav government in exile, and allied with the Western powers.[13]

Much of Croatia and Bosnia-Herzegovina was given over to an Ustasha-controlled *Independent State of Croatia* (or NDH) under the leadership of Ante Pavelic.[14] Many Croats at first saw the NDH as their liberation from over two decades of Serbian control. This initial support soon dampened, as Croatia was forced to cede most of Dalmatia to Italy, and northern Slovenia to Germany.[15] The poorly-trained Ustasha officers and soldiers, and Pavelic's distinct lack of charisma, reduced his exposure among the population. Nevertheless, the lack of credible resistance was also noticeable. Both the CPP and the Catholic Church remained largely passive.[16]

While Croatian writers have downplayed Ustasha crimes, the scale of atrocities was immense. Widespread massacres of Serbs, Jews, Gypsies, and Communists occurred throughout NDH territory.[17] Additionally, the Ustasha founded a series of concentration camps, ranging from smaller ones in Dakovo, Lepoglava, Lobor, and Sisak, to Jasenovac, the largest and best known.[18] Jasenovac was a complex of five camps, which operated from August 1941 to April 1945. Staffed by Croatian political police and Ustasha militiamen, conditions for prisoners were horrible, leading to the deaths of tens of thousands of Serbs and some 20,000 Jews.[19] The numbers of Serbian dead overall, not just as victims of Jasenovac, can never be known for certain. Historians, using a variety of statistics, give a range of between 200,000 and 750,000 deaths. The USHMM gives a figure of between 300,000 and 400,000 victims of Jasenovac alone.[20]

The Chetniks responded with massacres of Croatian and Bosnian-Moslem populations in Bosnia-Herzegovina, making them as hated as the Ustasha.

Chetnik reluctance to engage the Germans, for fear of reprisals, and their violent conflicts with Communist forces eventually lost them Allied favor.[21] While the wartime records of some Serbs and Croats were dubious, there were nevertheless qualitative differences between the Allied-backed Chetnik monarchists and their small-scale massacres, and the Nazi-backed Ustasha with their concentration camps.

The multinational Partisan force began recruiting large numbers of disaffected soldiers and civilians. Partisan ranks swelled as the Italians surrendered in 1943, and membership increased further as Germany began to weaken. Eventually, by the end of 1943, the Partisans gained Allied support and were able to score tangible hits against German and Ustasha targets.[22] By 1944 they had liberated most of the country, without Soviet help. By May 1945, with the end of the war, Tito and the Communist Party of Yugoslavia laid the basis for a new state.[23] The liberation of the country and the creation of the new state also involved bloodshed. The Partisans also carried out massacres, the best known being at Bleiburg (Austria), where retreating Croatian and Slovenian forces and their families were massacred. Bleiburg and later purges of suspected collaborators left bitter scars, fueling Croatian anger against the state and claims of genocide.[24]

Though there is indisputable evidence of Chetnik massacres of Croats and Moslems, there was no concrete proof that the Chetniks aimed to exterminate the entire Croatian nation – nor did they have the means to do so. The only letter to this effect, describing a plan to create an 'ethnically pure Greater Serbia', was a forgery.[25] There is likewise no proof of a Communist desire to commit genocide against Croatians as a people. However, it seems much clearer that the Ustasha aimed to exterminate at least a part of the Serbian nation. According to the Ustasha, one-third of Serbs were to be killed, another third expelled, and a further third converted. This famous equation is traceable to Ustasha Minister Mile Budak, in a speech delivered in June 1942.[26]

The legacies of this 'unresolved genocide' for many Serbs were profound. The lack of adequate discussion during the Communist era led to lingering anger and frustration. It is no surprise, then, that in the 1990s '[r]etaliation for what had been done earlier, and the fear of a renewal of genocide (irrespective of whether this fear was justified or not), were, at the same time, if not the moving force behind the war, then certainly and important element in motivating the masses'.[27] Others too have seen the 1941 'genocide' as an 'important contributory factor' in the uprising of Serbs in Croatia.[28] From a Croatian perspective, the feeling of persecution at the hands of the Partisans at Bleiberg and elsewhere was equally palpable, fueling claims of a 'Croatian holocaust' amongst Croatian Diaspora communities.[29]

The Socialist Federative Republic of Yugoslavia was created in 1945, with Tito in overall control. Both the Chetniks and the Ustasha were demonized in the SFRY, and free and frank discussion of wartime atrocities was impossible. Large numbers of collaborators and dissidents left the country, forming Diaspora organizations like the Serbian Unity Congress and the Croatian Liberation Movement. The Yugoslav state paid lip service to ethnic and national differences. Each major national group was given control over its own republic within the federation (six in total), but party bosses were loyal to Tito rather than their national constituencies. A rigid ethnic key was used in allocating government jobs, despite Serbian numerical dominance in the armed forces and Communist Party.[30] The state was fundamentally an artificial construction, designed to reign in nationalism through a series of overarching myths of 'Brotherhood and Unity'.

In coming to terms with the Communist period, there was certainly much to criticize. Tito's dictatorial rule relied on a corrupt base of power, and a personality cult of messianic proportions. The country was burdened by over-centralization, massive foreign debt, and a powerful secret police force which cracked down on internal dissent. Attempts to gain increased linguistic, cultural, and political autonomy were suppressed.[31]

These detractions aside, Yugoslavia was arguably the freest country in Eastern Europe, the most open to the West, and certainly one of the richest and most cosmopolitan in the Balkans. While most of the wealth was concentrated in Slovenia and Croatia, Yugoslavia's economy did come close to rivaling that of Czechoslovakia and the German Democratic Republic. Additionally, Tito was genuinely popular, despite his egomania and corruption (or perhaps in part because of it).

Yugoslavia was a founder of the Non-Aligned Movement, and played an important geopolitical role as a symbolic bridge between East and West, Capitalism and Communism. Yet the country entered a conservative phase in the 1970s. In 1974, Tito created a highly decentralized political structure to succeed him after his death. The 1974 Constitution created a presidium, where each republic, autonomous region, and even the Yugoslav People's Army (JNA) had a vote. The formerly Serbian-controlled provinces of Kosovo and Vojvodina were given autonomous status, and Yugoslavia was effectively made into the world's most decentralized federation.[32]

Nationalism in Yugoslavia

For most of the lifetime of the SFRY, Serbian nationalism was subordinate to Communism, and did not become an important factor until Tito's death in 1980. The Serbian capital Belgrade was the capital of Yugoslavia, and a high percentage of Serbs supported Tito's Communist system, even if they were dissatisfied with particular aspects of it. The crucial break came with Tito's death. The lack of any strong, articulate, non-nationalistic leader with Tito's charisma, capable of exercising the same level of control, created a power vacuum at the federal center. This vacuum would soon be filled by aspiring nationalists at the republic level.[33]

Albanians, not Serbs, were the first to articulate nationalist demands after 1980. Kosovar Albanian students demonstrated at Pristina University for autonomy and republic status, provoking riots.[34] The Serbian government clamped down the following year with a state of emergency.[35] In reaction to Albanian secessionism, amid fears of 'Greater Albania', the Serbian Academy of Sciences and Arts drew up a *Memorandum* in 1986 – a long list of Serbian grievances against their treatment within the Federation. In an unprecedented move, this Communist organization decried the 'genocide' of Serbs in Kosovo, and articulated the need for Serbs throughout Yugoslavia to assert themselves collectively. The 1974 Constitution was blamed for the loss of Serbian power and prestige. The *Memorandum*'s architects would eventually play a prominent role in spurring Serbian nationalism, and the dismemberment of the Federation.

Attempts by Serbian Party President Ivan Stambolic to deal with Kosovo's civil unrest through constitutional revision and consensus proved ineffective.[36] It was into this breach that an unlikely candidate asserted himself. Slobodan Milosevic, a former Belgrade banker and protégé of Stambolic, was in all respects a colorless Communist bureaucrat and a most unlikely nationalist. A clever opportunist, Milosevic allied himself with emerging nationalist figures at SANU, such as the novelist Dobrica Cosic. He embraced nationalism and used it to propel himself to power.[37] Milosevic opened the Pandora's box that forever changed the nature of Serbian and, by extension, Yugoslav politics. Milosevic soon ousted Stambolic, and took power in December 1987. He appealed to an emerging sense of Serbian unity, and claimed to speak for Serbs throughout Yugoslavia – a tacit warning to other republican leaders that their boundaries would provide little protection from Serbian intervention. He advocated a strengthening of the Orthodox Church and a privileging of Serbian cultural and social institutions.[38]

Another important aspect of this nationalist platform was the re-Serbianization of Kosovo and Vojvodina, which Milosevic accomplished by September 1990.[39] The lesson of Kosovo was obvious – the system was no longer strong enough or was unwilling to restrain belligerent republics, and it was unable to protect basic human and constitutional rights.[40] Milosevic's intimidation of other republics soon led to secessionist movements around the country. In December 1990, Slovenia declared its independence after holding a referendum. This later resulted in a short war, in June 1991, between Slovenian and the Yugoslav People's Army (JNA), which eventually led to Slovenian independence by 1992.[41]

War in Croatia

In Croatia, former general and historian Franjo Tudjman emerged as the head of the Croatian Democratic Movement (HDZ), which by 1990 had become the primary nationalist force in the republic, winning the elections in April.[42] Tudjman's party, while appearing Western and progressive, began discriminating against the republic's Serbian population.[43] Largely funded by Diaspora Croatians, the HDZ was anti-Communist and unsympathetic to Serbian demands. The 1990 Constitution conspicuously omitted Serbs as a constituent nation, and, on a practical level, jobs, property rights, and even residence status depended on having Croatian citizenship, which was not an automatic right for non-Croats.[44]

By 1990, Tudjman was trying to pull Croatia out of the Yugoslav Federation. Milosevic had not actively opposed Slovenian secession, on the grounds that there was no Serbian minority there in need of his 'protection'.[45] Croatia, however, contained a sizable Serbian minority – 13 percent of the population.[46] Moreover, certain regions of Croatia – Eastern Slavonia and the Krajina – were seen to be historically Serbian. Milosevic's legitimacy was based on uniting Serbian populations and historic lands, and this made confrontation with Croatia inevitable, even if he had privately assured Tudjman and other Croatian leaders that he had no interest in war.[47]

Tudjman's apparent discrimination against Serbs prompted the development of two Serbian nationalist parties within Croatia. A Serbian Democratic Party was formed in 1990.[48] A more militant party, the Democratic Union of Knin, was also founded in 1990. Leader Milan Babic soon began stockpiling weapons to create an 'Association of Serb Municipalities' – a nascent Serbian assembly which formed the nucleus of the eventual Republic of Srpska Krajina.[49] In 1990, with Serbia's backing, the Krajina Serbs declared a 'state of war' against the Croatian state. Open fighting broke out in April, and a referendum on Serbian independence was called for 17 April, which resulted in a call for Serbian secession.[50] Between February and June 1991, rebellion escalated. Serbian paramilitary units, such as Arkan's 'Tigers' and Vojislav Seselj's 'White Eagles', entered Croatia, both trained and funded by the Serbian Ministry of the Interior. The situation became more dramatic as JNA forces intervened, under the pretext of protecting Serbian minority rights.[51]

By September 1991, Serbian forces had leveled Vukovar and other eastern towns, and controlled almost one-third of Croatian territory; by October they had pushed southward to Dubrovnik, which they shelled with abandon.[52] Vatican and German recognition of Slovenia and Croatia by 1992 made the conflict an international one, as Serbs held that the independence of Croatia was illegal under international law. By January 1992, a ceasefire was agreed, UN troops created a series of buffer regions, and the fighting moved to Bosnia-Herzegovina. The seven-month campaign had cost some 10,000 lives and resulted in 700,000 displaced persons.[53]

War in Bosnia-Herzegovina

While bitterly fighting over Croatia, both Tudjman and Milosevic also dreamed of creating expanded national homelands. Both had their sights on parts of Bosnia-Herzegovina. Meeting together in one of Tito's former hunting lodges, Milosevic and Tudjman conspired together to dismember this multi-national republic.[54] While Serbs comprised some 31.1 percent of the population and the Croats some 17.3 percent, the Moslems (43.7 percent) were loyal to neither side.[55] Further problems with dismembering Bosnia concerned the paucity of homogenous enclaves. According to the 1991 census, Serbs could be found in 94.5 percent of the republic's territory, Moslems in 94 percent, and Croats in 70 percent.[56] Into this ethnic mosaic some 90,000–100,000 Serbian forces, including JNA units and irregulars, were moved down from Croatia after the January ceasefire, in preparation for the next phase of conflict. They surrounded the major population centers – Sarajevo, Mostar, Tuzla, and Bihac.[57] Clearly, any carve-up would be messy and dangerous.

While Alija Izetbegovic's (primarily Moslem) Party of Democratic Action (SDA) publicly favored the preservation of a tolerant and unitary Bosnia, Serbian and Croatian leaders were more hostile to the idea.[58] The Serbian Democratic Party (SDS) was founded two months after the SDA, led by poet and psychiatrist Radovan Karadzic. A Bosnian branch of the Croatian HDZ was formed under Stjepan Kljuic. This party would initially support the Bosnian government (due to Croatian numerical weakness within the republic), then undermine it.[59] Events in 1991 were to prove crucial to later developments. By April, autonomous Serbs established a regional Bosanska Krajina parliament at Banja Luka. By July, the SDS stormed out of the Bosnian Parliament, reacting sharply to Izetbegovic's call for a referendum on the future status of Bosnia-Herzegovina. After the referendum in August signaled Moslem and Croatian support for independence, Bosnian Serbs created four autonomous units which sprung up in the republic. Bosnian Serbs held their own referendum in November, which resulted in near-unanimous support for separation from Bosnia-Herzegovina and union with the SFRY.[60]

At the same time, the Croatian side was also working towards their autonomy. Only one day after the Bosnian Serb referendum, the Croats established a *Posavina* community of eight units, forming an autonomous area in northern Bosnia. They also formed Herceg-Bosna (with eighteen units) in western Herzegovina. In retaliation, the SDS in December announced the creation of the Serbian Republic of Bosnia-Herzegovina. In the same month, the Croats founded the Republic of Herceg-Bosna.[61] Thus by early 1992 both Serbian and Croatian leaders had created autonomous ethnic regions, and laid the ground for the bloody dismemberment of the republic.

A variety of paramilitary organizations began operating in the region, such as the Tigers and White Eagles (Serbian), and Autumn Rain and the Croatian Defence Forces-HOS (Croatian). Bosnian Serbs also formed a separate army, led by General Ratko Mladic and closely tied to the SDS. Fighting began in 1992 and quickly escalated into bloody fratricidal ethnic war; 'ethnic cleansing' for the first time entered the Western vocabulary as villages and towns were cleared of their 'enemy' populations.[62]

Cultural destruction played an important role in the campaign to destroy any traces of enemy history – some 1,400 churches and mosques were destroyed during the first years of the war. As Michael Sells noted:

> In many cases the mosques have been ploughed over and turned into parking lots or parks; every evidence of their existence has been effaced. Graveyards, birth records, work records, and other traces of the Bosnian Muslim people have been eradicated.[63]

At another level, organized rape was also common on the Serbian side, with rape camps established in many conflict zones. These were designed not only for perverse sexual gratification, but also to humiliate 'enemy' women, making them (in the eyes of their sometimes patriarchal society) unfit for marriage.[64] Sells uses the term 'gynocide' to describe the systematic and widespread rape of Bosnian women,[65] similar in kind to Adam Jones' 'gendercide'.[66]

Both Serbs and Croats also ran 'detention centers' and 'collection camps' where prisoners were housed, fed little to no food, frequently beaten and terrorized, sometimes sexually violated, and often killed. While one should note clearly that the majority of camps were Serb controlled (thirteen major camps), the Croats maintained four main camps as well. These, however, were only the largest. The International Red Cross, by 1994, documented a total of fifty-one camps run by the two sides, many small and impromptu – located in camp grounds, schools, even movie theaters.[67] Tudjman publicly admitted to the existence of Croatian 'collection centers', which housed, by 1993, an estimated 20,000 inmates in the territory of Herceg-Bosna.[68] While the camps were horrific, comparisons with the Holocaust in the Western media were exaggerated. The 10,000 innocents who died in these camps attest to the horrors they endured at the hands of the Serbs (primarily) and Croats, but the camps were designed to injure and humiliate perceived enemies, not to exterminate them.[69]

Serbian forces committed widescale atrocities during the conflict. They continuously shelled Sarajevo from April 1992 to 1995. Serbian shelling and sniper activity led to some 10,000 deaths, including approximately 1,500 children; 60 percent of Sarajevo's buildings were destroyed or severely damaged, resulting in $4 billion of destruction.[70] Wanton destruction like the Markdale Market bombing in August 1995 signaled the blatant disregard Serbian forces had for civilian life; thirty-eight Sarajevans were killed in a crowded marketplace, provoking again more international outrage and a concomitant sense of helplessness.[71]

The Serbs also committed genocide in Srebrenica, paradoxically in one of six UN safe havens created under a Security Council mandate in 1993. This was not the first time Serbs had deliberately attacked UN safe areas. In April 1994 Gorazde was shelled, and Muslim homes were burned while the British commanding officer did nothing.[72] General Mladic's goal was to ethnically cleanse the entire eastern portion of Bosnia, making it a Serbian preserve. In July 1995, Serbian forces launched a final attack on Srebrenica. After forcibly deporting 23,000 Moslem women and children between July 6 and 11, Mladic's forces massacred some 8,000 men and boys. Dutch peace-keepers were also taken hostage. Zepa, another putative safe haven, was sub-jected to ethnic cleansing a week later. Ironically, genocide helped Bosnian Serbs to accomplish their geostrategic goals. While the region was supposed to become Moslem-controlled under the US-brokered Dayton Peace Accords, both Srebrenica and Zepa became part of the Bosnian Serb Repub-lic after their Moslem populations were either forced out or killed.[73]

Srebrenica and the Markdale bombing spelled the end of Western com-placency. After sixteen months of failing to get Bosnian-Serb leaders to negotiate a peace agreement to end the conflict, America launched *Operation Deliberate Force* on August 30 – the largest military action in NATO's history. Bosnian Serb positions around Sarajevo were pounded by US planes, coupled with French and British artillery from Rapid Reaction Forces oper-ating in Bosnia.[74] Within hours, Milosevic secured the signatures of all the relevant high-ranking Serbian and Bosnian-Serb leaders to a document cre-ating a joint delegation to participate in negotiations.[75]

The Dayton Peace Accord was signed in November 1995, effectively dividing Bosnia-Herzegovina into a Serbian Republic and a Croato-Moslem Federation. The Accord gave Serbs much of the land they had cleansed by force, reinforcing the view that while democracy was a goal of the Accord, ethnic separation was a reality.[76] The legacies of ethnic cleansing, however, still remain; 60 percent of Bosnia's inhabitants were forced from their homes, and more than 1.3 million people (some 30 percent of the popu-lation) were dispersed to sixty-three countries.[77] This was in addition to a death toll of 280,000 at the war's end.[78] Croatia also achieved a measure of stability following the Dayton Accord. In 1995 Milosevic effectively aban-doned the Bosnian Serbs, standing back as Croatian forces re-took control of Croatian Serb strongholds.[79] In late April 1995 the Croatian Army launched an attack on western Slavonia, and within thirty-six hours managed to take back the region.[80] In August, the Croatian Army took control of the Krajina in just eighty-four hours.[81]

The Kosovo conflict and NATO intervention

While there were few real cultural and linguistic differences between Bosnian Serbs, Croats, and Moslems, Serbs and Albanians spoke different languages and were of different (and historically antagonistic) ethnic groups. While Milosevic happily sold out the Bosnian Serbs during Dayton, he was not prepared to give up Kosovo, which was seen historically to be Serbian – a topic I deal with in depth in the next chapter. Additionally, the reaction against Kosovar nationalism in the mid-1980s was crucial to Milosevic's rise to power. Kosovo made his reputation, and its loss would be his undoing.

Serbia was by the late 1990s awash with refugees from Croatia and Bosnia, and possessed an economy characterized by mismanagement, widespread corruption, and a flourishing black market.

In 1998, an asymmetrical civil war was taking place in Kosovo, pitting a ragtag but determined Kosovo Liberation Army (created in 1996) against units of the Yugoslav armed forces, loosely allied with Serbian paramilitary groups. In 1998 the conflict produced some 300,000 refugees and hundreds of dead, but hopes were raised when a ceasefire agreement was signed in October, calling for the reduction of Yugoslav military and police units in Kosovo and the creation of a 2,000-strong 'Kosovo Verification Mission'. However, by January 1999 fighting had resumed. Serbia was denounced after Serbian paramilitary forces massacred Albanian civilians in the village of Racak on January 15. Two weeks later, on February 6, the European Union, Russia, and the United States launched a series of negotiations at Rambouillet.[82]

The ninety-page Rambouillet Peace Agreement was dismissed by many impartial observers as a provocative document that Milosevic would never sign. Under the agreement, a NATO-appointed Civilian Implementation Mission would have had direct control over Kosovo, including 'the authority to issue binding directives to the Parties on all important matters he saw fit, including appointing and removing officials and curtailing institutions'.[83] Misreading the Bosnian precedent, American officials believed Milosevic would back down if threatened by force. This turned out to be a terrible miscalculation. On March 24 NATO began *Operation Allied Force*, a campaign which lasted seventy-eight days and saw nearly 40,000 aircraft sorties.[84] Unlike Bosnia, Kosovo was too strategically significant for Milosevic to cut loose, and the conflict dragged on for over two months.[85]

If the situation prevailing in Kosovo before *Allied Force* was serious, it would pale next to the full-scale catastrophe that the bombing campaign produced. By mid-April, after only two weeks of bombing, some 350,000 refugees poured out of Kosovo, fleeing south to Macedonia and Albania. By the end of the campaign the refugee total stood at 850,000, with an additional 500,000 people internally displaced within Kosovo.[86] The bombing soon became a backdrop for a program of systematic ethnic cleansing. Serbian forces began rounding up ethnic Albanians from Pristina, Qirez, and other cities.[87] Forced expulsions took place at gunpoint, with Serbian militia groups going door to door. In some instances, heavy weapons such as tanks, artillery, helicopters, and aircraft were used to promote an exodus. During the conflict, over 100,000 homes in 500 villages, towns, and cities were damaged or destroyed, most looted beforehand. Estimates of the death-toll hover around 10,000 Albanian casualties (mostly at Serb hands), along with thousands of soldiers and civilians.[88]

The campaign ended on June 2, when Milosevic finally signed a modified version of the Rambouillet Agreement, later codified as UN Security Council Resolution 1244. Kosovo would legally remain a part of

Yugoslavia, but would be subject to a separate international administration known as the United Nations Mission in Kosovo, or UNMIK.[89] Now Serbs and Roma were subject to Kosovar ethnic-cleansing campaigns in the province. By the end of 1999, the International Red Cross estimated that some 247,000 Serbs and Romani had fled the province. Pristine's Serbian population was reduced from 20,000 to 1,000.[90] By the end of 1999, Yugoslavia had the dubious distinction of supporting the largest refugee population of any country in Europe, while also being among the poorest and most reviled.[91]

The aftermath of war

By the turn of the millennium, the conflict in Yugoslavia neared a definitive conclusion. Croatia began to rebuild, and a divided Bosnia-Herzegovina was politically stable, although its economy was in tatters and has yet to recover. Kosovo – a tense UN protectorate – was the locus of continued violence, yet had little chance of achieving full independence.[92] In December 1999, Croatia's President Tudjman died of stomach cancer, ending his iron grip on the country. A new coalition government under Ivica Racan came to power during the January elections, spelling a temporary end to HDZ rule. In September 2000 Milosevic lost the Serbian presidential elections to Vojislav Kostunica, and he recognized Kostunica as the new president in early October.[93] In the December parliamentary elections, an eighteen-party coalition led by Zoran Djindjic won with almost two-thirds of the vote, making him the new Prime Minister. During this 'prudent revolution', the change in government occurred without bloodshed.[94] Kostunica soon declared that 'the years eaten by locusts', his term for the Milosevic era, was now over.[95] In June 2001, Djindjic handed Milosevic over to the ICTY to stand trial.

Created by the UN Security Council in 1993, the ICTY handed down its first verdict in 1997, convicting Serbian paramilitary leader Dusko Tadic of eleven counts of crimes against humanity.[96] In August 2001, the ICTY found Bosnian Serb General Radislav Krstic guilty of genocide for his role in the Srebrenica massacres.[97] By September 2001, Milosevic was indicted for grave breaches of the Geneva Conventions, crimes against humanity, and sixty-six counts of genocide.[98] As for Kosovo, the UN-supervised Supreme Court in Pristina ruled that while the Serbian regime did commit crimes against humanity and war crimes, 'the exactions committed by Milosevic's regime cannot be qualified as criminal acts of genocide, since their purpose was not the destruction of the Albanian ethnic group … but its forceful departure from Kosovo'.[99] Only in the Bosnian indictment was genocide expressly mentioned.

Milosevic's death in March 2006 allowed him to escape a life in prison and a clear understanding of his role in Serbia's crimes. The frustration of the prosecutors and the international community was palpable. Three hundred witnesses had appeared for the prosecution's case. Milosevic's death, in Chief Prosecutor Carla del Ponte's words, 'deprives the victims of the justice they need and deserve'.[100] However, Milosevic's many victims at least had the chance to accuse their persecutor. Those victimized by Tudjman had little such recourse. The ICTY is set to continue until 2008, with appeals allowed until 2010. Thereafter the ICTY will hand over the remaining cases to domestic courts, which are currently unable to handle even routine matters, let along war crimes trials.[101]

Clearly, there are links between Serbian victimization during World War II and their role as a perpetrator in ethnic cleansing and genocide in the 1990s. Yet Serbs were the clear aggressors in the contemporary conflict. Not only did they commit atrocities as Yugoslavia collapsed; Serbs were also primarily to blame for the collapse of the Federation. Milosevic's brutal strong-arm tactics in the late 1980s demonstrated clearly that if the Federation did stay together, it would be under Serbia's control. While he demanded democracy and referenda for Serbs in Croatia and Bosnia, he denied Kosovar Albanians the right to choose their own government or their own destiny. Milosevic destroyed Tito's illusion of Yugoslavia as a land of brotherhood and unity, murdering the Federation that had overseen forty years of peace in the Balkans.

11 Serbophobia and victimhood

Serbia and the successor wars in Yugoslavia

> The history of Serbian lands ... is full of instances of genocide against the Serbs and of exoduses to which they were exposed. Processes of annihilation of the Serbs in the most diverse and brutal ways have been continuous. Throughout their history they have faced the fiercest forms of genocide and exoduses that have jeopardised their existence, yet they have always been self-defenders of their own existence, spirituality, culture, and democratic convictions.
>
> (SANU, 'Declaration Against the Genocide of the Serbian People')[1]

This chapter addresses a terrible irony. From 1941 to 1944, a part of the Croatian and Bosnian Serb population was targeted with genocidal aggression by the Ustasha regime in Nazi-backed Croatia. Approximately fifty years later, Serbian paramilitary units conducted wide-scale ethnic cleansing, mass rape, and genocide in Bosnia-Herzegovina. Collective memories of past victimization and cynical manipulation by Serbia's leadership provided a moral cloak for some of the bloodiest acts of European state-building since 1945. Using the Holocaust as a lens through which to understand Serbian history and contemporary events proved an extremely useful strategy. It fed into pre-existing myths of victimization and loss, while tapping into a growing public awareness of the Holocaust and its significance. As Americans became Holocaust-conscious during the 1990s, so too did Serbs. Since part of the propaganda war was waged by Diaspora Serbs living in North America, this was hardly surprising.

An educated, relatively affluent people, Serbian ideologues made ready use of the Internet and other modern means of communication. Under the rule of Slobodan Milosevic, most media were actively subordinated to the war effort. Indeed, a dual war took place in the 1990s – a brutal war on the ground, and another equally insidious conflict for control of the hearts and minds of the Serbian people, a war which also targeted Western observers trying to make sense of the conflict.

Many Croatian and Bosnian Serbs arguably suffered from unresolved trauma as a result of their experiences during World War II. Some of that trauma became intergenerational. Five decades of Communist rule did little to help. Memories of past events were largely personal recollections – family stories of individual encounters with the enemy, painful losses of life and property. Of course, an important caveat applies when dealing with this period of history. The Ustasha did not operate in Serbia itself during World War II. Serbia was directly occupied by Germany, as discussed in the previous chapter. As such, Serbian victimization was considerably less 'global' in scope than Chinese and Armenian suffering at the hands of Japanese and Turkish forces.

The situation during the 1990s was qualitatively different. Croatian and Bosnian Serbs were not suffering from renewed genocide. There was no fighting in Serbia proper during the conflict, the exception being Kosovo. Certainly Serbs were subject to discrimination in Croatia, but there was no attempt to systematically kill anyone. Franjo Tudjman's regime did commit crimes against humanity in Bosnia-Herzegovina, but these were not genocidal crimes, and Serbian crimes were worse both in their frequency and severity. In the quest for territorial expansion, claiming to adopt a purely 'defensive' posture served the Milosevic administration extremely well. It helped justify thirteen years of corrupt dictatorial rule and economic impoverishment, and the destruction of decades of peaceful and cooperative life in Tito's Yugoslavia.

Serbians and the Holocaust

In Serbia, the use of Holocaust imagery began in the early 1980s, as Yugoslavia began to disintegrate. Psychiatrist Dusan Kecmanovic was one of the first systematically to analyze the widespread use of a victim complex, highlighting such themes as 'damage' (the historic deprivation of the nation), and 'victim and sacrifice', with Serbia being targeted from all sides, necessitating a vigorous (and pre-emptive) defence of its national interests.[2] In his more recent work, Kecmanovic rightly observes that claims of victimization were exploited to give Serbs 'the moral and material right to reprisal'. Indeed, victimhood could potentially excuse preparations for war, even pre-emptive strikes against a historic enemy, to prevent renewed bloodshed.[3]

Social theorist Ivan Colovic has also documented a deep-rooted sense of victimhood, where Serbs constantly feared their neighbors conspiring with one another to 'wipe them out biologically or destroy them spiritually'. He writes that 'false brothers and neighbours' as well as 'various traitors and degenerates among the Serbian people' made the need for vigilance acute. The Holocaust also formed a part of a Serbian 'mytho-political framework': 'The suffering of the Serbs today ... may be compared only to the persecution and annihilation of the Jews in the Third Reich'.[4] This was similar to Marko Zivkovic's paraphrasing of a Serbian view during the conflict: 'Both Serbs and Jews are the "chosen peoples" – slaughtered, sacrificed, denied expression, yet always righteous, always defending themselves, never attacking'. Zivkovic popularized the term 'Jewish trope' when discussing the seminal influence of the Holocaust on Serbian myth-making.[5]

Suffering and territory

Of interest to Serbian nationalists was the link between the Holocaust and the creation of Israel after 2,000 years of exile. In the literature on Israel and the Holocaust, links between disaster and deliverance are frequently made.[6] For Penkower, Israel was a crucial haven for Jewish Holocaust victims.[7] Similarly, Friedlander has stressed the links between 'catastrophe and redemption'.[8] Yet there are obviously major differences between Serbs and Jews. Even under the Ottoman Empire Serbs had limited autonomy over their own lands, and in 1878 Serbs gained an independent state and their own ruler. Even in Tito's Yugoslavia, Serbia controlled its own republic, and engaged in power-sharing at the federal level. When the Federation collapsed, and largely by Milosevic's own hand, Serbia gained yet more control.

On the surface, then, there seems no reason to invoke such imagery – Serbia already existed. However, Serbian nationalists did not simply crave *a* homeland. The goal of Serbian national movements since the nineteenth century has been to unite all co-nationals under Serbian government control, be they in Kosovo, Croatia, Bosnia-Herzegovina, or elsewhere. While the term 'Greater Serbia' has been much maligned, it was little more than a basic blueprint to unite all Serbs under a common state. For Serbian ideologues, any Serb not living within Serb-controlled territory was part of the Diaspora, and potentially vulnerable to genocide. This attitude was obvious in SANU's 1986 *Memorandum*. Much of this 1986 document dealt with the 'the physical, political and cultural genocide of the Serbian population in Kosovo and Metohije'. It cast doubt on Serbs' safety elsewhere in the Federation and created an impetus for territorial expansion.[9]

Another difference between Israel and Serbia was that the suffering of the Serbs helped determine the size and geography of the homeland, which was never the case for earlier or later Zionists. As Colovic has argued, persecution not only defined the character of the Serbian nation, but also helped to demarcate the nation's boundaries. Unlike Zionist claims, Serbian goals were more fluid and open to the possibilities of expansion into new territory never before part of Serbia. Colovic is perhaps the most evocative of Serbian writers in his analysis of the 'mytho-political' implications of Serbian blood and sacrifice in buttressing claims to land. Serbian blood, he argues:

> flows in a double bloodstream. Through one it is transferred from generation to generation, through the other, with the sacrificial blood of fallen heroes, it nourishes the body of Serbia, the native soil. That is why the places where this blood is spilled – battlefields, execution sites and pits, graveyards and graves – have exceptional symbolic value. They

preserve the germs of national renewal, which implies initial sacrifice and death, and the roots through which the nation is connected to the ancestral soil. Graves are therefore the natural frontiers of Serbia.[10]

Colovic is paraphrasing a key Serbian preoccupation of the 1990s. His work offers a cogent analysis of the cynical games played by propagandists during the war, quite content to wax lyrical about past heroes and mythical battles while Serbian militia forces ravaged women, gunned down families, and destroyed centuries-old houses, mosques, churches, and other public buildings.[11] A typical example of this type of Serbian thinking is evidenced in the work of novelist and politician Vuk Draskovic. For Draskovic, the true borders of Serbia were to be marked in the west by the Jadovno pits, the scenes of historic massacres of Serbs during World War II. These were to be 'pits that must become sacred places', while the eastern border was to be Kosovo, 'sacred places that must not become pits'.[12] While there are marked differences in the ways Serbs and Israelis approach national territory, Serbian ideologues saw the merits of promoting an axiomatic link between suffering and redemption. Suffering in the past and present would legitimate territorial expansion, to bring within the national fold any and all Serbs destined to be victims of renewed genocide. If that genocide could be proven to be like the Holocaust in its proportions and in its sinister aims, the case for preemptive action became stronger.

Serbia and the renewal of nationalism

Traditional victim-centered imagery in Serbia stems from nineteenth-century conceptualizations of the 1389 Battle of Kosovo. In this mythic battle, Serbian forces, led by Prince Lazar, were defeated in Kosovo by Sultan Murad's forces, subjecting Serbs to five centuries of Ottoman rule. In legend, Lazar is approached in a dream by a falcon from Jerusalem, who offers the Serbs a choice: earthly victory over Murad, or a heavenly victory if they allow themselves to be defeated. In legend, Lazar chooses the heavenly victory, and Serbia is thus elevated (after its defeat) to a chosen and especially favored nation. Modern manifestations of the myth stem from the nineteenth century, when linguist Vuk Karadzic transformed Lazar into a Christ-like figure. Enemies like Serbian warrior Vuk Brankovic (who in legend crossed over to the Turkish side) came to symbolize 'Christ killers' who converted from Orthodoxy to Islam.[13] This is an overtly Christian myth, which harkens back to Serbian views of the nation as a bulwark against Islamic expansion. Serbs could be likened to the suffering Christ – Lazar to a sacrificial lamb redeeming his people.

As Serbian nationalism arose following the death of Tito, the Battle of Kosovo was touted as a key moniker of Serbian identity.[14] It took on increasing salience by 1981, when Kosovar Albanians began to agitate for self-determination.[15] Kosovars were accused of ethnic cleansing, mass rape, of prolific breeding to out-birth the Serbs, even genocide. Kosovo's Christian symbolism was updated in the 1990s, and Jewish imagery was grafted onto emerging conceptions of the nation. Holocaust imagery pushed the envelope, allowing Serbian goals to gain wider, more universal appeal.[16] The use of strong Jewish imagery was first in evidence in 1983, when a petition was drawn up by Serbian Orthodox bishops, protesting Serbian persecution in Kosovo. They linked Serbian and Jewish suffering, and drew what later became common parallels between Kosovo and Jerusalem:

> The Jewish people, before the menace of their annihilation and by the miracle of the uninterrupted memory, returned to Jerusalem after 2,000 years of suffering, against all logic of history. In a similar manner, the Serbian people have been fighting their battle at Kosovo since 1389, in order to save the memory of its identity, to preserve the meaning of their existence against all odds.[17]

By 1985, Draskovic wrote his well-known 'Letter to the Writers of Israel', in which he argued that 'Serbs are the thirteenth, lost and the most ill-fated tribe of Israel'.[18] He saw both Serbia and Israel 'liv[ing] in a hellish siege where the sworn goal is to seize and then cover with mosques or Vaticanize the lands of Moses and the people of St. Sava [Serbia's patron saint]'.[19] Still others compared Kosovo to Masada, where approximately 1,000 Jewish Sicarii warriors committed mass suicide after a losing battle with the attacking Romans in AD 70.[20] Zarko Korac of Belgrade University promoted Serbs as a 'heavenly people' because of Kosovo, making it possible for them to 'identify themselves with the Jews. As victims yes, but also with the idea of "sacred soil"'.[21] During at least part of this time, Serbia was engaged in brutally suppressing Kosovar Albanian nationalism.

Few Serbs openly protested Milosevic's heavy-handed approach to Kosovo, which he ran like a military police state. The fact that Serbs had suffered 'genocide' gave him *carte blanche*. The links between an esthetic of persecution and state terror were not ignored by outside observers. Shkelsem Maliqi, in his study of Albanian nationalism, drew out the links between Serbs in Kosovo and the Palestinian problem, noting the militaristic capabilities and actions of each. Maliqi posited that Serbian nationalists and militant Zionists had much in common. Both, as he described, were 'persecuted and historically tragic people' who perceived local Moslem populations as a threat. Both used national mythology to claim 'the right to recolonise "sacred soil"'.[22] As an Albanian Moslem, Maliqi had clear sympathies with both Kosovars and Palestinians, and his denunciation of both Serbs and Israelis in one stroke is an interesting indication of how far he felt such parallels extended.

Croatia and the perils of Serbophobia

Serbian–Jewish connections also became important during the war in Croatia from 1991 to 1995. In 1991, Serbia was reviled internationally as the aggressor, with Croats presenting themselves as defenseless victims. For their stance, Croatia was rewarded with both Vatican and German recognition in 1992, as was Slovenia. During this perceived time of betrayal by the West, the concept of 'Serbophobia' was introduced. The term denoted a historic fear, hatred, and jealousy of Serbs, often likened to anti-Semitism. Dobrica Cosic would claim during the Croatian conflict: 'We Serbs feel today as the Jews did in Hitler's day. ... Today, Serbophobia in Europe is a concept and an attitude with the same ideological motivation and fury as antisemitism had during the Nazi era'.[23] For Milosevic advisor Smilja Avramov, 'The departure point for the genocide of the Jews was anti-Semitism, and of the Serbs, Serbophobia'.[24] Serbian invasion and aggression aside, Serbia seemed to be the irrational and inexplicable object of hatred in the West.

Tied to this, amusingly enough, was 'Slobophobia' – the supposedly Western idea that Milosevic was solely to blame for Serbian aggression. Anti-Milosevic rhetoric in the Western media was promoted as disguised Serbophobia, a means of demonizing Serbia without appearing racist. The only way to combat it was by showing support for the Serbian President and his policies.[25] Cosic also saw Tudjman's regime as an emerging Nazi dictatorship, urging Croatian Serbs to stand and fight:

> We see in Croatia, many aspects of a Nazi resurrection. This state is governed by a totalitarian and chauvinistic regime, which has abolished the elementary civil and national rights of the Serbs by simply erasing them from its Constitution. This provoked a Serbian insurrection in Croatia, those who justly fear a new program of extermination, the same as the one during the Second World War to which they fell victim.[26]

Because of their historical victimization, Cosic had little difficulty advocating a 'defensive war' to scotch Croatian attacks.[27] Other writers urged Croatian Serbs not to surrender any weapons to the Croatian police, since politics had blossomed into 'mass chauvinist hysteria'.[28] Even democracy was dismissed, since, after all, 'Hitler came to power in Germany within the framework of a multi-party mechanism but subsequently became a great dictator, aggressor and criminal'.[29] By 1991, as Serbian paramilitary forces were leveling much of eastern Croatia, Croatian Serbs began to complain of an 'ethnic tax' which they alone had to pay to the government.[30] Croatian Serb authorities followed this by identifying a 'formal brand' devised to separate Serbs from the rest of the population. As one writer reported, each Serb in Croatia was given the number three as the eighth figure of his personal identity number, which became 'nothing else for us than the David's star, our race label'.[31]

Added to this were outright conspiracy theories. Journalist Nikola Marinovic, searching for the Croatian version of the Wannsee Conference, traced the Croatian 'Final Solution' to a small cabal of HDZ leaders and representatives from Slavonia, who hatched a plot in 1991, bent on 'the extermination of Serbs from western Srem and Eastern Slavonija'.[32] Whatever Marinovic's original purpose, his book soon became part of a justification for Serbian military actions in Croatia. Towns and villages near the eastern border with Serbia (where Serbs were purportedly subjected to genocidal treatment) were the first to be overrun by Serbian forces.[33] This included Vukovar, where Marinovic described the 'hair raising savagery' of the manager of the Vukovar Hospital, Vesna Bosanac, who supposedly earned the title 'Vukovar Mengele', after threatening patients with guns, knives, and bombs.[34]

Serbian suffering would help define the boundaries of national territory, while endowing the nation with the moral right to take more territory than it could claim on a historical basis alone. While geographer Jovan Ilic claimed both the Krajina and Eastern Slavonia for Serbia on the basis of their Serbian populations, he also justified Serbian invasion of Dubrovnik and several islands in the Adriatic based on Serbian suffering. Ilic had to admit that 'according to the ethnic principle this area [Dubrovnik] should belong to Croatia'. However, occupying such regions could be justified as 'primarily a therapy for the treatment of ethno-psychic disorders ... primarily among the Croatian population'.[35] For Ilic, Serbs had an 'additional right to self-determination and uniting', because of their exposure to 'genocidal extermination many times'.[36] A mixture of compensation and punishment for past crimes was often held to be at the root of Serbian claims.

Historic Serbophobia

A key element of Croatian Serbophobia was Catholicism, and its putative hatred for Orthodoxy. The entirety of Catholic Croatian history could be encapsulated as a 'continuity of genocide' against the Serbs, something 'which has been carried out throughout history and is being implemented today'.[37] Like anti-Semitism, Serbophobia was said to be ancient and primordial, inspired by the Vatican's hatred of Serbian Orthodoxy. As Avramov asserted during the war:

> For [one] thousand years Croats have been in full political dominance by foreign factors, and have tried through them to achieve their own state.... Rome has planted an idea in the Croatian soul, that their land is 'Bulwark of Christianity' which turned them away from the Orthodox brothers, with the aim to exterminate Serbs on the religious basis.[38]

Seen as nothing more than historical slaves to the Vatican and their expansionist plans, Croatian nationalism and the killing of Serbs were inseparably tied together. 'Croatian national leaders', Avramov asserted, 'had no clear idea of national self-determination, unless it was founded on the genocide over Serbs'.[39]

The crystallization of Serbophobia in most accounts took place after the invasion of Yugoslavia in 1941, with the Ustasha presented as being little different from the Nazis in terms of their methods and morality.[40] Croats were lumped together with German Nazis as genocidal killers, Serbs and Jews as fellow victims of genocide. Avramov referred to a united 'Jewish–Serbian–Capitalist– Democratic front' that 'had to disappear forever from the world ... Jews and Serbs were struck with the same dagger'.[41] For Draskovic too: 'Jewish–Serbian martyrdom was sealed and signed in blood'. Both, after all, were 'exterminated at the same concentration camps, slaughtered at the same bridges, burned alive in the same ovens, thrown together in the same pits'.[42] Damir Mirkovic, writing in the *Journal of Genocide Research*, reflects a similar view, quoting Sava Bosnitch's argument, that 'The genocide, a joint enterprise of the Roman Catholic and Muslim Ustashas, was to Serbs what the Holocaust was to Jews across Europe'.[43]

Archbishop Alojzije Stepinac, head of the Roman Catholic Church in Croatia during the War, was a frequent subject of attack, as a lightning rod for Church collaboration with the Ustasha. For Serbian historians like Milan Bulajic, Stepinac was one of the most enthusiastic Ustasha supporters, 'the spiritual father' of the NDH, as well as a 'fanatical opponent' of the 'Masonic-Jewish state' – the rather strange moniker Bulajic used for Serbia.[44] Much of Bulajic's work consisted in debunking the Croatian myth of Stepinac's philosemitism.[45]

Alongside Stepinac, the Catholic Church was often portrayed as a genocidal collaborator. Historian Dusan Batakovic derided the Church for 'their own brand of religious exclusionism, intolerance, and a militant proselytizing', which formed part of a Church driven policy of extermination.[46] 'A very considerable part of the Croatian political elite', he concluded, 'strongly supported policies of clericalism and racism, marked by mass killings, forced conversions and the deportation of the Serbian Orthodox population as well the slaughter of the Jews and Gypsies'.[47] Other historians similarly described how the Ustasha state was 'soundly and joyously received by the majority of the Croatian people', and how the Catholic Church, and Stepinac in particular, were 'the most loyal [of] Hitler's collaborator[s]'.[48]

Epitomizing Ustasha crimes was Jasenovac, which some have called 'the dark secret of the Holocaust' and 'the suppressed chapter of Holocaust history'.[49] During the Milosevic era, the America-based Serbian Unity Congress would claim Jasenovac as 'the third largest concentration camp of the WW II occupied Europe',[50] while the Serbian Ministry of Information depicted events there as a Serbian 'holocaust'.[51] Bulajic, who served as the Director of the Museum of the Victims of Genocide in Belgrade, was the most vocal promoter of Jasenovac as a specifically Catholic death camp. Jasenovac's commandant, 'Friar Satan', was condemned alongside other priests, such as Friar Zvoniko Brekalo, whose supposed penchant for torturing and liquidating prisoners while engaging in 'orgies and immoral life' with his fellow priests was graphically described, along with the sadism, mass murder, and 'whoring' of other Catholic leaders.[52]

The numbers of Serbs killed at Jasenovac was also a frequent subject of debate, with numbers ranging (on the Serbian side) from 700,000 to two million casualties – way out of proportion to the numbers advanced by more impartial appraisals.[53] Revisionist novels and scholarly works were also designed to maintain or increase the Communist estimate of Serbian deaths.[54] Books and shorter surveys by Serbian academics perpetuated a high number of deaths, some describing a Croatian-led conspiracy after the War to reduce the official number of Serbian dead.[55]

Older studies were re-edited in line with new government priorities. Partisan historian Vladimir Dedijer's thought-provoking account of Jasenovac received a Holocaust-gloss designed primarily to heighten its propaganda value. The original Serbo-Croatian title, *Vatikan i Jasenovac*, had morphed by 1992 into *Jasenovac: The Yugoslav Auschwitz and the Vatican*.[56] In the process, Jasenovac gained some overt comparisons with Auschwitz, and the numbers of Serbian dead grew over three-fold. While Dedijer gives a figure of 200,000 people killed at Jasenovac, primarily Serbs (a figure echoed in Gottfried Niemietz's forward to the first German edition), Belgrade University's Mihailo Markovic, in his preliminary note, gives us a figure of 750,000 Serbian victims, followed by Jews and Gypsies. This was, he avers, to be a '"final solution" for Serbs'.[57] In order to give the book a timely wartime context, Markovic then argues of Tudjman's Croatia:

> The world must not forget that during World War II the fate of Serbs in Croatia was very similar to that of the Jews. With little imagination one can guess how a Jewish minority in Germany would feel if another pro-Nazi, racist government would come to power and begin to make militant anti-semitic moves. Serbian people in Croatia, described by a poet as 'the remnants of a murdered people', deserve a similar understanding.[58]

Presumably, one was meant to 'understand' the necessity of invading and occupying one-third of Croatian territory by the time Markovic's note was penned. Yet the Ustasha did not engage in genocidal acts outside of their own territory. There was no plan, for example, to exterminate all Serbs within the former Yugoslav kingdom, nor were all Serbs to be killed within the NDH itself. Further, unlike Jews, not all Serbs were innocent of wrong-doing. Chetnik bands also carried out atrocities which in turn provoked further Ustasha reprisals and increased Croatian support for Pavelic's regime. This should not detract from the reality of genocide against the Serbs during the 1940s. Nevertheless, each group on the territory it controlled carried out atrocities against perceived enemy civilians.

The Serbian–Jewish Friendship Society

Serbia attempted to create strong links with Jewish communities world-wide, especially Israel. A form of latent anti-Semitism was at work in some of these projects. Since many Serbs perceived that Jews 'controlled the world', it was better to cultivate them as friends than as enemies. History was revised with what Ellen Willis has dubbed 'the myth of the powerful Jew'.[59] Yet when many Jews proved to be unsupportive of Serbian goals, even critical, a backlash ensued towards the end of the conflict.

In 1988, a group of Serbian intellectuals formed the Serbian–Jewish Friendship Society, in the hope of paralleling the plight of Serbs and Jews. The SJFS was headed by Ljubomir Tadic, although its best-known representative was Secretary Klara Mandic, a Jewish dentist who had lost seventy-three members of her family in the Holocaust.[60] The SJFS was affili-ated with the Serbian government, and had its share of 'nationalistic hot-heads' in addition to several 'self-styled "Serbs of Moses faith"', as one reporter discovered at the founding meeting.[61] The Society had the backing of both Slobodan Milosevic and Radovan Karadzic, who composed a poem about Mandic and was even rumored to be her lover.[62]

The primary goal of the SJFS was to strengthen contact between Serbia and Israel – relations which had soured during the Communist era.[63] Activ-ities such as city twinning were popular (with twenty-two twinned cities), where mutual activities, from sporting events to commercial transactions, were encouraged. Mandic brought the mayors of fifteen Serbian cities to Israel during the first Gulf War, while Serbian Crown Prince in exile Alek-sander visited Israel.[64] Mandic was well known for her glowing portrayals of the Serbian people, and her constant invocation of their kindness and toler-ance to Jews: 'You are really one of the rare people of the world which can be counted on the fingers of one hand, a people that simply does not know how to hate'.[65]

By 1992, Mandic and her colleagues embarked on a lecture tour of the United States. The SJFS, together with other groups such as the Serbian Unity Congress and Serbnet, began actively trying to co-opt American Jewish public opinion. The campaign involved touting the Serbs' love of Jews, while demonizing Croats as Ustasha supporters.[66] The SJFS would promote awareness 'of the living historical memory about genocides com-mitted to Serbs and Jews since Medieval Ages till nowadays, especially during World War II…'. Comparisons between suffering Serbs and Jews became an emblematic part of the movement.[67]

In token of this philosemitic ideal, Belgrade dedicated its first public Holocaust memorial in 1990, created by Jewish sculptor Nandor Glid.[68] North of Belgrade, in Zemun, the ancestral home of Theodor Herzl's grand-parents was restored and turned into a museum to show the historic 'Jewish-ness' of Serbia.[69] SANU contributed by issuing two editions of Predrag Palavestra's *Jewish Writers in Serbian Literature*, which featured the work of sixty-seven Jewish writers based in Belgrade. As the Ministry of Information argued, the book was designed to stress that 'the Jewish challenge to all the Christians in the world, especially to the Orthodox Serbs, should be strengthening of one's own religious and national identity, a call to Serbs to be united, in order for them, just like the Jews, to preserve, strengthen and justify their existence in the world'. Jews were to be a crucial inspiration for how Serbs should present themselves.[70]

As the conflict progressed, Laslo Sekelj noted the increased 'functionaliza-tion' of Jews taking place through the SJFS, but also noted the overly polit-ical nature of the Society, how 'enormous quantity of public statements were made in support of Karadzic and Serb paramilitary groups in Bosnia and Croatia ... [e]specially in attempts to legitimize Serbian ethno-nationalism ...'. In reality, the SJFA enjoyed little support amongst Jewish groups and often harassed anyone critical of Serbian nationalism, including some Jewish intellectuals.[71] Some Jewish leaders did promote pro-Serbian policies, even seeing 'Serbophobia as a twin sister of anti-semitism', with others calling America 'a monster of this earth'. However, some coercion by the govern-ment seems to have taken place.[72] The Society fell from favor as the Milose-vic regime dragged on, and in 2001 Mandic was murdered in her apartment under mysterious circumstances.[73]

While American Jewish groups during the later war in Kosovo con-demned the Serbs, largely sympathizing with Kosovar Albanians, Serbian claims of philosemitism struck a chord with some segments of Israeli society.[74] Successive Labor and Likud governments maintained a pro-Serbian policy, as Auron argues, 'extending political and moral support to the Serbs' by refusing to condemn them. While Israeli Foreign Minister Shimon Peres did acknowledge that atrocities were being perpetrated in Bosnia, condemn-ing 'concentration camps, the killing, the shocking attacks on women and children', he mentioned neither the victims nor the aggressors by name.[75]

Larry Derfner, writing in *The Jerusalem Post*, noted a surprising ambiva-lence to the Serbian occupation of Kosovo. He cited a 'false perception', pro-moted by a 'Serbian lobby', that Serbs were completely pro-Jewish during the Holocaust, while the Croats were consumed with anti-Semitism. A further point of comparison concerned the belief that both Serbs and Israelis were unfairly condemned as 'neighborhood bullies'. For Haifa University's Arnon Sofer: 'Many Israelis see the West interfering with the Serbs' affairs out of ignorance and arrogance, just like they see the West interfering in Israel'.[76] Some Israeli politicians even saw NATO airstrikes as a 'dangerous precedent'.[77]

One might be tempted to draw similarities between Israeli support for Serbia and Turkey. However, this is misleading. Israel had no major mili-tary, economic, or other agreements with Serbia, and did not supply arms to that country during the war. Similarly, Serbia had no geopolitical signific-ance for Israel. There is little to suggest that the Israeli government felt pressured by the Serbian leadership, nor was there any evidence that they actively backed Serbia in their national goals. Nevertheless, Israeli passivity did surprise many American commentators, who saw clear parallels between ethnic cleansing and Hitler's policies of *Lebensraum*. For example, in 1993 Elie Wiesel, on the inauguration day of the USHMM, pushed for American involvement in Bosnia. In his view, Western governments had a duty to prevent the Yugoslav war from escalating.[78]

Operation Allied Force and myths of betrayal

In March 1999, NATO began bombing Yugoslavia in an effort to stop the ethnic cleansing of Kosovar Albanians by Serbian militia units linked to the Milosevic regime.[79] In the context of this air campaign, the need to stress Serbian–Jewish linkages increased. In 1990, author Brana Crncevic had argued that 'only friendship with Jews can save Serbhood'. It now seemed that, despite Serbian overtures, Jews had not extended the support Serbs felt they deserved.[80] Claims of Jews 'owing' the Serbs for their goodness in World War II emerged in SJFS rhetoric during this time, reinforcing Jewish duplicity. Thus Heather Cottin's position a month after *Allied Force* began: 'Today, the little nation of Yugoslavia is being bombed in a blitzkrieg more deadly then any the Nazis ever leveled at any nation in World War II. The Serbs, who were the only friends Jews had in Yugoslavia during World War II, have been demonized and accused of genocide'.[81] Cottin questioned why a 'false analogy' had arisen between Jews and Kosovar Albanians, concluding that a 'terrible manipulation' had been perpetrated.[82] Similarly, Ljubomir Tadic claimed Serbs as 'victims of monstrous lies and accusations. The inflamed Serbophobia is a new, modern form of Nazi racism'.[83]

A year after the Kosovo campaign, William Dorich would angrily accuse the World Jewish Congress of having 'set the stage for public relations spon- sored Serbophobia throughout the 1990s'. He further added, accusing Jews of ingratitude: 'Serbs can't count on the Jews to be honest anti-genocide brokers when they have never lifted a voice to recognize the thousands of Serbs who share common graves with Jews because those Serbs were caught hiding their Jewish neighbors in their attics, barns and basement during the Holocaust'.[84] Another popular argument concerned then Secretary of State Madeleine Albright's Jewish ancestry, and how Serbs had sheltered 'little Madeleine' and her family from the Germans during the Holocaust, only to be stabbed in the back.[85]

The most extreme accusation of Jewish ingratitude was leveled by the 'SACRU (Serbian–American Civil Rights Unlimited) Documenting Jewish Genocides on Serbs'. The ten-year history of the conflict was encapsulated in the actions of various American politicians, journalists, and lobbyists labeled as 'Jew', including General Wesley Clark.[86] The same names and arguments were present in a lengthy letter to Simon Wiesenthal published by the Serbian Unity Congress in late 2000. The letter highlighted the same names, asking Wiesenthal to explain 'the role these prominent Jews have played in trying to destroy the Serbian nation and [in] demonizing an entire people'.[87]

Sekelj does note the rise of anti-Semitism in Serbia during the 1990s, as the economic and political situation became desperate. The *Protocols of the Elders of Zion* were reprinted on several occasions, while various academics outlined Jewish conspiracies. The reprinted anti-Semitic works of Ratibor Djurdjevic and Orthodox Bishop Nikolaj Velimirovic were warmly received in some quarters, while rejected in others.[88] Even the Serbian Academy of Sciences bookstore began selling reprinted anti-Semitic works from the 1930s.[89]

However, most commentators are reluctant to see the Serbian peoples as excessively anti-Semitic by regional standards. Cathie Carmichael, in her study of ethnic cleansing, argues: 'Historical anti-Semitism in the Balkans, although it existed in popular culture, was by no means as developed in this region as it was in Central Europe or the Romanov monarchy'.[90] Sekelj too sees a *relatively* low level of anti-Semitism in Yugoslavia: 20.8 percent in Serbia (excluding Kosovo), and 15 percent in Montenegro. Like Carmichael, he argues: 'Antisemitism was not of major importance in the former Yugoslavia, unlike the case of Poland, the former Soviet Union, Hungary, Romania, and Slovakia'.[91] Zivkovic similarly argues that he did not experience any anti-Semitism in his own country.[92] Nevertheless, the overt and extreme manipulation of Holocaust imagery was a worrying phenomenon, and one which has been under-explored in histories of the Yugoslav conflict.

Serbian aggression and the West

To what extent did past memories of genocide and actual fear play a part in Serbia's decision to brutally wage war in Croatia, Bosnia, and Kosovo? Doubtless these personal memories were important. While to some extent Tudjman's discrimination against Croatian Serbs was worrying, his policies were not genocidal. Throughout the early conflict, he appeared willing to negotiate with Croatian Serb leaders like Jovan Raskovic if they agreed to live within an independent Croatia. Similarly, there is little evidence that the Bosnian Moslem leadership ever intended to create an Islamic state in Bosnia. The SDA was a secular organization, with few ties to fundamentalist Islamic countries until much later.

The frequent use of the terms 'Holocaust', 'death camps', 'death marches', 'exoduses', and 'pogroms' highlighted the history of Serbian victimization. Such imagery detracted from continuous media reports about Serbs 'rounding up' Bosnian Moslems, 'invading' territory, 'looting' property, while committing 'ethnic cleansing' and 'genocide'. Such rhetoric became doubly important when the Holocaust was used by Western media and politicians as a way of understanding Serbian actions. In 1992, journalist Roy Gutman published a lead article in *Newsday* – 'The Death Camps of Bosnia' – establishing the Moslems as victims of seemingly Nazi-esque atrocities at the hands of the Serbs.[93]

Indeed, Serbian-run 'collection centers' were little better than concentration camps, where prisoners were fed little to no food, frequently beaten and terrorized, sometimes sexually violated, and often killed. Yet Serbia could also legitimately cry foul, as Gutman's prize-winning dispatches notably omitted references to Croatian camps, which were equally horrific although fewer in number.[94] The feeling that there was a double standard in the Western media – that Serbs were 'misunderstood' – inspired many on the Serbian side to push Holocaust comparisons as far as they would go.

While Serbs were arguably the first to use Holocaust imagery in the Yugoslav conflict, Europeans and North Americans too began to interpret the escalating conflict through the prism of the Holocaust. As Levy and Sznaider observe, the debate about American intervention was largely framed by the Holocaust, which gave the imbroglio a moral clarity it hitherto lacked. On the right, Serbian treatment of Bosnian Moslems and Kosovar Albanians was likened to Nazi treatment of Jews, while the left compared German and American intervention to Nazi-style empire building. 'Holocaust iconography', the authors assert, came to play a dominant role, and the Kosovo crisis became 'a globally televised morality play'.[95]

Alan Steinweis has recently engaged with what he calls the 'Auschwitz analogy' and its role in framing US perceptions of the Yugoslav crisis. Since American administrations already had a tendency to view events in black-and-white terms, as previously discussed in Chapters 1 and 4, Holocaust analogies were an easy way of distinguishing victims from perpetrators. This dovetailed nicely with the growing awareness of the Holocaust amongst the American population.[96]

After Gutman's report, Congressman Tom Lantos, the only Holocaust survivor serving in Congress, lambasted the Clinton administration in 1992 for its lack of involvement in Yugoslavia. Prominent American Jewish organizations published an advertisement in the *New York Times* adding Omarska and Brcko 'to the blood-chilling names of Auschwitz, Treblinka, and other Nazi death camps'. They promoted swift government action to end the unfolding genocide. Several newspaper columnists compared Milosevic to Hitler, and Clinton to the appeasement-seeking Neville Chamberlain.[97] Then UN ambassador Madeleine Albright also pushed comparisons between Hitler and Milosevic, urging Clinton to conduct airstrikes.[98] Eventually NATO did intervene, but much later than most proponents of intervention desired.

In the case of NATO intervention in Kosovo in 1999, Clinton invoked the Holocaust in reference to Serbian ethnic cleansing. Both, he argued, were examples of 'vicious, premeditated, systematic oppression fueled by religious and ethnic hatred'.[99] German Foreign Minister Joschka Fischer repeatedly invoked the Holocaust when pushing the merits of NATO airstrikes.[100] It's clear from a reading of the events surrounding the 1999 intervention that Clinton, Fischer, Chancellor Schroeder, and British Prime Minister Blair overreacted to the situation on the ground. There was ethnic cleansing certainly, but the KLA was hardly a pacifist organization. Further, as I've argued elsewhere, the bombing campaign greatly exacerbated the speed of the ethnic cleansing, and led to a larger humanitarian crisis than was originally present. The Rambouillet Accords were also designed as a provocation to the Serbs. Milosevic could never have signed them and successfully remained in office.[101]

In the final analysis, Milosevic was not Hitler, possessing neither his charisma nor his deeply-rooted hatred. While Serbian crimes were horrific, they paled in comparison with those of the Holocaust. Srebrenica was one of the worst modern crimes against humanity, but Serbs did not commit this sort of genocide throughout Bosnia, either because they didn't want to, or because they did not possess the means to carry it out. Indeed, when it could be proven conclusively that the Bosnian Moslems were not suffering from Holocaust-like atrocities, the matter became more an issue of restraining a neighborhood bully than of 'bombing the rail lines to Auschwitz'.

Conclusions: Serbia's memory problems

Serbs, unlike indigenous or Armenian Comparativists, had little interest, at least at first, in denigrating Jews or the memory of the Holocaust. Indeed, the larger the Holocaust loomed in the popular imagination, the better. The Serbian strategy consisted of hitching their history to the Holocaust, transforming Serbs into Jews. Indeed, unlike most of the other cases I've reviewed so far, there was little attempt to systematically compare Serbian victimization with the Holocaust. Basic rhetoric and a plethora of accusations against Serbia's enemies seemed the preferred method. This was more a scattergun approach than a sustained scholarly analysis. The rise of Holocaust consciousness, many ideologues believed, could help sell the Serbian cause at home and abroad. Unlike some of the other cases examined in this book, Serbia's campaign to invoke the Holocaust was a domestic success. It was seamlessly grafted onto pre-existing myths of Serbia as the suffering Christ.

There is an almost complete lack of remorse for Serbia's role in the violent dismemberment of Yugoslavia. Amazingly, Serbs continue to see themselves as victims. Milosevic may be gone, but many of the values and attitudes he helped to instill remain. Even now, the Serbian Ministry of Information continues to promote Serbia as a victim of history rather than an aggressor. Its online *Encyclopaedia* perpetuates the claim that the 1974 Constitution was at the root of the 1990s conflict, and that much of the bloodshed was the fault of Slovenia and Croatia's illegal separation from the Federation.[102]

One might have assumed that Milosevic's handover to the ITCY would help Serbs engage with their nation's guilt. The reverse proved to be true. The trial fed into widely held perceptions that the West was punishing Milosevic as a way of punishing Serbia.[103] Yugoslav President Vojislav Kostunica, who was against the extradition of Milosevic, represented the view of most Serbs – that domestic trials needed to take place first. By charging Milosevic exclusively with crimes against non-Serbs committed outside of Serbia, many felt that justice had been denied.[104] As Ana Devic observed, the ICTY had not encouraged much soul-searching or self-reflection. It was viewed by Serbs either as an 'instrument for punishing Serbs', or alternatively as 'a national sports entertainment'.[105]

Despite the trials and massive media coverage of the events in Yugoslavia, the Serbian public remains surprisingly ignorant of Serbia's role in the conflict. Public opinion polls conducted in 2001 revealed that over 52 percent of respondents 'could not name a single war crime committed by Serb forces in Bosnia, Croatia, or Kosovo. Nearly half, however, could name at least three crimes committed against Serb civilians by other forces'. As the poll further revealed, Radovan Karadzic and Ratko Mladic continued to be heralded as the two 'greatest defenders of the Serb nation'.[106] The 2003 elections demonstrated clearly the memory problems still present in Serbia. The SRS party of warlord Vojislav Seselj was widely supported by the electorate. T-shirts of Mladic and Karadzic were sold throughout the campaign.[107]

Then, in June 2005, a video from the Srebrenica massacres stunned the Serbian public. The film captured the murder of six civilians by a Serbian paramilitary group known as The Scorpions. President Boris Tadic argued that 'Serbia is deeply shocked', further arguing 'Those images are proof of a monstrous crime committed against persons of a different religion, and the guilty had walked as free men until now'. Yet, as far as he was concerned, the crimes were committed 'in the name of our nation', but by *individuals* who did not represent Serbian interests.[108] Tadic's view is revealing – the crimes were a shocking aberration, not something Serbs normally did, nor knew anything about. It was a terrible surprise. A survey held in late May 2005 demonstrated that only half of Serbs believed the Srebrenica massacre actually took place anyway.[109] The Ministry of Information continued its oblique reaction to the video, referring to it in mid-2005 as 'a film of the crime in Srebrenica', following this up later by describing Srebrenica as 'that shameful crime'. No details were forthcoming about the crime, nor the guilty parties involved.[110]

Other issues are couched in similar terms. The Ministry of Information runs a web page on 'Terror in Kosovo-Metohija' stressing the destruction of Serbian Orthodox heritage by Kosovar Albanians. Searching its site under the key word 'apology' yields only a reference to how a US religious delegation felt it should apologize for the destruction caused to Kosovo during the NATO bombing campaign.[111] The Ministry seems interested only in crimes that happen to Serbs. Kosovar Albanians do not seem to deserve any apology for almost two decades of discrimination and ethnic repression.

As Kecmanovic has argued, the only way forward for Serbia in rebuilding society and in re-forging good relations with the other constituent peoples of the former Yugoslavia is to abandon its victim mentality.[112] This will not be easy. Serbia continues to see itself first and foremost as a victim of its neighbours. While it is now popular to denounce Milosevic and dream of membership in the EU, the basic beliefs of the Serbian people remain intact. Any crimes were the responsibility of aberrant individuals, and should in no way reflect on the Serbian nation. It will be interesting to see in the coming years if the EU, as it has signally failed to do for Turkey, attempts to place obligations on the Serbian state to confront its past squarely.

Conclusions

Do you think that men have always slaughtered each other the way they do nowadays? Were they always liars, cheats, traitors, brigands, weaklings, deceivers, cowards, enviers, gluttons, drunkards, misers, sycophants, butchers, slanderers, debauchees, fanatics, hypocrites and fools?

(Candide, in conversation with Martin the Manichæan)[1]

In its searing impact on Western consciousness, the Holocaust remains distinct from the genocidal and other crimes which preceded and followed it. First, the liberation of the death camps (albeit only a part of the Holocaust) was amazingly well documented at the time. Unlike later journalists and 'war junkies', reporters were untrained in atrocity reporting; they were caught by surprise by the sheer horror of what they witnessed. Radio, movie, and newspaper reports invoked the same message – what they were witnessing was unbelievable, the very depths of human depravity. General Eisenhower made his rounds, as did parliamentarians and Congressmen. As one historian put it: 'the significance of the Holocaust is that it not only confronted humanity with a previously inconceived horror, it also marked the beginning of documenting that horror'.[2]

Further, reporters covering these atrocities became passionately infused with a mission – to get the story out so that everyone would know what had happened. Unlike massacres in remote frontier provinces, the deliberate spread of disease, or forced marches such as the 'trail of tears', the Holocaust took place in the heart of Europe, during a conflict that was global in scope. Following on were the Nuremberg trials, exhibiting Nazi leaders for the world to see, documenting war crimes, while creating an archive which would form the basis of later academic reflection on the Holocaust.

Since 1945, almost every major conflict has been covered in graphic detail. If the Holocaust was a fresh and unprecedented horror, later wars were hardly that. We have become saturated with horrific images of death and destruction. I share Zeliger's lament that 'Despite ample evidence of atrocity as it is taking place, our response to pictures of horror often produces instead helplessness and indifference, by which we do little more than contextualize each instance of horror against those which come before and after'.[3]

We often understand past tragedies like the genocide of American Indians and Armenians, or more recent tragedies like Rwanda, Yugoslavia, or Darfur, indirectly. We also try to frame non-genocidal crimes, often colonial crimes, through the Holocaust. The subtext is revealing. Some tragedies deserve to be appreciated because they are like the Holocaust, not because of their own significant characteristics. Representation of the past and present can thus become a contest, with victimized groups repeatedly using the same imagery in the vain hope of provoking the same revulsion that accompanied reports of the liberation of the death camps. Yet activists are not solely responsible for these decisions. Since the Holocaust, the media bears some responsibility for creating an 'atrocity aesthetic', which comes complete with 'agonized collectives of survivors and victims, gaunt faces behind barbed wire, vacant stares of the tortured, and accoutrements of torture'.[4]

By framing each atrocity in relatively the same way, we lose the context and the details of each different event. The specificities of each new case thus elude the general public. Sadly, many of the activists and historians reviewed in my case studies consciously use a frame of reference easily at hand. In so doing, they trivialize both the Holocaust and the unique suffering of the group they represent. Thus CUP leaders must be likened to the top Nazi leadership, while their ideology must equally be Nazi-like. Bosnian Moslems become *real* victims only when they are pictured starving and standing behind barbed wire. Nanking's true significance only become apparent when compared to Nazi crimes; Rabe is only worthy of attention when he is Asia's answer to Schindler.

Yet the Holocaust is a poor guide for how bystanders should behave. Rabe and Schindler were exceptions at a time when most Jews and Chinese confronted the indifference of bystanders. Norman Geras has described a 'contract of mutual indifference', where we ignore the suffering of others in return for the tacit acceptance that if something horrible happens to us, we cannot expect any help in return.[5] This was true of the Holocaust, where most Germans, Poles and others did not care what happened to the Jews, nor did they want to know. 'Indifference' and the 'dead silence of unconcern' allowed the Nazis to carry on with their plans relatively unopposed.[6]

The Holocaust, unlike many other tragedies, has also been Americanized to appeal to a wider non-Jewish audience. The USHMM tried to make its displays relevant and accessible to non-Jews, while at the same time keeping the spotlight on Jewish suffering. Michael Berenbaum, who was project director of the Museum during its creation, has argued that 'instruction in the Holocaust had become an instrument for teaching the professed values of American society: democracy, pluralism, respect for differences, individual responsibility, freedom from prejudice, and an abhorrence of racism'.[7] Stressing both the unique *and* universal lessons of the Holocaust at the same time has been a difficult balancing act.

Since the 1970s, the Holocaust has also become part of high-school teaching curricula. Seven American states 'have passed legislation either mandating or suggesting that the Holocaust be taught in their public schools'. The purpose here is to inform and enlighten students about the horrors of the past, to convey lessons for the future, while promoting the commonalities between victims.[8] Yet Americanization has also performed the opposite role. It has forestalled efforts to prevent genocide in the present, has helped Western nations to excuse their past misconduct, and has become a useful means of demonstrating by stark contrast how 'nice' Western countries are *now*. Even Germany can play this game, contrasting its brutal past with its enlightened and peace-promoting present. This has provided it with enough moral capital (it seems) to criticize the US invasion and occupation of Iraq, while pouring scorn on Israel's treatment of the Palestinians.

Our fellow victims

Equally important for the Holocaust's significance was the fact that Nazi Germany was (alongside Fascist Italy and Imperial Japan) an enemy of the Western world. The Jews were 'our' fellow victims. Unlike the Holocaust's strongly fratricidal dimension, the victims of most other tragedies were distinctly 'other'. The Holocaust defied history because a Western group was actively demonized and destroyed.

In other cases, the treatment meted out at the hands of perpetrators was horrific, but stemmed from a long legacy of dehumanization and humiliation. As Peter Singer rightly argues: 'Racist assumptions shared by most Europeans at the turn of century are now totally unacceptable, at least in public life'.[9] We can now go back and re-humanize the victims, as Stannard and others have done, but the process of doing so is fundamentally different from telling the stories of Holocaust survivors. Holocaust scholarship is *relatively* easier because Jews were seen as fellow humans while the genocide was occurring. Jewish reactions to atrocities seemed reasonable and understandable – normal, urban, Western reactions. They remain accessible today.

As artist Judy Chicago makes clear: 'We have been able to articulate our experiences, and because we have been considered part of Western culture and have grown powerful enough to influence it, we have often been heard'.[10] Genocide in Australia, North America, and China, for example, remains under-explored, in part because of the paucity of survivor memoir and testimony. Strong literary traditions promote remembrance and help non-Jews to understand what Holocaust victims endured.

Ironically, when approaching colonialism, many cannot help but relate more to the colonisers than the colonised, in their motivations, tastes, and lifestyles. This is doubly so when ancestors may have participated in or acted as bystanders to the atrocities under discussion. As Jeremy Paxman has argued in *The English*, many share in nostalgia for the forgotten 'Breed' – those who created and maintained the British Empire. Such men were presented as:

> Fearless and philistine, safe in taxis and invaluable in shipwrecks ... men you could send to the ends of the earth and know that they would dominate the natives firmly but fairly, their needs no more than the occasional months-old copy of *The Times* and a tin of their favourite pipe tobacco.[11]

For many people, it is intuitively displeasing to dislike their own ancestors, to reject their national leaders, whose fundamental characteristics and motivations are seen to be not unlike their own, however paternalistic and potentially misguided. To attack the past of a nation is therefore to attack the linear descendents of that nation and its people in the present. Windschuttle's support is derived largely from such sentiments.

The Holocaust is readily identifiable as genocide because, as a collection of images and symbols, it is easily distinguishable as different from our own history and traditions. Demonization comes easily. As Finkielkraut has remarked of the Nazi era: 'Satan was incarnated in the person of Hitler, who from then on was merely the allegory of the demon'.[12] Minus the 'Swastika-wearing SS psychopaths, or crazed Black tribal Africans', genocidal destruction seems less easy to understand, the victims less obviously victims.[13] Since, as Paxman notes, we tend to like our own national leaders, we have a problem seeing George Washington, or Lachlan MacQuarie, or Kemal Ataturk, as Hitler-like individuals. The quest to compare elected leaders to a Nazi cabal thus falls on deaf ears most of the time. This is so, first, because the myths surrounding the construction of nations are carefully created, and resonate powerfully.

Based on undisputed Nazi evil, the Americanization process privileges genocide where a clear and obvious intent to destroy the group is present. For many academics focused on indigenous history, intent to destroy is difficult to discern, and official intent has been questioned, by Fein, Barta, and others, who emphasize instead 'relations of destruction'.[14] This *new look* for genocide studies is useful, insofar as it allows us to entertain the idea of applying the label where it has not readily been applied before. The application would of course be moral, not legal, since the UNGC is very strict about the importance of intent.

Yet in doing so, genocide as an emotive term loses some of its rhetorical suasion. This sort of intent-free genocide seems less evil; the motives of the perpetrators clouded or multifaceted, sometimes paternalistic and even well-meaning. 'Relations of destruction' is hardly as intuitively horrifying as the bald brutality of Hitler or Stalin or Mao.

In such cases we need to be very careful about bringing in the Holocaust. The moral absolutes it provides are not easily applicable to more nuanced cases of colonialism, where officials often focused on acquiring land and sub-jugating indigenous peoples, rather than exterminating them. In such cases, those who refute the label genocide are not always David Irving-style deniers. While some deny or suppress facts and others simply ignore them, not everyone who raises questions about the term 'genocide' does so from a position of malice. We have to be careful about framing all academic debates over past atrocities as being between gatekeepers of the truth and what Churchill so glibly calls 'holocaust deniers'.

A further problem in confronting and understanding the past is our inability statistically to quantify the suffering or deaths of non-European groups. The round total of six million Holocaust victims cannot easily be repeated in accounts of other atrocities. No realistic quantum of suffering has been agreed for the nineteenth or earlier centuries in terms of 'megadeaths'. Rummel has attempted to quantify the number of deaths committed by governments before the twentieth century, and arrives at a range of '89,000,000 to slightly over 260,000,000 million men, women, and children dead' for 'all pre-twentieth century killing – massacres, infanti-cide, executions, genocides, sacrifices, burnings, deaths by mistreatment, and the like'. This includes everything from the Mongol conquest of China to Medieval witch hunts and the Albigensian crusades. By contrast, he gives a figure of 262,000,000 dead from 1900 to 1999, suggesting (by a small fraction) that the twentieth century was worse than the rest of recorded human history put together.[15]

In the twentieth century, 'before' and 'after' population statistics (however imprecise) make it relatively easy to estimate the numbers of dead in a given conflict. Population losses during the Holocaust, ditto those in Cambodia and Rwanda, can be quantified with reasonable accuracy, even if there is disagreement about specifics. For political scientists obsessed with quantifying precise totals or calculating precise numbers of 'megadeaths', the imprecise death tolls of previous centuries can be frustrating, leading us to question the reality of past horrors. While the number of wars in the nineteenth century can be ascertained,[16] casualty rates are not always obvious – especially for non-White combatants. Researchers looking into past geno-cides must content themselves with ranges of numbers. Tatz, for example, has no accurate figures for Aboriginal populations before Cook's explora-tions. The range of pre-conquest figures varies from 250,000 to 750,000, even though we know that by 1924 only 31,000 remained.

Stannard's research has also involved a rejection of older statistics from the 'Berkeley School' which put the total population of the Americas at less than fifteen million (with only one million in North America). Yet even Borah and Dobyns' significantly higher totals of well over 100 million are dismissed as an underestimation.[17] Clearly, we will never know precisely how many people perished as a result of past atrocities, nor will we have completely accurate totals for evaluating population sizes before European conquest. The problem of bringing in the Holocaust is that we expect other atrocities to have the same impeccable provenance, and then proceed to discount them when they don't. This is an unrealistic expectation, and it is time we got over it.

Misreading the Holocaust

If pre-twentieth-century history is constantly misread and misunderstood, so too, sadly, is the Holocaust. If those from outside see the Holocaust as unimpeachable, monolithic, and established, Holocaust academics, survivors, and others approach matters in a starkly different light. Holocaust memory is not carved in stone, nor is its commemoration an unstoppable juggernaut. It is a vulnerable cluster of memories and experiences, constantly in danger of being eroded, trivialized, denied, and rejected. The battle for memory is not one between the guardians of a castle and its besiegers, but between two or more vulnerable groups of people whose competition for public recognition and posterity can threaten to erode the significance of each group. Manne, Tatz, and Chang, among others, understand this distinction; Stannard and Churchill do not seem to.

The 'Holocaust industry' promoted by Norman Finkelstein and others presents the Holocaust as an established entity, consciously nurtured by a large group of lobbyists or 'exclusivists' who promote the Holocaust at the expense of other historical tragedies. This is done primarily for political, nationalistic reasons – to advance Israeli power.[18] Finkelstein argues:

> Through its [the Holocaust's] deployment, one of the world's most formidable military powers, with a horrendous human rights record, has cast itself as a 'victim' state, and the most successful ethnic group in the United States has likewise acquired victim status.[19]

Finkelstein exhorts his readers to see the Holocaust as the tool of a cynical establishment that can and should be challenged. His is an extremely contentious proposition.

I answer as follows: Yes, the Holocaust has grown in importance with the spread of Holocaust scholarship, but Americanization is not the conspiracy Finkelstein suggests. Indeed, Holocaust studies in school curricula were not the result of an all-powerful Holocaust lobby. Support for Israel resonates more strongly in Christian right circles than it does amongst many American Jews. Certainly no lobby was present when hundreds if not thousands of Jewish inmates of ghettoes and camps took time to record what was happening to themselves as individuals and as a people. This, as Ben-Sasson rightly notes, is a testament to 'an impressive level of spiritual survival'.[20]

Nor was it ever certain that the Holocaust would resonate as strongly as it has. While the death camps were front-page news in 1945, Jews were not singled out as victims. Indeed, widespread anti-Semitism in America and Britain meant that highlighting the racial identity of camp inmates might dampen sympathy for them. The 'overwhelmingly Jewish nature of the victimization' was 'strategically understated'.[21] Jews returning to their European countries of origin were often shunned, sometimes violently attacked. Anti-Semitic attitudes remain a serious source of concern in Europe, sixty years after the War. As I made clear in Chapter 1, the Holocaust took decades to emerge for what it was. There was nothing automatic about its current status. Wiesel's *Night* was rejected many times before a small publisher picked it up. Anne Frank's house was almost bulldozed in the 1950s. Spielberg too was prepared for *Schindler's List* to lose money. Its iconic status surprised him as much as anyone else.

Similarly, Holocaust denial and anti-Semitism remain serious problems. While those promoting the relativization of the Holocaust may feel the events are secure and not subject to serious challenge, many Holocaust historians do worry about this problem. ADL Director Abraham Foxman's book *Never Again?* spelled out the renewed dangers of anti-Semitism in the wake of the terrorist attacks of 11 September 2001.[22] His tone was alarmist, but it did iterate a strongly-held view that Jews are not safe from the dangers of anti-Semitism. The post-Holocaust world hardly signals that Jewish communities are now safe. One only has to look at the recent Tehran conference to know that Israel and Jews have many powerful enemies. It was only in December 2006 that Iran's President predicted that 'The Zionist regime will be wiped out soon the same way the Soviet Union was, and humanity will achieve freedom'.[23]

Worryingly, while the Holocaust has become an iconic symbol and a standard of comparison, Jews themselves have become a lightning rod for attack – a stand-in in the Middle East for American power.[24] At an individual and community level, anti-Semitism has increased since the September 11 attacks and the 'war on terror'. France has witnessed an obvious rise in anti-Semitism since 2002, and indeed may be suffering from what French journalist Nicolas Weill has called 'Holocaust Fatigue'.[25]

In the wake of their hosting the 2006 Football World Cup, Germany too seems to be overcoming its past, reveling in newfound forms of patriotism, which include pride in being German. Does this mean that the Holocaust is more or less important in the contemporary world? Germany is often cited as a model of repentance, certainly when compared with Turkey or Japan. The sixtieth anniversary of the end of the Holocaust in 2005 touched off a vast project of commemoration and contemplation, with Berlin's 2005 Denkmal memorial as but one example.

Yet the anniversary has also allowed Germany to normalize its history, to celebrate German heroes like Claus von Stauffenberg, who led the assassination attempt against Hitler, and students like Hans and Sophie Scholl, who were executed for distributing pamphlets at Munich University critical of the Nazis. These Germans are now being celebrated as proof that there was 'another Germany' during the War.[26] Gunther Grass' novel *Crabwalk* is one of many books arguing that Germans suffered too during the War. Germans can now choose between two identities – the inheritance of the perpetrators, or of those who resisted or were victims. To what extent this will alter Germany's Cold War-era policy of repentance is unclear.

Israel as a reward

This view is a common one in the literature. Indigenous and other peoples argue that they have suffered, yet still wait to be territorially redeemed. Since Jews have a state, did they weather their genocide relatively better than indigenous peoples? This question is raised constantly by those challenging the predominance of the Holocaust. For example, Therrien and Neu's *Accounting for Genocide* compares Canadian indigenous residential schools to the Holocaust. They make the following (academically dubious) claim:

> Canadian Indian policy may not have been as overt or concentrated as the Holocaust would prove to be – but it was nonetheless violent and achieved much the same ends. Indeed, it might even be said that Canadian policy has been more effective than Nazi policy, since none of Canada's First Nations have yet to regain full statehood, whereas the Jews have Israel.[27]

Certainly, the authors are not concerned about comparing death tolls and degrees of horror. To engage in such comparisons would be to concede that the differences were more than marginal. But the point is clear – indigenous peoples have a trump card of sorts. Jews suffered and were redeemed by gaining a homeland – they thus have no more complaints, and should step aside to let other victimized groups gain their share of the pie. Unlike the Jews, other victims have not been able to regain control of their lands, while the perpetrators and their decedents continue to exploit them. If this is true in Canada, as the authors argue, then it is also the case in New Zealand, America, Australia, and elsewhere.

Such conclusions again support the notion that Israel is secure, and its proponents extremely powerful, able to uniquely shape and manipulate American foreign policy. Note, for example, Mearsheimer and Walt's claim that America has been pushed into war as the result of a 'Jewish Lobby' promoting its influence in Washington, in the process 'inflam[ing] Arab and Islamic opinion and jeopardis[ing] not only US security but that of much of the rest of the world'.[28] Certainly AIPAC is powerful, but it is so largely as a result of Christian fundamentalist support, as discussed in Chapter 4, and a general public sympathy with Israel, which often has little to do with Jews or the Holocaust per se. Ironically, one can be both an anti-Semite and a supporter of Israel. This is the paradox of conservative support for Israel.

Further, such claims assume that Israel was the first choice for Holocaust survivors, which was often not the case. Indeed, Israel was a haven precisely because many European Jews were not welcome in their former homes. The Holocaust was not only genocide, it was also ethnic cleansing, and Jews, from Poland to Holland and further south to Italy and Greece, found publics largely uninterested in their plight, and often hostile. Many languished for years in displaced persons camps before emigrating to Israel, North America, and Australasia. In part this reflected European anti-Semitism. However, it also reflected the guilt and shame of bystanders who did little to prevent Nazi atrocities.[29]

The way forward

Comparative work on genocide and other atrocities is important for providing context. It also demonstrates that all victims are part of the same human family, and that one individual's suffering should count for no more than another's. Yet each group reviewed here needs to find its own vocabulary, its own symbols, and its own ways of representing what it has endured. Groups do better to compare similar cases, to search for their own vocabulary and imagery, to make their emotional connection with the reader, viewer, or participant more direct and meaningful. Thus the *Holodomor* for the Ukrainian Famine-Genocide of the 1903s, the *Porrajmos* or 'devouring' for the Roma Genocide, the *Great Irish Famine*, the *Atlantic Slave Trade* or *Maafa* – these names stress the originality and uniqueness of the events they describe.

In researching this book, I was struck by the many commonalities in these cases – the dismal fate of *individual* victims of atrocities in the recent and distant past, the inability of survivors to engage fully with their experiences, the continued problems of denial, the palpable sense of injustice. Problems of individual, group, and intergenerational trauma persist amongst many victimized peoples. The symptoms are surprisingly similar, and we can make valid comparisons here, using such standard measures as the *Diagnostic and Statistical Manual* (DSM IV-R) of the American Psychiatric Association. This manual complements other studies of trauma, and allows us to understand that while the Holocaust was an extreme genocide in the collective sense, this does not mean that individuals from other groups have not endured levels of trauma comparable to those suffered by some survivors of the Holocaust.

In its most basic sense, trauma can be defined as 'an event in the subject's life defined by its intensity, by the subject's incapacity to respond adequately to it, and by the upheaval and long-lasting effects that it brings about in the psychical organization', to use a definition by psychoanalysts Laplanche and Pontalis.[30] Trauma can radically change one's perception of the world, moving a person from the feeling that the world is safe, to perceiving it as fundamentally unsafe and insecure. It can also make a person change his or her self-perception from 'good' to 'bad', recalling the traumatic experience constantly, and perhaps feeling helpless or guilty for not having done more to help others, or oneself.[31]

Some effects of trauma include 'disassociation', where salient chunks of information about the traumatic may be confused, mixed around, or even entirely forgotten. 'Emotional numbing' is also common, where sufferers are withdrawn and detached, and tend to over-intellectualize events. There is increased distance between friends and family as a result of trauma. Other potential effects, such as 'interpersonal vigilance', can lead to violence, injury, even death. 'Suicide thinking and risk-taking behavior' can also result from trauma, as the sufferer enters into a self-destructive spiral.[32] At the same time, forms of trauma can be passed on from one generation to the next, although the trauma will affect future generations in very different, and often not as serious, ways. Forced to deal with the psychological problems of a parent, offspring sometimes develop various psychological conditions of their own.[33]

And if individuals can suffer from trauma, so too sometimes can groups. As Vamik Volkan has observed: 'Members of a group who share the same loss collectively go through a similar psychological mourning process'.[34] Shared trauma can be profound, and can take years fully to express itself. He writes that 'memorial activities may be pronounced for many years', as in the Kennedy and King assassinations, or large monuments may need to be constructed to help the mourning process, concretely anchoring the group's trauma in something solid and tangible.[35] If the group has been unable properly to mourn and work through past tragedy, the past exerts itself powerfully on the present through a 'time collapse'. Here, 'people may intellectually separate the past event from the present one, but emotionally the two events are merged'.[36]

Collective trauma, in some ways similar to individual examples, can be transmitted through generations, although its effects on each generation will be different. Parents effectively externalize their unwanted trauma onto their children. The child then becomes 'a reservoir for the unwanted, troublesome parts of an older generation'. It then becomes the child's responsibility to absorb the expectations and frustrations of the parents, and eventually the child will feel obliged to 'mourn, to reverse the humiliation and feelings of helplessness pertaining to the trauma of his forebears'.[37]

While the events of the Holocaust are unique in some respects, the study of trauma allows us to see that the legacies of horrific events on individuals and families may be readily compared and the commonalities isolated. If one cannot understand the magnitude of six million Jewish deaths or 100 million American Indian deaths, it is easy to comprehend the individual suffering and trauma of one individual or a family struggling to cope with painful loss. And if we cannot perhaps relate to Jews or Tutsi or Maori as such, we can relate to these group members as individuals and as families. Movies like *Schindler's List* or *Rabbit Proof Fence* work because they focus on individual stories and emotional journeys. A focus on *people* is a more authentic means of understanding group tragedies, as well as the after-effects of such tragedies on survivors, their friends and family, and the generations who follow.

The study of trauma allows us to move away from a focus on the purely rhetorical, on comparisons between one group and another, and to begin to see everyone as an individual. This is where the actual healing of groups and individuals can occur. Bridges can be built based on what *people* have endured and tried to overcome. Such comparisons at an individual level may also help Holocaust survivors and their families make sense of their experiences.

An emphasis on individual, collective, and intergenerational trauma takes the emphasis off the group and its unique symbols and history, and stresses the human, psychological aspects of being a victim. Sensitivity to *all* victims is needed. For many activists reviewed in this book, sensitivity to Jewish victims is largely lip service. Their 'established' nature is taken for granted, which allows many activists to take extreme liberties with the Holocaust. Underwriting this is the belief that Jews are secure, that memory of the Holocaust is assured, and that Israel as the Jewish 'reward' provides Jews with a high level of security.

At the same time, Holocaust historians and Jewish community leaders need to do more than pay lip service to the suffering of other peoples. The examples of Lewy, Katz, and Rosenfeld come to mind here. These established scholars have taken aim at other victimized groups, denying them the chance to have their genocides recognized. These scholars are fortunately not representative. The USHMM has done good work publicizing the atrocities taking place in Darfur and elsewhere. Holocaust historians are often at the forefront of arguing for humanitarian intervention in cases of gross human rights abuses. Yet such scholars tarnish the reputation of their fellow Holocaust historians by forcing black-and-white comparisons which are neither academically nor socially fruitful.

Ultimately, the Holocaust is neither a window of opportunity nor a door slammed in the face of other victims. It is a unique and horrible tragedy, yet it exists in a world of other horrible tragedies, each possessing its own unique elements. We need to recognize that, at an individual and a collective level, people can suffer, can be traumatized, and can pass on this trauma, loss, and anger to succeeding generations. History is rich with examples of brutality, inhumanity, and genocide. It is also rich with kindness and everyday goodness. While the Holocaust clearly occupies a unique role in genocide studies, it is not (as the Australians would say) a 'tall poppy' that deserves to be cut down. We need to be careful about stepping on one victimized people to elevate another, even if seeking justice has been a long and arduous journey.

Notes

Introduction: the Holocaust and identity politics

1 B. Zeliger, *Remembering to Forget: Holocaust Memory Through the Camera's Eye*, Chicago: University of Chicago Press, 1998, pp. 226–7.
2 D. Frum and R. Perle, *An End to Evil? How to Win the War on Terror*, New York: Random House, 2004, p. 7.
3 R. Rubenstein, 'Religion and the Uniqueness of the Holocaust', in A. Rosenbaum (ed.), *Is The Holocaust Unique? Perspectives on Comparative Genocide Second Edition*, Boulder: Westview Press, 2001, p. 33.
4 M. Finnemore, *National Interests in International Society*, Ithaca: Cornell University Press, 1996, p. 22.
5 R. Posner and E. Rasmusen, 'Creating and Enforcing Norms, with Special Reference to Sanctions', *International Review of Law and Economics*, vol. 19, no. 3, 1999, p. 370.
6 M. Zivkovic, 'The Wish to be a Jew: The Power of the Jewish Trope in the Yugoslav Conflict', *Cahiers de l'Urmis*, no. 6, 2000.
7 O. Thomson, *Mass Persuasion in History: An Historical Analysis of the Development of Propaganda Techniques*, New York: Crane, Russak, & Company, 1977, p. 9.
8 See their conference book, especially p. 19. online. Available: www.holocaustforum. gov.ce (accessed October 10, 2005).
9 'The Stockholm International Forum on the Holocaust: A Conference on Education, Remembrance and Research', p. 15, online. Available: www.holocaustforum.gov.ce (accessed October 10, 2005).
10 Ibid., p. 6.
11 T. Cole, 'Nativization and Nationalization: A Comparative Landscape Study of Holocaust Museums in Israel, the US and the UK', *The Journal of Israeli History*, vol. 23, no. 1, 2004, p. 130.
12 S. Buckley-Zistel, 'Remembering to Forget: Chosen Amnesia as a Strategy For Local Coexistence In Post-Genocide Rwanda', *Africa*, vol. 76, no. 2, 2006, pp. 132–4.
13 American Jewish Committee, '"Holocaust Consciousness" Critics Chronicled, Countered – *Year Book: Threat to Holocaust Memory*', American Jewish Committee Press Release, December 9, 2001, online. Available: www.ajc.org/languages/
Spanish.asp?did=341 (accessed October 10, 2005).
14 To access the documents on this network of sites, see Hoffman's 'The Israeli Holocaust Against the Arab People', online. Available: www.revisionisthistory.org/ palestine.htm>l (accessed October 10, 2005).
15 For a full text of the Convention, see OHCHR-UNOG online. Available: www.unhchr.ch/htm>l>/menu3/b/p_genoci.htm (accessed October 10, 2005).

16 'Prosecutor v. Jelisic', IT-95–10, December 14, 1999, Trial Chamber, and July 5, 2001, Appeals Chamber, upheld that the killing of Bosnian Moslem men and boys in Srebrenica, 1995, was genocide, even if the entire Bosnian Moslem population was not targeted at that time. The issue was also debated extensively in 'Prosecutor v. Krstic', IT-98–33, August 2, 2001.

17 See, for example: 'Prosecutor v. Akayesu', ICTR-96–4, September 2, 1998.

18 D. Moshman, 'Conceptual constraints on thinking about genocide', *Journal of Genocide Research*, vol. 3, no. 3, 2001, p. 431.

19 H. Fein, 'Genocide, Terror, Life Integrity, and War Crimes: The Case for Discrimination', in G. Andreopoulos (ed.), *Genocide: Conceptual and Historical Dimensions*, Philadelphia: University of Pennsylvania Press, 1997, p. 94.

20 F. Chalk and K. Jonassohn, 'Introduction', in F. Chalk and K. Jonassohn (eds), *The History and Sociology of Genocide: Analysis and Case Studies*, New Haven: Yale University Press, 1990), p. 3.

21 W. Shawcross, *The Quality of Mercy: Cambodia, Holocaust, and Modern Conscience*, New York: Simon & Schuster, 1984, pp. 419–20; J. Petrie, 'The Secular Word HOLOCAUST: Scholarly Myths, History and 20th Century Meanings', *Journal of Genocide Research*, vol. 2, no. 1, 2000, pp. 35–6.

22 Petrie, 'The Secular Word HOLOCAUST', pp. 33–4; for another discussion of the history of the term 'holocaust', see M. Marrus, *The Holocaust in History*, New York: Penguin, 1989, pp. 3–4.

23 Ibid., pp. 39–41; 47.

24 Ibid., p. 48.

25 Shawcross, *The Quality of Mercy*, p. 420.

26 D. Ofer, 'Linguistic Conceptualization of the Holocaust in Palestine and Israel 1942–53', *Journal of Contemporary History*, vol. 31, no. 3, 1996, pp. 566–8.

27 O. Bartov, *Murder in Our Midst: The Holocaust, Industrial Killing, and Representation*, Oxford: Oxford University Press, 1996, pp. 59–60, (*italics his*).

28 Ibid., pp. 59–60.

29 Ibid., pp. 57–9. Works featuring this use of the term include G. Bensoussan's *Génocide pour mémoire*, Paris, editions du Felin, 1989; and F. Bédarida, *Le Nazisme et le Génocide*, Paris, Presses Pocket, 1992.

30 Shoah is very commonly used. *Le Monde* in 2005 featured a special series of articles as a reflection on the 60th anniversary of the liberation of the death camps. online. Available: www.lemonde.fr/web/sequence/0,2–641295,1–0,0.htm>1 (accessed October 10, 2005). A number of recent books, including Lanzmann's own *Shoah*, Paris: Gallimard, 1997, exemplify this trend.

31 Bartov, *Murder in Our Midst*, pp. 57–9.

32 See, for example, H.G. Adler, *Der Kampf gegen die 'Endlosung der Judenfrage'*, Bonn, 1960; G. Aly, *Endlosung: Volkerverschiebung und der Mord an den europaischen Juden*, Frankfurt: S. Fischer, 1995.

33 See M. Burleigh and W. Wippermann, *The Racial State: Germany 1933–1945*, Cambridge: Cambridge University Press, 1991, pp. 136–7.

34 See for example, www.holocaustforgotten.com/ and www.remember.org/forgotten/, both of which focus on the three million non-Jewish Poles killed by the Nazis (accessed October 15, 2005).

35 Interview with D. Lipstadt, 'Bookworld Live', *Washington Post*, 22 February, 2005, online. Available: www.washingtonpost.com/wp-dyn/content/discussion/2005/02/18/DI2005040201739.htm>1 (accessed October 15, 2005).

36 A. Levy, *The Wiesenthal File*, Grand Rapids: William Eerdmans, 1993, pp. 435–7.

37 J.E. Young, 'Germany's Holocaust Memorial Problem – And Mine', *The Public Historian*, vol. 24, no. 4, 2002, p. 80.

38 Moshman, 'Conceptual constraints on thinking about genocide', p. 433.

39   T. Schouls, *Shifting Boundaries: Aboriginal Identity, Pluralist Theory, and the Politics of Self-Government*, Vancouver: UBC Press, 2000, p. 2. See also I.M. Young, *Justice and the Politics of Difference*, Princeton: Princeton University Press, 1990.
40   S. Kruks, *Retrieving Experience: Subjectivity and Recognition in Feminist Politics*, Ithaca: Cornell University Press, 2000, pp. 83–7.
41   S.J. Hekman, *Private Selves Public Identity: Reconsidering Identity Politics*, University Park, Philadelphia: State University of Pennsylvania Press, 2004, p. 89.
42   S. Kinzer, 'Plans for Museum Buoy Armenians and Dismay Turks', *New York Times*, 24 April, 2002.
43   E. Zaretsky, 'Identity Theory, Identity Politics: Psychoanalysis, Marxism, Post-Structuralism', in C. Calhoun, *Social Theory and the Politics of Identity*, New York: Basil Blackwell, 1994, p. 199
44   Schouls, *Shifting Boundaries*, pp. 2–3.
45   C. Calhoun, op. cit., pp. 25–6.
46   J. Tosh, *The Pursuit of History*, 4th edition, Harlow: Pearson Longman, 2006, p. 12.
47   Ibid., p. 6.
48   Ibid., p. 191.
49   C. Brown and E. Ainley, *Understanding International Relations*, London, Palgrave MacMillan, 2005, pp. 48–9.

1 Cosmopolitanizing the Holocaust: from the Eichmann trial to identity politics

1   J. Tobin, 'From Silence to Cacophony: Holocaust Metaphors are the Coin of the Realm', *Jewish World Review*, April 9, 1999.
2   D. Levy and N. Sznaider, 'Memory Unbound: The Holocaust and the Formation of Cosmopolitan Memory', *European Journal of Social Theory*, vol. 5, no. 1, 2002, p. 92.
3   J. Young, 'Looking into Mirrors of Evil', *The Journal of Israeli History*, vol. 23. no. 1, 2004, pp. 161–2.
4   J. Torpey, 'Introduction: Politics and the Past', in J. Torpey (ed.), *Politics and the Past: On Repairing Historical Injustices*, Lanham: Rowman & Littlefield, 2003, p. 3.
5   P. Novick, *The Holocaust and Collective Memory*, London: Bloomsbury, 1999, p. 20. I have used the British version of the book, with the above title.
6   M. Lagerwey, *Reading Auschwitz*, London: Altamira Press, 1998, p. 47.
7   N. Levi and M. Rothberg, 'General Introduction: Theory and the Holocaust', in N. Levi and M. Rothberg (eds), *The Holocaust: Theoretical Readings*, New Brunswick: Rutgers University Press, 2003, p. 6.
8   A. Milchman and A. Rosenberg, 'Two Kinds of Uniqueness', in R.L. Millen (ed.), *New Perspectives on the Holocaust: A Guide for Teachers and Scholars*, New York: New York University Press, 1996, pp. 8–9.
9   M. Ignatieff, *Human Rights as Politics and Idolatry*, Princeton: Princeton University Press, 2003, pp. 313–15.
10   J.S. Nye, *Understanding International Conflicts: An Introduction to Theory and History*, 3rd edition, New York: Longman, 2000, p. 19.
11   L. Sekelj, 'Antisemitism and Jewish Identity in Serbia after the 1991 Collapse of the Yugoslav State', Jerusalem: Vidal Sassoon International Center for the Study of Anti-Semitism, 1998.
12   B. Dupuy, 'The Approach to the Question of Good and Evil in the Writings of Hans Jonas and Hannah Arendt', in J. Bemporad, J. Pawlikowski, and J. Sievers (eds), *Good and Evil After Auschwitz: Ethical Implications for Today*, Hoboken: KTAV Publishers, 2000, p. 180.

13 This was later translated as *Harvest of Hate*, London: Elek Books, 1956.
14 M. Gilbert, *Never Again: A History of the Holocaust*, New York: Universe Publishing, 2000, p. 174.
15 I.L. Horowitz, *Taking Lives: Genocide and State Power*, 5th edition revised, London: Transaction Publishers, 2002, p. 376.
16 P. Novick, 'Holocaust Memory in America', in J. Young (ed.), *The Art of Memory: Holocaust Memorials in History*, New York: Prestel, 1994, pp. 160–1.
17 Ibid., pp. 160–1.
18 H. Diner, 'Post-World-War-II American Jewry and the Confrontation with Catastrophe', *American Jewish History*, vol. 91, 2003, pp. 445; 466–7.
19 H. Greenspan, 'Imagining Survivors: Testimony and the Rise of Holocaust Consciousness', in H. Flanzbaum (ed.), *The Americanization of the Holocaust*, Baltimore: Johns Hopkins University Press, 1999, pp. 50–1.
20 H. Flanzbaum, 'Introduction: The Americanization of the Holocaust', in Flanzbaum, op. cit., pp. 2–3.
21 F. Lewis, 'Israel on the Eve of Eichmann's Trial', in B. Adler (ed.), *Israel: A Reader*, Philadelphia: Chilton Books, 1968, p. 80.
22 Z. Sternhell, *The Founding Myths of Israel: Nationalism, Socialism, and the Making of the Jewish State*, Princeton: Princeton University Press, 1998, p. 329.
23 See his discussion of their book *Civil Religion in Israel: Traditional Judaism and Political Culture in the Jewish State*, Berkeley: University of California Press, 1983; S. Friedlander, 'Memory of the Shoah in Israel', in Young, op. cit., p. 151.
24 G. Mosse, *Confronting the Nation: Jewish and Western Nationalism*, Hanover: Brandeis University Press, 1993, p. 126.
25 N. Ben-Yahuda, *The Masada Myth: Collective Memory and Mythmaking in Israel*, Madison: The University of Wisconsin Press, 1995, pp. 7–9, 18, 23.
26 A. Huyssen, 'Monument and Memory in a Postmodern Age', *Yale Journal of Criticism*, vol. 6, no. 2, 1993, p. 15.
27 Y. Zerubavel, 'The Death of Memory and the Memory of Death: Masada and the Holocaust as Historical Metaphors', *Representations*, no. 45, 1994, p. 80.
28 Friedlander, 'Memory of the Shoah in Israel', p. 151.
29 M. Marrus, *The Holocaust in History*, New York: Penguin, 1989: pp. 2; 4–5. Levi and Rothberg, 'General Introduction', pp. 6–7.
30 H. Arendt, *Eichmann in Jerusalem: A Report on the Banality of Evil*, London: Faber & Faber, 1963, pp. 7–8.
31 Novick, *The Holocaust and Collective Memory*, pp. 148–52.
32 Quoted in Novick, *The Holocaust and Collective Memory*, p. 150; J. Kugelmass, 'Why We Go to Poland; Holocaust Tourism as Secular Ritual', in Young, op. cit., p. 177; R. Rubenstein and J. Roth, *Approaches to Auschwitz*, Atlanta: John Knox, 1987, p. 189. For a more polemical assessment, see N. Finkelstein, *The Holocaust Industry: Reflections on the Exploitation of Jewish Suffering*, New York: Verso, 2000, p. 32.
33 Friedlander, 'Memory of the Shoah in Israel', p. 155.
34 E. Barkan, 'Restitution and Amending Historical Injustices in International Morality', in Torpey, op. cit., pp. 96–7.
35 A. Baumeister, *Liberalism and the 'Politics of Difference'*, Edinburgh: Edinburgh University Press, 2000, p. 5.
36 D. Cesarani, 'Holocaust Controversies in the 1990s: The Revenge of History or the History of Revenge?', *The Journal of Israeli History*, vol. 23, no. 1, 2004, p. 80.
37 J. Olick and J. Robbins, 'Social Memory Studies: From "Collective Memory" to the Historical Sociology of Mnemonic Practices', *Annual Review of Sociology*, vol. 24, 1998, pp. 107–8.

38 A.D. Smith, *Nationalism and Modernism*, London: Routledge, 1998; Section I, 'Varieties of Modernism', covers six chapters. pp. 25–142.
39 Olick and Robbins, 'Social Memory Studies', pp. 107–8.
40 H. Diner, *The Jews of the United States: 1645–2000*, Berkeley: University of California Press, 2004, pp. 265–9.
41 M. Gardell, *Countdown to Armageddon: Louis Farrakhan and the Nation of Islam*, London: Hurst and Company, 1996, pp. 247–8.
42 Diner, *The Jews of the United States*, pp. 270–1.
43 On the issue of Jewish socioeconomic advancement in the early 1960s, see N. Glazer and D.P. Moynihan, *Beyond the Melting Pot*, Cambridge, MA: MIT Press, 1963, pp. 143–55.
44 Gardell, *Countdown to Armageddon*, pp. 247–9.
45 Diner, *The Jews of the United States*, pp. 275–6.
46 J. Zeitz, 'If I am not for myself ... : The American Jewish Establishment in the Aftermath of the Six Day War', *American Jewish History* vol. 88, no. 2, 2000, p. 285.
47 Novick, *The Holocaust and Collective Memory*, pp. 148–52.
48 Diner, *The Jews of the United States*, pp. 323–6.
49 Novick, 'Holocaust Memory in America', p. 161.
50 K. Bischoping and A. Kalmin, 'Public Opinion about Comparisons to the Holocaust', *The Public Opinion Quarterly*, vol. 63, no. 4, 1999, p. 486. M. Levine, *African Americans and Civil Rights: From 1619 to the Present*, Phoenix: Oryx Press, 1996, pp. 202–4.
51 J. Young, 'America's Holocaust: Memory and the Politics of Identity', in Flanzbaum, op. cit., p. 70.
52 Diner, *The Jews of the United States*, pp. 334–5.
53 K. Ball, 'Introduction: Trauma and its Institutional Destinies', *Cultural Critique*, no. 46, 2000, p. 4.
54 Ball, 'Introduction', p. 5.
55 H. Greenspan, 'Imagining Survivors: Testimony and the Rise of Holocaust Consciousness', in H. Flanzbaum (ed.), *The Americanization of the Holocaust*, Baltimore: Johns Hopkins University Press, 1999, pp. 57–8.
56 E. Sicher, 'The Future of the Past: Countermemory and Postmemory in Contemporary Post-Holocaust Narratives', *History and Memory*, vol. 12, no. 2, 2000, p. 63.
57 Diner, *The Jews of the United States*, p. 331.
58 J. Varon, 'Probing the Limits of the Politics of Representation', *New German Critique*, no. 72, 1997, p. 83.
59 A. Hungerford, 'Surviving Rego Park: Holocaust Theory from Art Spiegelman to Berel Lang', in Flanzbaum, op. cit., p. 107.
60 Sicher, 'The Future of the Past', p. 57.
61 Diner, *The Jews of the United States*, p. 307.
62 B. Susser and C. Liebman, *Choosing Survival*, New York: Oxford University Press, 1999, pp. 55–6.
63 J. Doneson, 'Holocaust Revisited: A Catalyst for Memory or Trivialization?', *Annals of the American Academy of Political and Social Science*, vol. 548, 1996, p. 75.
64 Greenspan, 'Imagining Survivors', p. 45.
65 Ibid., p. 45.
66 Young, 'America's Holocaust', p. 73.
67 E. Linenthal, *Preserving Memory: The Struggle to Create America's Holocaust Museum*, New York: Columbia University Press, 2001, pp. 17–18.
68 A. Steinweis, 'Reflections on the Holocaust From Nebraska', in Flanzbaum, op. cit., pp. 178–9.

69 D. Schwartz, '"Who Will Tell Them after We're Gone?": Reflections on Teaching the Holocaust', *The History Teacher*, vol. 23, no. 2, 1990, pp. 98–9.

70 J. Micklethwaite and A. Wooldrige, *The Right Nation: Conservative Power in America*, New York: Penguin Press, 2004. On more recent manifestations of this trend, see M. Goldberg, 'Fundamentally Unsound', *Salon.com*, 29 July, 2002. online. Available: www.salon.com/books/feature/2002/07/29/left_ behind/ (accessed October 10, 2005).

71 C. Shindler, 'Likud and the Christian Dispensationalists: A Symbiotic Relationship', *Israel Studies* vol. 5, no. 1, 2000, p. 165.

72 F.M. Perko, 'Contemporary American Christian Attitudes to Israel Based on the Scriptures', *Israel Studies* vol. 8, no. 2, 2003, pp. 4–5; J. Beinin, 'The Israelization of American Middle East Policy Discourse', *Social Text*, vol. 21, no. 2, 2003, p. 129.

73 Perko, 'Contemporary American Christian Attitudes ...', pp. 3–4. For more commentary, see M. McAlister, 'Prophecy, Politics, and the Popular: The Left Behind Series and Christian Fundamentalism's New World Order', *The South Atlantic Quarterly* vol. 102, no. 4, 2003, pp. 775–6.

74 Shindler, 'Likud and the Christian Dispensationalists', pp. 167, 170.

75 R. Moeller, 'Germans as Victims? Thoughts on a Post-Cold War History of World War II's Legacies', *History & Memory*, vol. 17, nos. 1/2 (2005) pp. 150; 170. See also Cesarani, 'Holocaust Controversies in the 1990s', p. 81. For a good overall discussion of the incident, see G. Hartman's edited collection *Bitburg in Moral and Political Perspective*, Bloomington: Indiana University Press, 1986.

76 A. Finkielkraut, *The Future of a Negation: Reflections on the Question of Genocide*, Lincoln, NB: University of Nebraska Press, 1998, p. 59.

77 Ibid., pp. 99–100.

78 Ibid., pp. 59; 100–1. See also A. Finkielkraut, *Le juif imaginaire*, Paris: Gallimard, 1982, pp. 13–14.

79 Bischoping and Kalmin, 'Public Opinion about Comparisons to the Holocaust', p. 486.

80 Novick, *The Holocaust and Collective Memory*, pp. 248–9.

81 A. Stein, 'Whose Memories? Whose Victimhood? Contests for the Holocaust Frame in Recent Social Movement Discourse', *Sociological Perspectives*, vol. 41, no. 3, 1998, pp. 527–8.

82 See, for example, S. Graubard, *Mr. Bush's War: Adventures in the Politics of Illusion*, London: I.B. Tauris, 1992, pp. 3–4.

83 Excellent works in English are C. Maier's *The Unmasterable Past: History, Holocaust and German National Identity*, Cambridge: Harvard University Press, [1988] 1997; and P. Baldwin, *Hitler, the Holocaust and the Historians Dispute*, Boston: Beacon, 1990. In German, see A. Hillgruber, *Zweierlei Untergang: Die Zerschlagung des Deutschen Reichs und das Ende des europäischen Judentums*, Berlin: Siedler, 1986; and, from right and left perspectives, E. Nolte's *Das Vergehen der Vergangenhiet: antwort an meine Kritiker im sogenannten Historikerstreit*, Berlin: Ullstein, 1987, and H.U. Wehler's *Entsorgung der deutschen Vergangenheit? Ein polemischer Essay zum 'Historikerstreit'*, Munich: C.H Beck, 1988.

84 J. Olick, 'What Does it Mean to Normalize the Past?', *Social Science History*, vol. 4, no. 22, 1998, p. 562.

85 Moeller, 'Germans as Victims?', pp. 150, 172. German victims included the 600,000 civilians killed by Allied bombing, another 500,000 East Germans killed by the advancing Soviet Army, some five million Germans in uniform killed, and as many as 1.5 million German women raped by Soviet soldiers. For further details on Red Army atrocities, see H. Sander and B. John (eds), *Befreier und Befreite. Krieg, Vergewaltigung, Kinder*, Munich: Kunstmann Verlag,

1992. For a discussion of the devastation caused by Allied bombing, see L. Kettenacker (ed.), *Ein Volk von Opfern? Die neue Debatte um den Bombenkrieg 1940–45*, Berlin: Rowohlt Berlin Verlag, 2003.

86   Moeller, 'Germans as Victims?', pp. 148; 151–2.
87   Olick, 'What Does it Mean to Normalize the Past?', p. 562.
88   Sicher, 'The Future of the Past', p. 61.
89   Ibid., p. 56. The crucial importance of *Schindler's List* is also noted by A. Landsberg, 'America, the Holocaust and the Mass Culture of Memory: Towards a Radical Politics of Empathy', *New German Critique*, no. 71, 1997, pp. 63–4.
90   Since its opening, over fifteen million people have visited the Museum. Young, 'America's Holocaust', p. 80.
91   Young, 'America's Holocaust', p. 74.
92   Ball, 'Introduction', p. 14.
93   T. Cole, 'Nativization and Nationalization: A Comparative Landscape Study of Holocaust Museums in Israel, the US and the UK', *The Journal of Israeli History*, vol. 23, no. 1, 2004, p. 134.
94   Young, 'America's Holocaust', p. 73.
95   Cole, 'Nativization and Nationalization', p. 138.
96   D. Levy and N. Sznaider, 'Memory Unbound: The Holocaust and the Formation of Cosmopolitan Memory', *European Journal of Social Theory*, vol. 5, no. 1, 2002, pp. 97–8. *Schindler's List* as a morality play of good against evil functioned extremely well in the 'Americanization of the Holocaust'. See D. Levy and N. Sznaider, 'The Institutionalization of Cosmopolitan Morality: The Holocaust and human rights', *Journal of Human Rights*, vol. 3, no. 2, 2004, p. 152.
97   Flanzbaum, 'Introduction', p. 7.
98   Ibid., pp. 10–11.
99   E. Barkan, *The Guilt of Nations: Restitution and Negotiating Historical Injustices*, Baltimore: Johns Hopkins University Press, 2001, p. xv.
100 Ibid., p. 21.
101 Ibid., pp. 89–91.
102 R. Ludi, 'Michael Bazyler's Holocaust Justice', UCLA Center for European and Eurasian Studies Paper 1, 2003, pp. 2–3.
103 R. Ludi, 'Waging War on Wartime Memory: Recent Swiss Debates in the Legacies of the Holocaust and the Nazi Era', *Jewish Social Studies*, vol. 10, no. 2, 2004, pp. 121, 123.
104 S. Eisenstat, *Imperfect Justice: Looted Assets, Slave Labor, and the Unfinished Business of World War II*, New York: Public Affairs, 2004, pp. 5–6. As Eisenstat reminds us, other national lobby groups, like Greek-Americans and Cuban-Americans, also exert pressure on US foreign policy. Jewish lobbies, he argues, are little different.
105 Novick, 'Holocaust Memory in America', p. 159; a list of Holocaust and Jewish museums worldwide can be found at www.science.co.il/Holocaust-Museums.asp (accessed October 10, 2005).
106 N. Levin, 'The Relationship of Genocide to Holocaust Studies', in S. Friedman (ed.), *Holocaust Literature: Handbook of Critical Historical and Literary Writings*, New York: Greenwood Press, 1993, p. 197.
107 J. Doneson, 'Holocaust Revisited: A Catalyst for Memory or Trivialization?', *Annals of the American Academy of Political and Social Science*, vol. 548, 1996, p. 71.
108 Ibid., p. 76.
109 Eisenstat, *Imperfect Justice*, p. 7.
110 W. Lefeber, *America, Russia and the Cold War 1945–2000*, New York: McGraw Hill, 2002, p. 371.

111 Ludi, 'Michael Bazyler's Holocaust Justice', pp. 5–6.
112 J. Torpey, '"Making Whole What Has Been Smashed": Reflections on Reparations', *The Journal of Modern History*, vol. 73, 2001, p. 333.
113 M. Levene, 'Why is the Twentieth Century the Century of Genocide?', *Journal of World History*, vol. 11, no. 2, 2000, p. 305.
114 R.L. Nytagodien and A. Neal, 'Collective Trauma, Apologies, and the Politics of Memory', *Journal of Human Rights*, vol. 4, 2005, p. 465.
115 Torpey, '"Making Whole What Has Been Smashed"', p. 334.
116 J. Torpey, 'The Pursuit of the Past: A Polemical Perspective', Paper presented at Canadian Historical Consciousness in an International Context: Theoretical Frameworks, University of British Columbia, Vancouver, BC, 2001.
117 J. Olick, 'Introduction: Memory and Nation – Continuities, Conflicts, and Transformations', *Social Science History*, vol. 22, no. 4, 1998, p. 380. See also J. Olick, 'Collective Memory: The Two Cultures', *Sociological Theory*, vol. 17 no. 3, 1999, p. 333.
118 E. Barkan, 'Restitution and Amending Historical Injustices in International Morality', in Torpey, op. cit., p. 101.
119 Barkan, *The Guilt of Nations*, p. xvii. See also J. Olick and B. Coughlin, 'The Politics of Regret: Analytical Frames', in Torpey, op. cit., p. 37.
120 A. Cairns, 'Coming to Terms with the Past', in Torpey, op. cit., p. 65.
121 Ibid., p. 83.
122 I have translated the title from D. Levy and N. Sznaider, *Erinnerung im globalen Zeitalter. Der Holocaust*, Frankfurt: Shrkamp, 2004.
123 Levy and Sznaider, 'Memory Unbound', p. 89; Levy, 'The Cosmopolitan Figuration', pp. 6–7.
124 Levy and Sznaider, 'The Institutionalization of Cosmopolitan Morality', pp. 143; 146; 151.
125 Levy, 'The Cosmopolitan Figuration', pp. 9–10. See Delanty's book *Citizenship in a Global Age*, Buckingham: Open University Press, 2002, pp. 95–6.
126 Torpey, 'Introduction', pp. 6–7.
127 Torpey, 'Making Whole What Has Been Smashed', p. 338.
128 Torpey, 'Introduction', pp. 2–3.
129 J. Mowitt, 'Trauma Envy', *Cultural critique*, vol. 46, 2000, pp. 272–97.
130 Stein, 'Whose Memories?', pp. 521–2.
131 Torpey, 'Making Whole What Has Been Smashed', p. 342.
132 Rosenberg, 'Is the Holocaust Unique?', p. 150.
133 Nytagodien and Neal, 'Collective Trauma, Apologies, and the Politics of Memory', p. 471.
134 Stannard, 'Uniqueness as Denial', pp. 272–3, (*italics his*).
135 S. Wright, *International Human Rights, Decolonisation and Globalisation: Becoming Human*, New York: Routledge, 2001, pp. 18–19 (*italics hers*).
136 G. Lewy, *The Nazi Persecution of the Gypsies*, Oxford: Oxford University Press, 2000.
137 'An Address by Iris Chang, author of *The Rape of Nanking*', March 15, 1998, USHMM.
138 Moshman, 'Conceptual constraints on thinking about genocide', pp. 432; 444–8.
139 M. Berenbaum, 'The Uniqueness and Universality of the Holocaust', in M. Berenbaum (ed.), *A Mosaic of Victims – Non-Jews Persecuted and Murdered by Nazis*, London: I.B. Tauris, 1990, p. 34.
140 N. Levin, 'The Relationship of Genocide to Holocaust Studies', in Friedman, op. cit., p. 196.
141 Berenbaum, 'The Uniqueness and Universality of the Holocaust', p. 27.
142 D. Stannard, 'Uniqueness as Denial: The Politics of Genocide Scholarship',

A. Rosenbaum (ed.), *Is The Holocaust Unique?: Perspectives on Comparative Geno-cide Second Edition*, Boulder: Westview Press, 2001, p. 192.

143 A. Rosenberg, 'Was the Holocaust Unique? A Peculiar Question?', in I. Willi-mann and M. Dobkowski (eds), *Genocide and the Modern Age: Etiology and Case Studies of Mass Death*, Syracuse: Syracuse University Press, 2000, pp. 150–1.

144 See his interview with R. Rosenbaum, *Explaining Hitler: The Search for the Origins of his Evil*, New York: Random House, 1998, pp. 251–67.

145 R. Landau, *Studying the Holocaust: Issues, Readings and Documents*, London: Rout-ledge, 1998, pp. 3–5.

146 A. Rosenbaum, 'Introduction to the Second Edition', Rosenbaum, op. cit., pp. 13–14.

147 Rosenberg, 'Was the Holocaust Unique?', pp. 150–1.

148 Berenbaum, 'The Uniqueness and Universality of the Holocaust', p. 22.

149 Melson, *Revolution and Genocide*, p. 34.

150 Petrie, 'The secular word HOLOCAUST', p. 52.

151 Rosenberg, 'Is the Holocaust Unique?', pp. 151–2.

152 S. Katz, *The Holocaust in Historical Context Volume I*, Oxford: Oxford University Press, 1994. This book is based in part on an article Katz wrote in 1989, outlin-ing his methodology. See S. Katz, 'Genocide in the 20th Century: Essay: Quan-tity And Interpretation – Issues In The Comparative Historical Analysis Of The Holocaust', *Holocaust Genocide Studies*, vol. 4, 1989, pp. 127–48. For an insight-ful if polemical review of the book, see H. Huttenbach, 'The Katz Fallacy: The Art of Procrustes', *The Genocide Forum* vol. 3, no. 5. online. Available: www.chgs.umn.edu/Educational_Resources/Newsletter/The_Genocide_Forum/ Yr_3/Year_3__No__5/year_3__no__5.htm>1 (accessed October 10, 2005).

153 Katz, *The Holocaust in Historical Context Volume I*, p. 3.

154 Ibid., p. 10.

155 Ibid., p. 59.

156 Ibid., p. 128 (*italics in original*).

157 Ibid., p. 129.

158 S. Katz, 'The Uniqueness of the Holocaust: The Historical Dimension', in Rosenbaum, op. cit., pp. 21; 26; 30–4.

159 Katz, *The Holocaust in Historical Context Volume I*, p. 138. Katz's approach has called for comparing the Holocaust with a series of straw cases, doomed to failure from the onset: 'roman and classical slavery', 'medieval anti-Semitism', 'witchcraft and misogynism', 'persecution of homosexuals', and 'persecution of heretics'. While few if any scholars of genocide would claim these as cases of genocide, Katz plumps for including 'political, social and economic aggre-gates', without offering any sound reasons why such groups should be included other than to demolish them (p. 127).

160 Lewy, *The Nazi Persecution of the Gypsies*, pp. 10–14.

161 Ibid., pp. 141–2; 148–57. For a critique, see I. Hancock, 'Downplaying the Porrajmos: The Trend to Minimize the Romani Holocaust: A review of Guen-ther Lewy, *The Nazi Persecution of the Gypsies*, Oxford University Press, 2000', *Patrin Web Journal*, September, 2000, online. Available: www.geocities. com/Paris/5121/lewy.htm (accessed October 10, 2005).

2 Considering Holocaust uniqueness: from Hebrew peoplehood to the Americanization of memory

1 R. Kluger, 'The Camps', in N. Levi and M. Rothberg (eds), *The Holocaust: Theoretical Readings*, New Brunswick: Rutgers University Press, 2003, p. 51.

2 A.S. Rosenbaum (ed.), *Is the Holocaust Unique? Perspectives on Comparative Geno-cide*, Boulder: Westview Press, 1996.

3 A. Margalit and G. Motzkin, 'The Uniqueness of the Holocaust', *Philosophy and Public Affairs*, vol. 25, no. 1, 1996, p. 58.

4 P. Novick, *The Holocaust and Collective Memory: The American Experience*, London: Bloomsbury, 1999, p. 276.

5 I. Clendinnen, *Reading the Holocaust*, New York: Cambridge University Press, 1999, p. 11.

6 A. Hastings, *The Construction of Nationhood: Ethnicity, Religion and Nationalism*, Cambridge: Cambridge University Press, 1997, p. 187; for further discussion see also pp. 201–5.

7 C. Cruise O'Brien, *God Land: Reflections on Religion and Nationalism*, Cambridge: Harvard University Press, 1988, p. 141; S. Smooha 'The Model of Ethnic Democracy: Israel as a Jewish and Democratic State', *Nations and Nationalism*, vol. 8, no. 4, 2002, p. 484.

8 B. Cauthen, 'The Myth of Divine Election and Afrikaner Ethnogenesis', in G. Hosking and G. Schöpflin (eds), *Myths and Nationhood*, London: C. Hurst and Company, 1997, p. 113.

9 N. Frye, *The Great Code: The Bible and Literature*, Toronto: Academic Press Canada, 1982, p. 24. For a further discussion of cyclical nationalism and concepts of redemption, see N. Cohn, *The Pursuit of the Millennium*, London: Mercury Books, 1962.

10 H. Kohn, *The Idea of Nationalism: A Study in Its Origins and Background*, New York: Macmillan, 1945, pp. 37–8.

11 Y. Bauer, *Rethinking the Holocaust*, New Haven: Yale University Press, 2001, pp. 53–5.

12 Bauer, *Rethinking the Holocaust*, pp. 53–5.

13 B. Susser and C. Liebman, *Choosing Survival: Strategies for a Jewish Future*, Oxford: Oxford University Press, 1999, p. 3.

14 L. Greenfeld, *Nationalism: Five Roads to Modernity*, Cambridge: Harvard University Press, 1992, Chapters 1, 2 and 5.

15 See B. Cauthen, 'Covenant and continuity: ethno-symbolism and the myth of divine election', *Nations and Nationalism*, vol. 10, nos 1–2, 2004.

16 H. Trevor-Roper, *Jewish and Other Nationalism*, London: Weidenfeld and Nicolson, 1962, p. 12.

17 J. Trachtenberg, *The Devil and the Jews: The Medieval Concept of Jews and Its Relation to Modern Antisemitism*, New Haven: Yale University Press, 1943.

18 W. Laqueur, *A History of Zionism*, New York: Schoken Books, 1989, p. 590.

19 Y. Gothelf, 'Zionism's Adversaries at Home and Abroad', in Y. Gothelf (ed.), *Zionism: The Permanent Revolution of the Jewish People*, Tel Aviv: World Labour Zionist Movement, 1973, p. 81.

20 E. Wiesel, 'Opening Remarks: Conference on Antisemitism', in M. Rosensaft and Y. Bauer (eds), *Antisemitism: Threat to Western Civilization*, Jerusalem: Vidal Sassoon International Center for the Study of Antisemitism, 1988, p. 10.

21 D. Cohn-Sherbok, *The Crucified Jew: Twenty Centuries of Christian Anti-Semitism*, Grand Rapids: Eerdmans, 1997, pp. xiv–xix.

22 R. Steinhardt Botwinick, 'Prejudice and Anti-Semitism: Introduction', in R. Steinhardt Botwinick (ed.), *A Holocaust Reader: From Ideology to Annihilation*, Upper Saddle River: Prentice-Hall, 1998, p. 2.

23 P. Haas, *Morality After Auschwitz: The Radical Challenge of the Nazi Ethic*, Philadelphia: Fortress Press, 1992, p. 15; G. Kren, 'The Holocaust as History', in A. Rosenberg and G. Myers (eds), *Echoes from the Holocaust: Philosophical Reflections on a Dark Time*, Philadelphia: Temple University Press, 1988, p. 8.

24 Kren, 'The Holocaust as History', pp. 8–9.

25 R. Rubenstein and J. Roth, *Approaches to Auschwitz*, Atlanta: John Knox, 1987, pp. 31, 39, 45. See also D. Goldhagen, *Hitler's Willing Executioners: Ordinary*

Germans and the Holocaust, London: Little Brown and Company, 1996, pp. 38–45.

26 J. Carmicheal, 'The Satanizing of the Jews: Origin and Development of Mystical Anti-Semitism', in Steinhardt Botwinick, op. cit., pp. 11–13.

27 Trachtenberg, *The Devil and the Jews*, pp. 21–2.

28 M. Kleg, 'Hate Prejudice and Racism', in Steinhardt Botwinick, op. cit., p. 7.

29 Z. Bauman, *Modernity and the Holocaust*, Cambridge: Polity Press, 1989, pp. 1, 33, 39–41, 46, 50–2, 55 (*italics his*).

30 Rubenstein and Roth, *Approaches to Auschwitz*, p. 6.

31 R. Rubenstein, 'Afterword: Genocide and Civilization', in Willimann and Dobkowski, op. cit., pp. 291–2. For a further discussion see R. Rubenstein, 'Holocaust and Holy War', *Annals of the American Academy of Political and Social Science*, vol. 548, 1996, pp. 24–5.

32 Rubenstein, 'Religion and the Uniqueness of the Holocaust', pp. 33–5.

33 Ibid., pp. 35–8.

34 G. Steiner, *In Bluebeard's Castle*, London: Faber and Faber, 1971, p. 36.

35 Ibid., p. 45.

36 Ibid., p. 41.

37 Ibid., p. 46.

38 G. Heinsohn, 'What makes the Holocaust a uniquely unique genocide?', *Journal of Genocide Research* vol. 2, no. 3, 2000, pp. 416, 418.

39 Ibid., pp. 421–2.

40 Ibid., pp. 425–6.

41 Ibid., pp. 425–6.

42 See L. Poliakov, *Harvest of Hate: The Nazi Program for the Destruction of the Jews of Europe*, Westport: Greenwood Press, 1975 [1951], p. 5; H. Kaplan, *Conscience And Memory: Meditations In A Museum Of The Holocaust*, Chicago: University of Chicago Press, 1994, pp. 116–17; E. Bellamy, *Affective Genealogies: Psychoanalysis, Postmodernism and the 'Jewish Question' After Auschwitz*, London: University of Nebraska Press, 1997, p. 4.

43 Haas, *Morality After Auschwitz*, p. 28.

44 J.A. Gobineau, *Essai sur l'inégalité des races humaines*, Paris: Éditions Pierre Belfond, 1967.

45 Haas, *Morality After Auschwitz*, p. 2.

46 M. Burleigh and W. Wippermann, *The Racial State: Germany 1933–1945*, Cambridge: Cambridge University Press, 1991, p. 305.

47 Haas, *Morality After Auschwitz*, p. 2.

48 C. Koonz, *The Nazi Conscience*, Cambridge: Belknap Press/Harvard University Press, 2003, p. 1.

49 Ibid., p. 13.

50 Bauman, *Modernity and the Holocaust*, p. 68.

51 Poliakov, *Harvest of Hate*, p. 6.

52 Bauer, *Rethinking the Holocaust*, pp. 52–3.

53 R. Waite, 'The Holocaust and Historical Explanation', in Willimann and Dobkowski, op. cit., p. 165.

54 Bauer, *Rethinking the Holocaust*, p. 48.

55 R.J. Lifton, *The Nazi Doctors: Medical Killing and the Psychology of Genocide*, New York: Basic Books, 1986, p. 17.

56 Ibid., pp. 440–41.

57 These ideals existed well before Hitler's rise to power, in the writings of Julius Lehmann, Alfred Ploetz, Fritz Lenz, Ernst Haeckel and others. These arguments are fully developed in R. Proctor, *Racial Hygiene: Medicine Under the Nazis*, Cambridge: Harvard University Press, 1988, pp. 10–45. Burleigh and Wippermann, *The Racial State*, pp. 30–1; Lifton, *The Nazi Doctors*, p. 46.

58 Proctor, *Racial Hygiene*, pp. 30; 45; 47; 64.
59 Bauman, *Modernity and the Holocaust*, p. 70.
60 L. Friedberg, 'Dare to Compare: Americanizing the Holocaust', *American Indian Quarterly*, vol. 24, no. 3, 2000, p. 364.
61 Ibid., p. 364.
62 Clendinnen, *Reading the Holocaust*, p. 18.
63 A. Spiegelmann, *Maus: A Survivor's Tale, Volumes I and II*, New York: Pantheon, 1986.
64 Metselaar, Mennon, and van der Rol (eds), *A History for Today: Anne Frank*, Amsterdam: Anne Frank House, 1996, p. 5.
65 L. Kutler, 'Holocaust Diaries and Memoirs', in S. Friedman (ed.), *Holocaust Literature: A Handbook of Critical, Historical and Literary Writings*, Westport: Greenwood Press, 1993, p. 523.
66 Kutler, 'Holocaust Diaries and Memoirs', pp. 522–3.
67 *Des Voix Sous La Cendre – Manuscrits Des Sonderkommandos D'auschiwitz – Birkenau*, Paris: Calman-Levy, 2005.
68 M. Ignatieff, *Blood and Belonging: Journeys into the New Nationalism*, Toronto: Viking Books, 1993, p. 14. Even in the twentieth century, the Turkish and Kurdish genocide of Armenians in 1915 must surely rank as much a 'fratricidal' conflict as German against assimilated Jew. Yet earlier examples are common – brutal wars between Iroquois and Huron, Maori and Moriori, Scots and English, etc.
69 A. Rosenberg, 'Was the Holocaust Unique? A Peculiar Question?', in Willimann and Dobkowski, op. cit., p. 156.
70 G. Aly, 'The planning intelligentsia and the "Final Solution"', in O. Bartov (ed.), *The Holocaust: Origins, Implementation, Aftermath: Rewriting Histories*, London: Routledge, 2000, pp. 94–5; see also C. Browning, *The Path to Genocide: Essays on Launching the Final Solution*, Cambridge: Cambridge University Press, 1992, pp. 59–61. Such theories, while innovative, are not without their critics. While Browning hails the Aly and Hein study as a laudable one, he takes issue with the ideal of bureaucratic unity, which he argues glosses over the very real 'polycratic rivalries' within the Nazi system. He also raises doubts as to whether or not these planners were in favor of total genocide before 1941, and whether they in fact initiated it, as Aly and Hein have claimed. Browning, *The Path to Genocide*, pp. 64–5, 142–3.
71 A. Milchman and A. Rosenberg, 'Two Kinds of Uniqueness', in R. Millen (ed.), *New Perspectives on the Holocaust: A Guide for Teachers and Scholars*, New York: New York University Press, 1996, pp. 13–14.
72 Ibid., p. 14.
73 Kren, 'The Holocaust as History', p. 27; Rubenstein and Roth, *Approaches to Auschwitz*, p. 147.
74 V. Grossman, 'Preface', in I. Ehrenburg and V. Grossman (eds), *The Black Book*, New York: Holocaust Library, 1981, p. xxviii. For further elaborations of the same thesis see A. Rosenberg and P. Marcus, 'The Holocaust as a Test of Philosophy', in Rosenberg and Myers, op. cit., pp. 212–14; C. Sydnor, 'The Concentration Camps and Killing Centers of the Third Reich', in Friedman, op. cit., p. 75.
75 Bauman, *Modernity and the Holocaust*, pp. 89–90.
76 Ibid., pp. 21; 100–1.
77 Ibid., pp. 15, 17.
78 E. Black, *IBM and the Holocaust: The Strategic Alliance Between Nazi Germany and America's Most Powerful Corporation*, London: Little, Brown and Company, 2001, pp. 8–10, 56, 58–9.
79 Ibid., pp. 73–4.

80 Burleigh and Wippermann, *The Racial State*, p. 98.
81 Bauer, *Rethinking the Holocaust*, pp. 22, 27–8.
82 Ibid., pp. 48–9.
83 S. Katz, 'The Uniqueness of the Holocaust: The Historical Dimension', in A. Rosenbaum (ed.), *Is The Holocaust Unique? Perspectives on Comparative Genocide Second Edition*, Boulder: Westview Press, 2001, pp. 49–50; For discussion of Katz and his theory of the uniqueness of Nazi 'genocidal intent', see Seeskin, 'What Philosophy Can and Cannot Say About Evil', p. 98.
84 J. Roth, 'The Ethics of Uniqueness', in Rosenbaum, op. cit., p. 22.
85 M. Gilbert, *Never Again: A History of the Holocaust*, New York: Universe Publishing, 2000, p. 98. For more supporting views along the same lines, see Berenbaum, 'The Uniqueness and Universality of the Holocaust', pp. 31–2.
86 Gilbert, *Never Again*, pp. 70–1.
87 Ibid., pp. 70–1.
88 Haas, *Morality After Auschwitz*, pp. 157–9, 162; Clendinnen, *Reading the Holocaust*, p. 63; A. El-Hayek, 'The Major Texts of the Holocaust', in Friedman, op. cit., pp. 5–7.
89 Bauman, *Modernity and the Holocaust*, pp. 23, 118.
90 Ibid., p. 122.
91 T. Borowski, *This Way for the Gas, Ladies and Gentlemen*, London: Penguin, 1992.
92 Rubenstein and Roth, *Approaches to Auschwitz*, pp. 275–6.
93 Bauman, *Modernity and the Holocaust*, pp. 23, 130.
94 Ibid., pp. 131–3.
95 V. Frankl, *Man's Search for Meaning: An Introduction to Logotherapy*, London: Hodder and Stoughton, 1978, pp. 8–9.
96 P. Levi, 'The gray zone', in Bartov, op. cit., pp. 257–9.
97 Ibid., pp. 261–3.
98 D. Moshman, 'Conceptual constraints on thinking about genocide', *Journal of Genocide Research*, vol. 3, no. 3, 2001, pp. 433–4.
99 M. Marrus, *The Holocaust in History*, London: Penguin, 1987, pp. 19–20, 23.
100 Ball, 'Introduction', p. 11.
101 Clendinnen, *Reading the Holocaust*, pp. 15–16.
102 Margalit and Motzkin, 'The Uniqueness of the Holocaust', pp. 75–6.
103 Steiner, *In Bluebeard's Castle*, pp. 53–4.
104 A. Rabinbach and J. Zipes, 'Lessons of the Holocaust', *New German Critique*, no. 19, 1980, p. 4.
105 Steiner, *In Bluebeard's Castle*, pp. 55–6.
106 D. Diner, *Zivilisationsbruch. Denken nach Auschwitz*, Frankfurt: Herausgeber, 1989.
107 Bauman, *Modernity and the Holocaust*, p. 85.
108 A. Huyssen, 'Monument and Memory in a Postmodern Age', *Yale Journal of Criticism*, vol. 6, no. 2, 1993, p. 16.
109 Rosenberg and Marcus, 'The Holocaust as a Test of Philosophy', p. 209.
110 Rubenstein and Roth, *Approaches to Auschwitz*, pp. 14–15, 291.
111 J. Glover, *Humanity: A Moral History of the Twentieth Century*, London: Cape, 1999, pp. 2–4.
112 S. Wright, *International Human Rights, Decolonisation and Globalisation: Becoming Human*, New York: Routledge, 2001, pp. 18–19 (*italics hers*).
113 G. Robertson, *Crimes Against Humanity: The Struggle for Global Justice*, London: Penguin, 2000. Also L. Henkin, 'Human Rights: Ideology and Aspiration, Reality and Prospect', in S. Power and G. Allison (eds), *Realizing Human Rights: Moving From Inspiration to Impact*, New York: St. Martin's Press, 2000, pp. 7–18.

114 R. Goldstone, 'From the Holocaust: Some Legal and Moral Implications', in Rosenbaum, op. cit., pp. 41–2.

115 Ibid., pp. 43–5.

116 C. Brown, *Understanding International Relations*, London: MacMillan, 1997, pp. 21–7.

117 U. Makino, 'Final solutions, crimes against mankind: on the genesis and criticism of the concept of genocide', *Journal of Genocide Research*, vol. 3, no. 1, 2001, p. 53.

118 The lack of any international law protecting minorities from mass murder infuriated Lemkin, and inspired him in 1933 to propose an international law prohibiting the destruction of races, nations, and religious group. He relied on the Armenian massacres and the mistreatment of Jews in Hitler's Germany. In 1921, the assassination of former Turkish interior minister Mehmed Talaat by Armenian genocide survivor Soghomon Tehlirian had a profound impact on Lemkin as a young Polish law student. See S. Power, *'A Problem from Hell': America and the Age of Genocide*, New York: Basic Books, 2002, pp. 1, 17–19; and P. Ronayne, *Never Again? The United States and the Prevention and Punishment of Genocide Since the Holocaust*, Lanham: Rowman & Littlefield, 2001, pp. 14–17.

119 M. Ishay, *The History of Human Rights: From Ancient Times to the Globalization Era*, Berkeley: University of California Press, 2004, p. 151.

120 M. Ignatieff, 'Human Rights as Politics', and 'Human Rights as Idolatry', in A. Gutman (ed.), *Human Rights as Politics and Idolatry*, Princeton: Princeton University Press, 2001, pp. 313–15.

121 Ibid., p. 8.

122 D. Ofer, 'Linguistic Conceptualization of the Holocaust in Palestine and Israel 1942–53', *Journal of Contemporary History*, vol. 31, no. 3, 1996, pp. 582–3.

123 M. Rosensaft, 'Antisemitism Remains a Threat to the Jewish People', in M. Rosensaft and Y. Bauer (eds), *Antisemitism: Threat to Western Civilization*, Jerusalem: Vidal Sassoon International Center for the Study of Antisemitism/ University of Jerusalem, 1988, p. 4.

124 Y. Herzog, *A People that Dwells Alone*, London: Weidenfeld and Nicholson, 1975, pp. 140–2.

125 S. Friedlander, 'Memory of the Shoah in Israel', in Young, op. cit., p. 149.

126 Ibid., p. 152.

127 Y. Eliach, 'The Holocaust as Obligation and Excuse', *Sh'ma*, vol. 9, no. 181, 1979, online. Available: www.clal.org/e41.htm>l (accessed 23 June, 2004).

128 I. Pappe, 'Fifty Years Through the Eyes of "New Historians" in Israel', *Middle East Report*, no. 207, 1998, p. 14. See also A. Confino, 'Collective Memory and Cultural History: Problems of Method', *The American Historical Review*, vol. 102, no. 5, 1997, p. 1386.

129 D. Levy, 'The Future of the Past: Historiographical Disputes and Competing Memories in Germany and Israel', *History and Theory*, vol. 38, 1999, pp. 59–61.

130 Pappe, 'Fifty Years Through the Eyes of "New Historians" in Israel', pp. 14–15.

131 On this see M. Gerstenfeld, *Europe's Crumbling Myths: The Post-Holocaust Origins of Today's Anti-Semitism*, Jerusalem: Jerusalem Center for Public Affairs/Yad Vashem/World Jewish Congress, 2003.

132 Goldstone, 'From the Holocaust', p. 41.

133 K. Jonassohn, 'The Uniqueness of the Holocaust: Neglected Aspects and their Consequences', in F. Chalk and K. Jonassohn (eds), *The History and Sociology of Genocide: Analysis and Case Studies*, New Haven: Yale University Press, 1990, p. 326.

134 R. Wistrich, 'Anti-Semitism in Europe After 1945', in R. Wistrich (ed.), *Terms of Survival: The Jewish World since 1945*, London: Routledge, 1995, p. 269.

135 H. Kung, *Judaism: Between Yesterday and Tomorrow*, New York: Crossroad, 1992, p. 232.

136 J. Olick, 'What Does it Mean to Normalize the Past?', *Social Science History*, vol. 4, no. 22, 1998, pp. 547–8.

137 Gilbert, *Never Again*, p. 170.

138 The funds were designed not the compensate survivors for the deaths of loved ones, but were earmarked as reparations for the State of Israel, which had 'assumed the heavy burden of resettling so great a number of uprooted and destitute Jewish refugees from Germany and from territories formerly under German rule'. M. Gilbert, *Israel: A History*, New York: William Morrow, 1998, pp. 283–5.

139 Ibid., p. 284.

140 C. Koonz, 'Germany's Buchenwald: Whose Shrine? Whose Memory?', in Young, op. cit., p. 112.

141 W. Renn, 'The Holocaust in the School Textbooks of the Federal Republic of Germany', in Friedman, op. cit., pp. 481–2.

142 Olick, 'What Does it Mean to Normalize the Past?', pp. 551–2.

143 Ibid., p. 550.

144 Koonz, 'Germany's Buchenwald', pp. 118–19; For an excellent and recent overview of the Historians' debate, see D. La Capra, *History and Memory After Auschwitz*, Ithaca: Cornell University Press, 1998, pp. 43–70.

145 B. Bennett, 'The Holocaust: Denial and Memory', *The Humanist*, vol. 57, no. 3, 1997, pp. 2–3.

146 M. Hasian, 'Holocaust denial debates: the symbolic significance of Irving v. Penguin & Lipstadt', *Communications Studies*, vol. 53, no. 2, 2002, p. 7.; M. Shermer and A. Grobman, *Denying History: Who says the Holocaust never happened and why do they say it?*, Berkeley, CA: University of California Press, 2000, pp. 10–12.

147 D. Lipstadt, *Denying the Holocaust: The Growing Assault on Truth and Memory*, New York: Free Press, 1993, pp. 12–13; Shermer and Grobman, *Denying History*, p. 86.

148 Lipstadt, *Denying the Holocaust*, pp. 51–7, 62–4; Shermer and Grobman, *Denying History*, pp. 41, 58–9. For more detailed discussion, see P. Vidal-Naquet, *Les Assassins de la mémoire: 'Un Eichmann de papier' et autres essais sur le révisionnisme*, Paris: Seuil, 1995; and A. Finkielkraut, *L'avenir d'une négation: réflexion sur la question du génocide*, Paris: Seuil, 1982.

149 Lipstadt, *Denying the Holocaust*, pp. 65–6.

150 Ibid., pp. 67, 79, 85–6, 90–4, 123–7.

151 J. Najarian, 'Gnawing at history: the rhetoric of Holocaust denial', *The Midwest Quarterly*, vol. 39, no. 1, 1997, p. 4.

152 Shermer and Grobman, *Denying History*, p. 13.

153 Lipstadt, *Denying the Holocaust*, p. 157–9; Shermer and Grobman, *Denying History*, pp. 64–7. For information on his trials in Canada, see C. Winn and G. Weimann, *Hate on Trial: The Zundel Affair, the Media, and Public Opinion in Canada*, Oakville: Mosaic Press, 1986.

154 Lipstadt, *Denying the Holocaust*, p. 162–9; Shermer and Grobman, *Denying History*, pp. 128–33.

155 Rosenbaum, *Explaining Hitler*, p. 235.

156 Quoted in Hasian, 'Holocaust denial debates', p. 5.

157 Lipstadt, *Denying the Holocaust*, pp. 22–3; Najarian, 'Gnawing at history', p. 1.

158 E. Alexander, 'False witness: The Irving-Lipstadt trial and the New Yorker', *Judaism: A Quarterly Journal of Jewish Life and Thought*, vol. 50, no. 4, 2001, p. 454. S. Miller, 'Denial of the Holocaust', *Social Education*, vol. 59, no. 6, 1995.

3 Colonialism, genocide, and indigenous rights: America, Australia, and New Zealand

1 R. Hitchcock and T. Twedt, 'Physical and Cultural Genocides of Various Indigenous Peoples' in S. Totten, W. Parsons and I. Charny (eds), *Century of Genocide: Eyewitness Accounts and Critical Views*, London: Garland, 1997, pp. 372–4.

2 E. Barkan, 'Genocides of Indigenous Peoples: Rhetoric of Human Rights' in R. Gallately and B. Kiernan (eds), *The Specter of Genocide: Mass Murder in Historical Perspective*, Cambridge: Cambridge University Press, 2003, p. 117.

3 Ibid., p. 119. See also J. Wilson, *The Earth Shall Weep: A History of Native America*, New York: Atlantic Monthly Press, 1998, pp. xxii–xxiii; 45; B. Dippie, *The Vanishing American: White Attitudes and U.S. Indian Policy*, Middleton: Wesleyan University Press, 1982.

4 K. Bischoping and N. Fingerhut, 'Border Lines: Indigenous Peoples in Genocide Studies', *Canadian Review of Sociology and Anthropology*, vol. 33, 1996, p. 487.

5 F. Chalk, 'Redefining Genocide', in G. Andreopoulos (ed.), *Genocide: Conceptual and Historical Dimensions*, Philadelphia: University of Pennsylvania Press, 1994, p. 54.

6 Chalk, 'Redefining Genocide', p. 49.

7 As quoted in A.D. Moses, 'Genocide and Settler Society in Australian History', in A.D. Moses (ed.), *Genocide and Settler Society*, New York: Berghahn, 2005, p. 28.

8 M. Davis, *Late Victorian Holocausts: El Nino Famines and the Making of the Third World*, London: Verso, 2001, p. 7.

9 A. Hochschild, *King Leopold's Ghost: A Story of Greed, Terror and Heroism in Colonial Africa*, London: Papermac, 1998, pp. 225, 279–80. Hochschild argues that while the death tolls were of 'genocidal' proportions, they were not, strictly speaking, genocide.

10 P. Nicholson, *Who Do We Think We Are? Race and Nation in the Modern World*, New York: ME Sharpe, 2001, p. 118. For more information on these and other early genocides see B. Kiernan, 'Twentieth century genocides: Underlying Ideological Themes from Armenia to East Timor', in Gellately and Kiernan, op. cit.; K. Jonassohn, *Genocide and Gross Human Rights Violations*, New Brunswick: Transaction Publishers, 1998, pp. 72–4. M. Crocker, *Rivers of Blood Rivers of Gold: Europe's Conquest of Indigenous Peoples*, London: Jonathan Cape, 1998, pp. 269–358.

11 W. Hagan, *American Indians*, Chicago: University of Chicago Press, 1993, p. 73.

12 G. Morris, 'Vine Deloria, Jr., and the Development of a Decolonizing Critique of Indigenous Peoples and International Relations', in R. Grounds, G. Tinker and D. Wilkins (eds), *Native Voices: American Indian Identity and Resistance*, Kansas: University of Kansas Press, 2003, p. 108; W. Churchill and G. Morris, 'Key Indian Laws and Cases', in M.A. Jaimes (ed.), *The State of Native America: Genocide, Colonization, and Resistance*, Boston: South End Press, 1992, p. 18; see also J. Wickham, 'September 11 and America's War on Terrorism: A New Manifest destiny?', *American Indian Quarterly*, vol. 26, no. 1, 2002, p. 120.

13 Hagan, *American Indians*, pp. 80–1.

14 Hitchcock and Twedt, 'Physical and Cultural Genocides of Various Indigenous Peoples', p. 380.

15 L. Stiffarm and P. Lane, 'The Demography of Native North America: A Question of American Indian Survival', in Jaimes, op. cit.; A. Fleras and J. Elliot, *The Nations Within: Aboriginal–State Relations in Canada, the United States and New Zealand*, Toronto: Oxford University Press, 1994, p. 143.

16 F.P. Prucha, *American Indian Policy in the Formative Years: The Indian Trade and Intercourse Acts 1780–1834*, Cambridge: Harvard University Press, 1962, p. 198. For more details of the massacres see M.A. Jaimes, 'Sand Creek: The Morning After', in Jaimes, op. cit.

17 Similar tactics appear to have been used by the fledgling United States in its 1783 war against the Cherokee. Stiffarm and Lane, 'The Demography of Native North America', p. 32.

18 Stiffarm and Lane, 'The Demography of Native North America', p. 33; Hagan, *American Indians*, p. 130.

19 Stiffarm and Lane, 'The Demography of Native North America', pp. 33–4.

20 Fleras and Elliot, *The Nations Within*, p. 147.

21 D. Wilkins, 'From Time Immemorial: The Origin and Import of the Reserved Rights Doctrine', in Grounds, Tinker, and Wilkins, op. cit., p. 81.

22 J. Wilson, *The Earth Shall Weep: A History of Native America*, New York: Atlantic Monthly Press, 1998, pp. 303–4, 308.

23 J. Nagel, *American Indian Ethnic Renewal: Red Power and the Resurgence of Identity and Culture*, New York: Oxford University Press, 1997, p. 115.

24 Hagan, *American Indians*, pp. 152–6; Wilson, *The Earth Shall Weep*, pp. 315–18.

25 D. Adams, *Education for Extinction: American Indians and the Boarding School Experience 1875–1928*, Kansas: University Press of Kansas, 1995.

26 L. Poupart, 'The Familiar Face of Genocide: Internalized Oppression Among American Indians', *Hypatia*, vol. 18, no. 2, 2003, p. 92.

27 Hitchcock and Twedt, 'Physical and Cultural Genocides of Various Indigenous Peoples', p. 380.

28 B. Dippie, *The Vanishing American: White Attitudes and US Indian Policy*, Lawrence: University Press of Kansas, p. 345.

29 Hagan, *American Indians*, pp. 171–7.

30 Nagel, *American Indian Ethnic Renewal*, p. 119.

31 Fleras and Elliot, *The Nations Within*, p. 151; W. Churchill, *A Little Matter of Genocide: Holocaust and Denial in the Americas 1492 to Present*, San Francisco: City Lights, 1997, p. 32; Hagan, *American Indians*, p. 185.

32 Stiffarm and Lane, 'The Demography of Native North America', p. 37.

33 Online.   Available: www.cia.gov/cia/publications/factbook/geos/us.htm>1 (accessed October 24, 2005). Wilson, *The Earth Shall Weep*, p. xxiv.

34 Morris, 'Vine Deloria, Jr', p. 121.

35 Jaimes, 'Sand Creek', p. 8.

36 Poupart, 'The familiar face of genocide', pp. 87, 89.

37 Reuters, 'Lucky country's racism questioned', *The Press*, 27 August, 2001.

38 G. Greer, 'Whitefella Jump Up: The Shortest Way to Nationhood', *Quarterly Essay*, no. 11, 2003, p. 63.

39 F. Clark, *The History of Australia*, Westport: Greenwood Press, 2002, pp. 10–12; P. Clark, *Where the Ancestors Walked: Australia as an Aboriginal Landscape*, Crows Nest: Allen & Unwin, 2003, pp. 39–40; A.D. Moses, 'An antipodean genocide? The origins of the genocidal moment in the colonization of Australia', *Journal of Genocide Research*, vol. 2, no. 1, 2000, p. 92; R. Laidlaw, 'European Settlement and Aboriginal Society', in T. Gurry (ed.), *The European Occupation*, Richmond: Heinemann Educational, 1984, p. 61.

40 H. Reynolds, *Frontier: Aborigines, Settlers and Land*, Crows Nest: Allen & Unwin, 1987, p. 192.

41 Laidlaw, 'European Settlement and Aboriginal Society', p. 69.

42 Moses, 'An antipodean genocide?', p. 94.

43 C. Tatz, *Genocide In Australia*, AIATSIS Research Discussion Papers No 8, Canberra: Australian Institute of Aboriginal and Torres Strait Islander Studies, 1999, pp. 6–8. Manne estimates a pre-conquest population of between 300,000

and 1,000,000 and a figure by the 1920s of about 70,000 'full bloods' and 'half-castes' surviving. Manne, *In Denial* p. 103.

44 Reynolds, *Frontier*, p. 8.

45 Moses, 'An antipodean genocide?', pp. 95–8.

46 Reynolds, *Frontier*, pp. 13–18.

47 T. Keneally, P. Adam-Smith and R. Davidson, *Australia: Beyond the Dreamtime*, Richmond: BBC Books, 1987, pp. 140, 170.

48 Reynolds, *Frontier*, pp. 53–5.

49 Ibid., pp. 30, 53–5.

50 P. Knightley, *Australia: A Biography of a Nation*, London: Jonathan Cape, 2000, p. 108.

51 Manne, *In Denial* pp. 61–3; Reynold's and Broome's figures are discussed on p. 97. See also Clark, *A Short History of Australia*, p. 85; and P. Bartrop, 'The Holocaust, the Aborigines, and the bureaucracy of destruction: an Australian dimension of genocide', *Journal of Genocide Research*, vol. 3, no. 1, 2001, p. 76; J. Pilger, *A Secret Country*, London: Vintage, 1993, p. 28.

52 Reynolds, *An Indelible Stain?*, London: Viking, 2001, pp. 54–8, 67–85.

53 Moses, 'An antipodean genocide?', pp. 98–9. Reynolds, *The Indelible Stain*, pp. 84–5.

54 Laidlaw, 'European Settlement and Aboriginal Society', p. 57.

55 Pilger, *A Secret Country*, pp. 27–8.

56 Moses, 'An antipodean genocide?', pp. 98–102.

57 Reynolds, *Frontier*, pp. 47–8.

58 Reynolds, *The Indelible Stain*, pp. 105–18.

59 C. Tatz, 'Confronting Australian genocide', *Aboriginal History*, vol. 25, 2002, p. 23.

60 Manne is referring here to removals policies, but he also gives the example of state-sponsored sterilizations as another means of stopping the Aborigines from reproducing. Manne, *In Denial* p. 37.

61 Knightley, *Australia*, p. 112.

62 Reynolds, *The Indelible Stain*, p. 165.

63 Manne, *In Denial* p. 27; P. Bartrop, 'The Holocaust, the Aborigines, and the bureaucracy of destruction: an Australian dimension of genocide', *Journal of Genocide Research*, vol. 3, no. 1, 2001, p. 77. Tatz, 'Confronting Australian genocide', pp. 18–19.

64 Manne, *In Denial* pp. 17, 39. Bartrop, 'The Holocaust, the Aborigines, and the bureaucracy of destruction', p. 78.

65 A. Curthoys and J. Docker, 'Introduction: Genocide: definitions, questions, settler-colonies', *Aboriginal History*, vol. 25, 2001, p. 1.

66 MacIntyre, *The History Wars*, p. 154.

67 Manne, *In Denial* p. 35.

68 Bartrop, 'The Holocaust …', p. 79.

69 Knightley, *Australia*, p. 121.

70 Barkan, *The Guilt of Nations*, p. 262; D. Alves, *The Maori and the Crown: An Indigenous People's Struggle for Self-Determination*, London: Greenwood Press, 1999, pp. 3–5; R. Consedine and J. Consedine, *Healing Our History: The Challenge of the Treaty of Waitangi*, Auckland: Penguin, 2001, p. 79; A. Armitage, *Comparing the Policy of Aboriginal Assimilation in Australia, Canada and New Zealand*, Vancouver: University of British Columbia Press, 1995, p. 138.

71 K. Sinclair, *A Destiny Apart: New Zealand's Search for National Identity*, Auckland: Allen & Unwin, 1986, pp. 197–9.

72 C. Orange, *The Treaty of Waitangi*, Wellington: Allen & Unwin, 1987, p. 2; D. Williams, 'Te Tiriti o Waitangi – Unique Relationship Between Crown and Tangata Whenua?' in I.H. Kawharu (ed.), *Waitangi: Maori and Pakeha*

Perspectives of the Treaty of Waitangi, Auckland: Oxford University Press, 1989, p. 65; T. Simpson, *Te Riri Pakeha: The White Man's Anger*, Auckland: Hodder and Stoughton, 1986, p. 61; F. Brookfield, *Waitangi & Indigenous Rights: Revolution, Law & Legitimation*, Auckland: Auckland University Press, 1999, p. 137.

73 R. Walker, 'The Treaty of Waitangi as the Focus of Maori Protest', in I.H. Kawharu op. cit., pp. 263–72; and Orange, *The Treaty of Waitangi*, p. 1.

74 M. Jackson, 'Land Loss and the Treaty of Waitangi', pp. 70–7, in W. Ihimaera (ed.), *Te Ao Marama: Regaining Aotearoa: Maori Writers Speak Out*, Auckland: Reed, 1993, p. 70.

75 J. Williams, 'Back to the Future: Maori Survival in the 1990s, extract', pp. 78–82, in W. Ihimaera, *Te A. Marama: Regaining Aotearoa: Maori Writers Speak Out*, Auckland: Reed, 1993, p. 79.

76 A. Ward, *An Unsettled History: Treaty Claims in New Zealand Today*, Wellington: Bridget Williams Books, 1999, p. 167.

77 Jackson, 'Land Loss and the Treaty of Waitangi', pp. 70–1, 77.

78 Walker, 'The Maori People', p. 322.

79 R. Balzer, 'Hamilton Abuse Intervention Project: The Aotearoa Experience', in M. Shepard and E. Pence (eds), *Coordinating Community Responses to Domestic Violence*, London: Sage, 1999, pp. 342–3.

80 Armitage, *Comparing the Policy of Aboriginal Assimilation in Australia, Canada and New Zealand*, pp. 137–8.

81 Consedine and Consedine, *Healing Our History*, pp. 83–5.

82 Walker, 'The Maori People', pp. 321–2, 338; Orange, *The Treaty of Waitangi*, pp. 226–7; Ward, *An Unsettled History*, p. 114.

83 Walker, 'The Maori People, p. 323–4; Clark, *A Short History of Australia*, p. 177.

84 R. MacDonald, *The Fifth Wind: New Zealand and the Legacy of a Turbulent Past*, Auckland: Hodder & Stoughton, 1989, pp. 57–8.

85 Simpson, *Te Riri Pakeha*, p. 251; D. Colgan, 'The Maori: Integration or Subjugation' in G. Vaughn (ed.), *Racial Issues in New Zealand*, Auckland: Auckland University, 1972, pp. 20–2.

86 R. Walker, *Nga Tau Tohetohe – Years of Anger*, Auckland: Penguin, 1987, p. 96.

87 I. Ramsden, 'Borders and Frontiers', in Ihimaera, op. cit., p. 349.

88 Simpson, *Te Riri Pakeha*, pp. 198–9.

4 Uncle Sam's willing executioners? Indigenous genocide and representation in the United States

1 L. Peltier, *Prison Writings: My Life is My Sun Dance*, New York: St Martin's, 1999, p. 21.

2 T. Cole, 'Nativization and Nationalization: A Comparative Landscape Study of Holocaust Museums in Israel, the US and the UK', *The Journal of Israeli History*, vol. 23, no. 1, 2004, p. 139.

3 J. Ashley and K. Jarratt-Ziemski, 'Superficiality and Bias: The, Mistreatment of Native Americans in U.S. Government Textbooks', *American Indian Quarterly*, vol. 23, nos. 3/4, 1999.

4 J. Trescott, 'History's New Look', *The Washington Post*, 13 September, 2004, online. Available: www.washingtonpost.com/ac2/wp-dyn?node=entertainment/profile&id=831249&typeId=3 (accessed June 27, 2005).

5 Ibid.,

6 L. Friedberg, 'Dare to Compare: Americanizing the Holocaust', *The American Indian Quarterly*, vol. 24, no. 3, 2000, p. 367.

7 J. Boyarin, 'Europe's Indian, America's Jew: Modiano and Vizenor', *Boundary 2*, vol. 19, no. 3, 1992, p. 198.

8 Ibid., p. 207.
9 W. Churchill, *A Little Matter of Genocide: Holocaust and Denial in the Americas 1492 to the Present*, San Francisco: City Lights, 1997, p. i.
10 This included T. Todorov's *The Conquest of America*, 1982, E. Galeano, *Memory of Fire*, 1985, R. Thornton, *American Indian Holocaust and Survival*, 1987, and K. Sale, *The Conquest of Paradise*, 1990.
11 R. Drinnon, *Facing West: The Metaphysics of Indian-hating and Empire-building*, Minneapolis: University of Minnesota Press, 1980, p. xii.
12 Ibid., pp. 463–4.
13 Ibid., pp. 7–8, 36–43, 56.
14 Ibid., pp. 163–4.
15 Ibid., pp. 81–5, 93–7.
16 Ibid., pp. 100, 106–10.
17 Ibid., pp. 173–5, 180–1.
18 See R. Satz, *American Indian Policy in the Jacksonian Era*, Lincoln: University of Nebraska Press, 1975, p. 9.
19 B. Dippie, *The Vanishing American: White Attitudes and US Indian Policy*, Lawrence: University Press of Kansas, 1982, p. 351.
20 D. Stannard, *American Holocaust: The Conquest of the New World*, New York: Oxford University Press, 1992, p. 283.
21 D. Stannard, 'Preface', in Churchill, *A Little Matter of Genocide*, op. cit., p. xiii.
22 Churchill, *A Little Matter of Genocide*, p. 8.
23 Stannard, *American Holocaust*, pp. x, 128–9, 222–3.
24 Churchill, *A Little Matter of Genocide*, p. 4.
25 Ibid., pp. 1, 97.
26 A typical example is Iztapalapa in Mexico, a city with some 350,000 residents, five times larger than London or Seville at the time. The city possessed a network of canals, lavish gardens, markets teaming with exotic foods, and some 60,000 pale stuccoed houses, many of them multistoried. Stannard, *American Holocaust*, pp. 3–5.
27 Stannard, *American Holocaust*, pp. 3–8.
28 Ibid., pp. 30, 52–3.
29 J. Blick, 'The Iroquois practice of genocidal warfare, 1543–1787', *Journal of Genocide Research*, vol. 3, no. 3, 2001, pp. 406–8, 418.
30 D. Stannard, 'Uniqueness as Denial: The Politics of Genocide Scholarship', in A. Rosenbaum (ed.), *Is The Holocaust Unique? Perspectives on Comparative Genocide*, 2nd edition, Boulder: Westview Press, 2001, pp. 256–8.
31 Stannard, *American Holocaust*, pp. 71; 77–83.
32 Ibid., p. 222.
33 Ibid., pp. 58–9.
34 Ibid., pp. 85–7, 95, 101.
35 Major Sullivan later described how the Iroquois 'were hunted like wild beasts' in a 'war of extermination', a war of which Washington approved since he felt Indians deserved nothing from Whites but 'total ruin'. Ibid., pp. 119, 241.
36 Ibid., p. 120.
37 Ibid., pp. 121–2.
38 Churchill, *A Little Matter of Genocide*, pp. 211, 228–32.
39 Ibid., pp. 199–208.
40 Stannard, *American Holocaust*, pp. 130–3.
41 Churchill, *A Little Matter of Genocide*, pp. 2–3; M. Jaimes, 'Sand Creek: The Morning After', in M. Annette Jaimes (ed.), *The State of Native America: Genocide, Colonization, and Resistance*, Boston: South End Press, 1992, p. 6.
42 Ibid., pp. 81, 85, 88; see also W. Churchill, *Acts of Rebellion: The Ward Churchill Reader*, New York: Routledge, 2003, pp. 52–3.

43 Churchill, *A Little Matter of Genocide*, p. 88.
44 Ibid., pp. 117–18.
45 Stannard, *American Holocaust*, p. 184.
46 Churchill, *A Little Matter of Genocide*, p. 92.
47 Stannard, *American Holocaust*, p. 153.
48 Ibid., p. 246.
49 W. Churchill, 'The Earth is Our Mother', in Jaimes, op. cit., p. 145; He uses similar imagery in Churchill, *A Little Matter of Genocide*, p. 52.
50 Stannard, *American Holocaust*, p. xii.
51 Stannard, 'Uniqueness as Denial', pp. 255–6.
52 Ibid., pp. 258–60.
53 Stannard, *American Holocaust*, p. 89.
54 Churchill, *A Little Matter of Genocide*, p. 52.
55 Stannard, 'Uniqueness as Denial', p. 151.
56 Churchill, *A Little Matter of Genocide*, pp. 2–4.
57 Ibid., pp. 131, 135 (*italics in original*).
58 Ibid., p. 119.
59 Stannard, 'Preface', pp. xvii–xviii.
60 Ibid., pp. xvii–xviii. This was earlier elaborated in Stannard, *American Holocaust*, p. 256.
61 Churchill, *A Little Matter of Genocide*, p. 84.
62 Stannard, 'Uniqueness as Denial', p. 151.
63 Ibid., p. 167.
64 Ibid., pp. 272–3 (*italics his*).
65 Ibid., pp. 163–208. See p. 167.
66 W. Churchill, 'Forbidding the "G-Word": Holocaust Denial as Judicial Doctrine in Canada', *Other Voices*, vol. 2, no. 1, 2000, online. Available: www. othervoices.org/
2.1/churchill/denial.htm>l (accessed June 27, 2005).
67 Stannard, 'Uniqueness as Denial', p. 168.
68 Churchill, *A Little Matter of Genocide*, pp. 7, 11, 30–1, 36.
69 Ibid., p. 30.
70 Ibid., pp. 31, 52.
71 See Stannard, 'Uniqueness as Denial', pp. 250–1.
72 Churchill, *A Little Matter of Genocide*, pp. 157–8.
73 Ibid., pp. 426–7.
74 Ibid., p. 50.
75 E. Barkan, 'Genocides of Indigenous Peoples: Rhetoric of Human Rights', in R. Gellately and B. Kiernan (eds), *The Specter of Genocide: Mass Murder in Historical Perspective*, New York: Cambridge University Press, 2003, p. 122.
76 S. Katz, *The Holocaust in Historical Context Volume I*, Oxford: Oxford University Press, 1994, pp. 20, 133; G. Lewy, 'Were American Indians the Victims of Genocide?', *Commentary*, 2004, p. 56.
77 Stannard, *American Holocaust*, p. 57.
78 L. Stiffarm and P. Lane, 'The Demography of Native North America: A Question of American Indian Survival', in Jaimes, op. cit., p. 31.
79 Churchill, *A Little Matter of Genocide*, p. 30.
80 D. Lipstadt, *Denying the Holocaust: The Growing Assault on Truth and Memory*, New York: Free Press, 1993, pp. 214–15.
81 Ibid., pp. 212–13.
82 Ibid., p. 213.
83 Churchill, *A Little Matter of Genocide*, p. 31.
84 Ibid., pp. 68–9.
85 Katz, 'The Uniqueness of the Holocaust', pp. 49–50; For a discussion of Katz

and his theory of the uniqueness of Nazi 'genocidal intent' against the Jews, see K. Seeskin, 'What Philosophy Can and Cannot Say about Evil', in A. Rosenberg and G. Myers (eds), *Echoes from the Holocaust: Philosophical Reflections on a Dark Time*, Philadelphia: Temple University Press, 1988, p. 98.

86 Stannard, 'Uniqueness as denial' pp. 268–72; Churchill reaches the same conclusion in *A Little Matter of Genocide*, pp. 34–5.

87 Katz, *The Holocaust in Historical Context*, Volume I, p. 18.

88 Katz, 'The Uniqueness of the Holocaust', p. 51.

89 Ibid., p. 57.

90 Katz, *The Holocaust in Historical Context*, Volume I, p. 21.

91 Katz, 'The Uniqueness of the Holocaust', pp. 52–4.

92 Ibid., pp. 54–6.

93 Ibid., p. 51.

94 He is quite willing to recognize that the numbers indicate 'solely on statistical grounds' that the 'collapse' of indigenous populations in the Americas 'surpasses the destruction of European Jewry'. Katz, *The Holocaust in Historical Context*, Volume I, pp. 88–9.

95 Stannard, 'Uniqueness as Denial', p. 281.

96 W. Churchill, 'Some People Push Back': On the Justice of Roosting Chickens', 2001, online. Available: www.kersplebedeb.com/mystuff/s11/churchill.htm>l (accessed June 27, 2005).

97 K. Henley, 'Colorado case reopens debate about tenure', *The Christian Science Monitor*, April 11, 2005, online. Available: www.csmonitor.com/2005/0411/p03s01-ussc.htm>l (accessed June 27, 2005).

98 B. Bergman, 'Ward Churchill's Berkeley address: The reluctant poster boy for academic freedom defends his 9/11 comments, meets little resistance at campus forum', *UC Berkely News*, March 31, 2005, online. Available: www.berkeley.edu/news/berkeleyan/2005/03/31_churchill.shtm>l (accessed June 27, 2005).

99 L. Frank, 'Churchill denies sole authorship, plagiarized essay from Dalhousie University professor' *Rocky Mountain News*, March 14, 2005; S. Steers and C. Brennan, 'Talks hit snag: Claims of plagiarism, threat stall Churchill buyout negotiations' *Rocky Mountain News*, March 12, 2005, online. Available: www.rockymountainnews.com/drmn/local/article/0,1299,DRMN_15_361579 5,00.htm>l (accessed June 27, 2005).

100 S. Harjo, 'Why Native Identity Matters: A Cautionary Tale', *Indian Country Today*, February 10, 2005; H. Pankratz, 'CU prof affirms Indian heritage: Tribe says he's not full member', *Denver Post*, February, 2005 3, online. Available: www.denverpost.com/Stories/0,1413,36percent257E23827percent 257E2689334,00.htm>l (accessed June 27, 2005); S. Steers, 'Churchill's membership in tribe honorary only', *Rocky Mountain News*, February, 2005 4, online. Available: www.aimovement. org/moipr/cherokee.htm>l (accessed June 27, 2005).

101 W. Churchill, 'Ward Churchill Responds to Criticism of "Some People Push Back"', January 31, 2005, online. Available: www.kersplebedeb.com/mystuff/ s11/ward_churchill_responds.htm>l (accessed June 27, 2005).

102 B. Kiernan, 'Cover-up and Denial of Genocide: Australia, the USA, East Timor, and the Aborigines', *Critical Asian Studies*, vol. 34, no. 2, 2002, p. 165.

103 J. Angelo Corlett, 'Reparations to Native Americans?', in A. Jokic (ed.), *War Crimes and Collective Wrongdoing: A Reader*, Oxford: Blackwell, 2001, p. 239.

104 Corlett, 'Reparations to Native Americans?', p. 264.

105 Editorial, 'Churchill's Identity Revealed in Wake of Nazi Comment', *Indian Country Today*, February 3, 2005, online. Available: www.indiancountry.com/ content.cfm?id=1096410293 (accessed June 27, 2005).

5 Australia: Aboriginal genocide and the Holocaust

1 P. Knightley, *Australia: A Biography of a Nation*, London: Jonathan Cape, 2000, p. 107.
2 'First Nations Gallery', National Museum of Australia Canberra, online. Available: www.nma.gov.au/media/media_kits/permanent_exhibitions/gallery_of_first_australians/ (accessed October 12, 2005).
3 M. Glikson, 'A Censored Discourse: Contradictions in the Structure of the Gallery of the First Australians', Marxist Interventions/Australian National University, online. Available: www.anu.edu.au/polsci/marx/interventions/gallery.htm (accessed October 12, 2005); For more on the museum, see S. Foster, 'Yesterday and Tomorrow at the National Museum of Australia', *Borderlands*, vol. 3, no. 3, 2004.
4 K. Windschuttle, 'Submission to the review of the National Museum of Australia', March 3, 2003. online. Available: www.sydneyline.com/Nationalpercent20Museum percent20submission.htm> (accessed 12 October, 2005).
5 A.D. Moses, 'Coming to Terms with Genocidal Pasts in a Comparative Perspective', *Aboriginal History*, vol. 25, 2001, p. 106.
6 Ibid., p. 106.
7 B. Kiernan, 'Cover-up and Denial of Genocide: Australia, the USA, East Timor, and the Aborigines', *Critical Asian Studies*, vol. 34, no. 2, 2002, p. 179.
8 R. Gaita, 'Genocide and Pedantry', *Quadrant*, July/August, 1997; R. Gaita 'Genocide: The Holocaust and the Aborigines', *Quadrant*, November, 1997.
9 S. MacIntyre, *The History Wars*, Melbourne: Melbourne University Press, 2003, pp. 146–7.
10 Kiernan, 'Cover-up and Denial of Genocide', p. 180.
11 R. Brunton, 'Genocide, the "Stolen Generations", and the "Unconceived Generations"', *Quadrant*, May, 1998, pp. 19, 24.
12 Ibid., p. 22.
13 Quoted in Kiernan, 'Cover-up and Denial of Genocide', p. 177. See also Gaita, 'Genocide', p. 21.
14 K. Minogue, 'Aborigines and Australian Apologetics', *Quadrant*, September, 1998, pp. 13–14.
15 Minogue, 'Aborigines and Australian Apologetics', p. 15.
16 MacIntyre, *The History Wars*, p. 163.
17 R. Manne, 'In Denial: the Stolen Generations and the Right', *Australian Quarterly Essay*, vol. 1, 2001, p. 94.
18 MacIntyre, *The History Wars*, pp. 165–7.
19 W. Rubenstein, *Genocide: A History*, Harlow: Pearson Education, 2004, pp. 64–5.
20 Ibid., pp. 72–3.
21 Ibid., pp. 72–3.
22 Ibid., p. 112.
23 Ibid., p. 70.
24 Ibid., pp. 16–17.
25 Ibid., p. 17.
26 R. Manne, 'When Jewish loyalty meets the brutality of Israel', *Sydney Morning Herald*, December 6, 2004.
27 P. Bartrop, 'The Holocaust, the Aborigines, and the Bureaucracy of Destruction: an Australian Dimension of Genocide', *Journal of Genocide Research*, vol. 3, no. 1, 2001, pp. 75, 80–3.
28 Ibid., pp. 84–5.
29 'A Tour of Jewish History in Australia', Australian Jewish Historical Society, 2005, online. Available: www.ajhs.info/jha/historytour.htm (accessed October 12, 2005).

30 As Foley recalls, 'The Consul-General, Dr. R.W. Drechsler, refused them admittance'. G. Foley, 'Australia and the Holocaust: A Koori Perspective', The Koori History Website, 1997, online. Available: www.kooriweb.org/foley/essays/essay_8.htm>1 (accessed October 12, 2005).

31 Ibid.,

32 In 1999, Jonathan Morris, Executive Director of the Museum, had learned about the incident from Foley, and pushed for a commemoration. Henry Benjamin, 'Australian Holocaust Museum honors Aborigines' protest of Nazis', Jewish Telegraphic Agency, online. Available: www.kooriweb.org/foley/resources/jta.htm>1 (accessed October 12, 2005).

33 'Top 10 Questions and Answers: Q9. What is the state of the Jewish community's relations with the indigenous Australian community?', New South Wales Jewish Board of Deputies, 2003, online. Available: www.nswjbd.org/MintDigital.NET/
NSWJBD.aspx?XmlNode=/MainNav/FAQs/Top+10+Questions+and+Answers&view=9 (accessed October 12, 2005).

34 P. Kohn and A. Bard, 'Jews and Aboriginal reconciliation', European Network for Indigenous Australian Rights, online. Available: www.eniar.org/news/holocaust.htm>1 (accessed October 12, 2005).

35 'Top 10 Questions and Answers'.

36 'Aboriginal Reconciliation: A Jewish 3-Point Plan: Address By Rabbi Raymond Apple, Am, Rfd At The Great Synagogue, Sydney Shabbat, December 6, 1997', *Letters from Jewish Australia*, no. 56, December 9, 1997, online. Available: www.join.org.au/letters/reconcil.htm (accessed 12 October, 2005).

37 'Top 10 Questions and Answers'.

38 S. Lipman, 'Befriending The Native Aussies', *The Jewish Week*, 10 March, 2003, online. Available: www.join.org.au/media/Befriending_the_Native_Aussies_20031003.htm (accessed October 12, 2005).

39 C. Tatz, 'Confronting Australian genocide', *Aboriginal History*, vol. 25, 2001, pp. 18–19.

40 C. Tatz, *Genocide In Australia*, AIATSIS Research Discussion Papers No 8, Canberra: Australian Institute of Aboriginal and Torres Strait Islander Studies, 1999, p. 2.

41 A. Curthoys and J. Docker, 'Introduction: Genocide: definitions, questions, settler-colonies', *Aboriginal History*, vol. 25, 2001, p. 2. Their work is heavily influenced by Ward Churchill, who they cite ten times in their sixteen-page introduction.

42 Bartrop, 'The Holocaust, the Aborigines, and the bureaucracy of destruction', p. 76.

43 Document 139: 'Black Panthers of Australia, Platform and Programme, 1970', in B. Attwood and A. Markus (eds), *The Struggle for Aboriginal Rights: A Documentary History*, St Leonards: Allen & Unwin, 1999, p. 252.

44 'The Inquiry process', in *Bringing them Home: Report of the National Inquiry into the Separation of Aboriginal and Torres Strait Islander Children from Their Families*, Human Rights and Equal Opportunity Commission/Indigenous Law Resources Reconciliation and Social Justice Library, April, 1997, online. Available: www.austlii.edu.au/au/other/IndigLRes/stolen/stolen05.htm>1 (accessed October 12, 2005).

45 'ATSIC's Submission to the National Inquiry Into the Separation of Aboriginal and Torres Strait Islander Children from their Families', online. Available: www.atsic.gov.au/issues/law_and_justice/bringing_them_home_report/task_force/introduction.asp (accessed 12 October, 2005).

46 T. Barta, 'Discourses of Genocide in Germany and Australia: A Linked History', *Aboriginal History*, vol. 25, 2000, p. 37.

47 Ibid., pp. 37–8.
48 Ibid., pp. 47–8.
49 Ibid., pp. 50–1.
50 A. Markus, 'Genocide in Australia', *Aboriginal History*, vol. 25, 2000, pp. 63–5.
51 Ibid., p. 64.
52 Foley, 'Australia and the Holocaust'.
53 Ibid.,
54 Ibid.,
55 Barta, 'Discourses of genocide in Germany and Australia', p. 39.
56 Ibid., pp. 40–1.
57 Ibid., pp. 42–3.
58 Ibid., pp. 48–9.
59 A. Hebich, 'Between Knowing and Not Knowing: Public knowledge of the Stolen Generations', *Aboriginal History*, vol. 25, 2000, pp. 72, 74.
60 Hebich, 'Between Knowing and Not Knowing', p. 75.
61 Ibid., p. 79.
62 Ibid., p. 82.
63 A. Bonnell and M. Crotty, 'An Australian "Historikerstreit"? Review Article', *Australian Journal of Politics and History*, vol. 50, no. 3, 2005, pp. 425–33, online. Available: www.politicalreviewnet.com/polrev/reviews/AJPH/R_0004_9522_223_1004530.asp (accessed October 12, 2005).
64 Ibid.,
65 Ibid.,
66 Ibid.,
67 A.D. Moses, 'Coming to Terms with Genocidal Pasts in Comparative Perspective: Germany and Australia', *Aboriginal History*, vol. 25, 2000, p. 104.
68 Ibid., pp. 99–100.
69 'Marcia Langton responds to Alexis Wright's Breaking Taboos', *Australian Humanities Review*, online. Available: www.lib.latrobe.edu.au/AHR/emuse/taboos/langton2.htm>1 (accessed October 12, 2005).
70 Manne, *In Denial*, pp. 81–4.
71 Barta, 'Discourses of Genocide in Germany and Australia', p. 44.
72 Ibid., p. 50.
73 Markus, 'Genocide in Australia', p. 61.
74 Ibid., p. 67.
75 A.D. Moses, 'An Antipodean Genocide?', *Journal of Genocide Research*, vol. 2, no. 1, 2002, pp. 98–9.
76 Gaita, 'Genocide', pp. 18–19.
77 R. Gaita, 'Reply to Kenneth Minogue', *Quadrant*, November, 1998, p. 40. See also Gaita, 'Genocide and Pedantry', p. 44.
78 Tatz, 'Confronting Australian Genocide', p. 21.
79 Moses, 'Coming to Terms with Genocidal Pasts', p. 101.
80 Curthoys and Docker, 'Introduction', p. 1.
81 G. Davidson, *The Use and, Abuse of Australian History*, Crows Nest: Allen & Unwin, 2000, p. 8.

6 Indigenous history through the prism of the Holocaust: New Zealand Maori

1 This chapter is partially based on an article published in 2003. See D.B. Mac-Donald, 'Daring to Compare: The Debate about a Maori 'holocaust' in New Zealand', *Journal of Genocide Research*, September, 2003, pp. 383–404.
2 R. Walker, 'The Maori People: Their Political Development', in H. Gold (ed.), *New Zealand Politics in Perspective*, Auckland: Longman Paul, 1990, p. 330; W.

Ihimaera, 'Kaupapa', in W. Ihimaera (ed.), *Te Ao Marama: Regaining Aotearoa: Maori Writers Speak Out*, Auckland: Reed, 1993, p. 15.

3 E. Barkan, *The Guilt of Nations: Restitution and Negotiating Historical Injustices*, New York: W.W. Norton & Company, 2000, pp. 269–71; R. and J. Consedine, *Healing Our History: The Challenge of the Treaty of Waitangi*, Auckland: Penguin, 2001, p. 109.

4 'Report of the Waitangi Tribunal on the Orakei Claim', Waitangi Tribunal, Department of Justice, Wellington, online. Available: www.knowledge-basket. co.nz/search97cgi/s97> (accessed November 23, 2004) .

5 Ngati Paoa, 'Waiheke Island Claim', Waitangi Tribunal, Department of Justice, Wellington, online. Available: www.knowledge-basket.co.nz/search97 cgi/s97 (accessed November 23, 2004).

6 H. Riseborough, *Days of Darkness, Taranaki 1878–1884*, Auckland: Penguin, 2002; Edmund Bohan, *The Matter of Parihaka*, Christchurch: Hazard Press, 2000; James Frood, *Parihaka: Peace, Protest and Power*, Auckland: Elizabethan, 1994.

7 'The Taranaki Report – Kaupapa Tuatahi WAI 143 Muru me te Rauapatu – The Muru and Raupatu of the Taranaki Land and People', Wellington: Waitangi Tribunal Report, 1996, online. Available: www.knowledge-basket.co.nz/ waitangi/text/wai143/toc.html (accessed December 12, 2003). p. 253.

8 Ibid., pp. 251, 253.

9 Ibid., p. 78.

10 M. Kewley, *Going Public: The Changing Face of NZ History*, Auckland: University of Auckland Press, 2001, p. 107.

11 T. Turia, 'Speech to the NZ Psychological Society Conference 2000', Waikato University, Hamilton, August 29, 2000, p. 4.

12 Ibid., p. 3.

13 Ibid., p. 4.

14 Ibid., pp. 3–4.

15 I obtained an official copy of her speech on Labor Party letterhead shortly after the controversy erupted in early September, 2000.

16 A. Gregory, ' "Post-colonial stress" wins support from some psychologists', *NZ Herald*, August 31, 2000.

17 A. Young, 'Minister hammers colonial "holocaust", *NZ Herald*, August 30, 2000.

18 S. Scanton, 'Turia wrong on Holocaust, says survivor', *The Press*, August 31, 2000.

19 A. Young, 'Warning to Turia: keep "holocaust" opinions to yourself', *NZ Herald*, September 31, 2000.

20 N. Smith, 'Outbursts from Labour Minister Tariana Turia', *Nick Smith's Sunday news column*, September 2000 3, online. Available: www.ts.co.nz/~nicksmp/ pressrel/ 2000/09–03.html (accessed May 12, 2002).

21 Young, 'Minister hammers colonial "holocaust"'.

22 A. Young, 'Holocaust apology puts minister in hot water', *NZ Herald*, 6 September, 2000.

23 Young, 'Warning to Turia'.

24 Young, 'Holocaust apology puts minister in hot water'; See also 'Personal statement, Tariana Turia', September 5, 2000, online. Available: www.converge. org.nz/pma/tstate.htm (accessed May 12, 2002).

25 V. Small and A. Gregory, 'Lee defies PM by referring to "holocaust", *NZ Herald*, November 6, 2000.

26 Editorial, 'Ministerial psycho-babble', *The Press*, August 31, 2000.

27 NZPA, 'Meaning of "holocaust" lost in time', *The Nelson Mail*, September 7, 2000.

28 C. James, 'The ethnic factor in Clark's equation', *NZ Herald*, September 6, 2000.
29 H. Laracy, 'Was Colonisation Really That Bad?', online. Available: www.public
accessnewzealand.org/files/laracy_000915.pdf+maori+holocaust&hl=en&ie=UT
F-8 (accessed May 12, 2002).
30 M. King, *Moriori: A People Rediscovered Revised Edition*, Auckland: Penguin,
2000, pp. 58–60, 62–4, 66, 74, 77; F.M. Brookfield, *Waitangi & Indigenous
Rights: Revolution, Law & Legitimation*, Auckland: Auckland University Press,
1999, pp. 158–62.
31 W. Peters, 'The Way Ahead – One Country, One Electoral Franchise', New
Zealand First Speeches, September 13, 2000, online. Available: www.nzfirst.
org.nz/speech/wps1309000.htm (accessed November 23, 2004).
32 K. Rankin, 'Conquest and Trauma in our Archipelago', *Scoop*, 7 September,
2000, online. Available: www.scoop.co.nz/stories/HL0009/S00030.htm (accessed
November 23, 2004).
33 Ibid.,
34 NZPA, 'Race office puts Turia in clear over holocaust', *NZ Herald*, September
28, 2000.
35 E. Wellwood, 'MP raps Maori access to health', *The Press*, August 17, 2001.
36 E. Wellwood, 'Closing the gaps in a different guise', *The Press*, August 20,
2001.
37 A. Gregory, 'Clark behaving like Hitler, say Maori', *NZ Herald*, September 8,
2000.
38 'Corso Media release re: Indigenous Holocaust', Peace Movement Aotearoa
website, August 31, 2000, online. Available: www.converge.org.nz/pma/tcorso.
htm (accessed November 23, 2004).
39 J. Mitchell, 'A Field day for sticks and stones', *The Nelson Mail*, September 6,
2000.
40 Ibid.,
41 Ibid.,
42 Ibid.,
43 H. Turner, 'Whither the Maori?', *G21 ASIA*, online. Available: www.g21.net/
asia27.htm (accessed November 23, 2004) .
44 Ibid.,
45 'Post-Colonial trauma hits racists', *Class Struggle* no. 35, 2000, online. Available:
www.geocities.com/communistworker/CS35.htm>1 (accessed February 7, 2003).
46 Ibid.,
47 'Statement of the Indigenous Peoples Conference regarding "holocaust"',
Wellington: Peace Movement Aotearoa, September 8, 2000, online. Available:
www. converge.org.nz/pma/tstat.htm (accessed February 7, 2003).
48 Ibid.,
49 'New Zealand', Institute for Jewish Policy Research and American Jewish
Committee, 1997, online. Available: www.axt.org.uk/antisem/archive/archive1/
newzealand/newzealand.htm (accessed February 7, 2003).
50 For a larger contextual view of indigenous genocides and American indigenous
peoples' place within it, see R. Hitchcock and T. Twedt, 'Physical and Cultural
Genocide of Various Indigenous Peoples', in S. Totten, W. Parsons, and I.
Charny (eds), *Century of Genocide: Eyewitness Accounts and Critical Views*, London:
Garland Publishing, 1997.
51 W. Churchill, *A Little Matter of Genocide: Holocaust and Denial in the Americas
1492 to the Present*, San Francisco: City Lights, 1997, p. 66.
52 D. Fisher and J. Milne, 'Tamihere "sick" of Holocaust', *New Zealand Herald*,
April 10, 2005.
53 NZPA, 'Parliament's stance on anti-Semitism eases strains with Israel', *New
Zealand Herald*, August 13, 2004.

54 'Irving offers reward over NZ cemetery assaults, blames Mossad', *World Jewish Congress*, August 11, 2004, online. Available: www.worldjewishcongress.org/news/globalnews/gn_archives/2004/gn_arch_0408.htm (accessed December 12, 2005).
55 NZPA, 'Parliament's stance on anti-Semitism eases strains with Israel', *New Zealand Herald*, August 13, 2004.
56 'NZ launches first Maori TV station', *BBC News*, March 28, 2004.

7 The Armenian genocide: the politics of recognition and denial

1 'Ciller Denies Armenian Genocide', reproduced by the Center for Holocaust and Genocide Studies, online. Available: www.chgs.umn.edu/Histories__Narratives__Documen/The_Armenians/Ciller_Denies_Armenian_Genocid/ciller_denies_armenian_genocid.htm>l (accessed May 4, 2005).
2 T. Akçam, 'The Genocide of the Armenians and the Silence of the Turks', in L. Chorbajian and G. Shirinian (eds), *Studies in Comparative Genocide*, London: MacMillan, 1999, pp. 126, 139–41.
3 'Armenian Claims and Historical Facts: Questions and Answers', Ankara: Center for Strategic Research, 2005. The older work in question is Foreign Policy Institute, Ankara, 'The Turkish Argument: The Armenian Issue in Nine Questions and Answers', in The Permanent Peoples' Tribunal (eds), *A Crime of Silence: The Armenian Genocide*, London: Zed Books, 1985.
4 'Armenian–Turkish Dispute', *New York Times*, April 18, 2005, p. A3.
5 V. Dadrian, *The History of the Armenian Genocide: Ethnic Conflict from the Balkans to Anatolia to the Caucasus*, Providence: Berghahn Books, 1995, p. 4; R. Hovannisian, 'The Historical Dimensions of the Armenian Question, 1878–1923', in R. Hovannisian (ed.), *The Armenian Genocide in Perspective*, Chicago: University of Chicago Press, 1992, p. 251.
6 C. Walker, *Armenia: The Survival of a Nation*, New York: St Martin's Press, 1990, pp. 20, 28–31. F. Adanir, 'Armenian Deportations and Massacres in 1915', in D. Chirot and M. Seligman (eds), *Ethnopolitical Warfare: Causes, Consequences, and Possible Solutions*, Washington, DC: APA, 2000, p. 71.
7 Dadrian, *The History of the Armenian Genocide*, pp. 11–19, 22–4, 27, 30.
8 E. Weitz, *A Century of Genocide: Utopias of Race and Nation*, Princeton: Princeton University Press, 2003, pp. 3–4; H. Fein, *Accounting for Genocide: National Responses and Jewish Victimization during the Holocaust*, New York: The Free Press, 1979, p. 11.
9 Hovannisian, 'The Historical Dimensions of the Armenian Question', p. 255.
10 Dadrian, *The History of the Armenian Genocide*, pp. 114–19.
11 Ibid., pp. 119–20.
12 Fein, *Accounting for Genocide*, p. 12; Hovannisian, 'The Historical Dimensions of the Armenian Question', p. 256.
13 Adanir, 'Armenian Deportations and Massacres in 1915', pp. 74–5; Hovannisian, 'The Historical Dimensions of the Armenian Question', p. 257.
14 Walker, *Armenia*, pp. 180–1.
15 Hovannisian, 'The Historical Dimensions of the Armenian Question', pp. 257–8.
16 Dadrian, *The History of the Armenian Genocide*, pp. 182–4; Walker, *Armenia*, pp. 182–6.
17 Prominent figures included Eyub Sabri, Omer Najdi, Dr. Nazim, and Zia Gokalp. See Walker, *Armenia*, p. 189; Dadrian, *The History of the Armenian Genocide*, pp. 180–3.
18 Fein, *Accounting for Genocide*, p. 13.
19 Dadrian, *The History of the Armenian Genocide*, pp. 188–93.

20   Walker, *Armenia*, pp. 192–3; Hovannisian, 'The Historical Dimensions of the Armenian Question', p. 258.
21   Walker, *Armenia*, p. 197.
22   Dadrian, *The History of the Armenian Genocide*, pp. 195–7.
23   Walker, *Armenia*, p. 200.
24   Weitz, *A Century of Genocide*, pp. 4–5. See also A. Alvarez, *Governments, Citizens, and Genocide: A Comparative and Interdisciplinary Approach*, Bloomington: Indiana University Press, 2001, p. 48; I.L. Horowitz, *Taking Lives: Genocide and State Power*, 5th edition revised, London: Transaction Publishers, 2002, pp. 158–9.
25   Weitz, *A Century of Genocide*, pp. 4–5; Walker, *Armenia*, pp. 202–3.
26   Dadrian, *The History of the Armenian Genocide*, pp. 220–5; Weitz, *A Century of Genocide*, pp. 4–5; Fein, *Accounting for Genocide*, pp. 15–18; Horowitz, *Taking Lives*, pp. 158–9.
27   Dadrian, *The History of the Armenian Genocide*, pp. 236–7, 238–9.
28   Alvarez, *Governments, Citizens, and Genocide*, pp. 89, 93; Fein, *Accounting for Genocide*, p. 16.
29   Walker, *Armenia*, pp. 205–7; 210–15.
30   Dadrian, *The History of the Armenian Genocide*, pp. 384–5.
31   Ibid., pp. 242–3.
32   Walker, *Armenia*, p. 226; T. Hofmann, 'Annihilation, Impunity, Denial: The Case Study of the Armenian Genocide in the Ottoman Empire, 1915/16, and Genocide Research in Comparison', *Comparative Genocide Studies*, 2004, online. Available: www.cgs.c.utokyo.ac.jp/ws/sympo_040327/sympo_040327_Hofmann. english.htm (accessed November 12, 2005).
33   'Chronology of the Armenian Genocide 1918', Armenian National Institute, 2004, online. Available: www.armenian-genocide.org/1918.htm (accessed November 12, 2005).
34   S. Power, *'A Problem from Hell': America and the Age of Genocide*, New York: HarperCollins, 2003, pp. 14–17.
35   Dadrian, *The History of the Armenian Genocide*, p. xviii; V. Dadrian, 'The Comparative Aspects of the Armenian and Jewish Cases of Genocide: A Sociohistorical Perspective', in A. Rosenbaum (ed.), *Is the Holocaust Unique?* Boulder: Westview Press, 2001, pp. 159–61.
36   Walker, *Armenia*, pp. 304–5.
37   Dadrian, *The History of the Armenian Genocide*, pp. 358–63.
38   Alvarez gives a range of between 600,000 and two million. Fein echoes Toynbee's statistics that two-thirds of the 1.8 million were killed. Dadrian argues that over one million Armenians died during the genocide in World War I, while Libraridian gives a figure of 1.5 million. Lepsius argues for between 800,000 and one million. See Weitz, *A Century of Genocide*, p. 5; Alvarez, *Governments, Citizens, and Genocide*, p. 11; Fein, *Accounting for Genocide*, p. 16; Dadrian, *The History of the Armenian Genocide*, p. xviii; G. Libaridian, 'The Ultimate Repression: The Genocide of the Armenians, 1915–1917', in I. Walliman and M. Dobkowski (eds), *Genocide and the Modern Age: Etiology and Case Studies of Mass Death*, Syracuse: Syracuse Press, 1987, p. 206; J. Lepsius, *Archives du Génocide des Arméniens*, Paris: Fayard, 1986, p. 42.
39   I. Bremmer and C. Welt, 'Armenia's New Autocrats', *Journal of Democracy*, vol. 8, no. 3, 1997, p. 78.
40   Y. Shain, 'The Role of Diasporas in Conflict Perpetuation or Resolution', *SAIS Review*, vol. 22, no. 2, 2002, pp. 124–5.
41   R. Hovannisian, 'Etiology and Sequelae of the Armenian Genocide', in G. Andreopoulos (ed.), *Genocide: Conceptual and Historical Dimensions*, Philadelphia: University of Pennsylvania Press, 1994, pp. 128–30.

42 K. Scannell, 'Turk–Armenian fight over WWI History goes to a U.S. Court: Massachusetts Law Sparks A Free-Speech Debate About Teaching "Genocide", *The Wall Street Journal*, October 27, 2005, p. A1.

43 'Parlement Européen: La Résolution Du 18 Juin 1987 Resolution Sur Une Solution Politique De La Question Armenienne', online. Available: www.cdca. asso.fr/s/detail.php?r=1&&id=11 (accessed February 1, 2006).

44 Hovannisian, 'Etiology and Sequelae of the Armenian Genocide', pp. 115–16.

45 Bremmer and Welt, 'Armenia's New Autocrats', p. 77.

46 C. King, 'The Benefits of Ethnic War: Understanding Eurasia's Unrecognized States', *World Politics*, vol. 53, no. 4, 2001, p. 529.

47 Ibid., p. 532.

48 Bremmer and Welt, 'Armenia's New Autocrats', pp. 79–80.

49 King, 'The Benefits of Ethnic War', p. 532.

50 Bremmer and Welt, 'Armenia's New Autocrats', p. 78.

51 Z. Baran, 'The Caucasus: Ten Years after Independence', *The Washington Quarterly*, vol. 25, no. 1, 2002, p. 232. For further information, see US Department of State, 'Background Note: Armenia', Bureau of European and Eurasian Affairs, April, 2005, online. Available: www.state.gov/r/pa/ei/bgn/5275.htm (accessed February 1, 2006).

52 Shain, 'The Role of Diasporas in Conflict Perpetuation or Resolution', pp. 120–1.

53 Ibid., p. 130.

54 Ibid., pp. 120–21. For more on Kocharian's privileging of the genocide, see S. Totten, 'Does history matter? Ask the Armenians', *Social Education*, vol. 69, no. 6, 2005, pp. 328–9.

55 Shain, 'The Role of Diasporas in Conflict Perpetuation or Resolution', pp. 131.

56 They successfully lobbied, in section 907 of the 1992 'Freedom Support Act', to specifically ban US aid to Azerbaijan. S. Saideman, 'The Power of the Small: The Impact of Ethnic Minorities on Foreign Policy', *SAIS Review*, vol. 22, no. 2, 2002.

57 Baran, 'The Caucasus', pp. 225–7.

58 'Armenian Allegations of Genocide: The Issue and the Facts', Washington DC: Embassy of the Republic of Turkey, online. Available: www.turkishembassy. org/governmentpolitics/issuesarmenian.htm (accessed February 1, 2006).

59 Akçam, 'The Genocide of the Armenians and the Silence of the Turks', pp. 126, 139–41.

60 Ibid., pp. 140–1.

61 R. Smith, E. Markusen and R.J. Lifton, 'Professional Ethics and Denial of the Armenian Genocide', in *Holocaust and Genocide Studies*, vol. 9, no. 1, 1995, pp. 273–4.

62 C. Foss, 'The Turkish View of Armenian History: A Vanishing Nation', in Hovannisian, op. cit., pp. 250, 256–7.

63 Foss, 'The Turkish View of the Armenian Genocide', pp. 258–9.

64 Smith, Markusen and Lifton, 'Professional Ethics and Denial of the Armenian Genocide', pp. 273–4; see also R. Hovannisian, 'Denial of the Armenian Genocide in Comparison with Holocaust Denial', in Hovannisian, op. cit., p. 225.

65 Smith, Markusen and Lifton, 'Professional Ethics and Denial of the Armenian Genocide', pp. 274–5; see also O. Bartov, *Mirrors of Destruction: War, Genocide and Modern Identity*, Oxford: Oxford University Press, 2000, pp. 138–9; and Alvarez, *Governments, Citizens, and Genocide*, p. 34.

66 Hovannisian, 'Denial of the Armenian Genocide in Comparison with Holocaust Denial', pp. 208–9.

67 Ibid., p. 224. V. Dadrian, 'Ottoman Archives and Denial of the Armenian Genocide', in Hovannisian, op. cit., pp. 282–3, 288.

68 Shain, 'The Role of Diasporas in Conflict Perpetuation or Resolution', p. 132. See also 'Armenian genocide recognition spreads', *Signs & Sequels*, 2000, online. Available: www.isg-iags.org/oldsite/newsletters/25/signsseq.htm>1> #Armenia (accessed February 1, 2006).

69 L. Evans, 'Levon Marashlian: The White House Campaign of Silence on the Armenian Genocide', UCLA International Institute/Burkle Center for International Relations, 3 March, 2005, online. Available: www.isop. ucla.edu/article.asp?parentid=21398 (accessed February 1, 2006). The matter is discussed in detail in Yair Auron, *The Banality of Denial: Israel and the Armenian Genocide*, New Brunswick: Transaction Publishers, 2003, pp. 111–15.

70 M. Chapman, 'Never Forget the Armenian Genocide', Cato Institute, 6 May, 2003, online. Available: www.genocide1915.info/articles_view.asp?crypt=per cent86uper centA1per cent85aper cent7D (accessed February 1, 2006).

71 C. Morris, 'Bitter history of Armenian genocide row', *BBC News*, January 23, 2001; R. Fisk, 'Turkish TV Denies the Armenian Holocaust', *Independent*, January 26, 2001, online. Available: myweb.tiscali.co.uk/cragsite/2001Press-Report Articles/Article23.htm; R. Fisk, 'France passes Armenian genocide bill' UPI, 18 January, 2001, online. Available: www.atour.com/ ~aahgn/news/ 20010120g.htm>1 (both accessed May 14, 2006).

72 'Swiss accept Armenia "genocide" *BBC News*, December 16, 2003.

73 S. Kinzer, 'Plans for Museum Buoy Armenians and Dismay Turks', *New York Times*, April 24, 2002, p. E1. See Kinzer's correction dated May 2, 2002, online. Available: www.select.nytimes.com/gst/abstract.htm>1>?res=F7081 EFB345B0C778EDDAD0894DA404482 (accessed February 1, 2006).

74 'Statement by 126 Holocaust Scholars, Holders of Academic Chairs, and Directors of Holocaust Research and Studies Centers', March 7, 2000, online. Available: www.chgs.umn.edu/Histories__Narratives__Documen/Armenian_ Genocide/Public_Petitions/public_petitions.htm>1 (accessed May 4, 2005).

75 Smith, Markusen and Lifton, 'Professional Ethics and Denial of the Armenian Genocide', pp. 283–4.

76 R. Fisk, 'Peres stands accused over denial of "meaningless" Armenian Holocaust', *The Independent*, 18 April, 2001, online. Available: www.giwersworld. org/israel/fisk6.phtm>1 (accessed 4 May, 2005). See also Auron, *The Banality of Denial*, pp. 153–5.

77 Hovannisian, 'Denial of the Armenian Genocide in Comparison with Holocaust Denial', p. 225.

78 Auron, *The Banality of Denial*, pp. 62–5.

79 J. Vest, 'Turkey, Israel and the US', *The Nation*, August 23, 2002, online. Available: www.thenation.com/doc/20020902/vest20020823 (accessed February 1, 2006).

80 They also met with Moslem, Christian, and Jewish community and religious leaders. Press Release, 'Turkish Prime Minister Pledges to ADL: Will Fight Anti-Semitism and Promote Israeli-Palestinian Peace Talks', December 15, 2004, online. Available: www.adl.org/PresRele/Mise_00/4604_00.htm (accessed February 1, 2006).

81 Vest, 'Turkey, Israel and the US'.

82 Auron, *The Banality of Denial*, p. 117.

83 Information on the Institute-Museum is available at its website www. armeno-cide.am/ (accessed February 1, 2006).

84 '2006: L'année de l'Arménie en France', online. Available: www. patrimoinearmenien.free.fr/actualites_patrimoine.htm (accessed February 1, 2006).

85 Website of the The Zoryan Institute for Contemporary Armenian Research and

Documentation. Online. Available: www.zoryaninstitute.org/ (accessed February 1, 2006).

86 The film was banned in Turkey and roundly criticized by the Turkish media. For example, see S. Laciner's articles in *The Journal of Turkish Weekly*: 'Art and Propaganda: Ararat Case Study' Parts 1 and 2, and 'Armenian Propaganda and the Movie Industry', online. Available: www.turkishweekly.net/articles. php?id=88> (accessed February 2, 2006).

87 C. Reynolds, 'Armenians seek place in museum: Wiesenthal center's lack of an exhibition on the 1915 genocide is criticized' *Los Angeles Times*, February 3, 2003.

88 R. Hovannisian, 'The Armenian Genocide: An Eighty-Year Perspective' *USHMM*, October 31, 1995, online. Available: www.ushmm.org/conscience/ analysis/index. php?content=details.phpper cent3Fcontentper cent3D1995–10–24per cent26menu pageper cent3DHistoryper cent2Bper cent2526per cent2BConcept (accessed February 1, 2006).

89 Reynolds, 'Armenians seek place in museum'. On the hunger strike, see Ryan Carter, 'Armenians Fast For Recognition: Hunger strikers demand Museum of Tolerance fulfill its promise to put up a standing exhibit recognizing the Armenian Genocide', *Glendale News-Press*, April 19, 2003.

90 'Armenian Genocide Museum and Memorial in Washington D.C'., Armenian National Institute, online. Available: www.armeniangenocide.org/Memorial. 139/current_category.75/memorials_detail.htm>1 (accessed February 1, 2006).

91 Kinzer, 'Plans for Museum Buoy Armenians and Dismay Turks'. See also Nora Boustany, 'Armenians Save Their Tears For a New Museum', *Washington Post*, May 8, 2002, p. A18.

92 C. Shea, 'Turko-Armenian war brews in the Ivory Tower', *Salon.com*, 9 June, 1999, online. Available: www.salon.com/books/it/1999/06/09/turkish_chairs/ (accessed February 1, 2006).

93 D. Abeel, 'Turkish Scholars Acknowledge the Genocide', *Azg/Mirror On-Line*, 22 March, 2000, online. Available: www.omroep.nl/human/tv/muur/artikel_ chgo1.htm (accessed February 5, 2006).

94 V. Kechriotis, 'Politics: The Historian, the Philologist, the Minister, and the Traitors: Thoughts from Turkey on a Historical Conference', December 27, 2005, online. Available: www.greekworks.com/content/index.php/weblog/ extended/the_historian_the_philologist_the_minister_and_the_traitors_ thoughts_from_t/ (ac-cessed February 5, 2006).

95 For details, see their website. Turkish-Armenian Reconciliation Committee, online. Available: www.tarc.info/index.htm>1 (accessed February 5, 2006). For the issue of American promotion of the TARC, see E. Danielyan, 'Armenian Government "Endorsed" TARC', *RFE/RL Caucasus Report Radio Free Europe/Radio Liberty*, vol. 8, no. 5, February 4, 2005, www.rferl.org/reports/ caucasus-report/2005/02/5–040205.asp (accessed February 5, 2006).

96 E. Danielyan, 'Turkey/Armenia: Reconciliation Commission Off To Rocky Start', *RFE/RL*, August 13, 2001, online. Available: www.rferl.org/fea-tures/2001/08/13082001120048.asp (accessed February 5, 2006).

97 E. Danielyan, 'Turkey/Armenia: Panel Seeks Independent Study on 1915 Mass Killings' *RFE/RL*, December 4, 2001, online. Available: www.rferl.org/fea-tures/ 2001/12/04122001100222.asp (accessed February 5, 2006).

98 'Armenian–Turkish Reconciliation Commission Near Collapse?' *RFE/RL Newsline*, December 13, 2001, online. Available: www.rferl.org/newsline/ 2001/12/2-tca/tca-131201.asp (accessed February 5, 2006).

99 E. Danielyan, 'Fate of Turkish–Armenian Commission Still Unclear' *RFE/RL Caucasus Report Radio Free Europe/Radio Liberty*, vol. 5, no. 13, 12 April, 2002, online. Available: www.rferl.org/reports/caucasusreport/2002/04/13–120402.asp (accessed February 5, 2006); 'Turkish–Armenian Reconciliation Commission

May Resurface', *RFE/RL Newsline*, vol. 6 no. 70, April 15, 2002, online. Available: www.rferl.org/newsline/2002/04/2-tca/tca-150402.asp (accessed February 5, 2006); H. Melkumian and E. Danielyan, 'Turkish–Armenian Panel Seeks To Break Deadlock', *RFE/RL Caucasus Report Radio Free Europe/Radio Liberty*, vol. 5, no. 24, July 15, 2002, online. Available: www.rferl.org/reports/caucasus-report/2002/07/24–150702.asp (accessed February 5, 2006).

100 'Study Concludes That Killings of Armenians in 1915 Constituted Genocide', *RFE/RL Newsline*, vol. 7, no. 27, February 11, 2003.

101 'The Applicability Of The United Nations Convention On The Prevention And Punishment Of The Crime Of Genocide To Events Which Occurred During The Early Twentieth Century: Legal Analysis Prepared For The International Center For Transitional Justice', TARC, online. Available: www.tarc.info/ictj.htm> p. 4 (accessed February 5, 2006).

102 Danielyan, 'Armenian Government "Endorsed" TARC'.

103 E. Danielyan, 'Armenians Appear To Be Gaining Ground On Genocide Recognition', *RFE/RL Newsline*, vol. 9, no. 78, April 26, 2005, online. Available: www.rferl.org/newsline/2005/04/5-not/not-260405.asp (accessed February 5, 2006).

104 Kurds were also targeted. The *Vulpes Vulpes Kurdistanica*, or red fox, is now simply the *Vulpes Vulpes*. 'Turkey renames "divisive" animals', *BBC News*, March 8, 2005.

105 'Turk "genocide" author faces jail', *BBC News*, September 1, 2005.

106 S. Rainsford, 'Author's trial set to test Turkey', *BBC News*, December 14, 2005; 'Partial reprieve for Turk writer: Turkish state prosecutors have dropped one of two criminal charges against the best-selling writer Orhan Pamuk', *BBC News*, December 29, 2005; 'Court drops Turkish writer's case', *BBC News*, January 23, 2006.

107 Kechriotis, 'Politics'.

108 *Armenian and Turkish Citizens' Mutual Perceptions and Dialogue Project*, Turkish Economic and Social Studies Foundation and the Sociological – TESEV and Marketing Research Center – Armenia, 2005, online. Available: www.neevia. com (accessed February 5, 2006). Amazingly, several research interviewers were taken into custody and interrogated in Turkey. Others were deported from some districts.

109 *Armenian and Turkish Citizens' Mutual Perceptions and Dialogue Project*.

110 Akçam, *From Empire to Republic*, pp. 243–4.

111 Ibid., pp. 248–51.

8 The Armenian genocide and contemporary Holocaust scholarship

1 D. Lorenz, 'Hilsenraths Other Genocide', *Annual* no. 7, Simon Wiesenthal Center, 1997, online. Available: motlc.wiesenthal.com/resources/books/annual7/chap11.htm>1 (accessed November 25, 2005).

2 'Cannes film tackles Armenian "genocide"'. *BBC News*, May 21, 2002.

3 Y. Shain, 'The Role of Diasporas in Conflict Perpetuation or Resolution', *SAIS Review*, vol. XXII, no. 2, 2002, p. 116.

4 Further biographical details and a bibliography are available, online. Available: www.zoryaninstitute.org/Table_Of_Contents/genocide_bio_dadrian.htm (accessed November 25, 2005).

5 See the debate in *Armenian Forum* vol. 1, no. 2, 1998; for example, R. Suny, 'Empire and Nation: Armenians, Turks, and the End of the Ottoman Empire' and his 'Reply to My Critics', as well as Dadrian's piece, 'The Armenian Genocide and the Pitfalls of a "Balanced" Analysis'.

6 'Prof. Israel Charny Presents "Genocide Early Warning System" At Bay Area ANC/Holocaust Center Event', Armenian National Committee San Francisco Bay Area Chapter, November 20, 2002, online. Available: www.ancsf.org/press-releases/ 2002/11202002.htm (accessed November 25, 2005).

7 T. Hofmann, 'Annihilation, Impunity, Denial: The Case Study of the Armenian Genocide in the Ottoman Empire, 1915/16, and Genocide Research in Comparison', New Research Initiatives in Humanities and Social Sciences, 2004, online. Available: www.cgs.c.u-tokyo.ac.jp/ws/sympo_040327/sympo_040327_Hofmann. english.htm (accessed November 25, 2005).

8 Hofmann, 'Annihilation, Impunity, Denial'. For further discussion of Lemkin, including his defence of Soghomon Tehlirian, see S. Power, *'A Problem from Hell': America and the Age of Genocide*, New York: Harper, 2003, pp. 1–3, 17–21.

9 E. Weitz, *A Century of Genocide: Utopias of Race and Nation*, Princeton: Princeton University Press, 2003, p. 240; M. Marrus, *The Holocaust in History*, London: Penguin, 1987, pp. 20–1.

10 V. Dadrian, 'The Comparative Aspects of the Armenian and Jewish Cases of Genocide: A Sociohistorical Perspective', in A. Rosenbaum (ed.), *Is the Holocaust Unique?* Boulder: Westview Press, 1996, p. 133.

11 V. Dadrian, *The History of the Armenian Genocide: Ethnic Conflict from the Balkans to Anatolia to the Caucasus*, Providence: Berghahn Books, 1995, p. 395.

12 Ibid., p. 398.

13 Ibid.

14 G. Libaridian, 'The Ultimate Repression: The Genocide of the Armenians, 1915–1917', in I. Walliman and M. Dobkowski (eds), *Genocide and the Modern Age: Etiology and Case Studies of Mass Death*, Syracuse: Syracuse Press, 1987, pp. 221, 226.

15 Weitz, *A Century of Genocide*, pp. 3–4; A. Alvarez, *Governments, Citizens, and Genocide: A Comparative and Interdisciplinary Approach*, Bloomington: Indiana University Press, 2001, p. 49.

16 Dadrian, *The History of the Armenian Genocide*, p. 399.

17 Ibid., p. 400.

18 Ibid., pp. 399–400.

19 Dadrian, 'The Comparative Aspects of the Armenian and Jewish Cases of Genocide', pp. 156–7.

20 H. Dekmejian, 'Determinants of Genocide: Armenians and Jews as Case Studies', in R. Hovannisian (ed.), *The Armenian Genocide in Perspective*, New Brunswick: Transaction, 1986, p. 88.

21 C. Walker, *Armenia: The Survival of a Nation*, New York: St Martin's, 1990, pp. 191, 237.

22 Dadrian, *The History of the Armenian Genocide*, pp. 398–9.

23 Ibid., p. 397.

24 Dadrian, 'The Comparative Aspects of the Armenian and Jewish Cases of Genocide', p. 154.

25 Dekmejian, 'Determinants of Genocide', p. 87.

26 Dadrian, *The History of the Armenian Genocide*, p. 397.

27 Libaridian, 'The Ultimate Repression', pp. 203–4.

28 V. Dadrian, *German Responsibility in the Armenian Genocide: A Review of the Historical Evidence of German Complicity*, Blue Crane Books, 1996.

29 Dadrian, *The History of the Armenian Genocide*, pp. 395, 402.

30 Ibid., p. 409.

31 Ibid., p. 404.

32 Ibid., p. 407.

33 T. Hofmann, 'Note pour l'edition francaise', J. Lepsius, *Archives du Génocide des Arméniens*, Paris: Fayard, 1986. p. 15.

34 Dadrian, *The History of the Armenian Genocide*, pp. 91–4.
35 Ibid., pp. 91–4, 96–7.
36 Ibid., p. 252.
37 Ibid., p. 255.
38 Ibid., pp. 256–9, 277.
39 Ibid., pp. 285–6.
40 Ibid., pp. 411–12.
41 Ibid., p. 412.
42 R. Hovannisian, 'Denial of the Armenian Genocide in Comparison with Holocaust Denial', in R. Hovannisian (ed.), *Remembrance and Denial: The Case of the Armenian Genocide*, Detroit: Wayne State University Press, 1999. pp. 201–2.
43 Ibid., p. 203.
44 Ibid., p. 204.
45 Ibid., pp. 203–4; For denialist numbers of dead, see p. 218.
46 Ibid., p. 204–5.
47 Dadrian, 'The Comparative Aspects of the Armenian and Jewish Cases of Genocide', p. 135.
48 Ibid., p. 136.
49 Ibid., pp. 137–8.
50 Ibid.
51 Ibid., p. 153. Here Dadrian seems to contradict himself, in that he does note the importance of the convict element in the Holocaust. It is certainly more than implied that at an individual level and in terms of brutality, the Armenian genocide was worse.
52 Ibid., p. 137.
53 Ibid., pp. 138–9 (*italics mine*).
54 Ibid., p. 140.
55 Ibid., pp. 141–2.
56 Dadrian, *The History of the Armenian Genocide*, pp. 394–5.
57 Dadrian, 'The Comparative Aspects of the Armenian and Jewish Cases of Genocide', p. 143.
58 Dadrian, *The History of the Armenian Genocide*, pp. 400–1.
59 For details, see the *ISG Newsletter,* no. 35, 2005, and *ISG Newsletter,* no. 34, 2005, online. Available: www.isg-iags.org/newsletters.htm>1 (accessed November 24, 2005).
60 H. Fein, *Accounting for Genocide: National Responses and Jewish Victimization during the Holocaust*, New York: The Free Press, 1979, pp. 4–9, 16–18, 29–30; I.L. Horowitz, *Taking Lives: Genocide and State Power*, 5th edition revised, London: Transaction Publishers, 2002, pp. 160–1, 378–9, 157–8; R.J. Lifton, *The Nazi Doctors: Medical Killing and the Psychology of Genocide*, New York: Basic Books, 1986, pp. 470–73.
61 S. Katz, *The Holocaust in Historical Context*, Oxford: Oxford University Press, 1994, pp. 84–7.
62 Ibid., p. 22.
63 Ibid.
64 S. Katz, 'The Uniqueness of the Holocaust: The Historical Dimension', in Rosenbaum, op. cit., p. 62.
65 Ibid., pp. 62–3.
66 Katz here was both a source and the manuscript reviewer. A. Grobman, 'The Uniqueness of the Holocaust', Holocaust Teacher Resource Center, November, 2000, online. Available: www.holocaust-trc.org/uniqueness.htm (accessed November 24, 2005).
67 R. Melson, 'The Armenian Genocide as Precursor and Prototype of Twentieth-Century Genocide', in Rosenbaum, op. cit., pp. 120, 123.

68 R. Melson, *Revolution and Genocide: On the Origins of the Armenian Genocide and the Holocaust*, Chicago: University of Chicago Press, 1992, p. 73.

69 Y. Bauer, *Rethinking the Holocaust*, New Haven: Yale University Press, 2001, pp. 45, 266.

70 Ibid., pp. 266–7.

71 Ibid., pp. 45–6.

72 Marrus, *The Holocaust in History*, p. 22.

73 Katz, 'The Uniqueness of the Holocaust', p. 63.

74 Bauer, *Rethinking the Holocaust*, pp. 48–9.

75 Marrus, *The Holocaust in History*, pp. 21–2.

76 He concludes: 'Turkish policy reproduces medieval procedures of cultural homogenization, not modern procedures of physical genocide'. Katz, 'The Uniqueness of the Holocaust', pp. 64–5.

77 Melson, 'The Armenian Genocide ...', p. 123.

78 Ibid., p. 120; R. Melson, 'Revolution and Genocide: On the Causes of the Armenian Genocide and the Holocaust', in Hovannisian, op. cit., p. 82.

79 Melson, 'The Armenian Genocide ...', p. 120; Melson, 'Revolution and Genocide', pp. 89, 94.

80 Melson, 'Revolution and Genocide', pp. 88, 96–7. Melson, *Revolution and Genocide*, pp. 19–20, 140.

81 Melson, 'Revolution and Genocide', p. 95.

82 Melson, 'The Armenian Genocide ...', p. 124.

83 G. Lewy, 'Revisiting the Armenian Genocide', *The Middle East Quarterly*, vol. 12, no. 4, 2005. online. Available: www.meforum.org/article/748 (accessed November 24, 2005). His primary source for this is a pro-Turkish denialist work by Kamuran Gürün entitled *The Armenian File: The Myth of Innocence Exposed*, 1985. He also uses Bernard Lewis' *The Emergence of Modern Turkey*, 2002. Lewis, as some readers may recall, was convicted in a French court for denying the Armenian genocide. Such sources hardly demonstrate the existence of a genuine academic dispute. On the issue of Lewis' conviction under French law in 1995, see N. Herzberg, 'Bernard Lewis condamné pour avoir nié la réalité du génocide arménien: Selon le tribunal, l'historien a commis une <faute>', *Le Monde*, June 23, 1995, p. 11.

84 Lewy, 'Revisiting the Armenian Genocide'.

85 Ibid.,

86 Ibid.,

87 Ibid.,

88 Ibid.,

89 Ibid.,

90 In the case of the Holocaust, as we have seen, deniers often call themselves 'revisionists', arguing that they are simply participating in a legitimate debate, of their own creation, over the Holocaust's existence. Deniers often suggest – either obliquely or overtly – that there is some sort of amorphous conspiracy promoting 'some impenetrable cannon of the truth about the Holocaust', when this is simply false. Serious historians of the Holocaust reject Lewy's position and the entire premise that the facts of the Armenian genocide are open to refutation.

91 For a spirited attack, see V. Dadrian, 'Dr. Vahakn Dadrian responds to Guenther Lewy', *Armenian Genocide Forum*, October, 2005, online. Available: www. armeniangenocide.com/forum/showthread.php?t=1079 (accessed November 24, 2005).

92 Ibid.,

93 Melson, 'The Armenian Genocide ...', p. 123.

94 Hovannisian, 'Denial of the Armenian Genocide in Comparison with Holocaust Denial', p. 225. This quotation is reproduced from D. Lipstadt, *Denying the*

Holocaust: The Growing Assault on Truth and Memory, New York: Free Press, 1993, p. 212.
95 Bauer, *Rethinking the Holocaust*, pp. 45–6.
96 Quoted in L. Derfner, 'Jewish Split Marks Armenian Genocide', *Jewish Journal of Greater Los Angeles*, 22 April, 2005, online. Available: www.jewishjournal.com/home/preview.php?id=14011 (accessed 1 February, 2006).
97 Ibid.,

9 Nanking, the Chinese Holocaust, and Japanese atomic victim exceptionalism

1 K. McLaughlin, 'Iris Chang's suicide stunned those she tried so hard to help – the survivors of Japan's "Rape of Nanking"' *San Francisco Gate*, 20 November, 2004, p. E-1.
2 For additional background to this case and a theoretical appraisal, see my article on which this chapter is based: 'Forgetting and Denying: Iris Chang, the Holocaust and the Challenge of Nanking', *International Politics*, 2005, pp. 403–28.
3 'Textbook row stirs Japanese concern', *BBC News*, April 13, 2005.
4 There is an obvious political dimension to much of this. Japan recently pledged to defend Taiwan in case of attack, and both countries seek control over the same resources in the East China Sea. China's refusal to allow Japan to gain a permanent seat on the UN Security Council is another source of friction. 'Japan told to reflect on war past', *BBC News*, April 23, 2005; 'China–Japan ties at "30-year low"'; *BBC News*, April 18, 2005.
5 M. Shermer and A. Grobman, *Denying History: Who says the Holocaust never happened and why do they say it?* Berkeley: University of California Press, 2000, p. 232.
6 Y. Beigbeder, *Judging War Criminals: The Politics of International Justice*, London: Macmillan, 1999, pp. 52–4.
7 'The Project of the Preparatory Committee for Chinese Holocaust Museum in the United States, Inc'., Chinese Holocaust Museum in the United States, Inc., online. Available: www.chineseholocaust.org/committee.htm>1 (accessed May 25, 2005).
8 I. Buruma, *The Wages of Guilt: Memories of War in Germany and Japan*, London: Paperback Editions, 1995, p. 114.
9 D. Tao, 'Japan's War in China: Perspectives of Leading Japanese Sinologists', in D. Barrett and L. Shyu (eds), *China in the Anti-Japanese War 1937–1945*, New York: Peter Lang, 2001, pp. 32–3.
10 L. Eastman, 'Facets of an Ambivalent Relationship: Smuggling, Puppets and Atrocities during the War 1937–1945', in A. Iriye (ed.), *The Chinese and the Japanese: Essays in Political and Cultural Interactions*, Princeton: Princeton University Press, 1980, 293–5; for identical numbers, see E. Dreyer, *China at War 1901–1949*, London: Longman, 1995, p. 218.
11 Eastman, 'Facets of an Ambivalent Relationship', pp. 293–5.
12 J. Boyle, *China and Japan at War 1937–1945: The Politics of Collaboration*, Stanford: Stanford University Press, 1972, p. 54.
13 L. Jui-jung, 'Survival as Justification for Collaboration', in Barrett and Shyu, op. cit., p. 126.
14 M. Eykholt, 'Aggression, Victimization, and Chinese Historiography of the Nanjing Massacre', in J. Fogel (ed.), *The Nanjing Massacre in History and Historiography*, Berkeley: University of California Press, 2000, p. 11; C. Mackerras, 'From Imperialism to the End of the Cold War', in A. McGrew and C. Brook (eds), *Asia-Pacific in the New World Order*, London, Routledge/Open University, 1998, p. 39.

15 I. Chang, *The Rape of Nanking*, London: Penguin, 1997, p. 46.
16 Ibid., pp. 49, 52–3, 128. Others also advance the figure of 20,000. See M. Williamsen, 'The Military Dimension, 1937–1941', in J. Hsiung and S. Lavine (eds), *China's Bitter Victory: The War With Japan 1937–1945*, London: M.E. Sharpe, 1992, pp. 143–5; Dreyer, *China at War*, pp. 219–20; M. Bagish and H. Conroy, 'Japanese Aggression Against China: The Question of Responsibility', in A. Cox and H. Conroy (eds), *China and Japan: Search for Balance Since World War I*, Santa Barbara: ABC-Clio, 1978, pp. 325–7.
17 Buruma, *The Wages of Guilt*, pp. 118–19.
18 W. Morton, *China: Its History and Culture*, New York: McGraw-Hill, 1995, p. 196; Boyle, *China and Japan at War 1937–1945*, p. 55.
19 Eykholt, 'Aggression, Victimization, and Chinese Historiography of the Nanjing Massacre', pp. 14–15; R. Phillips, *China Since 1911*, London: Macmillan, 1996, p. 127. Writing shortly after the siege, Bisson locates Japanese 'excesses' in the connivance of officers, 'some of whom were seen directing the looting of street shops'. T. Bisson, *Japan in China*, New York: MacMillan, 1938, p. 287.
20 Beigbeder, *Judging War Criminals*, p. 53.
21 Bagish and Conroy, 'Japanese Aggression Against China', pp. 325–7; Williamsen, 'The Military Dimension, 1937–1941', pp. 143–5; Dreyer, *China at War 1901–1949*, pp. 219–20; E. Friedman, *National Identity and Democratic Prospects in Socialist China*, London: M.E. Sharpe, 1995, p. 135.
22 Chang, *The Rape of Nanking*, p. 4.
23 TOL, 'Guilty of Genocide', *Transitions Online*, August 7, 2001, online. Available: www.balkanreport.tol.cz/look/BRR/article (accessed June 2, 2005).
24 Shermer and Grobman, *Denying History*, p. 232.
25 Chang, *The Rape of Nanking*, pp. 199–214.
26 Chang, *The Rape of Nanking*, pp. 6–7.
27 G. Hicks, *Japan's War Memories: Amnesia or Concealment?* Aldershot: Ashgate, 1998, pp. 29–30; O. Yasuaki, 'The Tokyo War Crimes Trial, War Responsibility, and the Postwar Responsibility', in F. Li, R. Sabella and D. Liu (eds), *Nanking 1937: Memory and Healing*, London: M.E. Sharpe, 2002, p. 209.
28 T. Yoshida, 'Refighting the Nanking Massacre: The Continuing Struggle Over Memory', in Li, Sabella and Liu, op. cit., pp. 81–3.
29 Shermer and Grobman, *Denying History*, pp. 235–6; Yoshida pp. 87, 108–9; Buruma, *The Wages of Guilt*, p. 119.
30 L. Yoneyama, *Hiroshima Traces: Time, Space, and the Dialectics of Memory*, Berkeley: University of California Press, 1999, p. 5.
31 Yoshida, 'Refighting the Nanking Massacre', p. 85.
32 Hicks, *Japan's War Memories*, pp. ix, 44–6.
33 J. Dower, '"An Aptitude for Being Unloved": War and Memory in Japan', in O. Bartov, A. Grossmann and M. Nolan (eds), *Crimes of War: Guilt and Denial in the Twentieth Century*, New York: The New Press, 2002, pp. 218–19.
34 F. Godemont, *The New Asian Renaissance: From Colonialism to the post-Cold War*, London: Routledge, 1997, p. 147. Yoshida, 'Refighting the Nanking Massacre', pp. 74–5; Buruma, *The Wages of Guilt*, p. 119.
35 Dower, '"An Aptitude for Being Unloved"', p. 221.
36 Hicks, *Japan's War Memories*, p. 59; Dower, '"An Aptitude for Being Unloved"', p. 236; Godemont, *The New Asian Renaissance*, p. 180.
37 'Fury at Nanking "Lie" Claim', *BBC News*, July 13, 2003.
38 K. Tokudome, 'The Holocaust and Japanese Atrocities', in A. Rosenbaum (ed.), *Is The Holocaust Unique? Perspectives on Comparative Genocide*, Second Edition, Boulder: Westview Press, 2001, pp. 199–200.
39 J. Joseph, *The Japanese: Strange but not Strangers*, London: Penguin, 1993, p. 151.

For example, Chiune Sugihara, the Japanese Consul in Lithuania, saved the lives of some 6,000 Jews by issuing Japanese transit visas. For a brief discussion, see 'Chiune and Yukiko Sugihara', *Jewish Virtual Library*, online. Available: www.jewishvirtuallibrary.org/jsource/Holocaust/sugihara.htm>l (accessed January 12, 2006).

40 Rotem Kowner, 'Tokyo recognizes Auschwitz: the rise and fall of Holocaust denial in Japan, 1989–1999', *Journal of Genocide Research*, vol. 2, no. 2, 2001, pp. 266–9, Rubenstein, 'Religion and the Uniqueness of the Holocaust', pp. 35–8.

41 K. Tokushi, 'Remembering the Nanking Massacre', in Li, Sabella and Liu, op. cit., p. 91.

42 C. Fan, 'Chinese Americans: Immigration, Settlement, and Social Geography', in L. Ma and C. Cartier (eds), *The Chinese Diaspora: Space, Place, Mobility, and Identity*, Lanham: Rowman & Littlefield, 2003, pp. 261–2, 269–71.

43 Fan, 'Chinese Americans', pp. 264–5. H.M. Lai, 'The United States', in L. Pan (ed.), *The Encyclopedia of the Chinese Overseas*, Cambridge: Harvard University Press, 1999, p. 261.

44 W. Gungwu, *The Chinese Overseas: From Earthbound China to the Quest for Autonomy*, Cambridge: Harvard University Press, 2000, p. 95.

45 H. Yu, *Thinking Orientals: Migration, Contact, and Exoticism in Modern America*, New York: Oxford University Press, 2001, p. 203.

46 F. Wu, *Yellow: Race in America Beyond Black and White*, New York: Basic Books, 2002, p. 47.

47 Fan, 'Chinese Americans', pp. 282, 284–5; Lai, 'The United States', pp. 270–1.

48 P. Marino, 'Remember Nanking: With Global Alliance, Chang recounts the forgotten holocaust of the Chinese people', *The Cupertino Courier*, August 26, 1998, online. Available: www.svcn.com/archives/cupertinocourier/08.26.98/CoverStory. htm>l (accessed June 15, 2005).

49 C. Maier, 'Introduction', in J. Fogel (ed.), *The Nanjing Massacre in History and Historiography*, Berkeley: University of California Press, 2000, p. 3.

50 For a detailed analysis of this controversy, see C. Rose, *Interpreting History in Sino-Japanese Relations: A Case Study in Political Decision Making*, London: Routledge, 1988, Chapter 5: 'The Textbook Issue' provides a useful breakdown of the key points of contention. See pp. 80–120.

51 R. Chu, 'China Holocaust Museum – Update', *Rochester Chinese Association Summer Newsletter*, 2000, online. Available: www.rochesterchinese.org/Newsletter Summer.htm>l (accessed June 15, 2005).

52 Chang, *The Rape of Nanking*, p. 9.

53 For some basic information, see V. Hua, 'Activists keep focus on Japan's atrocities Chinese Americans lead effort to put pressure on Tokyo', *San Francisco Chronicle*, July 11, 2005.

54 Marino, 'Remember Nanking'.

55 P. Hung, 'Integrating the Sino-Japanese War, 1932–1945, into the World War II History Curriculum in High School', Chinese Holocaust Museum in the United States, Inc., online. Available: www.chineseholocaust.org/pubs. htm>l (accessed June 25, 2006).

56 Ibid.,

57 Ibid.,

58 Ibid.,

59 P. Chan, 'War in the Pacific: The Forgotten Holocaust'. Available at, Teachers' Asian Studies Summer Institute Web page, online. Available: www.csupomona.edu/~tassi/nanjing.htm>#supplement (accessed June 15, 2005).

60 Ibid.,

61 See Lipstadt, *Denying the Holocaust*, pp. 1–2.

62 Chu, 'China Holocaust Museum – Update'.

63 'Exhibition to Show Japan's War Crimes', *People's Daily*, 10 July, 2001, online. Available: www.fpeng.peopledaily.com.cn/200107/10/eng20010710_74590.htm>1 (accessed June 15, 2005).

64 'Exhibition to Show Japan's War Crimes'.

65 Chu, 'China Holocaust Museum – Update'.

66 'Exhibition to Show Japan's War Crimes'.

67 'Nanjing Massacre Exhibition to Open in San Francisco', Consulate-General of the People's Republic of China in New York, December 14, 2001, online. Available: www.nyconsulate.prchina.org/eng/22357.htm>1 (accessed June 15, 2005); '"Never Forget" tells days of hell', *China Daily*, 17 December, 2001, online. Available: www.chinaembassy.org.pl/pol/22726.htm>1 (accessed June 15, 2005).

68 'Press Release: American Museum of the Asian Holocaust World War II', Falls Creek, 2002, online. Available: www.geocities.com/amahwwii/ (accessed June 15, 2005).

69 Shermer and Grobman, *Denying History*, p. 237.

70 Chang, *The Rape of Nanking*, pp. 199–214. For more discussion on the commemoration and documentation of atrocities in Japan, see Hicks, *Japan's War Memories*, pp. 52, 104–6, 111–22; Joseph, *The Japanese*, pp. 227–9; and Yoshida, 'Refighting the Nanking Massacre', pp. 79–80, 98, 102–4.

71 Chang, *The Rape of Nanking*, p. 11.

72 Buruma, *The Wages of Guilt*, p. 126; See also I. Buruma, 'The Nanking Massacre as a Historical Symbol', in Li, Sabella, and Liu, op. cit., p. 8.

73 Maier, 'Introduction', p. 2.

74 Eykholt, 'Aggression, Victimization, and Chinese Historiography of the Nanjing Massacre', pp. 24–8; D. Shambaugh, 'Towards the Twenty-first Century', in C. Howe (ed.), *China and Japan: History, Trends and Prospects*, Oxford: Clarendon, 1996, pp. 88–90.

75 WWW Memorial Hall of the Victims in the Nanjing Massacre, 1937–1938, online. Available: www.arts.cuhk.edu.hk/NanjingMassacre/NM.htm>1 (accessed June 15, 2005).

76 Buruma, *The Wages of Guilt*, p. 127 Eykholt, 'Aggression, Victimization, and Chinese Historiography of the Nanjing Massacre', p. 35.

77 Eykholt, 'Aggression, Victimization, and Chinese Historiography of the Nanjing Massacre', p. 36.

78 Buruma, *The Wages of Guilt*, p. 126.

79 V. Schwarcz, 'The "Black Milk" of Historical Consciousness: Thinking About the Nanking Massacre in Light of Jewish Memory', in Li, Sabella, and Liu, op. cit., p. 187.

80 For more information and pictures, see 'Nanjing 1937', online. Available: www.nj1937.org/english/info.asp (accessed January 10, 2006).

81 'China Remembers Nanjing Massacre' and 'China to Expand Memorial Marking Nanjing Massacre', online. Available: www.nj1937.org/english/show_news.asp?id=44 (accessed January 10, 2006).

82 'Remember history, safeguard peace and mourn the victims of the Nanjing Massacre', online. Available: www.nj1937.org/english/show_massacre.asp?id=70 (accessed January 10, 2006).

83 D. Yang, 'Mirror for the Future or the History Card? Understanding the "History Problem",' in M. Soderberg (ed.), *Chinese–Japanese Relations in the Twenty-first Century: Complementarity and Conflict*, London: Routledge, 2002, p. 21.

84 Chang, *The Rape of Nanking*, pp. 5–6.
85 T. Tang, 'Chang details Chinese holocaust's horrors', *Daily Bruin*, 10 November, 1998, online. Available: www.dailybruin.ucla.edu/DB/issues/98/11.10/ae. chang.htm>l (accessed June 15, 2005).
86 Hung, 'Integrating the Sino-Japanese War...'.
87 Tokudome, 'The Holocaust and Japanese Atrocities', pp. 198–9.
88 Buruma, 'The Nanking Massacre as a Historical Symbol', p. 7.
89 Ibid.
90 A. Mills, 'Breaking the Silence', *Metro*, December, 1996, online. Available: www.metroactive.com/papers/metro/12.12.96/cover/china1–9650.htm>l (accessed June 15, 2005).
91 Mills, 'Breaking the Silence'.
92 Tokudome, 'The Holocaust and Japanese Atrocities', pp. 198–9.
93 Ibid.
94 P. Novick, *The Holocaust and Collective Memory: The American Experience*, London: Bloomsbury, 1999, p. 20.
95 Tokudome, 'The Holocaust and Japanese Atrocities', pp. 198–9.
96 Chang, *The Rape of Nanking*, pp. 12, 200.
97 Ibid., pp. 12, 200.
98 Ibid., pp. 13–14.
99 'The Project of the Preparatory Committee for Chinese Holocaust Museum in the United States, Inc'., Chinese Holocaust Museum in the United States, Inc. online. Available: www.chineseholocaust.org/committee.htm>l (accessed June 15, 2005).
100 T. Wu, 'New materials on the Pacific War disclosing Japanese army's germ attack on the United States and U.S. army's succession to Japan's biological warfare', Chinese Holocaust Museum in the United States, Inc., online. Available: www. chineseholocaust.org/pubs.htm>l (accessed June 15, 2005).
101 Wu, 'New materials on the Pacific War ...'.
102 Zhang, *Eyewitness to Massacre*, p. xiv.
103 'Japan vs Germany', Alliance for Preserving the Truth of Sino-Japanese War, online. Available: www.sjwar.org/ (accessed June 15, 2005).
104 Maier, 'Forward' pp. viii–xi.
105 Goldstone, 'From the Holocaust', p. 41.
106 Maier, 'Forward', pp. xii–xiii.
107 Eastman, 'Facets of an Ambivalent Relationship', pp. 293–5. For identical numbers, see Dreyer, *China at War*, p. 218.
108 Chang, *The Rape of Nanking*, pp. 109–16.
109 Schwarcz, 'The "Black Milk" of Historical Consciousness', p. 192.
110 Chang, *The Rape of Nanking*, pp. 122–3.
111 Ibid., pp. 155–6.
112 Ibid., pp. 83–6, 92.
113 Ibid., pp. 96–8.
114 Ibid., p. 83.
115 Ibid., pp. 182–3.
116 Novick, *The Holocaust and Collective Memory*, p. 180.
117 Chang, *The Rape of Nanking*, p. 195.
118 H. Huttenbach, 'Contra "Schindler" and his "List": A Warning', *Genocide Forum*, vol. 1, no. 4, online. Available: www.chgs.umn.edu/Educational_ Resources/Newsletter/The_Genocide_Forum/Yr_1/Year_1__No_4/year_1__no _4.htm>l (accessed June 15, 2005).
119 Godemont, *The New Asian Renaissance*, p. 141; J. Dower, 'The Bombed: Hiroshimas and Nagasakis in Japanese Memory', in M. Hogan (ed.), *Hiroshima in History and Memory*, Cambridge: Cambridge University Press, 1996, p. 121.

120 Dower, 'An Aptitude for Being Unloved', pp. 218, 228.
121 J. Orr, *The Victim as Hero: Ideologies of Peace and National Identity in Postwar Japan*, Honolulu: University of Hawai'i Press, 2001, p. 3.
122 Ibid., p. 7; Dower, 'The Bombed', p. 123.
123 Dower, 'The Bombed', p. 123.
124 Buruma, *The Wages of Guilt*, p. 92.
125 Dower, 'An Aptitude for Being Unloved', pp. 239–40; Dower, 'The Bombed', p. 135.
126 'The Hiroshima Peace Memorial, Genbaku Dome', online. Available: whc.unesco.org/sites/775.htm (accessed June 15, 2005).
127 'Introduction', The Hiroshima Peace Memorial Museum, online. Available: www. pcf.city.hiroshima.jp/virtual/VirtualMuseum_e/tour_e/tour_pro_e.htm>1 (accessed June 15, 2005).
128 Things have improved in recent years to some extent. The Peace Memorial Museum in 1994 began offering some background to America's decision to drop the bomb, including discussion of the attack on Pearl Harbor, a display on the massacre at Nanking, as well as some discussion of America's motives in using the atomic bomb. Claims Hicks, these were 'listed with some balance'. Hicks, *Japan's War Memories*, p. 89.
129 Yoneyama, *Hiroshima Traces*, pp. 1–2.
130 'Hiroshima Peace Site', online. Available: www.pcf.city.hiroshima.jp/peacesite/peaceculture/English/06E.htm>1 (accessed June 15, 2005).
131 The Hall of Remembrance', United States Holocaust Memorial Museum, online. Available: www.ushmm.org/museum/a_and_a/index.utp?content=inside_c/right. htm (accessed June 15, 2005).
132 Buruma, *The Wages of Guilt*, p. 97.
133 Ibid., p. 101.
134 Ibid., p. 103.
135 Dower, 'The Bombed', p. 129.
136 Buruma, *The Wages of Guilt*, pp. 37–8.

10 Serbs, Croats, and the dismemberment of Yugoslavia: war and genocide in the twentieth century

1 R. Holbrooke, *To End a War*, New York: Random House, 1998, p. 36.
2 R. Kaplan, 'Ground Zero', *The New Republic*, August 2, 1993, p. 15; 'History's Cauldron', *Atlantic Monthly*, June 1991, pp. 92–8; *Balkan Ghosts: A Journey Through History*, New York: St Martin's, 1993, pp. 3–48.
3 TOL, 'Guilty of Genocide', *Transitions Online*, August 7, 2001, online. Available: www.balkanreport.tol.cz/look/BRR/article (accessed June 27, 2001). For a fact sheet and summary of the charges, see 'KRSTIC, IT-98–33, Case Information Sheet', ICTY, July 8, 2005, online. Available: www.un.org/icty/glance/krstic.htm (accessed June 27, 2001).
4 W. Shawcross, *Deliver Us From Evil: Warlords and Peacekeepers in a World of Endless Conflict*, London: Bloomsbury, 2001, p. 347.
5 M. Mardell, 'Europe Diary: Serbian Radicals', *BBC News*, January 25, 2007.
6 M. Bakić-Hayden, 'Nesting Orientalisms: The Case of Former Yugoslavia', *Slavic Review*, Winter, 1995, p. 8.
7 M. Ignatieff, *Blood and Belonging*, Toronto: Viking, 1994, p. 14.
8 For a good brief history of the formation of Yugoslavia, see A. Djilas, *The Contested Country: Yugoslav Unity and the Communist Revolution*, Cambridge: Harvard University Press, 1996, pp. 10–14, 33–49.
9 M. Tanner, *Croatia: A Nation Forged in War*, New Haven: Yale University Press, 1997, pp. 119–26.

10 The *Sporazum*, Understanding, of August 1939 created a separate autonomous region for Croatia and Croatian parts of Bosnia-Herzegovina. B. Jelavich, *History of the Balkans: Twentieth Century*, Cambridge: Cambridge University Press, 1993, pp. 203–4.

11 Tanner, *Croatia*, p. 141.

12 B. Vankovska, 'Civil–Military Relations in the Third Yugoslavia', in C. Danopoulos, D. Vajpeyi and A. Bar-or (eds), *Civil–Military Relations, Nation-Building, and National Identity*, Portsmouth: Greenwood Press, 2004, pp. 20–21.

13 Jelavich, *History of the Balkans*, pp. 262–73.

14 S. Pawlovich, *Serbia: The History of an Idea*, New York: New York University Press, 2002, pp. 139–41.

15 J. Ridley, *Tito*, London: Constable, 1994, p. 164.

16 Jelavich, *History of the Balkans*, p. 264.

17 200,000 Serbs were forcibly converted to Catholicism. Ridley, *Tito*, p. 164.

18 V. Dedijer, *The Yugoslav Auschwitz and the Vatican: The Croatian Massacre of the Serbs During World War II*, New York: Prometheus Books, 1992, p. 227.

19 'Jasenovac', Holocaust Encyclopedia, USHMM; Dedijer, *The Yugoslav Auschwitz and the Vatican*, pp. 225–65.

20 To appreciate the enormous variance in Jasenovac statistics, see the following: B. Denitch, *Ethnic Nationalism: The Tragic Death of Yugoslavia*, Minneapolis: University of Minnesota Press, 1994, p. 33; E. Vulliamy, *Seasons in Hell*, New York: St Martin's Press, 1994, p. 23; E. Stitkovac, 'Croatia: The First War', in J. Udovički and J. Ridgeway (eds), *Burn This House*, London: Duke University Press, 1997, p. 154; T. Judah, *The Serbs*, New Haven: Yale University Press, 1997, p. 129; A. Dragnitch, *Serbs and Croats: The Struggle in Yugoslavia*, New York: Harcourt Brace Jovanovich, 1992, p. 103; M. Glenny, *The Fall of Yugoslavia*, London: Penguin, 1993, p. 81; Ridley, *Tito*, p. 165; *Genocide in Yugoslavia During the Holocaust*, Washington, DC: United States Holocaust Memorial Museum, 1995.

21 Tanner, *Croatia*, p. 160.

22 R.J. Crampton, *Eastern Europe in the Twentieth Century and After, second* edition, London: Routledge, 1997, pp. 202–3.

23 Djilas, *The Contested Country*, pp. 150–9.

24 A biased but illuminating study of this period is A. Beljo, *Genocide A Documented Analysis*, Sudbury: Northern Tribune Publishing, 1985.

25 Judah, *The Serbs*, p. 120.

26 Dedijer, *The Yugoslav Auschwitz and the Vatican*, p. 129.

27 S. Bogosavljevic, 'The Unresolved Genocide', in N. Popov (ed.), *The Road to War in Serbia: Trauma and Catharsis*, Budapest: Central European University Press, 2000, p. 146.

28 D. Mirkovic, 'The historical link between the Ustasha genocide and the Croato-Serb civil war: 1991–1995', *Journal of Genocide Research*, vol. 2, no. 3, 2000, pp. 366–7.

29 Beljo, *A Documented Analysis*, p. 281.

30 L. Cohen, *The Socialist Pyramid: Elites and Power in Yugoslavia*, Oakville: Mosaic Press, 1989, pp. 299–301.

31 S. Ramet, *Nationalism and Federalism in Yugoslavia 1962–1991*, Bloomington: Indiana University Press, 1992, pp. 81–135.

32 Ibid., pp. 72–4.

33 I. Banac (ed.), *Eastern Europe in Revolution*, Ithaca: Cornell University Press, 1992, pp. 173–5.

34 A. Pavkovic, *The Fragmentation of Yugoslavia: Nationalism in a Multi-Ethnic State*, Basingstoke: Macmillan, 1996, p. 78.

35 J. Seroka and V. Pavlovic, *The Tragedy of Yugoslavia*, London: M.E. Sharpe. 1992, p. 77; M. Thompson, *Forging War: The Media in Serbia, Croatia and Bosnia-Hercegovina*, London: Article 19/International Center Against Censorship, 1994, p. 128.

36 Denitch, *Ethnic Nationalism*, pp. 119–20.

37 Tanner, *Croatia*, p. 214.

38 B. Magas, *The Destruction of Yugoslavia: Tracing the Breakup 1980–92*, London: Verso, 1993, p. 110; and C. Cviic, 'Who's to Blame for the War in Ex-Yugoslavia?' *World Affairs*, Fall, 1993, p. 73.

39 Magas, *The Destruction of Yugoslavia*, p. 161; Ramet, *Nationalism and Federalism in Yugoslavia*, p. 78; Tanner, *Croatia*, pp. 215–16; A. Bebler, 'Yugoslavia's Variety of Communism and Her Demise', *Communist and Post Communist Studies*, March, 1993, pp. 75–6.

40 L. Silber and A. Little, *The Death of Yugoslavia*, London: BBC Books, 1995, p. 66.

41 M. Crnobrnja, *The Yugoslav Drama*, Toronto: McGill-Queens University Press, 1993, p. 154.

42 L. Cohen, *Broken Bonds: Yugoslavia's Disintegration and Balkan Politics in Transition*, Boulder: Westview Press, 1995, p. 95.

43 N. Cigar, *Genocide in Bosnia: The Policy of 'Ethnic Cleansing'*, Texas: A&M University Press, 1995, pp. 88, 98–9.

44 Cohen, *Broken Bonds*, p. 18.

45 Silber and Little, *The Death of Yugoslavia*, p. 169.

46 Ibid., p. 92.

47 S. Mesic, 'The Road to War', in B. Magas and I. Zanic (eds), *The War in Croatia and Bosnia-Herzegovina, 1991–1995*, London: Frank Cass, 2001, pp. 11–12.

48 Silber and Little, *The Death of Yugoslavia*, pp. 100–1.

49 Ibid., pp. 102, 104–5.

50 Ibid., pp. 107, 109–11.

51 Ibid., pp. 146–7.

52 Ibid., pp. 195–201.

53 S. Power, *'A Problem from Hell': America and the Age of Genocide*, New York: Harper Perennial, 2003, p. 247.

54 This surreal situation is described in S. Drakulic, *Cafe Europa: Life After Communism*, London: Little, Brown and Company, 1996, see pp. 188–94. For Bosnia's demographic composition, see T. Bringa, *Being Muslim the Bosnian Way: Identity and Community in a Central Bosnian Village*, Princeton: Princeton University Press, 1995, p. 26.

55 Bringa, *Being Muslim the Bosnian Way*, p. 26.

56 R. Mahmutcehajic, 'The Road to War', in Magas and Zanic, op. cit., p. 144.

57 J. Divjak, 'The First Phase: 1992–1993', in Magas and Zanic, op. cit., p. 155.

58 N. Malcolm, *Bosnia: A Short History*, London: New York University Press/Macmillan, 1994, p. 218.

59 Silber and Little, *The Death of Yugoslavia*, pp. 230–1.

60 D. Campbell, *National Deconstruction: Violence, Identity, And Justice In Bosnia*, Minneapolis: University of Minneapolis Press, 1998, pp. 58–9.

61 Ibid., p. 59.

62 R. Gutman, *Witness to Genocide*, New York: Lisa Drew Books, 1993, p. 23. G. Malic, 'Herceg Camp', *Feral Tribune*, April 29, 1996, online. Available: www.cdsp.neu.edu/info/students/marko/feral/feral31.htm>1 (accessed June 18, 1998).

63 M. Sells, *The Bridge Betrayed: Religion and Genocide in Bosnia*, Los Angeles: University of California Press, 1998, p. 3.

64 P. Ronayne, *Never Again: United States and the Prevention and Punishment of Genocide since the Holocaust*, Lanham: Rowman and Littlefield, 2001, p. 109.

65 Sells, *The Bridge Betrayed*, pp. 21–2.

66 A. Jones, 'Case Study: The Srebrenica Massacre, July 1995', Gendercide website, online. Available: www.gendercide.org/case_srebrenica.htm>l (accessed June, 2001).

67 Gutman, *Witness to Genocide*, p. 23.

68 Malic, 'Herceg Camp'.

69 Power, '*A Problem from Hell*', p. 269.

70 Ronayne, *Never Again*, p. 111.

71 Holbrooke, *To End a War*, p. 91.

72 Sells, *The Bridge Betrayed*, p. 138.

73 J. Honig and N. Both, *Srebrenica: Record of a Crime*, London: Penguin, 1996, Ronayne, *Never Again*, p. 111; Sells, *The Bridge Betrayed*, pp. 26–7; Holbrooke, *To End a War*, pp. 68–9.

74 Holbrooke, *To End A War*, pp. 101–2.

75 Ibid., pp. 102–6.

76 J. Udovicki and E. Stitkovac, 'Bosnia and Herzegovina: The Second War', in Udovicki and Ridgeway, op. cit., pp. 198–9.

77 Campbell, *National Deconstruction*, p. 221.

78 For a discussion, see J. Glover, *Humanity: A Moral History of the Twentieth Century*, New Haven: Yale University Press, 2001, pp. 127–9.

79 Holbrooke, *To End a War*, pp. 160–2.

80 Tanner, *Croatia*, p. 294.

81 Judah, *The Serbs*, pp. 195–8.

82 G. Bardos, 'Country files: Yugoslavia: Annual report 1999: War, intervention, and anarchy', *Transitions Online*, online. Available: www.archive.tol.cz/countries/yugar99. htm>l (accessed June, 2001).

83 Quoted in M. Parenti, *To Kill a Nation: The Attack on Yugoslavia*, London: Verso, 2000, p. 110. Of particular concern was the unpublicized 'Appendix B', which would have allowed NATO personnel complete and unrestricted access throughout the region, including airspace and waterways. Shawcross, *Deliver Us from Evil*, p. 329.

84 I. Daalder and M. O'Hanlon, *Winning Ugly: NATO's War to Save Kosovo*, Washington, DC: Brookings Institution Press, 2000, pp. 101, 143–4, 209; R. Greenberg, 'U.S. policy in the Balkans', in M. Honey and T. Barry (eds), *Global Focus: U.S. Foreign Policy at the Turn of the Millennium*, London: Palgrave Macmillan, 2000, p. 212.

85 T. Judah, *Kosovo: War and Revenge*, New Haven: Yale University Press, 2000, p. 229; M. Ignatieff, *Virtual War: Kosovo and Beyond*, London: Vintage, 2000, pp. 48–9.

86 N. Chomsky, *Rogue States: The Rule of Force in World Affairs*, London: Pluto Press, 2000, p. 34; Daalder and O'Hanlon, *Winning Ugly*, pp. 108–9; J. Crace, 'Fifty years and counting', *Guardian Education*, April 20, 1999.

87 R. Norton-Taylor, 'Weighing the military options', *Guardian*, May 11, 1999; I. Black and J. Borger, 'Serbs remain defiant as the missile attacks go on', *Guardian*, March 26, 1999.

88 Daalder and O'Hanlon, *Winning Ugly*, pp. 109–11; Greenberg, 'U.S. policy in the Balkans', p. 212.

89 Bardos, 'Country Files'.

90 'Horrors of Kosovo revealed: Mass graves containing the bodies of Kosovo Albanians have been discovered', *BBC News*, December 6, 1999; Judah, *Kosovo*, pp. 287, 289.

91 Bardos, 'Country Files'; Human Rights Watch, 'World report 2000: Federal

Republic of Yugoslavia', online. Available: www.hrw.org/wr2k/Eca-26.htm (accessed June 29, 2001).
92 The Kosovo situation continues to remain tense. See E. Pond, 'Kosovo and Serbia after the French Non', *The Washington Quarterly*, vol. 28, no. 4, 2005, pp. 21–2.
93 For details of this extraordinary change in Serbian politics, see D. Bujosevic and I. Radovanovic, *The Fall of Milosevic: The October 5th Revolution*, London: Palgrave Macmillan, 2003.
94 D. de Krnjevic-Miskovic, 'Serbia's Prudent Revolution', *Journal of Democracy* vol. 12, no. 3, 2001, p. 96.
95 Ibid., p. 110.
96 For basic information, see 'TADIC, IT-94–1, Case Information Sheet', ICTY, June 22, 2004, www.un.org/icty/glance/tadic.htm. For detailed commentary, see R. Wilson, 'Judging History: The Historical Record of the International Criminal Tribunal for the Former Yugoslavia', *Human Rights Quarterly*, vol. 27, no. 3, 2005, pp. 924–5.
97 'KRSTIC, IT-98–33, Case Information Sheet', ICTY, July 8, 2005, www.un.org/ icty/glance/krstic.htm.
98 For a fact sheet and summary of the charges, see 'MILOSEVIC Case Information Sheet (IT-02–54, 'Bosnia and Herzegovina' April 5, 2005, ICTY, online. Available: www.un.org/icty/milosevic/ (accessed June 29, 2001).
99 'Kosovo assault "was not genocide"', *BBC News*, 7 September, 2001.
100 Q. Peel, 'Lessons for Prosecutors of War Crimes Tribunals', *Financial Times*, March 13, 2006.
101 K. Zoglin, 'The Future of War Crimes Prosecutions in the Former Yugoslavia: Accountability or Junk Justice?' *Human Rights Quarterly*, vol. 27, no. 1, 2005, p. 41.

11 Serbophobia and victimhood: Serbia and the successor wars in Yugoslavia

1 B. Anzulovic, *Heavenly Serbia: From Myth to Genocide*, New York: New York University Press, 1999, pp. 123–4.
2 D. Kecmanovic, *The Mass Psychology of Ethnonationalism*, New York: Plenum Press, 1996, pp. 61–3, 66–7.
3 D. Kecmanovic, *Ethnic Times: Exploring Ethnonationalism in the Former Yugoslavia*, Westport: Praegar, 2002, pp. 54–6.
4 I. Colovic, *The Politics of Symbol in Serbia*, London: Hurst & Company, 2002, pp. 8–9.
5 M. Zivkovic, 'The Wish to be a Jew: The Power of the Jewish Trope in the Yugoslav Conflict', *Cahiers de L'URMIS*, no. 6, 2000, p. 73.
6 M. Rosensaft, 'Antisemitism Remains a Threat to the Jewish People', in M. Rosensaft and Y. Bauer (eds), *Antisemitism: Threat to Western Civilization*, Jerusalem: Vidal Sassoon International Center for the Study of Antisemitism, 1988, p. 4.
7 M. Penkower, *The Holocaust and Israel Reborn: From Catastrophe to Sovereignty*, Chicago: University of Illinois Press, 1994, p. 291.
8 S. Friedlander, 'Memory of the Shoah in Israel', in J. Young (ed.), *The Art of Memory: Holocaust Memorials in History*, New York: Prestel, 1994, p. 149.
9 SANU, (a group of members of the Serbian Academy of Science and Arts on current questions in the Yugoslav society), 'Memorandum', reprinted in B. Covic (ed.), *Roots of Serbian Aggression: Debates/Documents/Cartographic Reviews*, Zagreb: Centar za Strane Jezike/AGM, 1993, pp. 323–4. This is a Croatian publication, but the translated text is faithful to the Serbo-Croatian original.

10 Colovic, *The Politics of Symbol in Serbia*, p. 8.

11 Ibid., p. 9.

12 Zivkovic, 'The Wish to be a Jew', p. 72.

13 M. Sells, 'Religion, History and Genocide in Bosnia-Herzegovina', in G. Davis (ed.), *Religion and Justice in the War Over Bosnia*, London: Routledge, 1996, p. 31; T. Judah, *The Serbs: History, Myth and the Destruction of Yugoslavia*, New Haven: Yale University Press, 1997, p. 36.

14 B. Hall, *The Impossible Country: A Journey Through the Last Days of Yugoslavia*, Boston: David R. Godine, 1994, pp. 235–45; N. Malcolm, *Kosovo: A Short History*, London: Macmillan, 1998, pp. 75–9.

15 A. Pavkovic, *The Fragmentation of Yugoslavia: Nationalism in a Multi-Ethnic State*, Basingstoke: Macmillan, 1996, p. 78.

16 D. MacDonald, *Balkan Holocausts?* Manchester: Manchester University Press, 2002, pp. 76–8; J. Mertus, *Kosovo: How Myths and Truths Started a War*, Los Angeles: University of California Press, 1999, pp. 95–120.

17 A. Yelen, *Kossovo 1389–1989 Bataille pour les droits de l'âme*, Lausanne: Editions L'Age D'Homme, 1989. pp. 132–3 (*my translation*).

18 Zivkovic, 'The Wish to be a Jew', pp. 69, 73. For a fine example of Draskovic's thinking, see his novel *Le Couteau*, Paris: J.C. Lattes, 1993, pp. 5–6.

19 N. Cigar, *Genocide in Bosnia: The Policy of Ethnic Cleansing*, College Station: Texas A&M University Press, 1995, p. 236.

20 F. Levinsohn, *Belgrade: Among the Serbs*, Chicago: Ivan R. Dee, 1994, p. 16.

21 Judah, *The Serbs*, p. 37.

22 S. Maliqi, 'The Albanian Movement in Kosova', in D. Dyker and I. Vejdoda (eds), *Yugoslavia and After: A Study in Fragmentation, Despair and Rebirth*, London: Longman, 1996, p. 142.

23 D. Cosic, *L'éffondrement de la Yougoslavie: positions d'un resistant*, Paris: Age D'Homme, 1994, p. 44.

24 S. Avramov (ed.), *Genocide Against the Serbs*, Belgrade: Museum of Modern Art, 1992, p. 18.

25 N. Malic, 'Arrested! Milosevic's Seizure Unveils Hidden Agendas', *Balkan Express*, April 5, 2001, online. Available: www.antiwar.com/malic/m040501. htm>l (accessed September 20, 2004).

26 Cosic, *L'éffondrement de la Yougoslavie*, pp. 58–9.

27 Ibid., p. 78.

28 D. Vilic and B. Todorovic, *Breaking of Yugoslavia and Armed Secession of Croatia*, Beli Manastir: Cultura Centre 'Vuk Karadzic', 1996, pp. 14–15.

29 J. Ilic, 'Characteristics and Importance of Some Ethno-National and Political-Geographic Factors Relevant for the Possible Political-Legal Disintegration of Yugoslavia', in S. Ivanovic (ed.), *The Creation and Changes of the Internal Borders of Yugoslavia*, Belgrade: Ministry of Information of the Republic of Serbia, 1992, p. 93.

30 R. Nakrada, *The Disintegration of Yugoslavia and the New World Order*, Belgrade: Institute for European Studies, 1994–5, p. 378.

31 B. Zecevic (ed.), *The Uprooting: A Dossier of the Croatian Genocide Policy Against the Serbs*, Belgrade: Velauto International, 1992, pp. 8, 126.

32 N. Marinovic, *Stories from Hell: Confessions of Serbs, Tortured in the Concentration Camps in Croatia and Bosnia and Herzegovina in 1991 and 1992*, Belgrade: Serbian Ministry of Information, 1993, pp. 12–13.

33 Ibid., p. 14.

34 Ibid., pp. 21–2.

35 J. Ilic, 'Possible Borders of New Yugoslavia', in Ivanovic, op. cit., pp. 98, 100–1.

36 J. Ilic, 'The Balkan Geopolitical Knot and the Serbian Question', in D. Hadzi-

Jovancic (ed.), *The Serbian Question in the Balkans: Geographical and Historical Aspects*, Belgrade: University of Belgrade Faculty of Geography, 1995, p. 31.

37 Zecevic, *The Uprooting*, p. 10.
38 Avramov, *Genocide Against the Serbs*, pp. 10–11.
39 Ibid., p. 11.
40 Serbian National Defense Council of America, *Genocide in Croatia 1941–1945*, Chicago: 1993, pp. 28–30. See also R. Petrovic, *The Extermination of Serbs on the Territory of the Independent State of Croatia*, Belgrade: Serbian Ministry of Information, 1991.
41 Avramov, *Genocide Against the Serbs*, p. 32.
42 Zivkovic, 'The Wish to be a Jew', pp. 69, 73.
43 D. Mirkovic, 'The Historical Link between the Ustasha Genocide and the Croato-Serb Civil War: 1991–1995', *Journal of Genocide Research*, vol. 2, no. 3, 2000, p. 363.
44 M. Bulajic, *The Role of the Vatican in the Break-up of Yugoslavia*, Belgrade: Serbian Ministry of Information, 1993, p. 67.
45 Ibid., pp. 130–34.
46 D. Batakovic, 'Frustrated Nationalism in Yugoslavia: From Liberal to Communist Solution', *Serbian Studies*, vol. 11, no. 2, 1997, online. Available: www.bglink.com/personal/batakovic/boston.htm>1 (accessed June 18, 1998).
47 Ibid.,
48 Ilic, 'The Serbs in the Former SR of Croatia', p. 330.
49 Jasenovac Research Institute, 'What was Jasenovac?', Jasenovac Research Institute, 2004, online. Available: www.jasenovac.org/whatwasjasenovac/index.asp (accessed September 20, 2004); 'Jasenovac', Jewish Virtual Library, online. Available: www.jewishvirtuallibrary.org/jsource/Holocaust/Jasenovac.htm>1 (accessed September 20, 2004).
50 Serbian Unity Congress, 'Jasenovac', April, 1996, online. Available: www.suc.Suc.Org/~kosta/tar/jasenovac/intro.htm>1 (accessed June 24, 2004).
51 Serbian Ministry of Information, 'Facts About The Republic of Serbia', unpublished and undated from the Serbian Embassy, Switzerland.
52 Bulajic, *The Role of the Vatican in the Break-up of Yugoslavia* pp. 153–4.
53 For a full range of Serbian estimates, see Ilic, 'The Serbs in the Former SR of Croatia', p. 333; S. Durdevic, *The Continuity of a Crime: The Final Settlement of the Serbian Question in Croatia*, Belgrade: IDEA Publishing House, November, 1995, p. 15; Nouvel Observateur et Raporteurs sans Frontières, *Le Livre Noir de L'Ex-Yougoslavie: Purification Ethnique et Crimes de Guerre*, Paris: Publications Arlea, 1993, p. 277; D. Batakovic, 'Le génocide dans l'état independant croate 1941–1945', *Hérodote*, no. 67, 1992, online. Available: www.bglink.com/personal/batakovic (accessed November 15, 1999); P. Pavlovich, *The Serbians*, Toronto: Serbian Heritage Books, 1988, p. 226; Anzulovic, *Heavenly Serbia*, pp. 103–4.
54 See a synopsis of this at the Serbian Unity Congress Website, online. Available: www.suc.Suc.Org/~kosta/tar/knjige/atlas/index.htm>1 (accessed September 20, 2004); L. Kostich, *The Holocaust in the Independent State of Croatia: An Account Based on German, Italian and the Other Sources*, Chicago: Liberty Press, 1981.
55 S. Kljakic, *A Conspiracy of Silence: Genocide in the Independent State of Croatia and Concentration Camp Jasenovac*, Belgrade: Serbian Ministry of Information, 1991, p. 23.
56 V. Dedijer, *The Yugoslav Auschwitz and the Vatican: The Croatian Massacre of the Serbs During World War II*, New York: Prometheus Books, 1992.
57 Ibid., p. 11.
58 Ibid., p. 14.

59 A. Rabinbach and J. Zipes, 'Lessons of the Holocaust', *New German Critique*, no. 19, 1980, p. 6.
60 A. Lebor, *Milosevic: A Biography*, London: Bloomsbury, 2002, p. 331.
61 Helsinki Committee for Human Rights in Serbia, 'Reports: Antisemitism', online. Available: www.helsinki.org.yu/report_text.php?lang=en&idteksta=358 (accessed September 20, 2004).
62 Lebor, *Milosevic*, p. 331.
63 L. Pearl, 'Serb-Jewish commemoration disrupted by controversy', *Jewish News Weekly*, June 16, 1995, online. Available: www.jewishsf.com/content/2–0-/module/displaystory/story_id/20980/edition_id/432/format/htm>1>/displaystory.htm>1 (accessed September 20, 2004).
64 P. Cohen, *Serbia's Secret War: Propaganda and the Deceit of History*, College Station: Texas A&M University Press, 1996, p. 117.
65 K. Mandic, 'The European Hoodlum Democracy Will Not Break the Serbs', 1993, online. Available: www.srpska-mreza.com/library/facts/Mandic.htm>1 (accessed September 20, 2004).
66 Gruber, 'Our Yugoslavia'.
67 'Appeal By The Serbian–Jewish Friendship Society Of Belgrade', April 1, 1999, online. Available: www.vidici.com/NetClipping/Text_htm>/Politica/Kosovo/appeal.htm>1 (accessed September 20, 2004).
68 R. Gruber, 'Our Yugoslavia, Our Jerusalem', 1 June, 2003, online. Available: www.ourjerusalem.com/history/story/history20030601.htm>1 (accessed September 20, 2004).
69 Levinsohn, *Belgrade*, p. 199.
70 Serbia Info News, 'Work of the Jews in the Serbian literature', Serbian Ministry of Information, February 12, 1999, online. Available: www.serbia-info.com/news (accessed September 20, 2004).
71 L. Sekelj, 'Antisemitism and Jewish Identity in Serbia After the 1991 Collapse of the Yugoslav State', The Vidal Sassoon International Center for the Study of Antisemitism, 1997 acta no. 12, online. Available: www.sicsa.huji.ac.il/12sekelx.htm>1 (accessed September 20, 2004).
72 Other Jewish leaders were also co-opted into service. See D. Cadik *et al.*, 'Open letter to the American Jewish Committee', 1995, online. Available: www.emperors-clothes.com/articles/danon/YugoRabb.htm>1 (accessed September 20, 2004). For further claims of Jewish support, see Serbia Info News, 'Rabbi Asiel: deep sorrow for our fatherland', Belgrade: Ministry of Information, April 5, 1999, online. Available: www.serbia-info.com/cgibin/wwwwais?keywords=jewish&hideform=yes&headerver=.3.htm>1>&selection=News (accessed September 20, 2004).
73 Lebor, *Milosevic*, p. 336; 'Southeastern Europe', *RFE/RL*, 11 May, 2001, online. Available: www.rferl.org/newsline/2001/05/4-see/see-110501 (accessed September 20, 2004).
74 D. Plotz, 'Serbs, Kosovar, Israelis, Palestinians: The Bewildering Politics of Kosovo in Israel', *MSN Slate*, April, 1999, online. Available: www.slate.msn.com/id/25826/ (accessed September 20, 2004).
75 Y. Auron, *The Banality of Denial: Israel and the Armenian Genocide*, New York: Transaction Publishers, 2003, pp. 86–8.
76 L. Derfner, 'Love 'em or hate' em?', *The Jerusalem Post*, April 27, 1999.
77 Plotz, 'Serbs, Kosovar, Israelis, Palestinians'.
78 D. Levy and N. Sznaider, 'Memory Unbound: The Holocaust and the Formation of Cosmopolitan Memory', *European Journal of Social Theory*, vol. 5, no. 1, 2002, p. 99. D. Levy and N. Sznaider, 'The Institutionalization of Cosmopolitan Morality: The Holocaust and Human Rights', *Journal of Human Rights*, vol. 3, no. 2, 2004, p. 153.

79 I. Daalder and M. O'Hanlon, *Winning Ugly: NATO's War to Save Kosovo*, Washington, DC: Brookings Institution Press, 2000, p. 101.
80 Helsinki Committee for Human Rights in Serbia, 'Reports: Antisemitism'.
81 H. Cottin, 'Statement From The Jewish-Serbian Friendship Society U.S'., 12 April 1999, online. Available: www.vidici.com/NetClipping/Text_htm>/Politica/Kosovo/IZJAVA_jsfs.htm>l (accessed September 20, 2004).
82 Borba (Yu), 'NATO manipulates truth', August 5, 1999, online. Available: www.borba.co.yu/daily.htm>l (accessed September 20, 2004).
83 Yearwood, 'Another side to the story of Kosovo'.
84 W. Dorich, 'The Case Against the Vatican Bank', August 7, 2000, SUC, online. Available: www.news.suc.org/bydate/2000/Aug_28/7.htm>l (accessed September 20, 2004).
85 T. Emoff, Balkan Repository Project, 24 May, 1999, online. Available: www.balkan-archive.org.yu/kosovo_crisis/htm>l>/0524_emoff.htm>l (accessed September 20, 2004).
86 'SACRU Serbian-American Civil Rights Unlimited Documenting Jewish Genocides On Serbs', online. Available: www.compuserb.com/sacru/ (accessed September 20, 2004). For further discussion of Wesley Clark, see Zivkovic, 'The Wish to be a Jew', p. 79.
87 S. Marquette, 'Dear Dr. Wiesenthal ... A Letter Asking Why?' SUC, October, 2000, online. Available: www.suc.org/culture/history/wwii/Sandy.pdf (accessed September 20, 2004).
88 Sekelj, 'Antisemitism and Jewish Identity in Serbia'.
89 Helsinki Committee for Human Rights in Serbia, 'Reports: Antisemitism'.
90 C. Carmichael, *Ethnic Cleansing in the Balkans: Nationalism and the Destruction of Tradition*, London: Routledge, 2002, pp. 52–3.
91 Sekelj, 'Antisemitism and Jewish Identity in Serbia'.
92 Zivkovic, 'The Wish to be a Jew', p. 80.
93 P. Williams, 'The International Community', in Magas and Zanic, op. cit., p. 277.
94 R. Gutman, *Witness to Genocide*, New York: Lisa Drew Books, 1993, p. 23.
95 Levy and Sznaider, 'Memory Unbound', p. 99; Levy and Sznaider, 'The institutionalization of cosmopolitan morality', p. 153.
96 A. Steinweis, 'The Auschwitz Analogy: Holocaust Memory and American Debates over Intervention in Bosnia and Kosovo in the 1990s', *Holocaust and Genocide Studies*, vol. 19, no. 2, 2005, pp. 276–7.
97 Ibid., pp. 279–81.
98 On Albright's strong stance against Milosevic, see D. Doder and L. Branson, *Milosevic: Portrait of a Tyrant*, New York: The Free Press, 1999, p. 210.
99 Steinweis, 'The Auschwitz Analogy', p. 282.
100 A. Heinemann-Grüder, 'Germany's Anti-Hitler Coalition in Kosovo', *Mediterranean Quarterly*, Summer, 2001, p. 38. He comments further on the German strategy: 'The complexities of power games and clashing, violent nationalisms were reduced to the idea of crushing of a reborn Hitler by an enlightened German elite', p. 42.
101 D. MacDonald, 'The Fire in 1999? The United States, NATO, and the Bombing of Yugoslavia', in A. Jones (ed.), *Genocide, War Crimes, and the West: Ending the Culture of Impunity*, London: Zed Books, 2004, pp. 276–99.
102 See www.serbia-info.com/enc/history/sfrj.htm>l (accessed September 20, 2004).
103 M. Karadjis, 'Yugoslavia: The Milosevic regime without Milosevic', *Green Left Weekly*, 2001, online. Available: www.greenleft.org.au/back/2001/456/456 p19.htm (accessed September 20, 2004).
104 Ibid.,

105 A. Devic, 'War Guilt and Responsibility: The Case of Serbia: Diverging Attempts at Facing the Recent Past', *GSC Quarterly*, Spring, 2003, online. Available: www.ssrc.org/programs/gsc/gsc_quarterly/newsletter8/content/devic.page (accessed September 20, 2004).

106 Devic, 'War Guilt and Responsibility'.

107 D. Nikolic-Solomon and M. Tanner, 'Shadow of Hague Falls Over Serbian Election', *BCR*, no. 502, June, 2004, online. Available: www.iwpr.net/index. pl? archive/bcr3/bcr3_200406_502_1_eng.txt (accessed September 20, 2004).

108 'Serbian leader "shocked" by video', *BBC News*, June 3, 2005.

109 Ibid.,

110 'Del Ponte commends government's action in apprehension of Srebrenica suspects', Serbian Ministry of Information, June 2, 2005, online. Available: www.srbija.sr.gov. yu/vesti/vest.php?id=12880&q=srebrenica (accessed September 20, 2004).

111 'US religious delegation visits Devic monastery in Kosovo', Serbian Ministry of Information, June 2, 2005, online. Available: www.srbija.sr.gov.yu/vesti/ vest.php? id=4360&q=apology (accessed September 20, 2004).

112 Kecmanovic, *Ethnic Times*, p. 56.

Conclusions

1 Voltaire, *Candide: Or Optimism*, London: Wordsworth, 1993, p. 63.

2 B. Zeliger, *Remembering to Forget: Holocaust Memory Through the Camera's Eye*, Chicago: University of Chicago Press, 1998, pp. 12, 67.

3 Ibid., p. 203.

4 Ibid., p. 204.

5 N. Geras, *The Contract of Mutual Indifference: Political Philosophy After the Holocaust*, London: Verso, 1999, p. 28.

6 Ibid., pp. 17–18.

7 G. Weissman, *Fantasies of Witnessing: Postwar Efforts to Experience the Holocaust*, Ithaca: Cornell University Press, 2004, p. 11.

8 T. Fallace, 'The Origins of Holocaust Education in American Public Schools', *Holocaust and Genocide Studies*, vol. 20, no. 1, 2006, 96–7.

9 Peter Singer, *Practical Ethics*, Cambridge: Cambridge University Press, 1979, p. 14.

10 J. Chicago, *The Holocaust Project: From Darkness Into Light*, New York: Viking, 1993, p. 9. Chicago's conclusions are useful here, although I do have serious reservations about her art, which relativizes the Holocaust through comparison with many other tragedies.

11 J. Paxman, *The English: The Portrait of a People*, London: Michael Joseph, 1998, p. 177.

12 A. Finkielkraut, *The Future of a Negation: Reflections on the Question of Genocide*, translated by Mary Byrd Kelly, London: University of Nebraska Press, 1998, pp. 99–100.

13 C. Tatz, *Genocide In Australia*, AIATSIS Research Discussion Papers No 8, Canberra: Australian Institute of Aboriginal and Torres Strait Islander Studies, 1999, p. 2.

14 F. Chalk, 'Redefining Genocide', pp. 47–63, in G. Andropoulos (ed.), *Genocide: Conceptual and Historical Dimensions*, Philadelphia: University of Pennsylvania Press, 1994, pp. 49, 54.

15 R.J. Rummel, Statistics of Democide, Chapter 2, 'Statistics of Pre-20th Century Democide Estimates, Calculations, And Sources', online. Available: www.hawaii. edu/powerkills/SOD.CHAP2.HTM (accessed August 25, 2006).

16 E. Henderson and R. Tucker, 'Clear and Present Strangers: The Clash of Civilizations and International Conflict', *International Studies Quarterly*, June, 2001, pp. 317–38.

17 D. Stannard, *American Holocaust: The Conquest of the New World*, New York: Oxford University Press, 1992, pp. 267–8.

18 N. Finkelstein, *The Holocaust Industry: Reflections on the Exploitation of Jewish Suffering*, New York: Verso, 2000, p. 32.

19 Ibid., p. 3.

20 H. Ben-Sasson, 'The Human Spirit in the Shadow of Death: The Central Theme for Holocaust Remembrance Day 2006', *Vad Vashem Quarterly Magazine*, vol. 41, 2006.

21 Zeliger, *Remembering to Forget*, p. 80.

22 A. Foxman, *Never Again? The Threat of the New Anti-Semitism*, San Francisco: HarperCollins, 2003.

23 'Holocaust deniers finish conference in Iran', *CTV News*, December 13, 2006.

24 R. Israeli, 'Antisemitism Parading as Antizionism', Paper from the International Conference on the Global Dimensions of Contemporary Antisemitism, Montreal, March, 2004, p. 6.

25 C. Dean, 'Recent French Discourses on Stalinism, Nazism and 'Exorbitant' Jewish Memory' *History & Memory*, vol. 18, no.1, 2006, 44.

26 C. Murphy, 'Forging a Future After Auschwitz'. *BBC News*, 24 January, 2005.

27 R. Therrien and D. Neu, *Accounting for Genocide: Canada's Bureaucratic Assault on Aboriginal People*, Blackpoint: Fernwood Publishing, 2003, pp. 23–4.

28 J. Mearsheimer and S. Walt, 'The Israel Lobby', *London Review of Books*, vol. 28 no. 6, 23, 2006.

29 Manfred Gerstenfeld, *Europe's Crumbling Myths: The Post-Holocaust Origins of Today's Anti-Semitism*, (Jerusalem: Jerusalem Center for Public Affairs, 2003, pp. 27–8; 129–30.

30 C. Hendershot, 'From Trauma to Paranoia: Nuclear Weapons, Science Fiction, and history' *Mosaic*, vol. 32, no. 4, 1999.

31 T. Spiers, 'Trauma: An Integrated Model', in T. Spiers (ed.), *Trauma: A Practitioner's Guide to Counselling*, London: Routledge, 2001, p. 17.

32 A. McFarlane, J. Golier, and R. Yahuda, 'Treatment Planning for Trauma Survivors with PTSD: What Does a Clinician Need to Know Before Implementing PTSD Treatment?' in R. Yahuda (ed.), *Treating Trauma: Survivors with PTSD*, Washington, DC: American Psychiatric Publishing, 2002, pp. 10–13.

33 P. Lerner and M. Micale, 'Trauma, Psychiatry, and History: A Conceptual and Historiographical Introduction', in P. Lerner and M. Micale (eds), *Traumatic Pasts: History, Psychiatry, and Trauma in the Modern Age, 1870–1930*, Cambridge: Cambridge University Press, 2001, p. 4.

34 V. Volkan, *Bloodlines: From Ethnic Pride to Ethnic Terrorism*, London: Farrar, Strauss and Giroux, 1997, p. 38.

35 Ibid., p. 40.

36 Ibid., pp. 34–5.

37 Ibid., p. 43.

Index

Lightning Source UK Ltd.
Milton Keynes UK
UKOW040349061012

200136UK00002B/16/P